YOUR ETERNAL HOLOGRAM

New discovery is a key to Access and Enlighten your Consciousness

BY
AVATAR SVADI HATRA

photo: Tim Orden, www.timorden.com

Your Eternal Hologram – New discovery is a key to Access and Enlighten your Consciousness
Amelia Earhart Spirit Journey
Copyright © 2017 by Avatar Svadi Hatra
SECOND Edition

All rights reserved. No part of this book may be used or reproduced by any means, graphic, electronic, or mechanical, including photocopying, recording, taping or by any information storage retrieval system without the written permission of the publisher except in the case of brief quotations embodied in critical articles and reviews.

First published in 2008
The Re-birth of an Atlantean Queen © 2009 by Julia Svadi Hatra
ISBN: 978-1-4401-4115-7 (pbk)
ISBN: 978-1-4401-4116-4 (ebk)

Published by : www. CreateSpace.com

Editor, transcriber: Roxane Christ, www.aribert-editinghouse.com
Reader: Birgit Lang, www.release4you.com
Reader: Eliot James Estep
Back Cover photo: Tim Orden, www.timorden.com
Back Cover text: Boccaccio di Chellino
Translation: Olga Lipovskaya
Cover design: Tony Ariawan, http://area105.deviantart.com/gallery
Front Cover image: Tony Ariawan, **http://area105.deviantart.com/gallery**
Back Cover image: Sven Geier, www.sgeir.net

The luxury and privilege of a Goddess is now within your reach. Let this unique and magnificent book create an ocean of feelings that will touch the deepest layers of your Spirit and Soul.

Discover the treasure of your inner harmony, peace and power. It is a precious gift of rare knowledge and experiences about the existence of a much BIGGER Eternal Spirit LIFE, outside the present one, which each of us is living right now.

YOUR ETERNAL HOLOGRAM chronicles the magnificent Spirit Journey of an ancient Spirit Being. In this book you will find the complete story about all his past lives as a Priest of Chichen Itza, an Atlantean Queen, Ancient Egyptian Royal Priestess, Amelia Earhart, Julia Svadi Hatra and even one future life.

YOUR ETERNAL HOLOGRAM

In the Chapter **"THE PRIEST"**, you will find details of a SPIRIT Journey from his life as an Ancient Mayan Priest of Chichen Itza. 2000 years old secrets revealed: how he performed ceremonies and rituals on top of the pyramid, the Spirit world, sacrifices, symbols and the life of the ancient Maya people in Chichen Itza – a Message from them to the present-day civilization passed on to us. Meeting with God and angels, contacts with ancient Goddesses, Persian Goddesses, new Atharvan images, Zaratustra, ghosts, visiting a real Buddhist temple ... are all in Ancient Priest of Chichen Itza reincarnated by Avatar Svadi Hatra.

In the chapter, **"DREAMS of an ATLANTEAN QUEEN"**, you will find who the Ancient Priest meets in Chichen Itza! Guess who it was? He was a Giant Atlantean man! A Mexican hero, Chak Mol! You will find out who he was; where he came from before arriving in Mexico and Chichen Itza and even who his mother was! You will find out where he lived and where he played in Chichen Itza. Was Avatar Svadi an Atlantean Queen in her past life? Did she carry with her secrets of the crystal pyramid and how to re-ignite its energy? In this book, Spirit Avatar Svadi went back to her past life in Atlantis and her abilities began to emerge in this life time in a new re-born person!

In the Chapter, **"AMELIA RETURN?"** Amelia Earhart is talking to us. Astonishing secrets are revealed: echoes from the past and future. Was Amelia meant to die according to some "secret plan"? Through the author's past life experience, Amelia is able to describe the last minutes before her death, how she enters Heaven, her hopes and dreams, which come true in her next life. Why was she lost? Why is it impossibly difficult to find her? Is it a curse by ancient Egyptian or Mexican Spirits on those who are "playing games" around Amelia's disappearance?

What is common between Avatar Svadi, Amelia and the Ancient Priest of Chichen Itza?

In the Chapter, **"EGYPT"** you will read about Avatar's SPIRIT Journey from there life in Ancient Egypt. Did Ancient Spirit Avatar belong to a royal family of Ancient Egypt or was she a Priestess there? A unique Egypt's ancient initiation ceremony of a Goddess, meeting with Egyptian Goddesses and the magic of the Holy Spirit of Bast, the Royal Cat Goddess, intriguing Anubis, communication with an Ancient Priest & Pharaoh, swimming in the efir oils, present to the Great Cheops pyramid, ancient ritual inside the tomb, talking to mummies, GIANT Pharaohs ... are all in this truly Mysterious Magic Egypt.

These chapters **"VIOLET FIELD"** and **"KUKULCAN"** an Ancient Maya Priest comes to you through thousands of years and giving rare knowledge what you can expect after your own death. All people will live in Spirit world between lives. The spirit world is full of amazing colors, lights, dynamics speed and magic things which do not exist in our world. BUT it could be very dangerous sometimes. These chapters will show another side of the same Spirit - a very unusual part of the Spirit, which we know as the High Priest from Chichen Itza, the Atlantis woman, Amelia the pilot, and the royal girl from Egypt and Avatar Svadi. Yes, all of them have the same consciousness, thoughts and actions. It is one solid strong crystal. And this crystal will not be complete in your vision until you read these chapters and open one more granule of that Spirit-and-Soul crystal, **Eternal Hologram.**

It is good to know that another side of human nature exists and that you study some ultra-human possibilities for yourself. Travel in Time? Teleportation? Meeting with Kukulcan-Quetzalcoatl. Who is he? From where GIANTS come on Earth? Who is Svadi and what is Hatra? Why people built pyramids? The Earth will be wiped out soon? Do we live in the Past or in the Future?

Let's go now through the door, to the room where dreams are waiting for you. In these dreams, Spirit travels to another multidimensional world. Spirit contacted and met other spirits from our Galaxy and other parts of the Universe. The body looks and feels different in this other world. Instead of a body it was sometimes just one solid point or a pulsation of energy, with sparks of quantum particles. So let's take the first ride...

Fascinating!

Customer Reviews: November 28, 2009
Reviewed by Paige Lovitt for Reader Views (11/09)
By Reader Views "www.readerviews.com" (Austin, Texas)

As I read "YOUR ETERNAL HOLOGRAM," found myself totally fascinated with Julia Svadi Hatra's life journey. Julia writes about her awakening into knowing who she really is. Her path has been an intriguing one. As she has gone through her life, she has experienced memories and dreams of who she was in her former lives. Three key people stand out in her recollections, Amelia Earhart, a Mayan Priest and an Atlantean Queen. Not a person just to sit back and recollect, Julia has journeyed to places where she feels she has been before. Included in her story are some incredible pictures that are reflective of her personal experiences in prior lives. She also discusses dream states that she has been in where she recollects some incredible events, including many of which involve initiations.

To back up her experiences, Julia includes testimonials from people who were there when fantastic events were taking place around her. As a scientist, she also has researched and extensively referenced much of the material that she offers. She discusses correlations of her experiences to actual scientific events or possible explanations, and she offers interpretations of her dreams. In addition to extensive referencing, Julia offers some incredible photographs to illustrate what she is talking about. I found myself getting goose bumps over and over.

I had two initial impressions upon reading this book. The first was admiration and the second was appreciation. I admired the author's willingness to take on the task that she has in writing her story. Just as this is not a book to be read in one sitting, it was also not a story that could be told in one lifetime. The feeling of appreciation came from being appreciative that Julia was willing to put her story out there for the people of the world to read and to be inspired to discover their own stories.

YOUR ETERNAL HOLOGRAM

Julia Svadi Hatra strikes me as a phenomenal woman who has not allowed her human shell to hide the essence of who she truly is. She has not allowed a mundane façade to cover up her real beauty and essence. She radiates beauty and strength from the inside out. By reading about her experiences, and the incredible dreams that followed me in my life, she made me want to get up and shake off my fears and apprehensions about really allowing who I am to emerge.

I highly recommend "YOUR ETERNAL HOLOGRAM" by Julia Svadi Hatra to people who are feeling compelled to explore their pasts and use that knowledge to take the next step in their evolution. As you read it, you will find yourself letting go of the shackles that you are allowing to hold yourself back. **Ready, get set, go...**

© Josephine Wall. All Rights Reserved. www.josephinewall.com

About the author

From an early age, Julia was waking up and continued talking in other languages – the ancient languages of her dreams. During her life she saw thousands of very detailed dreams about her life in Atlantis, Ancient Egypt, Ancient Mexico and Persia. It had been puzzling her for many years until she visited the Chichen Itza pyramid. She felt that she lived there before! Soon upon her return to Vancouver, she visited a past-life regression specialist and everything she described during the hypnoses sessions supported her dreams and her feelings of déjà-vu.

Julia is a scientist. She carried out in-depth investigations and research; she visited 11 countries – all of the cradles of ancient civilizations on the planet. As a result she compared her life with those of other people from the past. Lucky, one of them was the pilot, Amelia Earhart. Due to Amelia's popularity, her life's descriptions are available in detail on various websites and books, which made the comparison much easier. It was priceless!

As a result from Julia Svadi Hatra's research, an astonishing conclusion came to light; after death our Spirits do not die! It transfers to the newborn baby and it continues its journey through the centuries. Habits, experience and knowledge people collect during their lifetime is preserved in the Spirit Body, which is a multidimensional hologram. In this book, for the first time in human history, it has been scientifically proven that people have many lives. **Our Spirit is ETERNAL.**

YOUR ETERNAL HOLOGRAM

Dedication

Dedicated to the creativity of the people who lived on Earth, living now and will be living in the future.

Leonardo Da Vinci, Wolfgang Amadeus Mozart, Alexander Pushkin, Johann Sebastian Bach, Tchaikovsky, Lev Tolstoy,Michelangelo, Rembrandt van Rijn, president John F.Kennedy, president Franklin D. Roosevelt, Eleanour Roosevelt, pilot Amelia Earhart, George P. Putman, admiral Richard ByrdSouthPole expedition, Charles Lindbergh,Linda Finch,Capt Hilton H. Railey, scientist David Sinclair, attorney David Tanzer, healer Alfons Ven, George Friedrich Händel, "Abba", Elvis Presley, Rimsky Korsakov,Nostradamus, Tesla, Mendeleyev, Buryl Payne,Marie Curie, Louis Pasteur, Carlos Castaneda, Stephen Hawking,Jan Van Hyusum, artist Shahla Homayoni, Shawn Sviridovgalleryss.com, Jan Davidsz de Heem, Edvard Grieg, artistPeter Breughel, Kathryn Raaker,designerGrace Bardin,David Icke, M.V.Hartevelt, Pierre-Auguste Renoir, Frans Snyders,Lord Steven Christ,William Shakespeare, pilotAnna Egorova, conductor Igor Golovchin, photographer Tim Orden, artist Darlene Lurr Sviridov, opera singer Vecheclav Osipov, Budhist Supreme monk Won Dam, artist Josephine Wall,Simon Dewulfaulive.com, singer Zzak (Irving) Grinwald, healer Samir Ali Baba, Cherokee Marc Eagle Eyes, Tim Stephens astralreflections.com, father of wave genetic P. Gariaev, healer Djuna Davidashvili, Jon of God and his Entity&Spirits, Adrianne, doctor Sally Williams, financier JayHaldeman, attorney Peter Dimitrov, Mexican spiritual leader and healerJulio Luis Rodriguez,Gloria Elizabeth Sanchez, Simon Parkes, William Tompkins, Corey Goode, David Wilcock, Alex Collier, Kerry Cassidy Project Camelot,Hans Donker,Valery Uvarov,healer Howard Wills, past life specialists: Marianne Notschaele-den Boer,Dianna Cherry, Douglas D. Settles, Kevin Williamswww.near-death.com; Eliot James Estep, photographer David Holiday, editor Roxane Christ, screen writer Barb Doyon, artist Hoteya, artist Tony Ariawan, artist Sven Geier, child prodigy artist Akiane Kramarik, Hansjörg Wyss&Wyss foundation, president Donald Trump, FedEx founder and chairman Fred Smith, Spencer King, David W Jourdan & NAUTICOS, Jon Thompson
success /Titanic venture, Elgen Long "Crash and Sink" theory explaining the disappearance of Amelia Earhart ….

To Creators of our beautiful amazing Earth, Solar system and Universe.

You can add any creative person you know at www.ameliareborn.com

Table of Contents

Dedication
The Dreams

Chapter 1 – The Priest
    Ancient Priest of Chichen Itza Reincarnated

Chapter 2 – The Dreams of an Atlantean Queen
    Part 1 – Chak Mol, Giant Atlantean man in Chichen Itza
    Part 2 – Giants, Chak Mol facts
    Part 3 – Atlantis

Chapter 3 – Amelia Return?
Table of Common Characteristics
Conclusion
WHAT DOES SPIRIT LOOK LIKE?
Trinity
Reincarnation as a group

Chapter 4 – Egypt

Chapter 5 – The Violet Field

Chapter 6 – Kukulcan

POWER of REINCARNATION
MIND OVER Matter
Who am I?

Reincarnation and the Bible
Reincarnation and Early Christianity
Reincarnation and the Secret Teachings of Jesus
Scientific Interpretation
Sources
Acknowledgements
How to purchase this book and CDs, CD List
Testimonials

Dreams

Translated by Olga Lipovskaya

The Priest

1. THEY PULLED MY BODY OUT OF ME, April 25, 1996
2. HIEROGLYPH ON THE PALM, September 12, 1992
3. ATHARVAN, October 13, 1989
4. BABY FROM THE RIVER, April 11, 1992
5. THE UPPER KINGDOM, October 24, 1993
6. THE QUEEN OF A CRYSTAL KINGDOM, December 4, 2007
7. ARABIAN AND AMERICAN MOUNTAINS,
   (2 pyramids: Egypt and Mexico, October 25, 1990)
8. I RETURN TO THE LAND WHERE I LIVED BEFORE, November 23, 1992
9. THE POWER OF THE FOUR, August 21, 1992
10. GREAT HARMONY OF NATURE, October 8, 1991
11. LUMINOUS BODIES OF PLANTS, January 8, 1992
12. SPECTRUM, February 23, 1992,
13. GOD'S BLESSING, ANGELS, July 20, 1995
14. THE GRAIN OF DIVINITY, January 4, 1992
15. A MESSAGE FROM THE MAGNIFICENT MAYA PEOPLE, June 24, 2008

The Dreams of an Atlantean Queen

16. DESTRUCTION OF THE CRYSTAL SPHERE, February. 19, 1992
17. ELEVATORS WERE RINGING BECAUSE OF ME, September 12, 1992
18. ZARATUSTRA IN WATER, September 6, 1993
19. RUBY EMERALD, February 11, 1988
20. WOMAN ON A RED CRYSTAL, September 25, 1994
21. THE LILAC WORLD, March 4, 2001
22. THE WOMAN-DOUBLE AND A WISE MAN, July 8, 2004
23. THE CITY OF CRYSTAL PYRAMIDS, June 13, 1993
24. I WAS VERY THIN AND EXTREMELY TALL, February 11, 1997
25. HISTORY – PYRAMID IN A PYRAMID, August, 1994
26. HUNDREDS OF FOLLOWERS. RUBIES, November 8, 2003

Amelia Return?
27. WOMAN-PILOT DISAPPEARED, June 22, 1992
28. RAYS COMING FROM THE EYES, April, 1994
29. BIFURCATION SIMILAR TO A "VIBRATING" RULER – May 13, 1991

Egypt
30. THE BLUE VESSEL OF AN EGYPTIAN PRIEST & PHARAOH – January 10, 1992
31. CROWN, September 6, 1991
32. THE FOX and the SARCOPHAGUS, February 23, 1992

The "Violet Field", KUKULCAN
33. VIA GOS CAME INSPIRATION, April 25, 1998
34. BIG CREATURE OF A HOLY RELIGION, October 31, 1993
35. BUSINESS IN THE CENTER OF THE GALAXY, July 16 1991
36. THE GUIDE OF MY LIFE, February 22, 1996
37. YOUR COSMIC SISTER, March 20, 1992
38. MAN OF THE FOREST – HIS NAME – December 13, 1991
39. THE DRILLING FROM BELGIUM BOTHERS ME, October 16, 1992
40. THE SWIRL OF COMAS, May 1, 1992
41. GRAY DUMB-BELL IN THE HEAD, September 4, 1991
42. DOWEL BAR IN TO THE HEAD, September 15, 1991
43. THE BELT BUCKLE. THE LAW OF TIME, March 16, 1992
44. THE PEOPLE STOPPED in the PRAIRIE, November 26, 1991
45. HUGE GOD WAS DICTATING INTO MY EARS, January 7, 1983
46. A WARNING FROM THREE AUSTRONAUTS, March 22, 1988
47. THE EARTH CURLED UP, February 12, 1992
48. CANYON OF LUMINESCENT ELVES, June 21, 1992
49. BELOW – THE TRANSPARENT MEDUSAS OF AIR, November 19, 1992
50. MEDUSA IN STREAMS OF ENERGY, July 22, 1992
51. THE VIOLET FIELD or *The Stalker*
52. KUKULCAN (Human Lizard), September 19, 1991
53. STARSHIP WITH FISH SCALE, October 21, 1991
54. YOU ARE SVADI HATRA FROM GALAXY KVAZI IN!

YOUR ETERNAL HOLOGRAM

55. MEETING MYSELF FROM THE FUTURE

"In this book, the knowledge comes to the surface, which was unknownto people until now. This book was a revelation. People did not evensuspect it - it opened up, revealing itself like an old secret, atreasure, as if someone dugit out of the earth. A very rare animal, adiamond animal was buried there thousands and thousands of years ago..."

Chapter 1

THE PRIEST

Strange and amazing things have happened in my life since I visited the Chichén Itza archeological site in Mexico in January, 2008. Before that day, I was a scientist, a business person with a mother's responsibility, just like millions of people around. My life changed forever after this visit.

Julia – the Little Priest

The way I saw the world changed dramatically! The way people saw me also changed. The most amazing thing was that wild animals started to accept me as if I was part of their world and nature. Suddenly, I wanted and I started talking to them in the same way we talk between humans and they started listening to me, following me and even doing what I asked them to do. It surprised me and other people who became witnesses of this occurrence. In one sentence, I can describe it this way: Wisdom has come to me and touched my soul and I became wise.

Here is my story.

"Equinox! Equinox! Equinox!" I woke up and continued to say this strange word over and over again.

I see, in front of me, huge, beautiful, orange tulips inside a green vase with gold drawings on it. The morning sunlight is shimmering through the water in the vase ... and I smell the sweet fragrance of spring.

At the time, we lived near the Tibet Mountains, it is part of the Shambala triangle and my father, every year, gave these tulips to my mother as a gift on her Birthday. He was a scientist, studying plants. He told me that these kinds of tulips grow very high in the mountains. Their name is *Greg's Tulips*.

My mother lifted me from my bed, took me into her arms and hugged me... I studied her face, her eyes. I knew she was worried, because I woke up again with the same dream, with this strange word in my mind and I didn't have any idea what it meant. I felt guilty, because I loved my mother and father so much that I didn't want them to worry because of me. My mother told me always that I was a very good child...

Suddenly, I remembered that I just saw a huge snake in my dream; a snake slithering through the street at the back of our house. It was maybe 5 to 8 houses long. I became all excited and wanted to escape from my mother's embrace. I needed to jump from her arms and run to the street to check if the snake was still there...

YOUR ETERNAL HOLOGRAM

"Mommy, I need to run fast outside now. Please let me go, big snake there... Let's go with me, I want to show it to you... It is a very nice big snake. She is kind and wise like an old king in the book you read to me. Today in my dream she talks to me with her soft voice... Please Mommy, please let's go!"

It first started when I was two and half years old and my parents were really worried – they didn't know what this word "Equinox" meant. I grew up in the country where no one was using it and no one knew what it meant. No one spoke English there.
I had hundreds of dreams during my life about pyramids and white, beautiful palaces, huge crystals, turquoise oceans with white sand beaches, animals, birds and fruits, which did not exist in my country and in our world. I also saw strange people with unusual outfits and drawings like tattoos on their faces and hands. I saw very big, tall people and I saw myself the same size as they were.
I saw ancient Gods, Goddesses, those always of extremely big sizes... Sometimes, I woke up and continued talking in another language; repeating again and again the same word, the meaning of which I didn't know.
Some of my dreams reoccurred – I saw them a few times, for example this one about a pyramid: In my dream, I am inside the temple, on the top of the pyramid. The pyramid is cut on top. Lots of people below are waiting for me to start something very important – some kind of ritual. Everything is ready. I see, on a tray, amazing orange see-through fruits and unusual ritual things. I sneak, kind of hiding, and try to look through the white curtains. Down below, I see people waiting. I am ready to start ... and I woke up each time.
I always knew that pyramids existed in Egypt, but they all had a pointed top. When I moved to Canada 20 years ago, my friend told me that she also saw some pyramids near Mexico City. I asked her if these pyramids were cut on top. She said, "NO, they're kind of round on top."
I continued to think that it was just one of my dreams, nothing more...

On January 2, 2008, I visited Mexico and Chichén Itza for the first time in my life. When I walked through the alley, where local people sell souvenirs, I instantly knew that I lived here before. My whole body was covered in goose bumps! I recognized these white-barked trees and this special light going through the trees and the white soil.
When I saw the pyramid, I knew – I felt it instantly – this is it! Here I am. This is the pyramid I saw in my dreams so many times during my life. It was impossible to explain, but I felt a connection with the Maya people around me, the people who were selling souvenirs. I immediately felt an affinity toward them and I liked them a lot. This young boy tried to sell me some masks. A small-size, wrinkled grandmother walked toward me in the crowd. It just felt as if I had returned home, to my mother land, and I felt that these people around me were almost like my relatives! I bought some souvenirs just to make them happy and I enjoyed seeing the happy smile on this boy's face.
It was a very short visit in Chichén Itza that day, less than a few hours. Most of the time, I stayed with the group of tourists, gathering around our tour guide and listening to him. Waves of goose bumps continued to flow through my body during his talk. The problem was that I knew nothing – zero – about Mayan history, culture or architecture prior to this day. I bought this travel package shortly before my departure and there was no time to study anything. Now it all started to be really interesting. I tried to remain close to the guide and sometimes I asked questions.

At one point during the tour, the guide started describing the Maya leaders. He told us that they were wearing sandals, big bracelets on their legs and hands and big jewelry around the neck made from shells, jade and feathers, short cotton dress, sometimes with jaguar skin on top. Also he mentioned that there was a legend saying that a very long time ago; some man came here with blond hair and green eyes...
Suddenly, a German tourist pointed directly at me and said that the tour guide may have made a mistake because he was describing me. It was funny, but it was exactly what he described. I was

wearing my favorite jaguar print jacket on top of a short cotton dress, sandals and big bracelets on my legs and hands made from shells and jade, and my hair is blond and I do have green eyes. When I was packing in Canada I felt that this outfit would be best in case I visited the pyramids in Mexico!

Deep inside, I was a little bit worried about this visit, because of all my previous dreams. For some reason, I wished to have my favorite outfit with me for support... At the same time I felt like I was going to some kind of important celebration or party and I might meet someone I knew a long time ago. Two weeks later, I returned to Canada and told my friend that I saw the pyramid from my dream! She advised me to visit a hypnosis specialist, who was doing past life regression. As a scientist, I didn't believe that we have another life and that it would be possible to travel back to that time or even remember it. It sounded really silly to me, so I decided not to do this. Period. But this strange coincidence and feeling regarding the pyramid continued to invade my thoughts at every turn...

http://500px.com/NataNaz/photos
http://nanaz555.ya.ru/e-mail:nanaz@mail.ru

The next day I was sitting, as usual, on my favorite bench in Stanley Park, reading a magazine. One article attracted my attention. It was about a very famous doctor, **Alfons Ven,** [1] from Holland. He discovered that our body has an invisible control system. This system controls the functions of our body, our metabolism and health. Most people are born healthy. During their lives people experience stress and as a result this control system goes "out of order", breaks down and cannot control the body anymore. So the body starts to develop all kinds of illnesses. This amazing doctor prepares pills for his clients made of pure lactose. He uses them like a container for the important information he puts inside them to fix the control system, and to return it to normal. But not only this, Alfons also says: *"The intelligence of the preparations is so highly evolved that you are gently reconnected with your origin, with your authenticity, with the real you, your inner power."* WOW! This doctor is a genius!

There was a story in this article about a boy who had a big problem. He simply did not want to attend school. At all! Because his own father was working in that school and the boy did not feel comfortable; he was shy. Alfons asked him to do one thing while he prepared the treatment for this boy. He asked him to say aloud to the open window: **"I am not more than somebody else, I am not less than somebody else, I am myself.** And then you say your first name." It worked great with perfect result for this boy. As a scientist, all my life I have experimented with everything new. I looked around... I was alone in this park. Only some Canadian wild geese were eating grass between rosebushes and cherry trees, and one big white-head eagle was sleeping on the pine tree across the rose garden. I repeated the magic words, aloud...! Suddenly, it struck me as a lightning from the sky directed to my origin. A miracle happened. I felt a heavenly, beautiful energy coming to me...

Doctor Alfons Ven is a real magical person living on Earth right now. GOD talks with people through him and sends this ray from heaven to each and every one who is in touch with him! Just by reading this article I felt instantly – the very same day – that some amazing changes were beginning to take place. I organized my day like never before, full of energy and happiness. And this feeling of pure, fresh and dynamic energy is amazing!

I decided that day that I would visit my past life with the assistance of the hypnosis specialist and find out WHO I AM. Because when I tried to repeat this sentence at that moment, when I needed to say my name, my own name did not sound right! I needed to know WHO I AM! Soon after that, I am sitting in the chair in front of the famous hypnosis specialist, Diana Cherry. This woman is 85 years old with 60 years' experience.
****
I came for the appointment 15 minutes early. It was a cute house with a sign on the door saying that her office was at the back of the house. I went there and decided to wait. I looked around. It was early spring and many plants around the backyard and patio were still dry and grey. It gave me the feeling that maybe no one lived here for a very long time.
A black cat arrived softly to the step ladder, sat near me and looked into my eyes; he sat for a while and then left. A squirrel ran to the patio and I noticed that there were lots of nuts on the ground waiting for it. It was silent and very peaceful in this backyard. Suddenly, out of nowhere a lot of black crows started landing on the neighbor's huge pine tree. They were cawing and screeching and it created such a big loud noise that I put my hands to my ears to avoid the deafening sound. There were way too many of them, maybe hundreds. I never saw so many all at once. At 10 a.m. precisely, I knocked on the door....
A woman with silver hair and turquoise, aquamarine eyes opened the door. She was wearing an aquamarine top – the same color as her eyes – it was a beautiful harmony! Smiling, she said, "Welcome, I am Di Cherry."

Diana (Di) Cherry, President of the hypnoses association, Canada

She invited me to sit in front of her in a big comfortable chair. She gently put my legs up on a stool with a big pillow and covered them with some very brightly knitted blanket called an "afghan" to keep them warm. And we started. Di Cherry told me to relax and we went step by step through this process into a deeper and deeper relaxation level... My feet and hands felt very heavy ... my eyes were closed.

Reading # 1, 13th of February 2008.

It felt as if Di's voice came through water to me.

(Note: The text below is a literal transcription of the first session –no editing.)
She began…
In your dream, you are in the temple on the top of the pyramid ready to start some ritual. You look down below; there are many people waiting for you to start...
What do you see around you?

I see instantly big huge eagle head near me!!! With bright yellow orange beak! WOW! A man is wearing a cape, made from many feathers; he wears sandals, bracelets, on the legs and hands, short skirt... Another one across of me wearing long, kind of trench coat down to the floor, made like a snake skin. It is a very well done coat, looks really neat and beautiful! It is made from dark grey colored polished scales, one to one. I see him from the back at that moment. He turns and looks directly at me very serious. He has high cheekbones, long slim eyes and he is tall, handsome man in his 40's. He has long spears in his hand... He is magnificent.

I see man staying near him with square-shaped hat, same shape as Nefertiti from Egypt had. Another man with mask like a fox or coyote... After I visited Egypt, I have no doubt that this is an Anubis mask. I recognized it instantly when I saw it in Egypt. This Goddess is responsible for the mummification and protection of the dead on the Other Side. All these men wearing masks and an enormous amount of very big size jewels made from stones, rocks. Looks very beautiful and luxurious... I look down and I see my muscular legs with toned skin and, like everyone else around, I wear short skirt and sandals. And I wear coat made from soft jaguar skin sides down to the floor and I feel this softness and see it from both sides... To my big surprise I see them all wearing round big earrings! It is strange and funny. I never saw before men wearing earrings that look like big white buttons! I start laughing. I am sure that this part was a creation of my mind!

I was sure about it... until I visited Chichén Itza for the second time and saw pictures of men everywhere on the walls, who were all wearing this kind of round button earrings! What does it mean? What I saw during the hypnosis sessions was a real jump into my past!
God Kukulcan, who looked like a man lizard, had these round circles on his earlobes such as all iguanas have. Since the Maya nobles and warriors were copying Kukulcan, they also copied these round circles at the side of its head and wore these white button-like earrings. (See chapter: Kukulcan.)

Where were you an hour before?

I am inside in some building with white carved walls.
In front of me, there was a very big book with jaguar skin cover.

What kind of book? Touch the page...
It is heavy, it is yellow color pages, and it is opening wide, like accordion folder paper. I saw two guard people staying near the open door ... with long spears in their hands.

YOUR ETERNAL HOLOGRAM

Why do you read this book?

An incredibly strong feeling come over me... my voice suddenly changed... and now it was full of emotions. Suddenly, I was drawn deeply into these emotions...
It is such a hard responsibility for me! ... I need to make the right decision today... I am the one who make decisions... my people are waiting. And I saw the page and their round Maya calendar and I studied it... It is very hard to make decision today ... big responsibility to make announcement when to start to plant seed to the ground ... rain needs to be short after ... I need to know when rain season will start ... we have a drought.

Suddenly, I started talking much louder, almost screaming: *"WATER! WATER!!! People need water to have harvest! They need harvest! They work so hard... Their life so difficult..."*

Streams of tears started running down my face; my tears were two rivers of tears... I never had such tears in my whole life! The muscles on my face, which I never used before, made a sorrow mask... I feel an ENORMOUS spirit PAIN come out. I was talking in a different voice and used different muscles on my face!
It was overwhelming and I didn't have any control over what was going on. I never experienced something like this in my entire life...

*At this point I am the **Highest Priest** in this pyramid and I am full of emotions and feeling...*

"Let's back up to the pyramid," Di Cherry's voice told me.

What is the reason for this gathering?

I see round shape, it come again and again in my vision ... now I see it. It is a ball. I see stone table and I saw a light coming from an entrance.
On the table, I see a man lying down...
He is the winner today! He is very proud!! And happy. And he is ready to die now to help people ... and to be sacrificed ... and I continue crying and talking with great emotion. These people will give everything what they have to GOD, most best what they have ... best of their people ... in order to have harvest.

Come close, look into their eyes. People can change gender, the color of their hair or skin, their whole looks, BUT if you look into their eyes, you will recognize who the person is. Maybe it is someone you know from this life.

I step closer... I am afraid to look into his eyes ... tears run down my face and suddenly a loud scream come out from my throat...

Di Cherry stopped the session. She decided that this was excessively emotional for me.

The last question she asked was:

Let's go to the end of your life there, your last year, where are you, what do you see?

I see head of big huge grey snake made of stone...
YOUTUBE: Avatar Svadi 7, Hypnoses Di Cherry

Chichen Itza pyramid, calendar

It was a very strange feeling to see, to look at people around me on the street right after my past life readings... They were all so preoccupied with this present life!

I wish that all of these people on the street could have the possibility to see themselves for a moment from the side of the road where one life follows another and another. Such possibility can give them a new way of evaluating their present life and enjoy it much more. It is very important for them to know that, YES; they have this life in this body. BUT when they die, the Spirit they have inside them will not die! Never! It just does not work that way. Spirits cannot die! Spirits will continue to exist in a new body in the next life, period. Now that I know this, I am guarantying it for each and every one. Spirit's life will go on and continue to live in many future lives. Those special skills a person is developing now will be useful in his/her next life. It is important for everyone to visit a past life regression specialist at least once to make adjustments for their development. Who was I before? What kind of skills did I have? Our problems in this life can have roots in our past lives. Most people just don't know this and are suffering not in one life, but maybe throughout a chain of lives by carrying this emotional baggage with them from one life to the next. The only way to fix it, to get rid of this burden, is to visit a past life regression specialist. We all have a doctor for the body; I am glad that doctors for the Spirit exist as well.

I really wish to say to all of these people on the street that we have many lives and that the life we have now is really easy to live, not that bad at all! Enjoy your life! Make people around you happy in your presence! Skip fighting with your close friends, with the people you love... These problems, which you are facing today, right now, and which look BIG to you, are really NOTHING when compared to the problems people had a long time ago during their lives in ancient Mexico. You have food and water and you will have water tomorrow and after tomorrow and for a long, long time. You are very lucky that you don't know what the word **DROUGHT** really means... I wish to tell people: **WATER** is the most important part of people's lives. Please, each and every one, take care of **WATER** now and of the future water supply. Do what you can to be sure it is safe, clean and will be always available to everyone who needs it on our planet.

****

YOUR ETERNAL HOLOGRAM

When I left Di Cherry's place and I look back one more time at this cute house, I had a different view of this place, compared to how I saw it before. Now I see this house as a secret Star Gate to the past – to the ancient world, thousands of years ago. And this smiling, innocent, angelic-looking Di Cherry, in reality, is a wise, magic person; she is making such magic for everyone who consults her.

I never had entertainment like this! This is the best possible quality entertainment on Earth! You can be inside of your life, back thousands of years ago and you can see everything in color, you can touch things around you and you are part of your real past life! It is much better then to see movie with 3D glasses in theatre.

I had arrived that day at Di Cherry's place alone. When I left her house, there were two people inside me... It was an astonishing feeling – me and myself as a Priest, altogether as one person.

When I returned home that day and looked in the mirror I could not recognize my own face! After a few hours of exercise during the past life session this muscle, which I never use before, created a new "mask" on my face. This "Stamp" from my past was there for 3 or 4 days, and even now, people see a shadow of it and tell me that something changed in my face!

After the first two hypnosis sessions, I was staying again at the same hotel in Rivera Maya, Mexico. It was just 2.5 months later. The people who worked there and remembered me from my first visit told me that my face had changed somehow and that it looked different. I guess I just started to be older – by 2000 years.

The Priest was a guest in my mind during the next 2 or 3 weeks after the hypnosis sessions. From time to time, during the day, I had visions and feelings. During the night, in my dreams, I saw myself in Chichén Itza carrying on with my daily routine. I enjoyed the Priest's presence and continued to remember more and more of my life as a High Priest in ancient Mexico.

I remembered my two hairdressers, who worked my hair into such an unusual hairstyle every day. They lifted up my black, long, thick hair and attached all this heavy jewelry and feathers to it. It was similar to the hairstyle that Japanese women have on ancient pictures.

Once, I started remembering that I had received a very special gift from the far north city. It was a little baby jaguar, which was white – a very rare color! He was born with twisted, bended toes in his front right paw. It was impossible to fix. He was small and never grew to its full size. This baby followed me everywhere and slept nearby. I guess he accepted me as his mother because I always wore a jaguar cape. He had green, jade jewelry on the collar around his neck. I loved him and gave him the name of "White star". The word **Zolkin** or **Zolkan** came often to my mind after I woke up those days and I didn't know what it meant in Mayan, until December 2008 when I was in Australia and found the same word in a book, but with a T in front! It was name for the Mayan Calendar! I remember that I had a live turtle as a pet as well. This turtle lived with the previous Priest and we had it in the temple for many years. The turtle had a round, tattoo-like mandolin drawing on her carapace. I brought this turtle to the observatory **Caracol,** because the jaguar had begun hunting it and had tried to bite her.

I remember living in the white carved building, now named the Annex to the Nunnery. Near the entrance, on the wall there is a bas relief of me as a Priest with luxuriant hair including two pony tails.

YOUTUBE:
Avatar Svadi 3, Angels & Giant

****

I often walked in the dark to the observatory after a sauna, and enjoy staring at the night sky, studying the stars. I love studying sounds. Maybe Priest was the one who knew the secrets of the sounds produced in the pyramid of Chichén Itza? I even wrote a manuscript about the sounds of the rocks. Once, I found a stone – it was my favorite limestone – a big flat, white, grey rock. I found it deep in the cave and it produced a beautiful sound. I tried pounding this rock with different size shells and other pebbles and it made beautiful sounds – like many bells made of glass or crystals. This often put me in a trance somehow.

****

The mystery around the sounds echoing from the Chichén Itza pyramid is still not solved. *"Where else in the history of the world have an ancient people preserved a sacred sound by coding it into stone so that a thousand years later people might hear and wonder,"* (An archaeological study of chirped echo from the Mayan pyramid of Kukulcan at Chichén Itza by David Lubman)[8].

It is interesting that every spring, for many years, I bought the smallest size turtle for my sister, Elena's birthday on April 10. In the fall, we would return the turtle back to nature. The place where I bought the turtles belonged to a company, which caught wild animals to send them all over the world to different Zoos. There were snow-jaguars among the lot. They looked exactly like regular jaguars and belong to the same family, but their fur is white and their eyes are icy blue. Their local name is *Irbis*. The Latin name is *Uncia* (Shreber, 1775). They are very rare and part of the "RED book" of protected species. They live in Tibet, Altai, in Central Asia. During my early school years, I visited that place and stared at the white jaguars for many hours. That species is the largest among the panther's family and they are very powerful. Sometimes it was very scary to be right near the cage, when they jumped or roared.

I was very lucky that the director let me go into the company's territory, because he knew my father very well. It was also interesting that the workers at that place brought back lots of turtles from the desert and kept them as live-meat to feed the snow jaguars.

Now I found a reason for having such an attraction to the jaguars and – I had my own little, white jaguar in my past life as a Priest! This is what attracted me as a magnet near the cages of these huge, scary, white cats. Same about turtles.

Some time ago, my daughter asked what I was doing; what kind of book was I writing? So I gave the first few pages of the book about the Priest for her to read. She returned to me and asked, "How long did you sleep with Sweetheart and turtle?"

10 years ago, at the age of two, she got two very nice cat-toys that looked almost real – one black and one white. The white one, which she named Sweetheart, she gave to me. Ever since then, I sleep hugging the big white cat every night. For Christmas, I got a sea turtle and now I sleep with my right hand on her soft, velvet smooth shell. And now, here is my daughter pointing out that the Priest had a white jaguar and a turtle and that I am sleeping with a white cat and a turtle! Well..., I had not notice this until today. It is amazing how many things follow us from one past life to another.

Word **Tzolkin** – sounds of the rocks – is an unusual hair shape which also supports what I saw during the hypnosis sessions. This is a real event from my past life and it is described in many historical accounts about Chichén Itza and the Mayan culture.

YOUR ETERNAL HOLOGRAM

A young white jaguar

Reading # 2 & 3 – 20th of February and 25th of March 2008

You can hear this reading, as well as Reading # 4, April 29, 2008, on the CD at www.ameliareborn.com

Reading # 2

(Note: This literal transcription from the recorded reading – no editing, for the comfort of the readers here short version)

Di Cherry:
We are leaving this room, to eternity ... through the centuries back... Back to the land we called Mexico. This is the day when you are in the temple, way on top of the pyramid. You are ready to start some ritual and look down below, lots of people waiting for you to start.

(I start talking with a voice that sounded strange even to me...)

I see this room, on top it is very cool walls. But it's crazy hot outside and so dry land, like powder all leaves on the trees around ... very dry, and its very hot ... it sunshine killing...
Yes so many people waiting and it is very hot for them to wait and I need to start soon.

Are you up already or are you ascending those steps?

I see myself; I can run to this pyramid very fast! I see myself one morning, I am running up to this so fast, like almost flying. I remember each of these steps and I am not afraid to run fast, fast, fast down. And I am enjoying actually run through this pyramid up and down...

So you have a speech or duty today, something important to do...

(Suddenly, my voice changes)
I am a Priest, I am a Priest in this pyramid and it is such a big responsibility to be Priest, it is hard, impossibly hard! It is my people, so many people, they waiting for me, I care about this people... It is

big responsibility; it is hard to be Priest... They waiting for me, it is so dry, they don't have food, we need rain season. We need WATER.

I understand.

They need to know when to start planting seeds. And I need to know and I cannot make mistake. We need to put seed right before rain season. We need rain. We need to pray to have rain. People waiting ... they ready give everything what they have, best what they have ... to have water.

Right.
And this day is so important, we pray God to help us and we need to make sacrifice... We need to give; gift to the God.

And what is to be the gift today?

It is so hard ... it so hard... (My voice is very, very sad.)
We have game today, we have big game today.

YES.

We choose best people to play in this game ... and we have winner, we already have winner. It is all about ball, it is beautiful blue ball and this is the winner of the ball.

And the winner, you're going to take him up to the pyramid?

Yes, he's so proud today, he so happy. He win the game ... But he going to die ... he going to die!

But, he knows this, doesn't he?

Yea... Everybody knows this and this is so hard...

This is the way of the people honoring the God ... he is going to give himself – great honor for himself...

YES... (Crying)

Being fine young men ... and so ... this sacrifice needs to be done in this room?

In this room, they bring him up and he has garlands of flowers, he has flowers ... it is droughts... People find flowers and they make for him ... flowers ... they washed him ... like a shower ... and put on him all kind of oils, they have nice smell oils, he all with this like perfume things ... He's very beautiful, he have short skirt, and very tone muscles ... and sandals ... and necklaces and bracelets and on the legs he have bracelets and it is very rich and beautiful... It is so much stones, very beautiful many stones, I guess it is very expensive, very beautiful outfit he has...

I like you to look to this young man for a moment. Does he have dark blue eyes like you?

YES, he has blue eyes like me...[1] (Pause)

---

[1] During another reading we found that the Priest had dark blue eyes...

YOUR ETERNAL HOLOGRAM

It is very hard day, it so hard day for me ... difficult day for me...

But this is the great honor?

O ... No! ... No ... no... (I start screaming, crying and talking through the crying.)
This is my son ... this is the son, my son ... the only one son I have... (I start crying hard.)

I am going to take you back before this day, I am going to take you to time when you were with your son and you were happy.

... I am fine ... we still up ... I need to do my job now... I need to do my job now...
He is on the table, he on the right side, I turn him to the right side... I have in front of me men with Eagles mask, big Eagle mask... I saw another man, he has long coat and he has slim eyes, very slim eyes and high cheek. And he look at me right now, he looks at me; because now most important moment ... and we look to each other ... we talk with our eyes...

He has long coat and this coat is made from huge snake ... with many, many scales, beautiful! The scales are side by side. And he has a long stick on the top sharp, with black sharp end. And many feathers and skins of all kinds of animals around... And I have a long coat and this one is made from Jaguar, it's a jaguar coat ... and now..., and now most important moment... (Voice trembles)

... I say bye to my son and I kiss him and I touch him and say to him bye and this is so stressful...
(Crying) *And now he on his side ... and now...*

And now...

I give him some kind of plants juice to drink, something makes him sleep and he just sleeps. And it's made from kind of mushrooms and kind of bulbs from the flowers and roots all together and he sleeps now...
(My voice start to be strong and solid)

But his Spirit aware, his spirit aware and ready... And ready to start...

Right.

We pray and we make some rituals ... some kind rituals, kind of strange things people doing ... and they brings cups and they already have cups around, I don't want see these cups ... they have this white cups for the blood ... to collect blood...

That's right.

I need to make this Spirit FREE; I need to talk with his spirit now. It is very important to be very organized and cold minded to make it right. He is the winner ... from all people who was in this game. They all try; each of them tries the best to win... Each of them tries hard to win, very hard to win.

They all try to concentrate on this ring. They try to concentrate as much as they can ... and I see level of the concentration of energy. I see this energy near each person who plays. I see color of energy also ... and they are all playing and I am sitting and all my people and EAGLE and SNAKE and all other guards and warriors and we look. My people see color of concentration, and we know: those who win have today most strong highest level of concentration of energy. And we need someone, we need MESSENGER to the GOD, we need him who will reach GOD ears.

YES.

Symbol of the BALL is the message to put to GOD ears, and we need someone who best with this today. Yes, he sleep, his spirit strong, his spirit ready to bring the message to GOD, he is waiting now for action. I see his body now with many layers ... many layers, you can see them through, but it's one, two, tree, four, five six, seven, maybe eight ... layers of his body, up and up, one by one, kind of his body also and ... one of those more round ... round. This one I need to start with, this one most important ... and now ... all my concentration going to him. I need to take out from his body his spirit, his Spirit Body.

YES.

And, and it is heavy work... My hands start to be so heavy ... very heavy ... my hand near his back and I'm opening it and I take out from inside this round sphere and I try to take it out and it is very difficult and going out very slow ... very slow ... it's going out. It's kind of light when it's inside ... but when it's coming out, it starts so stuffy, heavy, like a honey, strong. And I take out and I make effort and I make it like with help of strongest vacuum. Out, take it out this thing and now it's in the air right near me ... it comes out finally all. It's a flat, big huge gong or disk, like a gong. Chinese people have gong like this and they make sound with this ... this things now very heavy and it make sound ... Hmmmmm ... wuuuuuuu ... heavy, down sound ...very low deep sound. I put it in big container for now, like a vase ... until I will deliver it to GOD.

YES.

And all people, all my people around already closed their noses and ears to avoid that spirit goes in to their body.

Interesting!

So it's closed now, they breathe through their mouths very little. Spirit runs to anyone's body around trying to find new body.

YES.

And this is more than a live thing now, so all closed their noses and their ears. Guards, these warriors they're waiting and they have the same... (Pause)

This part, I don't want to talk... (Sad voice) I see blood; I see they collect blood from his neck to these white containers, to this big bowl... I see this... (Pause)
They're giving me his heart... I have his heart, in my left hand his heart and I have ball in my right hand and I am going down to people and I show them the heart and ball.

This is Heart of the Winner...
This is heart of my son... (Crying)

All these people below have little containers. Little white cups, round cups. And to each cup only one drop of his blood coming, each cup one drop, only one drop. They will bring this cup to their homes, to their plants, to their fields. They will mix with water and they will put this Holy Water to the plants to have harvest, to have plants to grow.

YOUR ETERNAL HOLOGRAM

This Sacrifice Blood, Holy Blood will turn to Plants and Flowers and Fruits... and give them LIFE to live...

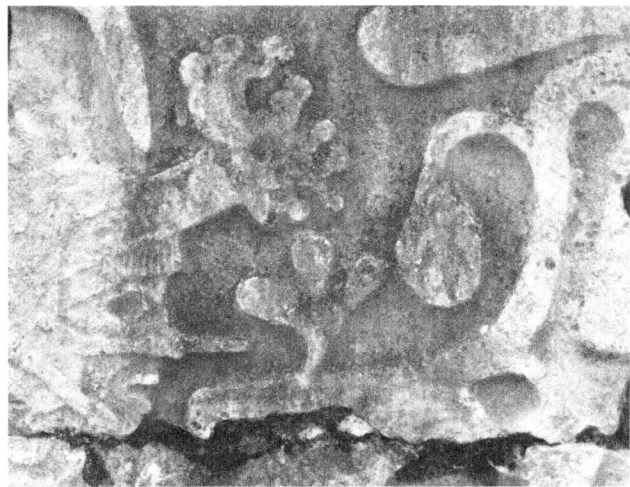

Details of the bas-relief from the wall in Ball court in Chichén Itza

This supports what I saw during the hypnosis sessions: warriors have their noses closed to avoid the spirit going inside their bodies. They are near plants, the symbol of harvest, growing from bulbs into fruits from the sacrificed blood. The spirit of the winner was connected through his energy from his blood to all plants in the fields in that area. When he asked God for help, rain would fall on that territory.
Right.

Can I ask you who teaches you to do these rituals?

I will tell now. I am Priest in this temple, in this big beautiful temple. My responsibility is to take care of the plants and harvest and agriculture. And astrology. I have many students, I have people who only study planets and they study in Caracol, our observatory. This is my responsibility. Sometimes, I bless little children, very little children, newborn children.

And I like to heal little children and I just heal yesterday an old, very old and sick and slim old man and I remember him. Sometimes I am a doctor and I have KNOWLEDGE. My knowledge comes from a far ... far away time ... my knowledge split between maybe 10 people, they're carrying this part through their lifetime and if I am dead, they all come to one, new Priest, and they each give their part. I am the only one who knows everything about this; my responsibilities. This is my subjects, deep...very deep.

I have a book, I have a big old book, it comes from previous Priest and it is a heavy book. I can hardly lift this book, it's so heavy. Many numbers in this book and I see calendar... I see this big calendar; this is astrological round calendar, the size of the whole page and many calculations, math and some drawings, and letters...

Eternal Spirit by Shahla Homayoni
http://www.homayoni.com/
Shahla.ht@gmail.com

****

The first few days after this session were very hard. I tried to avoid my thoughts about this sacrifice. Emotions and tears kept invading my mind. I tried to avoid people. Imagine if someone would ask me why I was crying – how could I answer? "O ... yesterday I sacrificed my son, because we had droughts..." What would people think? Imagine the expression on their faces? They would think I had gone completely out of my mind.

People who heard this hypnosis session were also touched emotionally...

"Reading your book but I am crying so much reading I can hardly read it. Your book resonates so much with me, so much emotions it brings up. You put your heart in this book to touch the hearts of the readers." **Buryl P.** A few months later, I found this description of the game I visualized during my life-regression session. Di Cherry and I were surprised to read this. It supports again everything I saw during hypnoses sessions!

The more ancient type of sacrifice in Maya – is an idea of sending a messenger to the deity in the name of the whole community. The soul of the sacrificed person after his death was freed from the body and went to gods and delivered requests and prayers of people. The human sacrifice by no means represented any kind of "exceptional brutality". This act was perceived as sending of the selected, best of the best person to gods – similar to Jesus Christ the Savior. Indians were constantly surprised by brutality of the inhabitants of the Old World, who crucified Jesus without any special drug thus causing his unbearable physical suffering. Indians perceived Him as a messenger to the Only God. More than that, in ancient times, messengers to gods were sent only in exceptional or difficult situations. Messengers were supposed to solicit for wellbeing and prevention of disasters. Messengers to gods were either regular (in particular feasts) or in exceptional cases, like: crop failure, draught, epidemics, etcThe soul of a person in order to transcend another space should separate itself from the body. Naturally, it was happening most often after the death of the body. But sometimes the soul could leave the body in a time of sleep or sickness. And in very particular moments the selected magicians were able to do it – priests and naguali – by using special practices and devices, for example, taking psychedelic substances. The mountain lord of the darkness – jaguar was the chief purifier of souls in the underworld. (Ref. 29 "Ancient America: Flight in time and prostransive. Mezoamerika" Excerpts from the book by GG Ershovoy UnCopyrighted©Sam, 2003-2006) [30]

Once after the first hypnosis readings with Di Cherry, I was walking through the Duty Free stores at the international airport. Suddenly, I saw something which took my breath away – literally – I stopped breathing. I saw through the store window some jacket with the exact snake skin coat, which I saw during my hypnosis session! It was an astonishing feeling! It was a Zilli store for luxury men's clothes and shoes. I went inside and ask the clerk to show me the jacket. It was made from real python skin! Now I know for sure that in my hypnosis session I saw an ancient Maya man who was wearing a cape from real snake skin. It looked very similar to this one in the Zilli store![2] [18] – with only two differences; the scales on the coat were smaller than those on the cape I saw in the ancient Chichén Itza temple. And 2000 years ago, there were no seams on the garment. It gave me the idea that, at that time, the snakes which existed then were much bigger than the pythons are today! Or maybe they used special techniques, which do not exist today.The jacket was available only for men. Wow! How lucky they are, they can feel themselves almost as a Kukulcan, the Serpent Snake God of Maya in this amazing Zilli jacket! When I started going through my clothes, I noticed that many had this scale pattern: dresses, purses, shoes and even my Japanese kimono have it!

Below are dreams which I had at different times of my life. I didn't have any idea before, WHY I had these unusual dreams. I decided to add them here, because I know now that, in these dreams, there is an echo from my past lives. They also support what I saw and felt during my hypnosis sessions. They add some information and interesting details.

These dreams are exactly – word for word – how I told them after I woke up.[3]
In the dream below, for example, I experienced the process by which the SPIRIT BODY was taken out from my physical body.

---

[2]   www.zilli.fr

[3]   It will be very interesting to meet scientists who study Chichen Itza. I wish that they would ask me questions about the mystery that still surrounds the place. Perhaps I will be able to answer them – if these questions cover the time I lived in Chichen Itza.

AVATAR SVADI HATRA

Snakeskin jacket

Dream # 1
They pulled my body out of me, April 25, 1996

After a long time of suffering I dozed off at 6 am. It went on for many days. I could not have enough sleep. I asked to be helped falling asleep. It had been happening many times that my body turned off, became heavy as lead, dull, but my mind went on thinking. After that, a strange thing happened – it seemed that, I began falling asleep very deeply, as if falling into some pit, but the mind was not sleeping yet and partly in control. It happened immediately. It was horrible. I was lying there – inert. My entire body was heavy, I didn't feel it and suddenly some force began sucking me out of my body, pulling out like a pump, sucking milk out of the breast, forcefully, pulling out something out of me ... but the shell of my body stayed there. They were pulling out my soul. It was a purely physical sensation and I observed it with my brain. At the same time, I was feeling how it was being pulled out of my self. All the while, I was still feeling my physical body. At the beginning I thought that it was simply a huge suction cup pulling my body up, but then, I noticed, that my body rested in its place...

I remembered how it was! I was lying on my right side, and everything was coming out from here, it is like when the sky is covered with clouds, and then an opening appears – it was in the middle of my back, over the waistline, closer to the left side, in the heart area. They were pulling slowly and with great force – the spirit body was coming out of the skin with difficulty. There was a moment, when this thing almost came out, but had not separated completely; a laden, heavy thing was hanging over me. It may have not been heavy, but it was pulled out with such difficulty, tightly – that is why I felt this laden heaviness. It was like a sphere, like a shape of the spiral galaxy, the thing being pulled out, larger than a meter. It was hanging over my body. My mind was on its own, I was looking from the inside and from the outside at the same time. Then I experienced some sensations, which I can neither describe, nor tell about. I felt with my eyes some rounded protruding surface, some drops of temperature, then I crashed out totally and didn't remember anything afterwards.Maybe the body in the dream was dead after this "experiment"...?

Dream # 2
Hieroglyphs on the palm, September 12, 1992

I was sitting on the hill, the hill of yellow clay, leaning my back against the hill. There were similar hillocks around, the size of about two meters, not more. Some oval form. I realized that I looked at my palm, the left one. There was a drawing on the palm – a sign almost as big as the palm. As if it was stamped by a stamp of a very good quality. There were no chiromancy lines on the palm. There was a white rim, like a closed circle. And some colors. Such colors are painted on cakes – meringue – rosy, protuberant and dried on. And it was like that; each line very clear and they stuck out over the skin.[4] Apart from white, there also was red, and, maybe also brown-beige and black. It was a three-dimensional, complicated figure. The lines did not merge, as if they were drawn under a microscope. It looked very much like a hieroglyph, but a hieroglyph is always based on a square frame – this one was rounded. At least one side was curved.

I was looking for a long time, and then I saw two women approach me, Indians, wearing clothes of a fabric with streaming, iridescent pattern. I recognized them. I said, "Oh, I haven't seen you for a long time." I said, "Look, I have a sign," and stretched out my hand to them. They started looking. (I remembered all this with difficulty, as if through thick honey, or layers of water; every word was hard to utter.) They also said about me: **"You are a Goddess, and there is also one more person."**

I asked them, "Where are you, where are you coming from, what is your life like?"
They said, "We can show you," and laughed with a rustling sound. **"You probably should know yourself."They said, "Because you have capabilities, energy," (specific energy in dreams).**
I know I am used to make a plan, and remember everything in my dreams. I break everything in my dreams into parts, fragments. And I have a capacity of automatically storing in my memory major moments, coordinates. However, since I was 16 then, I always threw out of my memory all the unnecessary information and I controlled my thoughts. They knew this. And they told me, that if I wanted to, I could keep all of my dreams in my memory. And I could wake up, coming back to them years and years later.
They said, **"You will see and remember all of the details, every hour."** (And this will enable me to change the past and the future – if I would go to them often then I would see and remember the future more clearly.)
They also said that people cannot remember this even if they get there. And this would make no sense to them, and they would not get their experience there. From that comment, I thought that maybe people do not have enough energy.[5] If I knew which step brought me to what, then it would become possible for me to plan my own life and change my life.

Dream # 3
ATHARVAN, October 13, 1989

In the morning, I remembered the word from yesterday – EQUINOX, I was repeating it yesterday all the time. It was there before my waking up, always like a drop of water pecking the stone. EQUINOX ... EQUINOX ... EQUINOX...Now I have the same sensation. But this time the word is different. This was like a flow, repeating the same word... It was only one minute. I woke up, looked toward the window and closed my eyes again. And at this moment (I felt a shiver on my skin); I immediately saw the face of a man of a huge size. Maybe it was an enormous statue. My field of view captured an eye, a cheek, the chin on the left side. I was so staggered, shaken, that it disappeared. Afterwards, it appeared again, and again – I am stunned – it disappeared.
It was the face of a man, made of grey marble. But there was a feeling that he was alive. On the side there was a pattern, something I saw on Chinese walls in China, and on his face there were many, many manuscripts of a very fine design. The face was of a single-color, and the pattern on the edge of the chin – a darker shade. The curvy writing was on the cheek in a triangle shape. He had Persian,

---

[4] The Maya word Tlappalan means land of red and black. Black, red, brown-beige are the colors the Maya usually used for their tattoos. All tattoos on the face are flat drawing, but they are as if embossed over the skin surface.

[5] You will find Scientific Interpretation at the end of the book.

almond-shaped eyes. And there was a word, which stuck with me, much harder than the word EQUINOX – it was repeating again and again ... constantly, rapidly. In my dream I thought that I would forget it, when I woke up. So I tried to remember. Maybe two words – avatar. And the word "vat" or "tar". I composed it from three words "vat", "tara". Something that was repeating all the time – "avatar", and somewhere there was also the word, "hat". A V A T A R A ... A H A T A V A R A ... - Atharvan, maybe?

Yes! Exactly that word! I think it was the word. It was this one, whose face I saw. But I could not bear it, only for a moment, then everything blurred, I could not bear to look for a long time. I was there for an instant – a few times. Just like a quantum of light[6] of grey-dim color. It was not a marble – marble shine. I could draw it, how it was, what proportions there were. The finest drawing, as if his face was the size of a room, but traced with exquisite precision. (I drew this picture immediately after I woke up. I never expected that it would be featured in a future book.) Was he sleeping? I don't remember. He radiated the sensation of a living being. And I did not feel that I was sleeping.

Atharvan

Vedic atharvan is cognate with Avestan Atharvan, "priest", but the etymology of the term is not yet conclusively established. (Boyce, 1982:16)

Dream # 4
Baby from the river, April 11, 1992

High up in the mountains there was a giant castle, the Palace. Inside, there was a ball. I was the principal queen there. Some noble mothers brought their newborn babies there. It was some kind of tradition; they would bring their babies, and the ball is in honor of that. They are either initiated, or it is some sort of a ritual. The babies are nice, beautiful. They all are my people, and I have a right to do anything with anybody. I could keep any of their babies as a tribute.

I went outside, unnoticed. It was grey dawn and I saw a deep, deep canyon with a river running down at the bottom. The river was flowing out of the mountain; you could hear the sound of running water. And I found a baby there. He was lying in something like a nutshell – comfortable, in a good sleeping berth lined with silk and jewels. He seemed not to be dressed at all, but decorated all over! His body was entirely covered with something that resembled hieroglyphs, probably painted. His face, as if Mexican – eyes like olives, the nose as if Indian. There were similar wavy lines on his lips and nose. He had an unusual face with dark blue eyes. I brought him into the Palace, to keep him. They all surrounded me, surprised.

---

[6] You will find Scientific Interpretation about quantum light at the end of the book.

YOUR ETERNAL HOLOGRAM

As you noticed in the last three dreams the tattoo subject is repeated. There are tattoos on the palm of the hand, on the face and on the entire body of the baby. I asked myself why I had these dreams many times in my life? I never had any interest in visiting any tattoo parlor. However, now I know; I was simply a Maya Priest a few thousand years ago. And for Maya people, this was part of their lives.

****

Here is the amazing story of a Miracle Man living in our time in Brazil. What I saw during my hypnosis sessions and in my dreams – how the Spirit Body leaves our physical body – is the real thing. It is happening every day in the life of this Miracle Man. In this particular story, there are many Spirits who were doctors in their earthly lives and who are now helping this special man heal hundreds of people daily! He is the proof that Spirits exist and do not die after their earthly death. Below is only an excerpt from the book.

The Miracle Man

We humans are strange creatures. Sometimes we see the evidence but reject the explanation, grappling instead for our own one to fit with our narrow, limited knowledge; preferably an explanation that isn't going to rock our 'conscience boat' too much, that does not require too much in the way of a radical life-change, and that does not shake the shell of security that is our understanding and perception. In light of the evidence in this book, there is no alternative explanation.

João Teixeira da Faria *is the living proof. He has been tested and examined by the best scientific minds this planet can muster. He permits and welcomes these investigations in the hope that they will prove to everyone the existence of the spirit world and the importance of living correctly in this life so as to elevate ourselves in the next, instead of enduring a karmic penalty. João dedicates his life to healing the sick and incurable, without payment and without prejudice. João Teixeira da Faria is arguably the most powerful medium alive at this time and must surely rank amongst the greatest of the past two thousand years. A "medium", as defined by the Oxford Dictionary, is a person who is "a spiritual intermediary between the living and the dead". João not only communicates with spirit, he incorporates the spirit entity; he is literally taken over by the spirit and, in doing so, loses consciousness, 'waking' a few hours later without any knowledge of his actions during the incorporation. Whilst 'in entity', his body is used as a means of conducting physical surgery and seemingly miraculous healing of the sick by the spirit entities who work through him.*

João meditates in a small room at the rear of the complex before entering the main current room. To incorporate the spirit entity he simply stands before a table containing a wooden cross. He begins by asking that his hands be guided in the work of the day. Then, as he recites the Lord's Prayer, the entity enters him and takes control of his body. At the end of the daily program, he then stands up, begins a small prayer and the entity leaves his body with a visible shudder of his heavy frame. João Teixeira da Faria is a medium of extraordinary capabilities.

His mediumship enables him to take on, or incorporate, thirty-three entities, all of whom were remarkable people during their own physical lives. The entities are spirits of deceased doctors, surgeons, healers, psychologists and theologians who are of such high soul elevation they need no longer reincarnate to our physical plane. They do, however, continue to elevate in the spirit plane by the extent of their benevolence and charitable works.

João is capable of incorporating only one entity at a time, although he can change entity at any time as the need arises. It does not preclude any number of entities performing operations at the same time outside his body. During incorporation, each entity carries with him his own personality from the past life and, to those who work in the house regularly, each one can be recognized in João's behavior. (The Miracle Man: The Life Story of João de Deus, by Robert Pellegrino-Ostrich.). [5]

Dream # 5
The Upper Kingdom, October 24, 1993
Part 1 – the clash

It was some terrible, black, big and hairy creature. I was feeling it. It was approaching, coming closer to me in order to kill me and some of my cute creatures, who were standing behind me, behind my back. I realized with my mind, that the beast was approaching but it was still far away. I went with my creatures to the woods, through strange brushwood, they were not woods, or bushes – they were just branches growing right out of the soil, interwoven, like barberry ... and white sand; they were growing on white sand. I brought my creatures to this THING. Then something crawled out to meet me. It had green spots all over his white body. The wise one. It appeared, suspended in front of me. It was speaking with a soft voice, like Kaa (the huge snake in the cartoon about the Indian boy, Maugli). It said to me, "I will save yours, the little ones." And it began to unwind, unroll, as if it was crawling out of an invisible crack in the wall. There was an opening and it crawled out – I didn't see the inside of the place. It was growing in size – expanding, and became as big as a Hercules plane. From the tail, a huge crack opened across its body leading my creatures inside it. Its head was flat, like a leaf. The crack was in the lower side – and my creatures started walking inside IT. And here I saw them with my eyes, I knew beforehand that I had them; that they followed me, and the snake spoke about them, but now I saw them, finally. I was very much surprised.

There were less than ten of them, maybe seven or eight. They were little animals, different from each other, sweet, nice. Spirits or Creatures... I cannot describe them. I cannot even name them. Once in my dream, I went with Kaliostro – there was such a tiny elephant, and a semi-plant – None of them walked, but floated over the ground ... the spirits. They were like spirits and similar to the creatures from another dream, which looked like that little magic hen, like those two birds, which are not really birds that were coming to me, such as that shaggy-haired one that lived in my castle – that's what they looked like. Very strange, no legs, no arms, just their individual essence – very nice, very cute. Then they started walking in a line, like children in kindergarten. They did not mix up. When they were all inside it, the snake closed up, curled inside itself, slithered behind the invisible wall and disappeared.

Then suddenly this horrible beast came upon me – to kill me and my spirit-like creatures. The beast had something very sharp – something between a scythe and a sickle in its hand. Besides that, he held two more sharp things – one like the sharpest arrowhead or spearhead, a lance maybe. The second weapon was a semi-round object, similar to a fishhook, which had been inserted into a wooden stick. Once inserted into the stick, you could not pull it out. It was easier to leave it there. But it was protruding from the stick slightly. I had a feeling that it was not supposed to be put on the stick *(or it was perhaps "retractable")*, because, when you inserted the hook in it – just *a print* in a shape of the letter ЭC was visible – and no one could notice it. The other weapon had a heavy ball attached to it, similar to a spiked ball attached to the end of a chain. The sharpness combined with incredible heaviness made for a dangerous weapon. It was similar to a medieval flail – a spiked ball stuck to the stick by a chain.

His armor was round-shaped, curved. I was rather afraid of him. I would have rather run away from him. I cannot describe him – when someone comes to kill you, then you fix your attention on the thing that is supposed to kill you. He was like a blurred, dirty, heavy, wet woolen spot – a very hairy Siberian bear; big – about two to three meters high. But I knew that I should not run away, but defend my creatures, I had to fight. Then something surprising started to happen. I was looking at everything as if from some other, second sight. **Suddenly there was two of me.** Everything ended up very quickly – looking from the outside – incredibly simply and easily. The other me, who was fighting did this – she was standing away at about two to three meters and then the beast lunged in my direction – at that same moment, that same second, an air stream appeared in front of him, very thin, it captured him then lunged and turned in the right direction. In front of him, there was something invisible, similar to a veil with gold threads, fibers, but incredibly taut and strong, like laser rays, twisted.

Medieval Flail

There was a breath inside the veil, or something like a stream of air, invisible. This was in the air in front of him right at the moment he lunged at me with his armor. He hit the veil around him. His body was pulled into the threads, bending around and twisting to escape. It turned up, he hit, cut himself. Meanwhile, I did nothing. I just stayed there and watched from the side. Yet I knew that I had created this air-wall with threads in front of him. And I noticed that the sickle, that had stricken him and was in his hands, looked actually like a laser disc, but larger, and incredibly thin and sharp.

So, when this all happened – I was surprised, but the other me, who was doing all this, went and found it immediately. She knew where to look, where it was, I felt them – the other two weapons. They were at a distance, hidden in two different places. It is hard to explain; why they were there. I approached and found the flail, without the wooden end, large – ten to fifteen centimeters long. I went to the other place and – in a strange small wooden construction, on the steps of a small house – I found a wooden box that was not touching the ground, floating in the air, just like the first weapon. While they were in such a condition, they were still dangerous – I knew this. I felt that I must level them. They could be unloaded – and I did it.

Part 2, Palace, celebration

The dream went on. After I finished with the third weapon, I went to the palace, to check what was going on there. Everything that happened occurred just before the great, magic celebration.
There was to be a feast of magical enchantment with the participation of many creatures; some ritual with celebration. I was in this palace before, it is very high in the sky, and there were no more clouds.

I started checking if everything was all right, everything prepared. The white columns reached to the sky as if there was no ceiling. In the center, a wide marble staircase, with white steps, suddenly emerged, like a road, stretching into the distance – so far – you could not see what was downstairs. The staircase was very wide. On the sides, there were those who were waiting for the feast to begin.

I was checking two big silver trays standing on both sides – there were strange fruit on those trays[7] – like huge amber tangerines with their skin peeled away, without white particles, just little lines. But these were not tangerines, they were divine fruit. Without peel, shining through like amber – they

---

[7] All the way in the dream we were escorted by a guide, someone orange (later I said – of amber color), a tangerine without peel. His name was YAN, or ZWING, ZWIANG – hard to say in human language, just like some clanking sound.

were prepared, about ten on each tray. They were the most important items for the ritual. I started looking. While I was away to fight the monster – I could not understand how someone could commit a sacrilege – about three fruit were missing on each tray. But I was checking at the last moment, because the number of them was very important. I knew clearly, that it was a dainty piece – but not for humans. People were far away downstairs; I went to them later, for I knew the fruit was for my retinue.

There was a king in the palace. God was in the church, but he was not there, and the manager was a priest. The same as me. The symbol was a spirit, He would have come to the feast, and I was a manager, the executive. The other executives were around me. The spirit would have come, or His thoughts, or His light... I was the lady of the kingdom. There were some creatures – not people – around me, very tall, of huge stature. The tall-sized creatures were very different, their essences were different, like the birds, the grass, as if one would have a head of an Eagle, and the other of a Snake. I knew that for some of them these dainty pieces of orange fruit were important for magic, for consecration, and maybe later they would have eaten them.

In short, I noticed it, I checked the fruits that were left and went downstairs to the people. But maybe, because there were not enough of them, they were losing their quality, and they did not have the same quality together. So I gave both trays to the people around me. Maybe they had eaten them. I went down the stairs. Downward, the staircase opened wide, like in Rome's amphitheaters, and at the open side there was a stormy ocean. It was a sunny day. I was up on the columns, talking – up there, where the stairs were coming together with the upper colonnade like amphitheater. There were crowds of people downstairs. They all were wearing strange clothes – ancient Roman togas, and fabrics fastened by a buckle on the shoulder, and in short iron skirts, in chain armor – all different designs. But there were no wild ones, everybody was normal.

They were standing in the amphitheater, and on the beach – but they were not swimming, not sunbathing. I was looking at the sea – the sea was important. It was stormy, I looked carefully – it was dangerous. It was boiling from something inside it. Some herds were coming out of it by groups – some elephants, and other creatures. They were not animals. I went down. When I found myself in some narrow corridor just before the amphitheater , I saw that some new creatures began to appear from the ocean – they were some kind of deer, or rather goats – a huge mass, they were walking very closely to each other – horns, hooves, many hooves. And I understood, that it became dangerous – many hooves. They were coming one after another, you could not stop them. And then I told to my surrounding to leave. Actually, I was not talking – I had a sign. But in that corridor people were running towards me – they all were rushing to the ocean. I was telling them, that it is dangerous, "don't do it" – but they were running, and blocking my way and the way of my people up... I don't remember, what happened afterwards...

"So those goat-deer disturbed your celebration?"

Not at all. It is like if you prepare yourself for a feast, invite some guests, and then in a free moment, you go to the window to look outside – I was watching the scene from somewhere above it.

****

It is interesting that in 1988 I was introduced to Nina, a psychic. As soon as she looked at me she told me, "I see you sitting in front of an enormous book and you are reading it."

Two years later, I met the opera singer, Slava, who also has physic ability – the vibration of his voice is healing people. Suddenly he told me that he sees me as a Priest on the steps of big pyramid...

When I saw this picture in the book "The Origin of the Advanced Maya Civilization in the Yucatan", by Douglas T. Peck, I was truly amazed! Because this ancient picture on the wall of Chichén Itzá was portraying exactly the four people, including me, who were in that sacrifice ceremony! [6] From left, there was a SNAKE, next an EAGLE and next, ANUBIS, and the Priest JAGUAR stood on the right – they were my "colleagues."

YOUR ETERNAL HOLOGRAM

*Bas relief sculpture in Chichén Itzá
showing captive rulers or nobles involved in a ritual ceremony.*

I don't think they were captive; this is the position these nobles assumed right before the ritual ceremony. In my vision, following the hypnosis sessions, I remember how each of us had a very thin rope and string in our hands to fill at first with our own energy, and afterwards we traced a circle and connected these ropes with each other through the top layer of the skin up to the navel area. We needed to be ALL as ONE at the same time. Each of us had a little blood trickling onto this rope, coming from the skin and our blood was then mixed...

When you read this, you may have a clear picture of what I describe and what you think about it... You may ask, "Why are they doing this? Are they insane maybe?"

No, I found that they were smarter than we are – they were wise. What we just discovered now, using the most advanced science is what these people knew and used successfully in their daily lives thousands of years ago.

After we prayed and supported each other with combined energy, we had the ability to talk to Spirits, to GOD, and maybe check the Hall of Records for information about the Past and Future.

I talked to the famous scientist, Peter Gariaev, the father of wave genetic. Here is how he explained this ritual:

DNA phantoms can be perceived as means of genetic-metabolic communications between organisms on the wave level. It is something like "immaculate conception". DNA not only passes information in a form of wave replicas, but it also records information from the environment (replicas of the parts of apparatus, lamp). Thus the replicas get to know the surrounding and translate this information onto genetic level in the chromosomes, the organism, alienating probe-replicas and returning back to the organism with new knowledge. People united by a "blood rope" form a hyper-personality; build an antenna and become the acceptors of information from OUTSIDE, the Universe. They are capable of assimilating it because they are all united by the common quantum entangled blood of each other and because of that, being a hyper-personality; they are capable to accomplish something much bigger, together then separately.

YOUTUBE
Russians Change DNA with Frequency Experiments (1/2)
DNA Awakening - Universal Consciousness
The DNA Phantom Effect

For those interested in studying the subject, he advises to read also the article "Quantum Magic" by S.I.Doronin. *DNA Found to Have "Impossible" Telepathic Properties, Journal of Physical Chemistry.*

DNA has been found to have a bizarre ability to put itself together, even at a distance, when according to known science, it shouldn't be able to do so. Explanation: None, at least not yet. [28] Scientists are reporting evidence that contrary to our current beliefs about what is possible, intact double-stranded DNA has the "amazing" ability to recognize similarities in other DNA strands from a distance. The recognition of similar sequences in DNA's chemical sub-units, occurs in a way unrecognized by science. There is no known reason why the DNA is able to combine the way it does, and from a current theoretical standpoint this feat should be chemically impossible.
The "telepathic" effect is a source of wonder and amazement for scientists. **(You will find more details of scientific explanation at the end of the book)**

In their book "Vernetzte Intelligenz" (Networked Intelligence), Grazyna Fosar and Franz Bludorf explain these connections precisely and clearly. The authors also quote sources, presuming that in earlier times, humanity had been, just like the animals, very strongly connected to the group consciousness and acted as a group. To develop and experience individuality we, humans, however, had to forget hyper-communication almost completely.[8]

Interesting that when I was a Priest, I accepted all people around me like my close relatives. Today, I found proof of this again: the Mayan people had marriages between close relatives, so finally the whole village was one big family!

Ancient Maya had a common type of marriage, called cross-cousin. The familial clan was presented by constantly intersecting lines of cousin sisters and brothers, thus all members of the clan had common ancestors, beginning with grandfathers. (Ref. 29 "Ancient America: Flight in time and prostransive. Mezoamerika" Excerpts from the book by GG Ershovoy UnCopyrighted©Sam, 2003-2006) [30]

Dream # 6
The Queen of a Crystal Kingdom, December 4, 2007

It was a strange dream. I got to bed at 11:50 p.m., and woke up at 2:30 a.m. Then the dream continued. There were three parts to it.

1. First Kingdom It was like they were preparing me. They sucked out every material out of me, piece by piece. They were purifying me. They pulled out everything from inside my body. I became as light as a bubble, and transparent. They were doing some rituals with me. After purification I entered the Kingdom of Transition. It was more structured than mine was. It consisted of two huge spaces. I was in one of them, and in the other, there was God – an old man, speaking in human language. I understood that he was a Master here. I was afraid to move, to take a step, to break anything, to spoil anything by my presence here. He also did something to me, some ritual with a space, maybe with clouds. We were talking (he was speaking, and I was listening). He did not leave His territory. Afterwards, I was ready – all my psychic structures were ready. For in my next Kingdom it was much finer. They moved me to this 2nd kingdom after the ritual was completed. They were purifying me, in a way, but they could not enter the place themselves.

2. Crystal spaces The first sensation – there is ice everywhere. Everything is transparent. The person becomes like a blue-gray colloid. Large crystals – all made of ice – like finely streamlined ... such a pleasant bliss. I was alone. And they told me – in my mind – that I am a tsariza (queen) in this kingdom. Well in our language the words tzarstvo (kingdom) – they are bulky, sharp, and heavy. But there – everything was like air, harmonious, beautiful. Everything here was perfection itself,

---
[8] You will find DNA phantoms and Scientific Interpretations with more details about this at the end of the book.

completeness. Nothing in excess. All was completed, when I was brought in. I felt "complete" – I was full. At the beginning I was getting accustomed – everything was light-blue-crystal-clear-turquoise. But there was a feeling, that all this was frosted, sparkling with snowflakes. The kingdom was similar to the huge stadium-sphere in Vancouver, as if the kingdom was situated in the sphere.

3. Alexandrian and New York kingdoms I went down by the sphere – and I saw beside me some elevation on one side and on the other. In one of the spheres an old lady appeared – like that old man from Indiana Jones, who was guarding the water of life. Her arms and legs were not visible; her body appeared to be just a stream of veils beneath her head. She said, "These two Kingdoms are Alexandrian and New York. They are your assistants. They can fly over to you from their places – two persons, two souls." I could address them as my assistants, my secretaries. They are the two lightest spirits from those kingdoms.[9]

Dream # 7
Arabian and American Mountains - 2 pyramids: Egypt and Mexico, October 25, 1990

I was escorted by a laden-gray doughnut, of a strange square-round shape – either round outside and square inside or vice-versa.[10] There were mountains in front of me. The voice in my ear, this doughnut-guide reported: "Arabian peninsula..." and was telling me about the future of this place, what it is called now, how it will be called, what will go where, which people will pass by, and which will die. *He* was speaking from over my head and his voice was enveloping me. The mountain in front of me was not material, but maybe made of psychic emanations from the people assembled in the shape of a pyramid. And right after that we flew to America, to the other mountain – also a pyramid. *When you fly over an area you can't remember rivers, lakes, seas, but you can remember the similarities between two places.* The doughnut-guide was with me all the time.

His voice was talking to me very quickly – humans cannot talk that fast – it was saying different things, which I could not memorize. The views were replacing each other, the voice followed with information – very even; all phrases were similar, spoken like a robot. The letters were like little beads tumbling down through my ears at incredible speed.[11] It was impossible to understand the meaning, if there are no mistakes in the speech and no human details. I mean when there is no timber or inflection, pauses, tonality, etc. in the voice; you cannot understand what the person is saying. One view was followed by another followed by the text. When I said "stop" to myself, in order to memorize and put fragments together, I was confused; I lost the train of thought. I worried. And I even forgot this. When I started to try to fly from one mountain to the other – slowly, since slowly is what I could remember, the voice began talking more slowly, 5 to 10 times more slowly. There was a feeling that it was speaking through water. The words came to me evenly and clearly.

---

[9] I understood it not as a New York City, but some new city, so Alexandria was the old city, built earlier. I think there were two sets of pyramids, the ones in Egypt (Alexandrian) and the second one in Mexico, New York being a new city.

[10] Another famous Egyptologist, Arnold de Belizal, later inherited the ring. He was a well-known expert in radio-aesthesia, the science concerned with the energy of shapes. De Belizal's found that the ring emits electromagnetic waves capable of creating 'energy fields' which work as a force of energy. This energy protected the wearer, gave him increased psychic abilities and the ability to heal, and brought the person good luck.
The Atlantis Ring, http://www.crystalinks.com/atlantisring.html

[11] Scientific interpretations can be found at the end of the book.

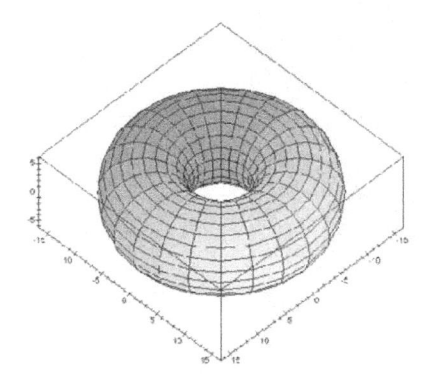

http://www.crystalinks.com/gordianknot.html
Science began using this model and, THIS is what I meant in my dream!

Sacred geometry: - an ancient mystery schools teaching, stressed the one force or consciousness behind existence through the laws of geometry, made extensive. According to ancient teachings in the beginning there was a great void. This void is the creator, with no body shape or definition. Creation requires a definition of space (as well as direction). The Torus tube provides this kind of definition by using the inside, the outside, and infinity. In that way it can be the shape that also represents the idea of The one and only God and the holy trinity relation, which comes from the one **God and exists in everything (positive, negative and neutral, for example). The word "one" in Hebrew, "Echad" as well as the word "love" – "Ahava" in Hebrew, has a numerological value of 13. The number 13 contains the one and the three. [1+3=4=time].**

Many people claim they had dreams in which they were able to solve difficult karmatic personal relations or situations during the daytime after wearing a Gordian knot pendant. The reason for this might be that the pendant symbolizes the idea of unity which binds everything into one.

Wikipedia: http://en.wikipedia.org/wiki/Knot_theory
http://www.ka-gold-jewelry.com/p-products/gordian-knot-silver-big.php#ProDetails

YOUTUBE: Who lives in the eleventh dimension? - Parallel Universes - BBC science
I found one more website with Sacred Geometry: www.akaija.com. The Akaija is a cosmic jewel made in co-operation with the Divine Lightworld. Wim Roskam, the maker of the Akaija, has been given this object by his girlfriend Linda, who died in 2001. She was sending him many dimensional images and inspired him to start producing them as jewelry! This jewelry carries amazing power![12]
http://www.ka-gold-jewelry.com/p-products/gordian-knot-silver-big.php#ProDetails
Akaija = The Oneness of 'We'

http://www.akaija.com/info/UK/UK06_3D.shtml
http://www.akaija.com/info/UK/UK05_gallery.shtml

---

[12] More information regarding Akaija can be found at the end of the book in the Scientific Interpretation section.

YOUR ETERNAL HOLOGRAM

Acajia symbolizes universal Love. Gordian-knot.

Dream # 8
I return to the land where I lived before, November 13, 1992

This is a short version of the dream. It was about me arriving to America, Mexico. In my dream I walked on this land and my grandmother tells me that this is the land where I was living before.... When we were driving through Canada, from Toronto to Vancouver, during the night in the prairies, I started feeling that some spirit was near me. I knew at that moment that this was a native Indian spirit, who owns all of this land... I started talking to him and asked permission – it's a blessing to settle down in this North American land.
The other day, I was under a hot shower – I love hot showers – and I started remembering that I had this dream, and suddenly I was covered with goose bumps – like a hoar-frost covering my skin – under a hot shower! I was shaking. It was surprising to me to feel frozen under a hot shower!

I never had such goose bumps, so often, such as I had this spring while I was writing this book and reading the dreams which I collected over the years. The energy was coded in the words of the dreams. When Di Cherry started reading my dreams, while I was under hypnosis, the doors of the past opened for me instantly. I could see, feel, smell, and touch such as I did all those years ago. Psychic people know that when something real comes from the past or another side of life, they are often covered with goose bumps.

****

Today I received an envelope from Dr. Alfons Ven from Holland with the custom-made pills – made especially for me. I am totally healthy; these are really "miracle pills".

I opened the instructions and read this magic sentence: ***The aim of the Ven-Cure is to elicit a better attunement with your evolution and being freer with your original selves.*** When I was reading those words, I was near a window, looking at cherry blossoms, pink rhododendrons and brand new emerald-green leaves on an apple tree, and I started smiling... It was a very unusual smile, which I never experienced in my life. I wish I could have watched myself from the side. I was very surprised.

I have no words to describe what I really felt. There were waves of the wise, heavenly, and beautiful – the kindest, softest sort of energy – invading me such as a tide of happiness and contentment, and it was coming out with this smile through my eyes. I continued looking at the flowers and continued to smile blissfully. It was an astonishing pleasure to feel God's touch. It was something amazing and unusual! I wish I had a witness to this magical experience at that moment or a video camera to record the look in my eyes. I wish that someone saw it and told me what it looked like.

I decided to keep these miraculous, pure lactose pills near my pillow. When I look at them from the side right now, they look like little lilies-of-the-valley or snow-drop flowers – they're the cutest round, white balls. I feel harmony and connection with this special, beautiful, glowing energy, which makes them so appealing. I know why! They have my own pure energy from heaven, which GOD gave me at the moment He created me. They connect me with God and will guide me to return to my own original self. I think everyone should make such an adjustment once during their lifetime with Dr. Alfons Ven's unique help.

****

I find lots of things in common between the Priest and me. I am sure there will be a list of items in your present life that you will be able to compare with those of your past lives. The next pages should enable you to see that we not only have genes from our real relatives, but also that our personality is strongly affected by our previous life. My idea is simple: people have genes which carry some skills, abilities; we can have cellular memories from our mother and father, since we are built from their cells, but we also have spirit memories from our past lives. People collect many skills and experiences from their past life which they can use in their present and future lives. What we are developing now will be useful in our next lives.

When I was studying plants during my post-graduate courses, my teacher was an 85-year-old professor, academician A. A. Prokofiev. I was his last student in this lifetime. When this extremely smart, amazingly wise man died, on top of the deep sorrow and sadness I felt, I had one thought, which always came to my mind that day: "How unfair that people exercise their brain throughout their lives and when it is rich and at the highest point in its development, the person dies and all of these skills are lost forever."Now I know that nothing is lost and that these skills will be transferred with the Spirit to his next life.

There are many cases of talented, gifted people who were born with rare skills which they were able to apply from a very young age, such as Connie Talbot, Akiane Kramarik, Joshua Johnson, Carlos Blanco, Jackie Evancho; the world's most talented kids.

(Akiane Kramarik http://www.artakiane.com) [7]
http://www.tagtele.com/videos/voir/19214/1/Connie

Here is a page from the book, the **"The Miracle Man"** with some of the most important, basic knowledge about the nature of our own Spirit and the Spirit world.

1) *"We have all lived many lives before this one. We are incarnated, and after this life we will be reincarnated again into another life. (There are many well-documented cases of hypnotists taking countless numbers of people back into past lives. They speak languages totally foreign to them and they describe in detail places and lifestyles of long ago, which are frequently proven correct by subsequent investigation.)*
2) *If you remove the physical shell we call the body, what is left is the real you: your soul, your spirit. This eternal essence is in a perpetual state of improvement or deterioration, depending on what you do in each of your physical lives.*
3) *Free will is the only means by which the physical you, and subsequently your soul, can improve its position after your demise.*
4) *Karma is the means by which you will pay your debt for wrongdoings or be rewarded for your free-will choice of good in each life. If you have killed, stolen, lied or cheated in a past life, chances are that you will be suffering some malady or conflict in your current life. Conversely, if you have been caring, considerate, honest and moral, then your soul will have elevated and you will probably be a healthy, well-balanced person.*
5) *There is a spirit world! It is much more complex than our physical world. It is much more powerful and decidedly more beautiful for those who have earned a place in it. It is multi-leveled and multidimensional, to cater for the infinite number of development stages through which souls pass. Of over 150 out-of-body, near-death experiences surveyed by Kenneth Ring (author of Heading Towards Omega: In Search of the Meanings of Near-Death Experience), all reported similar observations, feelings and experiences to support this belief.*

6) Spirits, both good and bad, are with us all the time. So many of those strange coincidences we experience (usually when we most earnestly wish for them) are the result of thought generation picked up and acted upon by your guides, your spirit guides. It adds new meaning to the biblical quotation, "Ask and ye shall receive".

7) Our human bodies are generated from and protected by energy fields. There are seven corresponding layers, each with its own density or frequency, and seven major chakras (spinning vortexes). Some people can actually see these layers as auras. If we live healthy, clean lives, our energy fields protect us very well. Conversely, if we abuse ourselves with excesses of alcohol, drugs or unclean living, the fields become weakened, will be attacked and will attract undesirable attachments. Disease begins in these outer layers and the fields lose their vibrancy.

The endless line of people pass through the room and are spiritually prepared to meet João-in-entity who sits at the far end in a large chair covered in white linen. At the moment of meeting there is a split-second recognition by the entity of each person's 'blueprint': past lives, current situation, illness and spiritual awareness. Depending on what is seen, the person will be dealt with according to the requirement. Some are given herbal prescriptions. Some are sent to the intensive care room for surgery or treatment at a later time. Those who need spiritual strength may be told to sit in current, whilst others are given concise instructions on necessary life changes. Each person is dealt with in less than twenty seconds.

In this life the Priest's Spirit continues his habits.

Here is a list of "inheritance", which Spirit, who lives in my body, got from past life as a Priest. I guarantee that you will find some of these "habits" crazy or at least shocking.

1. **Ball court & Basketball,**
2. **Healing,**
3. **Intuition, Predictions,**
4. **Jaguar pattern outfits,**
5. **Leadership,**
6. **Astrology,**
7. **Numbers,**
8. **Plants, Agriculture,**
9. **Masks,**
10. **Caracol – the observatory – talking on ancient Maya, word Equinox, Tzolkin**
11. **Aztek God Xochipilli,**
12. **I always wanted to be Priest!**
13. **Tortoise,**
14. **Connection with the Goddess Bodhisattva, Meeting with God, Ghosts.**

1. Ball court & Basketball

Our teacher, Margarita, asked each of us to take the ball and throw it up to the basket 10 times and then she would grade our performance. When it was my turn, my classmates ran to watch me throw the ball. I could throw the ball into the basket 10, 20, 40 times, without fail. The ball always went through the hoop easily. In the end, our teacher said, "Okay, enough!" But my classmates were screaming for me to be allowed to continue. All of the kids in school and my neighbors knew about my talent. I guess the Priest's spirit remembered how he played in the ball court in Chichén Itzá, a few thousand years ago. Believe me; it is much easier to do this with your hands than with the knees and elbows, such as the ancient Maya players did.

2. Healing

The Priest applied his healing power to his people often. I always paid attention, asked about the health of each person around me and gave advice. Today, it comes out automatically as if I have some program set up inside me to do this. Interesting that I catch myself many times, scanning people's health during my dreams and I heal them. I care about all of my friends, relatives and business partners' wellbeing. I try to keep all of them in good health while preventing them from catching some diseases with homeopathy, herbal treatments and advice. My Diagnostic machine always with me.

Numerous people have told me that I had an amazing way to heal them without my knowledge. It is facts, but it still strange for me to know this.

Tree last cases were in Thailand, Australia and Europe.

In **Thailand hotel**, a Belgian boy asked me to heal him ... He had a serious problem with breathing, sleep apnea. He said it in very emotional way, it was call for help, and apparently, my Spirit heard it.
 At night in a dream I saw this boy with 6 items similar washers (pucks) attached like magnets ... I did something and they fell.... On the back, in the place of attachment washers (pucks) remained reddish spots, like dry blood. In the morning, during breakfast, I told him that the problems will be no more! Four people feeding on his energy, these were real people.

I said that they will contact him during the day. Four girls called him and sent letters through the Internet, said that they do not feel comfortable and they need to talk to him. They were all his former girlfriends.

Two other entities were not human. Spirits told me that from that day he will be happy and healthy!
 Since the disease - is not always a real disease. This may be a loss of energy, which can pass from one person to other people.

Case # 2.

We was working on the editing of the film with the editor Monty at his home in Victoria, **Australia.** Suddenly in came Monti's wife. Monti told her that she should return to her room and go to bed. His wife was sick, she had pneumonia. Much to our surprise, she pointed at me and said that I had healed her, and she feels great! But I did not get up from the chair during the last 3 hours!

She was sleeping in the bedroom next to mine. Turns out she had a dream that I walked into her room and walked over the bed past her sleeping husband Monti, and healed her! Then she said that she saw me in the church with the red short hair in clothes worn before the war in 30-40 years ... This is the exact description of Amelia! This is my past life. (Read the book Amelia). Wow, she saw 1 a layer of my HOLOGRAM!

Case # 3.

One woman had a surgery in **Europe** and during that surgery someone named Julia (a voice), instructed the surgeon what to do. When he ask that woman if she know Julia from Canada, she told that she did meet her 3 years ago...Surgeon admitted that help of Julia wasimportant for him, because by mistake he got somebody else's x-ray before surgery!

Well, I was sleeping in London, there was 5 am when surgery start in other country at 8 am.

3. Intuition, predictions

I am sure the Priest had stronger intuitions, with his hyper-communication ability and being in harmony with nature, than I ever did. I got good intuition too. I got it as an "inheritance" from him. I had lots of predictions about big events, which have come true.

Once, I woke up deeply depressed. I saw, in my dream, the horror of the Twin Towers' collapse in all of its disastrous details – I was right there. It was exactly one year before it happened. I told the

people around me at the time, and one replied to me, saying, "There was an explosion under a building before. This is what you saw in your dream."
On September 11, 2001, I was walking through a little street in Rarotonga, Cook Islands in the middle of the South Pacific Ocean. The local doctor, Wolfgang, who was also the German consul there, waved at me from his office and said, "I was rushed to work today and I saw on TV that a small airplane hit one of the Twin Towers in New York."

I asked him, "Have both building already collapsed?" He looked at me curiously and replied, "How can you even imagine this: that two huge, concrete buildings will collapse?"
I said, "If they are not both destroyed yet, they will be soon and there will only be debris left." I remembered wishing that I could have said to him, "I know it, because I saw it in my dream...," but I just walked across the street to the internet café. Letters had arrived already from everyone: "Remember what you said about the Twin Towers? Terrible things have happened..." In those days, in Cook Islands news arrived late – at least 12 hours or a day late...
I remember how I woke up around 4:00am one morning and told my grandmother: "Indira Gandhi has just been killed – right now!" I found out later that day she had indeed died on October 31, 1984. The dream had occurred at the exact moment when the Indian Prime Minister, Indira Gandhi, had been assassinated. I liked her!
I woke up from a dream about a huge earthquake in Armenia. I saw trucks full of frozen, dead bodies. People were sliding the corpses into the trucks as if they were on an ice sheet after they had pushed them inside. About 100,000 people died in that terrible, devastating earthquake. It happened the day after I had the dream.
For around 10 days I felt that a terrible earthquake would be soon. I told and sent to everyone about that. Last evening I talked with my friend, I told her that there would be an earthquake in a matter of hours and we may not see each other again. The feeling of a coming disaster was enormously strong ... suddenly I broke to tears, I told her goodbye ... few minutes later I felt a sudden INSTANT relief. I opened my computer and sign arrived in front of my eyes:
Major Earthquake Haiti - Wednesday evening « on: January 12, 2010, 11:26:46 PM » ... huge release of emotional pressure happened was just minute later. It was the same Pacific Rim fault of fire, where my city located.
Once, I started writing my dreams on a list, where I only noted the predictions as I saw them in each dream. I wrote the list down in November 1991. When I had about 30 of them, I stopped. All 30 came true. They all happened during the next one and half to two months afterwards. I marked near each one: happened, come true today, etc. and Wow – this one also happened! And so on...

I try avoiding seeing the future; because of dramatic events. I avoid looking at people's faces, because, some days, I can see how they will die. I check the future only when it is really necessary. For example, I often see in my dreams what will happen the same day or the next.

Once, we needed to travel 1200km in one day by car. This was a long road...When I woke up early that morning, I started envisioning the road. I saw a crossing, where the roads in all directions were covered with a red liquid. "How could an accident create so much blood?" I asked myself. I was worried. We arrived at the crossing at nightfall. The roads were indeed covered with the blood ... of tomatoes! There had been an accident at this intersection earlier that day. A huge truck full of boxes of tomatoes had turned over on its side, spilling its entire content on the road! Before the truck had been hauled off from the site, many cars had passed through smashed tomatoes. There was juice everywhere. This was a funny case of prediction turning out all right.

Another time, we were to travel through Poland. When I started checking the road ahead in my mind, I heard a screeching metal sound. I had no idea what it could be – except perhaps my car was going to be dragged during an accident. When we drove that day, the front license plate fell down to the side, scratched the surface of the road, and began making the same screeching, horrible sound as the one I had heard before leaving on our trip.

I traveled in my dreams, through time, to the future and I made lots of predictions along the way, which have come true.

Here are just a few examples of the technological developments which I saw in my dreams and later became a reality.

In 1980, I dreamed that I was in an airport. I went to the TV screen on the wall, touched it and entered the data from my diary, which I had left home in another city. I did some writing, closed the screen and went to the gate to board my plane. In 1980, personal computers did not exist yet, and they were certainly not available or accessible to the public. As for the **internet** or transferring one's diary from one terminal to another was beyond anyone's imagination. However, now, 28 years later, you could go to any airport, use your laptop, your phone, access the internet at any "internet café" and access your diary wherever you are in the world.

In another dream, I am in some field far away from town – it is some kind of sandy desert. I have a phone in my hand; I start dialing and calling a girl, who suddenly appears in front of me in three-dimension – a **hologram** – and who starts talking to me with a clear voice. It was absolutely real, except that I put my hand *through* her and could not *feel* her – the space she seemingly occupied was empty. I decided to check the date at which it occurred – because I remember the exact year, how old I was at that time – the

dream was on the night before my birthday! It was thirty years ago. Cell phones did not exist at that time and I did not see "Star Trek" until I moved to Canada in 1990.

Last year my business partners introduced me to a very interesting researcher in the Department of Surgery, at the University of British Columbia. It was an unforgettable day, meeting the Professor of Surgery, Dr. Karim Qayumi, Director of the Centre of Excellence for Surgical Education & Innovation (CESEI).

He started his research with a study of the memory and later found that medical students remember only 10% of what they studied during the lecture after they finished medical school. After four years, students remember a little bit more when they also read the material and much more when they practice what they have been taught.

Memory depends on one important factor: how many areas of the brain are activated – sound, vision, movements of the hands, problem solving participation and so on. He found that the best results were obtained when the students participated fully in all of the activated memory areas. Dr. Qayumi created an interactive, computer-assisted instructions program that looked like a video game in which students visit their patients, define the symptoms, diagnose the problem and perform real surgery.

During our visit I had the opportunity of performing a surgery through this computer-assisted program – right there on that day. The students are usually performing three surgeries a day. Even grade 12 students study on this program, very successfully.

Doctor Qayumi is an amazing and very talented man. He even created robots for the students to practice their surgical skills. This robot lies down on the operating table, in the operating theatre – he looked like a real person to me. I felt his pulse and observed his breathing. After giving the patient an adrenalin injection, we scanned the level of adrenalin in his system and I observed that his pulse started racing at an incredible rate! I had mixed feelings at that moment. I didn't know who should run first – me from the room, because my patient seemed to be very agitated, or him by jumping off the table and running down the hallway. I asked, "Will he stand up and run out now?"

"No," the professor replied, "but if we give him a bigger dose he will die, his heart will stop!" Well, what could I say?

At that moment, when I was near the robot, I remembered a dream I had many years ago, and related this dream to my business partners when I went home. In that dream, I arrived at a company to receive what I ordered from them. My order was a boy. There was a couple – two old people who ran the company. They came out with him and started showing me his abilities. We went through the whole list of abilities. I expected him to have the abilities which I ordered from the beginning. He was excellent, he looked perfect, and he smiled. I made a mental note that he also had very positive emotions. I was happy with the order and paid them extra.

This boy was a **robot boy.** I ordered him to do the work at home: cooking, cleaning, teaching my child and entertaining, giving medical diagnoses in case a member of my family was sick and preparing custom-made food for each of us, with minerals, vitamins, and applying creams, giving a bath, a massage to the ones who needed it, and so on. He was to be that special someone in the family who cares for everyone – someone which we no longer employ these days. He also had some secretarial responsibility.

In the house, there was some special sound and healing room with specific vibration... I remember, on the way to the car, I stopped and looked at the peacock walking around in the garden. He looked so beautiful that I tried to decide if I should order one like this as well. The bird was also a robot, you understand.

When I returned home, I found that this dream occurred 24 years ago!

Well, I expected that all of this would come true during this present life. I have a reason for this. My friend, a genetic scientist, opened the code of longevity and proved scientifically that people after "his treatment" could live up to 800 to 1000 years now. He started his research many years ago and observed that people after his "treatment" even started "a rejuvenating process". In one case, a 76-year-old grew five brand new teeth! I saw the X-rays of her mouth myself. Amazing! (By the way my daughter got as an "inheritance" same ability and she is child psychic, indigo child)

4. Jaguar

From a very young age, the jaguar has always been my favorite animal. Today, I favor the jaguar pattern in any of the clothes I buy. It makes me feel very comfortable – as if it were my own skin. I guess when the priest was wearing his jaguar coat for forty or fifty years, it created a DNA phantom, which seeped through and into the "cellular memory" of his Spirit.[13].

I am also attracted to the animal's movements and energy flow. The jaguar moves are often associated with ancient martial arts such as Kung Fu. When people come to me, asking for help with the Kung Fu association in the former Soviet Union, I agree instantly. In fact, I helped legalizing the first martial art, Kung Fu & Tai Chi Association in the country. Martial arts had been illegal and prohibited for 72 years. I was even Vice President of this association in Moscow!

"My sister, Julia, visited me and my family, in Germany. She lives in Canada and I live in Europe. After many years of living apart, we decided to meet and go to town to celebrate this event in some fancy restaurant.

To my surprise on such a special and happy occasion, instead of wearing one of her many luxurious and glamorous outfits, she chose to wear her jaguar jacket and she even attached a tail to it for fun! I noticed she even had a jaguar mask in her hands!

I felt really uncomfortable by this and I started to tell my husband that I was afraid that people around us would think that we hired her as the entertainment person. I love her, but that evening I felt really ashamed for her. She, instead, was extremely happy with this jacket – she was always wearing it and I guess could even sleep in it. It was a quality garment, the kind of silk like jacket from "Victoria's secret catalogue". Still, I couldn't take it. I didn't understand why it made her feel so excited and happy or why she was so attached to it. Anyway, I asked her remove the tail at least, and not to use the mask. After all that, the celebration on the day was a very happy time for us!"

Elena Neimark, Germany

---

[13] It sounds really strange, but if you are interested, please read the scientific part, with the latest research at the end of the book. It will clarify some of the questions you may have on the subject, I'm sure.

"Julia loves leopard and jaguar print clothing. Every Halloween she wears this outfit. It makes her extremely happy! It seems to make her happy to have the opportunity to wear a jaguar costume once a year. She walks around with a jaguar mask, long tail, and jaguar print gloves – the entire costume. She is always a Jaguar. People love her outfit. It is always fun lots or joy for kids to be near her. I guess she was even offered a free home at the "big cat" reserve in California."

Lawrence De Lange, Canada

5. Leadership

This martial arts association was the first independent, private sports' association in the country when PERESTROIKA and democracy began to emerge in Russia. I had a big fight with the Sports Committee who had kept sports' people on a small salary and used to collect all of the money from the Olympic Games. Finally they agreed, but with the condition that the president would be a very bureaucracy former KGB general! When I went to China for the competition with the first group, he tried to close the association. As soon as I returned I called a big meeting with all the masters – 4 thousand attended the meeting.
I asked those present: "Do we need a president like this? NO!" They agreed. I then turned to this shameless president and told him, "You're free to go..." And he left.
The world chess champion, Garry Kasparov, was the first who came to us and asked for advice. "How did you do it?" he asked. "I wish to open a school for the children and teach them how to play." Hockey, chess, soccer, and many other sports' associations followed in our footsteps afterwards. Today, in Russia, millions of people study Martial Arts. In Moscow alone, our Kung Fu Association counts over 50 thousand members. I helped them and as soon as they were stable on their "legs", I left this association to help others.

The organization skills I had acquired during my life as a Priest and leader were used in this present life.

6. Astrology

Astrology was a very important part of the Priest's daily life.

I never believed in astrology until a famous astrologer predicted my future and everything came true! As a scientist, I wished to understand how it was possible. Therefore, I decided to study it a little and now I understand the main principles. By the way, Astrology was also illegal for 72 years in the former Soviet Union. Many things were illegal then, even such things as innocent as astrology. I was the leader who opened the door for astrology and created the first association in Russia.

When we published our first astrology book in 1989 about Nostradamus and another six most famous astrologers, with their predictions, instead of my real name I used the **pen name "Magician".**

I didn't have any idea what it meant in those days – remember the Russian alphabet is quite different than our alphabet – and for me to compose such a name meant that it must have been imprinted in my "memory" beforehand. I just didn't feel comfortable with my own last name, it did not sound right for this book. So I used the word, "Magician".

I wrote it letter by letter from my mind, because I felt in harmony with this word. I even took my membership in the astrology association under this name. A few months ago, which is 15 years later, I found that the name **"Magician"** was used to designate the **Highest Priests in ancient Mexico!**

Pyramid of Magician

When I was due to give birth to my daughter, I consulted the charts and noticed that if she were to be born on July 4, her horoscope would not be that great. So, I decided to delay her birth by a couple of weeks and turned the clock back until the time was right. She was born on July 21 with a fabulous astrology chart. Each planet in her chart was in the strongest, most powerful configuration.

There are planets that stay in their own particular place – the Moon, Venus, Jupiter, Saturn, Uranus, and Neptune. These planets are inscribed in a perfect hexagram – an extremely favorable aspect. This hexagram connects all of the planets on the map, and not one stands out of it. Long before now, this hexagram represented the key principle of the Universe – harmony and balance. Regulus, the star of the kings, is a guiding star for it. Very rare. It looks like a perfect star. In fact, my daughter's chart is always a surprise to astrologers. And it looks like it helped her! From the day she was born, she could keep her head straight! Usually, children can't do this until they are one and half or two months old. But the most amazing thing to me was that she was able to stand instantly on her legs! She just needed to hold my hand a little bit for balance. The nurse, was speechless... "Usually, kids start to stand at eight or ten months," she said. She also told me that I should apply for the Guinness world record. (I still have pictures and video.)

My daughter started reading by herself when she was two and half years old. No one taught her to read. Once I went out with her and she started reading the names of all the stores around the mall. I asked her how come she could read. She replied, "Remember I asked you to read me every evening a fairy tale story and you sometimes were too busy? You told me that if I knew my letters, I could read anything in the world. I was very happy that evening and I started studying..."

I remember after her first day in kindergarten, the teacher stopped me and said, "Your daughter ... your daughter...," I asked her, "What's wrong?"

She then told me that my five-year-old girl brought "The Lord of the Rings" with her to school and was reading the entire day! The teacher was amazed that a child of that age could read so fast when other kids don't even know their alphabet and cannot read.

A few days later the teacher asked me to go and see the principal. He said that my daughter already went through all of the school programs up to 4th grade! At age five, she had finished the computer programs – preschool format, kindergarten schooling, and that she had completed grade 1, 2, 3 and 4 tests successfully! I asked the principal to put her in grade 5, but since she was only five years old, he told me, that she would feel very uncomfortable studying with the older kids. At that point, I wanted to find out how she was studying and how she could have attained such an intellectual level so rapidly.

Her playthings and toys consisted mainly of a computer that I had put in front of her when she was only 17 months old. She received many study games and toys that developed her brain very early. Her first game was Catz. In this game, there were cats which she could feed, paint, and play with. It was very interesting to see a child, who couldn't talk yet – from the way she was doing things on the computer – you would know how a child at this age was thinking.

**Such a serious child for a 3-year-old!
She has adult eyes here...**

Every outline and everything was different: the way she was drawing, playing with her cats, feeding them, painting them, put clothes on them or hunting for the mouse with 30 water sprays or build a wall from hundreds of pillows!

My business partners were amazed with her memory ability when, at age seven, in London, she started listing each capital city in each country of the world.

Once at age eight, in Los Angeles, when a translator was sick, she translated the whole day's business meetings for the airline company regarding equipment for the airplanes. People were amazed at her level of concentration and her ability to study airplane parts instantly, while putting her knowledge in English to build an order. The Los Angeles Company then gave her a "huge gift": she visited Disney Land during the next five days. On one of the days, Donald Nixon, the co-owner of Disney Land and nephew of Richard Nixon, personally went through all of the best attractions with her, sometimes carrying her on his shoulders. Afterwards, he invited us for dinner in Walt Disney's private restaurant.

Last year, at age 13, she was a gold medal a winner in geography, coming first in front of all the kids, up to grade 12, from the whole of Vancouver.

Yes, astrology definitely affects people's lives. See proof of this in the section: ***biofield*** at the end of the book.

7. Numbers

a. Interesting that the Priest decided to be re-born in this present life where the day, year, hour and minute comprised only the numbers 8 and 5.

Meaning of **#5** and **#8:** The Priest, The Hand of God, Body and Soul.

In Mayan contexts, each number from one to nine had a sacred value, and since the Mayan number system was based on the number 20, there is given meanings to numbers, and the figures and patterns that they were inscribed upon:

1. *God, Goddess*
2. *The Maker, Parents*
3. *The Created, Life*
4. *Venus, called Kukulcan*
5. **The Priest, The Hand of God**
6. *Life and Death*
7. *God and Divine Power*
8. **Body and Soul**
9. *The Nine Drinks*

The Mayans designed their mats in many patterns; their craftsmen wove and carved these patterns into stone and cloth. The patterns became known for their specific numbers, power and significance (Daniel Clark Orey, Ph.D. The Mayan Mat: Mathematical Modeling of an Ancient Number Pattern). [10] [16]

When I got the ISBN for my book, The Priest, I noticed the last 6 numbers: the numbers of the year, month and day I was born!

The following day, I talked with my friend, Marianne, over the internet about the numbers **5 and 8** in my life. She lives in Holland and I in Canada. Hours later she sent me the following message:

"Julia, you are not going to believe this... This afternoon I registered my 2 books for
ISBN number over internet and the book that 'will smash like a bomb' ends at... ***8-5****!!!*
(I could choose out of 8 numbers I once got assigned and I knew it must end 8-5!) Creepy!!
Marianne, Netherlands   http://www.vorigelevens.nl/

I added to a letter to my editor: *PS:*
*Dear Roxane, strange unexplained things continue... a person asked when I was born. I sent her a message about **8 and 5** numbers, an hour later she registered her own book with ISBN. It goes automatically by computer over internet. All the numbers 8 and 5!!!*

Roxane to me:

*"Hi Julia, Did you know I was born on the **8th** of the **5th** month? Maybe that's why you chose me your editor?"* Well..., I never had any idea about that!

Roxane, Christ, editor for the book

Here is more!
8 plus **5** will be **13**! My lucky numbers are **85**, **58** and **13.** Bad number is **87**. 100 minus 13 = 87. Number **13** was extremely important number and lucky according to the Maya people. For example, Maya 260 days' year was **13** month, with 20 days and each week was **13** days. The universe in the Maya legends had **13** skies
****

PHI, the "**gold ratio**" of 1.618, found in many plants and human proportions, in relationship between planets orbiting around our Sun is mathematically derived through the Fibonacci sequence of numbers - 0, 1, 1, 2, 3, **5, 8, 13, 21** and so on. When you divide the larger number by the preceding smaller one, you gradually approach the phi constant. Venus is a very important planet in Maya astrology. As John Martines writes in a "LITTLE BOOK of Coincidence": "Venus rotates extremely slowly on her own axis in the opposite direction to most rotations in the solar system. Her day is precisely two-thirds of an Earth year, a musical fifth. This exactly harmonized...so that every time Venus and Earth kiss, Venus does so with the same face looking at the Earth". **8** Earths equals exactly **13** Venus years, the five kisses between them crafting a perfect pentagon, carved out of space. The numbers **5, 8** and **13** belong to the Fibonacci sequence, defining phi."(Daniel Pinchbeck, 2012 The return of Quetzalcoatl).

Here is another description of the **5, 8,** and **13** according to the Maya culture.
Communicating (5) through time, (Past, Present & Future, (3) becomes the number 8, indicating harmony and balance, and the infinite playing out of duality between all of what exists in the universe and what does not exist except as potential creation. It is my perception that each and every individual consciousness exists at the very center of its own individual Universe. Your consciousness (1) continually communicating (3) with your creation (1) from an established center is 5 plus (8) for infinity creates the number 13.
The Maya had a very clear understanding that all Creation is divided by the number 13. The Mayan priests and kings had a system of time-keeping for each day. A day was equally divided into 13 sections that we would call hours. Each section was divided into 13 segments that we would call minutes, which were further divided by 13 to create "seconds." Each second was further divided by 13, and divided again and again to infinity. So, each and every moment experienced by a Mayan was divided infinitely by the number 13.
My daughter was born 21 of July, number 21. Number 21 which is 7, 7, 7, - 3 times and the month is also 7. Now, years later I know that in Chichén Itzá the number 7 was a very important number.

Desk or counter top was a representation of all of infinity. Let's make that flat surface stand for the number 8 with the 13 on it. So, if all infinity (8) is consciously divided or individuated out (13) by the Witnessing Creator, this creates the number 21. As described by the Mayan calendar, the number of different aspects of creation equals 20. The number 21 is all of those aspects plus, once again, the Witnessing Creator looking over Its Creation. This number, 21, could be called counting your blessings or gratitude. It could also be seen as a completed step in the ascension of Consciousness.(Ref. 11; Sacred Geometry and the Mayan Calendar, Ian Xel Lungold. http://www.mayanmajix.com/3nn02_01_04.html) [10]

b. Everybody has lucky and bad numbers, right?

Yet, in my life, numbers play a mystery role! **YOUTUBE:** AVATAR SVADI 5, Mystery numbers?

Maybe it was a daily routine for the Priest, but I never got used to it; on every occasion it still amazed me. Numbers connected with me in some strange way and always advised me of what to do. In my case, if I wish to make an important decision, I ask a question and see what happens. The most extraordinary of these occurrences is when I am on or near a road. I ask the question that needs an answer and instantly cars will start showing up with license plates either with bad or good numbers. Not only that, but they seem to come out of nowhere in great numbers and their license plates always add up to the same number! Good ones are **085, 058, 013-->5+8.** Bad ones; **087-->100-13.**
Who sent them? How can it be possible that someone knew ahead of time what I would think about at that exact moment? How is it possible for all of the cars to assemble in one place, all at once? And I

am not the only one who witnesses this unbelievable event – when it occurs, the people around me could testify to this truly amazing moment. It works in any part of the world.

****

*Saturday morning I picked up Julia from Lihue and we drove to Hanalei for the interview with Kauai Community Radio station KKCR. The trip is about 23 miles and takes about 40 minutes. We talked about spiritual things and each time we would say something important, a car or sign with the number **085** or **058** would appear before us. I was amazed at the amount of cars and signs with these numbers that kept appearing. And the car in front of us for the whole trip from Lihue to Hanalei's license plate number was also Julia's lucky number, **013** (8+5=13). We stopped at the farmers market and when we continued on our way to the radio station, a car with plate #**013** was in front of our car again!*

It looked to me like the Spirits were trying to show their existence and support for Julia on this day, which was the kick off interview to publicize her new book. It was Amazing!

Captain JD Gott
(Volunteer programmer @ KKCR)
Hanalei, Hawaii, USA

NUMBER 13

"I don't know Julia very well. I have seen her 2 or 3 times at the Chinese New Year. We started talking with her about her cute ferret that she always has with her. I give her advice regarding homeopathy for the ferret.

*We decided to meet for a short meeting. Our first meeting, on Sunday at 9 a.m. was at English Bay. We talked and walked near the road. Julia mentioned that numbers play an important part in her life. They kind of speak to her. When she had a question or thought about something and tried to make a decision, her numbers started showing up. If it was a lucky number, she knew that her decision was correct. Or if her bad numbers started showing up it meant that she should avoid something. I listened to this and told her that I too have a lucky number, it is **#13.***

*While we were walking near the road, at the crossing of Beach Avenue and Davie, we were close to the main entrance to the beach. The street was empty, it was a Sunday morning and suddenly one car arrived and stopped near the crossing and the car license plate number was **013**.*

*Next, the following car came and its license plate was also # **013**! It stopped after the first one. A third car arrived with the same number 013 on the license plate! All three cars stayed one after the other:* **013, 013, 013!!!**

She pointed and said to me, "See! Again, as usual! All my business partners know this... it happened when I was in the cars anywhere in the world." I was in shock and didn't know what to think.

The Universe really speaks to her and proved to me that YES some high power is talking with her! It was an astonishing feeling and kind of scary.

How it can be possible that someone sent at the same moment 3 cars with the same number right at the same time that we were discussing it...? These cars arrived from the road, which goes through the park and there was not much traffic as it was not a busy time of the day. For three cars to arrive simultaneously with the same number, it is impossible to understand. It is impossible to understand with our logical mind, it has to be felt with your heart.

I know that the Universe keeps talking to us using every media possible, but it can use language that we are able to understand. In Julia's case numbers are one of the media, she really tuned into. There is a very special aura around her; it is really hard not to notice the higher energy levels in her presence. I met her again, after about a year had passed, and decided to mention this incident in the book she is writing."

Istvan Orodan, Thailand

*"This is just an example of one day in Julia's life... In October 2007; I was driving Julia, to the airport as she was catching a flight to Spain. When we arrive I looked down at the odometer, which I had reset at some point earlier in the week. However, as I was there and the exact distance that I had traveled since resetting it was at **87.1**km, which is usually a negative number that Julia has always mentioned and always appears just before some kind of trouble. Obviously, it was a warning sign for her.*

She asked me to wait and give her a few minutes to think. She continued walking into the airport building. She returned almost instantly and told me: "I will not fly, I want to go back home now". I was literally shocked by her immediate decision!

On the way back in to town, she told us that at the moment when she started thinking about the possibility of not to flying that day, she started feeling easy and light, as if she was in heaven. It's like she ran away from hell or from some terrible disaster – like a weight was lifted off her shoulders.

The next day we learned that horrible, severe flooding had started during her scheduled flight in this area and by the time she would have arrived in Spain, 14 hours later, all the roads were washed away, they were closed by flooding, and the bridge over the river collapsed in Alicante, where she should have landed. This caused huge damage and people were dead and missing.

The Universe or some higher power protected her, like a guardian angel speaking to her through numbers and prevented her from taking this deadly trip. Those numbers on that day could have saved her life or obviously from lots of stress. I feel now that it will be safe for anyone to be near her, because she has some high power protecting her and those around her."

Shawn, Canada

Here is one of the dreams about numbers. I guess this is how the Priest felt the energy of number **4**. Remember it was 4 nobles on the top of the pyramid?

Dream # 9
The power of the four, August 21, 1992

I was lying on a mounted bed. Around me, there was nothing, only space and emptiness. On my right, four creatures started to move away diagonally. Somehow, I had a 360-degree vision. At that moment, on my left side, a crowd of black creatures started approaching, moving sideways (the Roman army moved like that – it's called "a pig"). Everything was black, they were moving straight, all covered in black. First line, there were three, and then the second, and then the leader – number one – in front. They were only waiting. I knew that when the lead-creature would leave, they would tear me apart – into pieces.

I am lying on something like a platform or pedestal – it is my bed; I am not allowed to run away, I am a noble person. I am lying on this bed, in a noble position, like someone self-confident and strong – similar to Buddha. Leaning on my elbows, I "called" the number ones – the leaders. (Not with my voice – I don't have a voice in my dreams). Then they turned and get done with all this quickly.

Now, I understand, what the digit 4 means. In different dimensions, it has different meanings. In one-dimensional space (on a line) they cover the sides, they are of a different color, and then inside the ones – between them – was my place, number 5. Internal distance is filled with a different color. Between them, the connections were very strong and stable (that is why the others were able to scatter). I could see my power. I knew why these four were stronger than the others were.
The four-figure is stronger, than 7 or 9. I don't know why it is very stable. These golden threads through all the space were there again... When I woke up, I had a strong feeling; these golden threads were spreading, and the body was lying somewhere by itself. It was like a dualization (bifurcation). It was an eternal bliss. I did not feel my body at all. In my dream, when those ones were approaching me... I should not pronounce the words – I am afraid to start worrying, to get irritated. It is dangerous and it pulls me away from the stable, powerful condition in which I live currently. And I never got irritated in my dreams and awake. Irritation brings enormous destruction.

This was the most unusual thing that I saw – before that, I had a flight of spirit, or creativity, or we were somewhere in nature. As a result, at night in my dream, I am rewarded by even larger waves – High Spirit, in a dream, comes to me in stronger waves.

Four is seen as the first solid number; it represents wholeness, totality, completion; a solid foundation. There are four cardinal points; four seasons; four winds; four directions (as in North, South, East, and West); four elements (Fire, Water, Air, Earth) in the western culture. There are four sides to a square; four arms to a cross. There are four rivers in Paradise forming a cross.

In the Mayan culture, four giants support the celestial roof. Four is seen as the number of support.

8. Plants, agriculture

Plants and agriculture were the main responsibility of the Priest.

In my present life I love plants, all of them! I can't live without plants and I spend every single day in the Stanley Park, walking for close to two hours. This park merges into a wild forest. On my desk, in front of me, right now there are lily-of-the-valley blossoms, lilacs, jasmine and three kinds of wild flowers. I spend lots of time in my life studying plants at the university, while taking post-graduate courses. I know how plants live, breathe, grow, feel.

We have a secret, deep, tender love between us – between me and plants. As soon as I start talking about plants, I radiate with a waterfall of happiness. Anyone who has a good relationship with plants and nature will be healthy, strong, optimistic and full of energy.

I cannot live without plants, period. I remember when I moved to a new city, I lived in an area where there were almost no plants. After two weeks, I felt as if I was "dying" there. I really missed them. It felt almost as if I didn't have enough water or air to survive. I decided to move ASAP. As soon as I moved I was restored and began living in harmony with myself and nature again.
The famous Aristotle said that plants have souls, but do not have feelings (Genady Belimov, "Soul and Intelligence of the Plants", TD 2005). [31]
Today scientists have proved that plants have memory, music ability, consciousness, they even feel people or animals' pain.
New version of the book I'm doing now in 2016, I decided to check it out.
I got rose bush and when I was watering the plant I was thinking about my daughter. That one day I will give this rose to her. I could not believe my eyes when this rose bush grew 18 branches and in each of them at the end was one perfect red rose.
Later but around a month before her 19th birthday it began to grow another new branch and new flower opened, just days before Birthday!!!

I read in a magazine about a couple, who was checking their very big garden in autumn, and decided which tree they would cut down in the spring. They marked 35 trees with white chalk. In the spring, they were surprised to see that each tree, which they marked, was dead! None of them had budding leaves on their branches. By the way, ancient people asked a tree for forgiveness before cutting it down.

AVATAR SVADI HATRA

© Josephine Wall. All Rights Reserved. www.josephinewall.com

Rose with 19 branches

Some orchids can imitate the color of the female insect trying to attract the male insect to pollinate them. In some cases, plants can imitate the smell of rotten meat, trying to attract insects for the same reason. It means plants can see and smell.

During the last century, the famous Luter Berbank created many new kinds of plants by talking to them! For example, he talked to a cactus and told it that it would not need needles in its new growing parts because there was no danger in his place; and in case there was looming danger, Luter would protect the cactus. The cactus started growing without needles! In the same manner, Luter Berbank created new kinds of potatoes, fruit trees, flowers, which are now carrying his name. All he did was just to talk to the plants!

Plants react to music; pineapples from Hawaii and Antilles have different taste. The difference was that on Antilles Islands, people sing songs while they are working in the fields!

A garden filled with roses is literally singing, making vibrations, which our ears can't hear, but our spirit, aura can. In Scotland, scientists found that red and black gooseberry prefer Mozart and Giedne music. Strawberry love Brahms and Dvořák. Potatoes increase production by listening to Bruckner and Milleara symphonies. It means plants can hear!

Plants can even read people's thoughts. Scientists have put that theory to the test by thinking positively and wishing the plants good health. These plants showed excellent reactions to "positive thinking" and grew healthy, and happy! Production increased up to 30% with potatoes, for example. The opposite is also true; when a negative person lives around plants, the negativity seems to stem their growth.

© **Ballerina in Green Theater. Marius1988Roma. All Rights Reserved.**
As you can see I can talk about plants forever...

I was studying the famous Vavilov's wild wheat collection, which he collected from all over the world for future selection. During the Second World War, in Leningrad, thousands of people died from hunger, but no one took any grain from this rare collection – not a single seed. They preserved it for the benefit of future generations. What a strong spirit these people had! Now all over the world, those priceless seeds have produced new generations of wheat, growing and feeding millions of people!

Dream # 10
The Great Harmony of Nature
That evening, I knew that I would have a dream... Something special. I saw some two or three kinds of "men" (not human) – more like some "guides". Maybe they were the spirits of people. I seem to be reporting to them.

You and me – we are reporting to these "guides". It was some kind of "valley", by that I mean there is nothing there... It's as if this valley is covered by fog. I seem to be walking "in" a cloud – only to my waist. And that is all, there is nothing more; not on top not at the bottom. The fog is like vapor, steamy – something monotonous, no landscape. We are together with you in this valley, and you were helping me, we had to find maybe six or ten plants that I had planted there. We were looking for them, were picking them and had to show them to those "spirit-ones" as if it were some sort of a test. They were somehow strange flowers, like a big flower on a pedicle. I remember one of them close to me. When I took it to put together with the others, I made an adjustment to it. And when I looked at it closely, it was a sphere – a divided sphere (I repeated it to myself later, it was important) 20 centimeters in diameter. They had a white background with lilac diagonal lines crisscrossing them. I moved my finger on one of them and made the diagonals longer. These diagonals divided the sphere in 12 sections, like an astrology chart. After I lengthened these diagonals, we carried the spheres to those creatures. It seems to me, that there was also a woman there, a female spirit, like an angel, very light. Then suddenly, when I carried all this to them, I turned around and looked back, and the entire place was covered with emerald leaves. It looked like a rice field I saw in Japan. They all were covered with large beads of dew – as big as grapes. The beads of dew attracted my attention. I saw, that on the side, on the edge, the valley was surrounded by vertical rocks. Clear, fresh water came out from these rocks – waterfalls. The water was purified as it passed through the rocks.

Afterwards something unusual, beautiful started to happen... Water, rocks – all this was tentative, not real, and the grass as well... Those were symbols. It was like the fog was taking different shapes and qualities in different places... And all this started to talk to me... (I got goose bumps all over my skin). It was tremendous, astonishing law... Nature itself was telling me its law, but "law" is a very strong word... Nature was telling about its ... way of living ... how they all are existing in harmony ... and their energy in such harmony, all in brilliance. At the same time, I felt the soft, warm energy of the sun... Everything is so transparent, clear, harmonious... It was telling me all this step by step... And when in one moment it seemed to me that something was missing, they told me more, and it turned out to be the key to all that was said before... Something from the humans, something very fine and fragile, indistinguishable, very harmoniously flowed into it... All this is one life... And I thought that I should write a book about it. And then I looked and saw in front of me a large book, and one page is written – dedicated to what I was told, and already clearly, and explicitly written, as if by myself... Curly letters, very-very beautiful calligraphy. I started reading it... I remember that it was a dream, and I had to remember it well. I tried to find human words and even tried to remember the order of words. Step after step. It was hard work, very strange. After all these efforts, I woke up.

What is most interesting, when I woke up and got out of this condition, a part of me was bigger than the ones that live here. The large one was from somewhere above, from far away. It was watching when I, the little one, was coming back. It was like the sun and one ray coming from it... In what condition of life am I coming back this time? It was a very strong and very real sensation. And so this sun, the main part, saw my life with its own eyes – that is, I saw it with her eyes – that I am returning to such a warm, cozy, soft untroubled spot; something like a nest, something calm, like a pool or a lake. There was neither satisfaction, nor anything else from the one, BIG part of me that I was here, only a very clear, cold observation...

Then, I woke up. I was lying on my back, trying to remember who I am, and how I fell asleep... It seemed to me, that the BIG side of me told me that a human being could exist without food, while being in harmony with nature. He told me specifically not to eat animals. There was energy of water, energy of rocks, and energy of plants. They were not real plants, rocks, water – this was all clearly symbolic. The water was extraordinary. There were no animals, birds, fish, or insects. There was something very fine, something of a human sort, very specific – and we especially should not eat them. The humans should not eat at all! If a person is placed in this harmony, s/he does not need feeding.

© Josephine Wall. All Rights Reserved. www.josephinewall.com

Dream # 11
Luminous Bodies of Plants, January 8, 1992

I hadn't slept all night. Again, like the other times, I was dreaming of unusual things within five minutes of my being asleep. I can remember it, because I woke up right after that. It was maybe 5:00am. I was lying in bed. At this moment a terrible sound, a terrible click made me open my eyes – as if some shot went off in my room. I remembered my dream – and at the same moment, there was this shot, a terrible sound, like dry wood cracking. I jumped, opened my eyes, and I could still hear the shot. Something like that used to happen with my piano. I fell back to sleep and again something unusual came to my dreams. Again, this shot, and I woke up again. Very strong sound.

I was dreaming that I approached the window, there was some space in front of me, and different kinds of trees had been planted in rows. There were some apple trees, pines, birch-trees, a whole variety, and rare breeds as well. I looked at them. In my mind, I knew what kind of trees they were, but with my eyes, I saw them in colors. I was shocked – I hadn't seen this before. The trees of the same breed were of the same color. They had approximately three spectra. I remembered what apple trees looked like, their color was orange; what the fir trees looked like – they consisted of three lines of the spectrum, I think, bright blue. If the blue is responsible for dynamic of growth, it should be on the top, where the new growth is. But it turned out to be not so, the fir tree had it in the middle, 2/3 from the bottom – a blue line, then bright-yellow, and perhaps a red one. I don't remember now, I cannot remember clearly. The apple tree had a soft orange tone, coming into rose, but two separate colors, like on those balloons.

You opened a book and started reading – a prologue. You were reading aloud with my voice. At the same time, the other me, was observing the scene from outside. I interrupted your reading. I knew what was written there, right away, although I heard it for the first time. **In this book, the knowledge came to the surface, which was unknown to people until then. This book was a revelation. People did not even suspect it – it opened up, revealing itself like an old secret, a treasure, as if someone dug it out of the earth. A very rare animal, a diamond animal was buried there thousands and thousands of years ago. I interrupted myself and started dictating the already specific things from this book (you had only the introduction). You started to write down what I was saying immediately.**

I am sure that if scientists would make a list of questions about ancient civilizations like Sumerians, Atlantis, Ancient Egypt and Mexico, and started asking me these questions during some hypnosis sessions, I would shift in to this "diamond animal", which would be a rare and unique source for people to receive treasure from many Ancient civilizations: their deep secrets, knowledge about super human possibilities, ultra-advanced technology and deep, wise connections that exist between people and nature.

I am a *human time bullet*. I did remember my past lives through the centuries and now, this current life will be added, which will enable me to tell people in the future about our civilization.

YOUTUBE: Scientist photographed a soul leaving in the body in death – 2nd part

****

Dream # 12
Spectrum, February 23, 1992

Many trees, large clearing, they were growing not one by one, but as if united for some purpose. I thought – well, what a clearing, and I saw it in my dream for the first time. However, I knew that it is not a dream, but a reality. After that, some living creature appeared in the clearing – either a dog, or a person, I don't remember now. And it was also consisting of those spectrums. It was going on for so long, that I could look for as long as I wanted, at all of the details, transformations of colors, and I divided all this into a system. I counted how many breeds of trees there were, how many colors, everything. It was very unusual, beautiful, and at the same time more real than the trees ever were. Incredible!

YOUR ETERNAL HOLOGRAM

9. Masks.

The priest always had his mask with him. I always wished to have a mask, but the type I needed, I could never find in any store. I wished to have a full size mask, covering my entire face. Now I am wearing one – it is a jaguar mask; it makes me very comfortable and happy. It is always in front of my eyes, on the wall or on my head... My business partner Desmond Bloom in London wished to give me something as a souvenir, and he was very surprised when I asked him to find a jaguar mask for me.

10. Word Caracol.

Caracol - the name of the observatory in Chichén Itzá, where Priest spent most of his time.
Also the town of **Caracol** is near Tibet where my parents were born and where I grew up. It seems as if Spirit before I was born searched for a place with a similar name. It is interesting that in 1987, I saw the name **Caracola** on the map of Turkmenistan and I was attracted to this place like a magnet. I felt as if someone called me to come. Caracola is like a quad – a meeting place. I flew there. I went through the Time Gate to the many dimensional worlds and I had an astonishing contact there. Guess what? It was a meeting with my own Spirit from the future in a new body! You can see in another chapter, KUKULCAN, a drawing from this "spirit". This place is close to the place where the Spirits, creatures from my dreams contact me from time to time. (You name them if you can. It is not easy for me to find words to describe them or give them a name, because some of them are different from our world and I don't have anything to compare them with.)
Also, since an early age, when I was waking up from a dream-filled sleep, I continued talking in ancient Maya, using words like Equinox, Tzolkin, Caracol, which I pronounced often.

11. Aztec God Xochipilli

For many years, I often held a little wooden man in my hands. It was a gift, which was carved for me by a handsome boy, soon after we met. I inspired him to make this little wooden man. After many years, a week ago, I found that this little statue is the Aztec God, Xochipilli, the God of flowers, corn, and love. I find lots of them selling as a souvenirs in Chichén Itzá!

12. I always want to be Priest – during my present life!

My best friend is a High Priest from Asia.
Three years ago, I was living in Asia in a Buddhist temple. I loved harmony, meditation, nature and the wise Buddhist philosophy they taught there. In this ancient, beautiful temple, every evening the monks play huge drum, the size of a wall, maybe 2.5 to 3 meters in diameter. Instead of drumsticks, they use the trunk of a tree! The magnificent sound they produce comes out in waves of strong, powerful vibrations, which flows far away to the valley and mountains around.

On the opposite side, in front of the main temple, the monks play on big gongs and on a few drums. I am sure these monks are the best drummers in the world. You know why? Each of our moves is an impulse from the brain connected through the nervous system.

The monks' brains are extremely organized due to the many hours of daily meditation, which last sometimes for weeks, so all of this energy moves through the channels smoothly, without friction, onto their drums. A few years ago, I read an article about some research done in San Diego about the brain of the Buddhist monks. The scientists found that the monks' portion of their brains dedicated to pleasure and happiness is 25% larger! Wow! They must be the happiest people on the planet.

They enjoy life much more than we do. I think this is the reason for the light of happiness and kindness, which shines from their eyes.

There were 250 Buddhist monks, men and women living in the Temple. They have a big kitchen where monks and guests share their meals. One day I was sitting near two monks. I heard one telling the other; "Today, in my dream, I will travel to galaxy," naming the exact galaxy where he intended to journey during his dream. Then the second monk replied, "I will join you." To this, their teacher, who was sitting nearby, said, "I will follow you both, and I will check on you today." Apparently, this is part of their daily routine. I was very envious! All they do is sleep and meditate...! Afterwards they talk for hours about their dreams...

I even asked the Supreme monk to accept me as a monk into this temple and he asked me if I was ready to cut all my long, golden hair. I agreed instantly!

YOUR ETERNAL HOLOGRAM

He told me that my great purpose in this life time was to be in front of millions of people around the world with an important mission, not in an isolated temple. That summer, I cut 70 cm and still had another 50 cm flowing down over my shoulders.

That was not a problem for me, since my hair grows very fast as if I were a "wild animal", with lots of thick, long hair, down to my hips. Supreme monk told me that this is a sign of strong energy. I always receive many compliments about my hair. However, when I was modeling my agent asked me to cut my hair many times, because women just do not have such strong, long hair when they are in their thirties. I remember ending up buying a short wig to try to hide my hair under it! It was funny!

I discovered during my studies that each little hair is a long tube, inside which there is a channel filled with electro conductivity mass. On the cover of the hair, charges are besieged with a thin coat of what we call PRANA energy. Women with long hair bring this energy to the fetus during pregnancy. It is interesting that in my past lives (see next chapters) as a Priest, a woman from Atlantis, a girl from Egypt, everyone had very long, thick hair. Amelia, who had good, long hair when she was young, but cut short later, which was suitable for her woman-pilot image, and which was in fashion at that time.

While I was living in that temple, the monks asked me about my dreams: what I saw, where I went, how many times I had been in the same places and how many times I saw the same dreams – in as many details as I could. This analysis gave them an idea as to the amount and level of special spiritual energy I have, and about the stage of my spirit development. They complimented me many times about my energy, and as a result, I got a Blessing from the Honorable Supreme Buddhist monk, who is the leader of 13 million monks in Asia. We developed a very good friendship between him and me. He told me that in one of my past lives I was in this temple as a High Buddhist monk. It looks like this is what attracted me always to the Buddhist part of Asia.

As for me, this Supreme Buddhist monk is the wisest man on the planet. Each of his words and sentences is filled with deep spiritual meaning. Some special, heavenly, beautiful, white, glowing energy fills the space and the whole room around him. After talking to him, when you go outside, it feels as if you are returning from Heaven – from the sky down to Earth's reality. To me, he is a **"Live Buddha"** here on the planet.

He drew something for me – a gift – a painting with hieroglyphs, which meant **"One of a kind"**.
I asked him, "Why?" He told me that I am very rare, because of some special qualities my Spirit has. It is human, but also **multidimensional Supreme Being.**

As for me, I think that every human is *one of a kind* and this belongs to the same kind of idea. Remember Mr. Alfons: "I am who I am, I am not more then somebody else, I am not less then somebody else. I am myself." I am one of a kind here on Earth. Period.

I don't belong to any religion; there was a time in my life when I was searching for it. That until I saw in a dream a special place – I called this place White Emptiness. I returned to this dream from time to time, and this glowing white, pure energy place, which is absolutely empty – nothing around, nothing under or on top – is the most sacred place for me, because, this place gives me the most amazing, beautiful feeling I ever had in my whole life. The monks also know about this place and they asked me to give them every detail about my travels there.
There is NOTHING there, right...? My advice to you is to start meditating, and you might discover the door leading to this new world, bright and beautiful like a "sky full of stars and galaxy in eternity".

13. Tortoise

I like turtles a lot! I have a collection of them. From a young age, until now, I always have a live one near me, around 5 to 6 cm in diameter. When I didn't have a little turtle during my first few years in Canada, I often had many dreams where I tried to find my tortoise. Then I called Tibet asking them to find the smallest one in the desert and to send it to me. As soon as I got it, everything went back into harmony. My little turtle usually loves to sleep on my desk under the cozy, green lamp, while I am typing. It looks like a little, shiny rock down there. In this Buddhist temple, there were tortoises everywhere, carved in wood and rocks, but not a real, live one in sight. So I gave a little live-turtle to my friend for his 80th birthday.

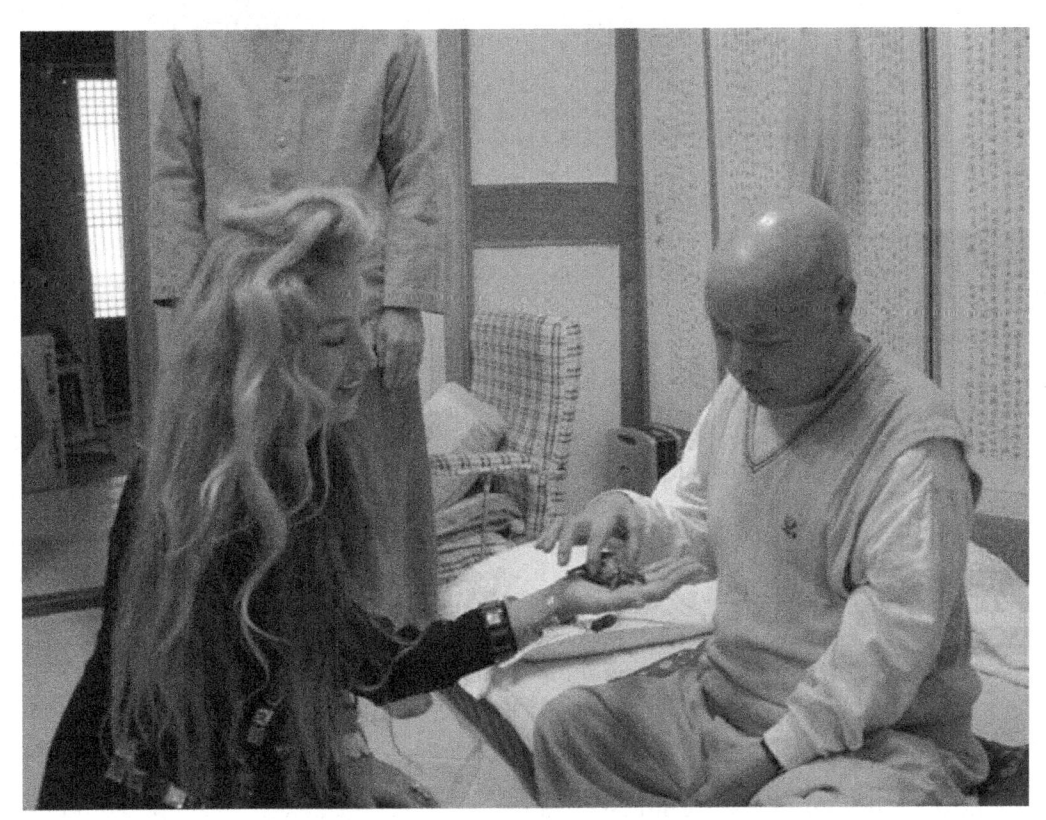

Meeting of two High Priests: from Asia and Ancient Mexico, turtle gift exchange.

I always travel with my turtle. This is the main reason I always have very small size ones. Once, I was at the Frankfurt airport going through customs. When it came time for me to go through the checkpoint, I was asked to put everything through the X-ray. Since I didn't want my turtle to be subjected to radiation, I kept her in my pocket. The officers then asked, "What do you have in your pocket?" I told them it was a toy. Next, they asked me, "Why is your toy moving?" I was traveling, as usual, in my silky jaguar cape and no one would imagine that I had a live turtle in my pocket – however, this time it looked like my tortoise woke up and was making a fuss. I pulled my little pet out. Everyone around me then started screaming and yelling for assistance. Yet, since I have all thedocuments necessary to go through any border – veterinarian passport, etc. – and a little cage for her, there was no problem. We all ended up laughing.

Julia's latest friend, a Sulcata tortoise, Drayga

14. Connection with the Goddess Bodhisattva, meeting with God.

Goddess Bodhisattva

In this old, ancient Buddhist temple, there is a 1,500-year-old legend.
The monks found this place, high in the mountains. There was a very special, pure energy about the place and they started dreaming of building a temple there. However, they didn't have money to erect the temple. They prayed for many months for somebody to help them realizing their dream. One day, a girl came and told them that she would work and help them in the kitchen. She was a magnificent, beautiful creature! Soon people started to come from the villages around, just to see her beauty and began donating money for the temple. More and more people came every day. One day, a rich man arrived with his son and gave the money necessary to build the temple. His son, on the other hand, fell in love with this girl. The wedding and the Temple's inauguration were scheduled for the same day. Many people gathered for the celebration. At the moment, when everyone stood in front of the temple and the wedding ceremony was about to start, the girl suddenly decided to change something in her outfit. She ran straight into a huge rock near the temple and disappeared in front of hundreds of people! In the middle of this rock her little sock got stuck. Since then, every year one flower blossoms in the place where she lost her sock.
The monks believe that she was Goddess Bodhisattva – the best among all Gods and Goddesses when it comes to serve people's needs and help them in their pursuits. This is why, on the

statues, sometimes she is represented with many hands to help everyone. From time to time, she visits Earth as a human. The monks invited me to visit the huge rock where she disappeared. I wore my golden outfit for this ceremony. They told me that if I would tell her name three times and ask for something, it would happen. I did it all according to their rituals; I stayed on my knees on this marble floor in front of her statue and began to concentrate. Suddenly, I saw Goddess Bodhisattva standing on a big turtle!

Wow! When I saw this, I felt an instant connection with her, as if she was my friend and we knew each other forever, and we have the same interests – she loves tortoises! Then I started calling her, by repeating her name: "Kwansaeum Bosal, Kwansaeum Bosal, Kwansaeum Bosal." Next, I told her in one sentence: "Please make me successful in my business, so I will be able to help this temple."

Suddenly, the air around me began to feel very hot! I found myself in the middle of an enormous flame and it sparkled! I experienced heavenly, beautiful energy around me. I enjoyed being in this sparkling cloud, which wrapped around my body like a cocoon. It continued to surround me for 2 to 3 minutes.

The monks, who had stayed near me, saw it; felt it and they were in total shock! They decided that this was a sign that maybe I am the **Goddess Bodhisattva and that I had come to visit the temple again**..., and they reported what happened to the top Supreme monk.

As for me, I don't know how to explain this. It is evident that she came and was around me... The monks asked me what I did. I told them that I started calling for her to come to me. Perhaps I didn't understand the translation that I should just pronounce her name and say my wish. Maybe it was the Spirit of the Maya Priest which is inside me who intervened. He used to be in connection with God and he would know exactly how to deal with Goddesses.

During the next three weeks, the monks brought me the best Korean pears and some of the fruits, which are usually given to the three Gold Buddha statues in the main temple. Most importantly, though, I got a blessing and special prayers in the temple on my birthday and I was showered with Buddhist presents! It was a happy time!

Meeting with God

It was Christmas Morning.
Red carnations and white chrysanthemums filled the biggest Catholic Church in Vancouver and it was packed with people. The priest was talking and talking... but as for me, I didn't feel any energy, I didn't feel any life in it... His speech was empty...
What kind of message is he sending to people on this special day? I guess he just tried, but he must not have had enough sleep after the midnight service. Suddenly he decided to ask people to say something special... I was right! He needed help today. I got up and found myself talking to 300-400 people on Christmas day. I told them:
"It was the day when I should have given birth to my baby. I did not sleep all night except for a few minutes. I had a dream, but everything in this dream was very real! Two angels arrived, two real angels with white wings! I remember flying with them and they guided me from both sides. They brought me to the church on the hill... A tall priest came to me from this church with the parishioners following him... He stopped in front of me and he blessed me... I saw his face... I recognized him instantly!" (As I am typing these lines, I am covered with goose bumps again...)
"I woke up at 8:00am and the contractions started... Exactly 24 hours later, I gave birth to a healthy baby girl."
The next part of my dream, I did not tell the people in church but I will relate it to you now. When intellectual people who do not believe in astrology, and especially those who visit the Catholic Church – if I were to tell them this part, they would start thinking that I am crazy and they would lose interest in the priceless gold dime in this story. Doctors were worried about the baby and me. The problem was that I turned my body clock to give birth to my baby three weeks later in order for her to

have a perfect astrology chart on the day she was born. I had locked the door for the baby to come out into the world. I just needed one more day... I went through all of the stages of labor and imminent delivery, but the situation was still the same and the doctors could do nothing about it. After the birth, they called me a hero and told me that I went through all possible and impossible phases of birthing and they thought I would die. All the while, I felt Him nearby, He held my hand...

YES, I told all these people in the church that, "I grew up in a country where people were atheist, no one went to church for 75 years. Until that day, when I had this dream, I never thought about GOD, I never visited a church. Since it happened, I know that GOD exists. Angels exist. And they take care of each and every one of us. I then began to respect people who never met GOD during their lifetime or in their dreams, BUT believe that He exists and have His Holy Faith in their hearts!"

People liked my story; some of them ran after the service to talk to me. I like this church, especially for the beautiful cut-glass windows, with scenes portraying God's life, and for the wonderful organ music.

Here is the exact dream with all of the details, for those who are interested.

Dream # 13
God's Blessing, angels, July 20, 1995

There were two dreams. I remembered only one. I slept from 5:00 to 8:00. It was at the time, when I was expecting a baby. I had a dream, but everything in this dream was very real! Two little children appeared beside me – small, up to my knees, but they understood everything, as if they were not five years old, but much older. They started pulling me on both sides – as if I should go with them somewhere; they should bring me to some place. It was two real angels with white wings! They took me and I remember flying with them and they guided me from both sides. I started moving, and they stayed with me, floating in the air, not touching the ground but floating beside me at my waist. They brought me to the church, the cathedral on the hill. Near this cathedral, I saw a priest surrounded by other people. He saw me and immediately came to meet me, as if he was expecting me.

He was very tall, very thin, very strict in his manner and clean. Young – as if he was in his 30th, but wise, as if he were thousands of years old – not a person, but a Saint. I looked around. The cathedral was snow-white, very severe. I looked up. It had one cupola, but it went very high up, in eternity. It was shining – snow-white, clear and high. I don't know with what to compare it – some mountains are like that, crystal-clear, untouched, virginal.

He approached me and started saying something. I knew that it was some kind of ritual, an important ritual. There was a feeling, that this day was a day of sacral feast. I was wearing something; I put it on to go to the hospital – what I wore before falling asleep. He made some movements around me with his arms and something, a cover, shiny as snowflakes came down on me from above. When it fell down on me – my shoulders and my back were covered with soft white fur, like swans' feathers, very fine.

Then he made a roundish move in the air with his arms, as if making a circle downright, and completed it as if by drawing a line under my breast. And I understood that women's breast is a symbol of maternity, and not something else. My breast swelled. It was filled with a sensation of elasticity. Then he made a gesture with his hand, with a finger – some sign in front of me – he raised the forefinger of the right hand and moved it to the side. I suddenly understood what he was doing – he was blessing me. I just had enough time to tell him, that I liked very, very much his cathedral, of eternal beauty, splendid, clear, white... I opened my eyes – it was eight o'clock. And my first contraction started...

As for me, I think God exists and He is the only one. However, through human eyes he can be perceived in a variety of shapes and forms, depending on the religion and beliefs of each person.

Something very odd happened to me in **Rome, at the Vatican,** in the summer of 2008. We went with my daughter through St. Peter's Basilica with crowds of tourists and we needed to rush back to the tour bus. While we were inside, I saw, not far from the exit, a statue with two baby angels, exactly the same size and looks as what I saw in my dream! I asked my daughter to take a photo and I asked her to take a few photos outside. When we went outside, I started to cross the square. As soon as I was alone and somewhat separated from people, I instantly felt the very strong presence of someone near me! My whole body was covered with goose bumps ... and I started talking to this Spirit. I told him that I felt him and so on, and so on... My daughter didn't notice it! Since we were very rushed, she ran ahead and turned to take some pictures while I was totally in shock with this astounding feeling of talking to this Spirit! In the middle of a sunshiny day! And with thousands of people around!

At first, I stopped agape, as if the ground in front of me suddenly opened and there was no place for me to take the next step. Afterwards, I talked to this Spirit as if he were a long lost friend... Wow! I have no idea who he was...

I remember, when I stopped I was not worrying about our bus anymore; I just looked around me as if in a daze. When I turned around, I saw Jesus holding a cross in his hand and with his apostles surrounding him. Surrounding the square in front of the St. Peter's Basilica, there are many statues of "Holy" people, they are very special to the Catholic faithful, and the Church pronounced them "Holy" or canonized them. Perhaps it was a "Holy" man who guided me through my dreams. Or maybe it was the spirit of Michelangelo who came to me in front of St. Peter's Basilica? He invested his creativity and an enormous amount of energy everywhere around this place, into the paintings and the statues. Maybe Michelangelo wanted to *thank me* for dedicating this book to him and other creative people? Or maybe it was Jesus? It is possible – since this place resounded of such a strong energy. Maybe right there, in another dimension, which is invisible to us, this is the church where the real GOD, Jesus exists and where I was invited, guided by two little angels, and blessed by God right before my baby was born?

Julia in front of Jesus in the Church of the Holy Wisdom, known as Hagia Sophia, Istanbul
Photo by Darlene Lauren SV

It is interesting that since it happened, as soon as I started remembering that moment, I experienced again the same sensation: my body was covered with goose bumps. It means that the **Spirit** knew I was thinking about him at that exact moment – and it's happening again right now, while I am typing these words...
The scientist who led the team responsible for cracking the human genome says he has found GOD. Francis Collins, the director of the US National Human Genome Research Institute, has written a newbook: "The Language of God," arguing that there is nothing in science that contradicts the existence of God. On the contrary, Collins says his research has convinced him that God is real!

In this book, the pioneering geneticist argues that, *"Today we are learning the language in which God created life"*. He believed that sequencing of the human genome is in fact the most remarkable of the texts, offering a detailed view of the mind of the creator at work.
"Science is not threatened by God. It is enhanced" and "God is most certainly not threatened by science. He made it all possible." In staking out a position in support of the existence of God, Collins joins some of the history's most influential scientists – Isaac Newton, and Albert Einstein *(Magazine, "Atlantis Rising", number 59, "Genome pioneer discovers God")*.

YOUTUBE: Angels are taking away the soul of the dead child
j^ ^j^ Angels Angels Angels ^j^ ^j^
Evidence of God: Physics
Evidence of God: DNA

****

15. Ghosts

When people die, their Spirit goes to Heaven. However, some are stuck in between for different reasons: some are attached to the house, where they live, or to a real person, or things they had in this life... Some worry that God will not accept them because they were not baptized or did something wrong in this life, and some don't know that they are actually dead. God will accept everyone. People should go directly to the white glowing light. Simple – and they will be taken care of. People who die and Spirit in heaven show up to me usually very nicely, beautiful, in the best shape they had during their lives. Ghost are instead not here and not there, they are stuck in the space between Heaven and Earth and show up ugly, deformed, partly decomposed even ... yak!

It is easy for a ghost to appear in a humid climate. I lived in Tokyo many times, always for a few months. I remember the first time I went to Japan; I arrived at this building from the airport very tired and went to sleep instantly. Someone, during the night, touched me and patted me lightly on the back, without stopping – no break, no rest – and he laughed all night long into my ears! It was exhausting. I remember ending up screaming, "Go away! Go away! Stop it! Stop it! Stop it!" I asked this "someone" to go away all night long! When I woke up in the morning, I told my friend, Lisa, about it. She replied, "This is our ghost; it bothers everyone in this building!"

I asked her, "What you mean ghost?"

She said, "Look out the window." Near the building was a huge cemetery! She told me that everyone in the building knew about ghosts and there was not a thing they could do about it. This building, with its adjoining cemetery, was located in the middle of modern Tokyo, near the TV station.

I returned to my apartment in the same building at around 7:30 p.m. My mother, who was a doctor, from an early age taught me to wash my hands as soon as I returned home. Seeing that the light was on in the washroom, I thought someone was in there. A few minutes later, I called, "Anyone home?" No answer. I then decided to put the kettle on the stove to make some tea and waited for a few seconds. At the same moment, a drawer and a door from the kitchen cabinets popped open loudly! The drawer on top contained spoons, forks, knifes; the cupboard below stored big things like pots. In order to open it, someone should have pulled the first drawer near the wall, and the other door needed to be pulled from inside, where I stood in amazement.

I returned to my seat at the kitchen table and began thinking about this like a scientist. "How can it be possible? I just put the teakettle on the stove and it didn't start boiling yet. It would be impossible for the difference in temperature to create this." I really didn't have any explanation. I then looked at the bathroom door. Still no sign of anyone being in there. I pulled on the door; it did not open. I started calling, "Someone inside?" No reply. I pulled on the door harder and opened it. No one inside! It was empty!

My first thought was, "What a silly girls live here," because the entire floor was covered with unrolled toilet paper... Next, I was amazed! Really amazed! Someone inside had taken the toilet paper from the roll, which was located near the door, dragged it along the wall and wrapped it many times around the towel bar, on the door, until the roll was empty. There had been many layers wrapped around the towel bar, and when I had pulled the door hard, the ball of wrapped paper had ripped in the middle and had unraveled itself across the floor!

"How can this be possible?" – That question came back to mind immediately. There is only one way for someone to unravel an entire roll of toilet paper and roll it around the doorknob – with time and very patiently. Secondly, what really hit me: someone did it from inside, but there was no one, nobody inside! Our apartment was located on the fourth floor and there was NO window – no access to the washroom except through the door. How this can be possible?I was totally lost with two unexplained events. Then I remembered the previous night's disturbance and Lisa's comments about the ghosts in this building.

Lucky for me Lisa returned home soon and told me that many strange things happened in this apartment. She told me that sometimes the curtains blew up in front of her and blankets were ripped off her bed, or someone had scratched her hand while she was eating...

The second night I did not sleep again. Again, someone try to "play" with me all night long. I began remembering that in Russia people from far away villages called this sort of spirit "chekotilki" – those who tickle people to death.

However, an even more horrible thing happened close to the morning. In my dream, I saw my friend, the famous opera singer, Slava. Slava had a voice, which could heal people. When friends came to see him, he always asked the person to stay in front of him while he adjusted their energy. Sometimes during this procedure, people started to levitate and ended up only being supported by their toes. After this procedure, people felt like they were newborn babies, full of energy and harmony. In the dream, I did what he asked and my feet started lifting. Suddenly something horrible happened! Something came inside me from under my feet, went through my body, up to my chest and stayed there – some sort of enormous pressure, like a two-ton-truck had settled against my chest and was compressing my lungs. I couldn't breathe. I saw my mother, she was calling my father, she was screaming for help! The pressure was finally released with a terrible blow and it left me with the most awful pain in my lungs. I woke up and I could hardly breathe! Each breath was painful for me. This ghost pretended to be my friend and I trusted him. This allowed him to do these horrible things!

That day I called Canada but I couldn't really talk – my voice was but a whisper. People asked why I talked like that. I tried to tell them that a ghost had come during my dream and had settled on my body. They didn't believe me; instead they told me to "get some sleep!"

"I wish I could," I said, "but it's impossible." When I told them that I could not sleep because of some ghost, they started worrying about my mental health...

YOUR ETERNAL HOLOGRAM

It was already the third night since I left Canada and I had not slept a wink in four days. I was sick and tired of that damn ghost! I was even thinking about people who die because of lack of sleep. My neighbors told me that many people had moved from this building because of the ghosts. Some of them tried to sleep during the day. In my condition, in my deeply tired state of mind, it was impossible for me to start looking for another apartment in a country where I arrived only three days ago.

I returned home the next day, no one was there. After the previous night's events I was afraid to fall asleep. I understood clearly that even if someone is not alone in the apartment, while you are sleeping, in your dream you are still alone – one on one with the ghost!

I went to the neighbors, the girls who lived on the seventh floor. Only one was there and she told me that my friend and her roommate went to a party at Hero Park! "They'll return maybe in the morning!" she said. I spent the whole night reading magazines at her place. She told me that what happened with my lungs happened also, in exactly the same way, to one girl living with her. It took three weeks for her to return back to normal.

At 6 a.m. the girls returned and I finally went back to the 4th floor to my home. It was twilight already when I lay down on my bed. As soon as I closed my eyes, I saw a Japanese girl standing near my bed! I sat up and looked at her. She looked at me in total silence. No emotions, nothing. I only remember that I thought, "What a sick girl!"

I woke up... I am not sure that I even went to sleep at all ... and I went to my roommates. The two of them, and one from the 7th floor, were sitting in the living room next to the open door to my room, eating. I asked them, "Who is this Japanese girl? Why has she come to visit us so early? Is she our neighbor? I need rest!" They looked at me and replied, "You went to sleep ten minutes ago, when we were already eating right here, no one came in. No one went to your room. The only way to go to your room from the entrance door is through the living room where we are all eating right now."

They were right – the only other way to my room was from the balcony – on the 4th floor. I told them, "This is impossible! I saw her right here, a minute ago! I remember her in all the little details!"

"Okay! Tell us what she looks like."

I described her. She was 26 years old maybe, a modern girl, but her face was very pale, ashen. Usually, Japanese girls have very nice white face. But this one seemed very sick; she had dark, really dark, black circles under her eyes and cheeks.

One of the girls told me, "You describe someone from the "Adams family!"" It was obvious to everyone that a ghost was visiting us – no one else... Again, the word "obvious" sounds strange when talking about ghosts.

I was fed up! I needed rest. It was the fourth morning after another sleepless night. That day I decided to go to the cemetery. No two ways about it, I wanted to talk to these ghosts and stop this harassment! Especially, I wished to talk to that Japanese girl. I know that it was her who was playing during the night trying to attract my attention. And I wanted to talk to those who "sat" on my lungs!

I don't like ghosts, you never know what to expect from them. They're kind of sticky, grand masters at creating fear and existing on it. They're very creative in the way they trick people. They are lost souls ... nothing to add.

I invited the girls to go with me to the cemetery, but they were afraid to death! No one wanted to go. I told them that in their dreams they were on their own with this ghost and I could not help them if that were to happen. The goal was to let the ghosts know that we were aware of them, that we were not going to pay attention to them, that we would have no part of their games and that we would not support them or feed them with our fearful energy – so that they would have to leave us alone.

So here I am. I left Canada four days ago and now **I am in a Tokyo cemetery talking to ghosts!**

I was wearing my beautiful red sari, a silk dress from Nepal, maybe five meters long if you opened it. I lit a candle, and started calling the ghosts to come to the meeting by knocking on the little wooden monk bells from China. And I started talking to them with my full voice. It was almost dark now. I told them that I came here to Japan for a modeling job and that I was here because I did not sleep for four days, that I was sick and tired of them and that I couldn't take it anymore! "It needs to stop!" I hollered.

I told them again that I needed rest to look good for my work. I repeated that they should stop their tricks, never come to me again, and never bother me! I said that I didn't want to hear them, feel them and know about them. Period. I told them that all of them were dead and their place was in heaven ... instead of being stuck here and creating problems for all the people in this building. I also said that they should feel really ashamed of what they were doing.

It was starting to get really dark now – no light – except for the light from a window on the second floor of the building. Suddenly I saw a bunch of them standing near me – they were surrounding me! Perhaps more than ten kind of white people's shadows! Like pieces of fog... To my surprise, instead of being scared, I was glad that I made my speech in "public", not to the empty air. I told them, "I see that you all were listening to me carefully. Very good! BYE forever," and I returned home.

And you know what? They never, ever bothered me again. They never came to me! When my friend slept during the day or I woke up early, I saw that she tossed and turned all the time in her bed, in her room – as if someone was pinching her without stopping...

****

Hold on! The fire alarm just came on – on our floor – it's ringing right now!
"Bye for now... I need to run and see if the house is on fire..." My daughter is already in the hallway with our ferret in her arms...
I am back; it was the fire alarm on our floor alright. Our neighbor ran for the manager. He checked everything and told us that he doesn't have any idea why it was ringing... I am suspicious that this Japanese girl showed up. Really! Because at the moment it started ringing I decided to be done with the ghosts and said, "Bye for now" to the Japanese girl!

When I am reading now the last sentence I wrote before the fire alarm started ringing..., "They never, ever bothered me again. They never came to me!" Wow! I know why the fire alarm started ringing! The Japanese girl – right! She doesn't bother me in my dreams now, but I was connected to her for a long time. Okay, I will tell you the full story about my "friendship" with ghosts.

****

The next day I talked to the priest at the cemetery and asked him about the Japanese girl. He told me that, YES, a week ago there was a funeral for a girl. She was 28 years old, she was very sick before she died. He showed me her grave, which was still covered with fresh flowers. Poor girl, it looked like she didn't know she was dead! She was walking among the living, a stranger trying to attract attention, but no one ever saw her!

Now I have a question for you: How many girls, especially a modern girl, a model, would go alone to the cemetery to talk to dead people, ghosts in the dark? Maybe one in 100, one in 500, maybe one in a million? I am sure no one will do this intentionally...I am sure the Priest in me went to the cemetery – not me. I still don't believe I did it...Another one of those "inherited characteristics" to put on the list...

I remember that one of the girls I lived with always did the cleaning, wash the dishes, did the laundry – she was always working for everybody. One day she was up before everyone and wrote a note on a piece of paper: *"Please clean after yourself or I will kill you. Signed: Ghost."*

You know what? Since that day, our apartment was squeaky clean...

Okay; back to that Japanese ghost girl.

YOUR ETERNAL HOLOGRAM

My contract finished with that modeling agency and I moved to another area, working for another agency. And again there was a cemetery nearby! It was interesting that in Tokyo, the agencies put foreign people to live in places near cemeteries – because the rent was much cheaper. Tokyo has lots of old cemeteries right in the middle of town. This time, I was living in a wooden house on the second floor. During the weekend I visited a Japanese family in Yamanachi. Taky, his wife, Mammy, and I went to the South of Japan for two days. I returned from that trip with a big, green pray-mantis, which I kept in a cage. I was glad that the cemetery was nearby because it was the end of the summer andgetting cooler and there were not too many insects left to feed the mantis. There was a time when I couldn't find any insect at all!

When I went to the cemetery to collect some insects for the mantis, I only saw a huge butterfly flying around some old tombs. I thought of what to do...? It is hard to kill such a beautiful creature to feed a mantis... Yet, I thought the butterfly would die soon anyway since it was too cold for her and she was weak, but still so beautiful. I needed to spray her with some perfume to put her to sleep... I couldn't do it... It was very hard to start... At that same moment, I remembered that my friend, Professor Taky, told me that a butterfly, in Japan, is the symbol of the dead people's spirit... I brought it home. It was asleep, maybe it was dead already. I then took a needle, and when I stuck it in her heart, suddenly, the house started shaking! With a terrible sound!!!

I ran outside with the mantis in my hand. Many people came out as I did. I asked a neighbor, a Japanese woman: "Our house will fall down?"

She said, "Maybe not..." It had been a short earthquake tremor – 4.5 on the Richter scale. Obviously for me it was a sign of punishment for the killing of this butterfly. Since that day and for a week afterwards I carried a bag with my passport, the ticket back to Canada, some money, and jewelry. It was the fourth earthquake in the last three months and I was worried that one day I would return to my apartment to find the house destroyed.

Soon, it was time to return to Canada. It was Friday, and I was flying home on Monday. I decided to go to buy some presents, souvenirs for my relatives and friends. I went to Yokohama, because they have everything there but much cheaper than in the middle of Tokyo. I remember I was in the sky train, sitting near an old Japanese man, who was carrying a very beautiful, hand-carved umbrella. Suddenly, I saw that he went out at the station and forgot his umbrella!

I was sure he loved this umbrella, and I ran out to try to find him, but he had disappeared in the crowd already! So, I dropped the umbrella at the "Lost and Found" place and continued my journey for a few more stations. When I arrived at my station I realized that I needed to pay some extra money for the trip. I went to an automatic exchange machine, but it was broken. Then, I went to make the change. Anyway, when I was finally outside the station, instead of two things in my hands I had only one! I forgot my bag near that machine. I ran back... no bag! I ran to the Lost and Found – but nothing!

My passport, tickets, money, everything valuable and important was in that bag! I called the police and asked them to see the tape of the security camera. We saw that a woman took the bag. The police told me that there was a mafia ring in this part of town, hunting for foreign documents and that they would probably re-sell my passport. I put an ad everywhere around that station, asking to return the passport, promising a reward - nothing. In the meantime, I was stuck in a hotel near the Canadian embassy, waiting for my new passport. Within a couple of days, they received all of my documents from Canada, but how could I prove that me was me? Some others could look exactly like me; conversely, I can look the same as someone else. They did it in a very smart way. I was asked the type of questions that only a Canadian living in that city would know. For example, they asked me how much is a bus ticket or general knowledge question such as, "What is the name for the dollar in Canada?"

"The Loonie," I replied, because on the Canadian dollar there is a picture of the magic loon, on its face.

I learned my lesson, though. Tourists should never carry their passports, only copies. It was very interesting when I had the interview. First, they showed me a plastic bag full of Canadian passports, stolen in that area. One passport was of a very nice looking woman – she killed her husband and two kids in some country and arrived in Japan, to buy a Canadian passport and to try to go to Canada. The second was that of a man, who was a drug dealer – he also arrived in Japan from somewhere else, trying to go to Canada.

Anyway, three months later at the end of November, in Canada, I had a dream. That Japanese girl-ghost from the cemetery took me by the hand and brought me downstairs to some kind of basement. There was an empty, dark room. Inside, near the walls, there were bones of the dead people, each wrapped in some blankets. She brought me to the far left corner and opened one of the blankets. Inside, there was a skull and bones of the person who had presumably taken my passport since it was lying on its chest! She told me that the person who tried to use my passport was dead!

Perhaps the room where she brought me was under the cemetery. Maybe she wanted to show me how it looks under the ground in the world of the dead – her world ... bones here, bones there... Since then and for some 4 or 5 years she appeared in my dreams and delivered information about my life and my future. I have not seen her in the last few years... But today when the fire alarm sounded, maybe it was her again ... maybe I will see her in my dream today...

****

The Mexican Connections

There were interesting *coincidences* in connection with reincarnation that happened when I flew and arrived in Mexico, all of them occurred during the first 24 hours.

1. Numbers

On the way to the airport, all the cars around had license plates which had triple numbers! I gathered that the Universe or Mexican spirits tried to talk to me. It was some kind of coding with numbers 888, 444, 555, 111, 888, 555, 666, 444, 333, and they appeared repeatedly during the next 30 minutes. Our friend, Peter, my daughter and I didn't know what to think, what did it mean? Obviously, somebody was talking and trying to say something to us.

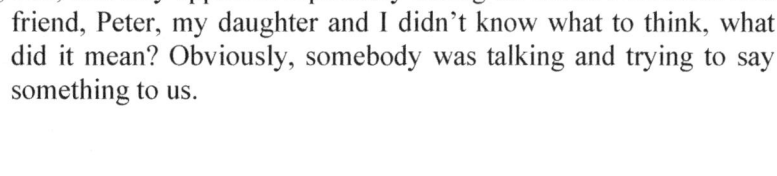

2. Hotel of Lord or King Pakal

When I arrived at the Cancun airport, it was late at night and there was only one hotel with rooms available. When I stepped inside, I felt as if I was a guest of the Lord King Pakal from Palenque Chiapas! This entire hotel was about him. His statues could be found inside and outside; there were beautiful bas-reliefs on the walls and even a fountain with his face carved at the base of it!

3. Restaurant of reincarnation

Next stop, when we arrived in the morning at Acumal, I went to eat in the local restaurant. All of the statues and pictures on the walls were symbols of reincarnation and of spirits! I found big and small skeletons of humans, animals, and hundreds of calabashes, which the Mexicans keep as the containers of the Spirits.

Restaurant of the reincarnation, Calabashes – containers of the Spirits

4. Blessing by a Maya priest

While I was there, I saw a marriage ceremony starting on this beautiful, white, sandy beach. The Maya priest or maybe a shaman was conducting this ceremony and the blessing of the newly wedded couple. When he finished and passed near me, we felt some instant connection between us, which stopped him. What happened is impossible to explain. Although he couldn't speak English or Spanish – only Maya – he invited me to the beach and performed a full ceremony with a blessing connecting me with the God Kukulcan and other Maya Spirits. It was powerful and it touched me deeply.

Blessing from a Maya Shaman

A Maya Shaman

5. Coba pyramid

The next day, early in the morning, I went to the Coba pyramid. I just enjoyed running up to the pyramid! I ran fast, without stopping and I even ran much faster coming down all these stairs! I did it few times.

I was very excited for some reason. The tourists around were staring at me and took many photos of my running up and down the stairs..., because in order to come down from the pyramid they all crawled on their hands and knees like babies – that's how steep it was. It was not funny to see adult people in this embarrassing position. Yet, I was laughing, but I began showing them how easy it was to go down the stairs.

6. Rock from the past

The same day, I found a rock, which I believe was my favorite rock to play with as a Priest.

I was walking and I stopped suddenly. I felt it! I felt something very special in this place! I sat down and stretched my hand in front of me; it landed on this rock. Next: I took another, smaller rock and started to play the two. It all went automatically without thinking. My hands knew what to do. This white limestone rock produced the amazing sounds of crystal bells! I couldn't stop playing...

It is astonishing that this rock was waiting for me; no one had taken it or moved it in 2000 years! It was in a place, which is protected from any of nature's changes. I guess I started to feel my own energy in this rock, which I was playing daily, a long time ago for many years before meditation, to relax myself and to go into a trance.

We are calling this "energy", but according to scientist Peter Gariaev[14] it was my DNA phantom, which made an imprint on this rock many years ago. The same happened when I started walking for the first time in Chichén Itzá and suddenly recognized everything around me, without even seeing the pyramids themselves. It was my phantom DNA which had stayed there since my past life and I started to be connected! By the way, I had a different DNA when I was a Priest. However, I guess, the phantom DNA soaked into the Spirit, making a print on my Spirit, which was reborn in my body. I continued playing on this rock now, every day. As I type this book, my feet are lying on my past, on this rock – on Mexican soil – I feel wonderful!

This rock is 38 by 25cm and the taxi driver at the airport asked me, "Why is your suitcase so heavy? You've got rocks in there or what?" I replied, smiling from ear to ear, "YES, a very cool rock!" He didn't believe it, of course.

Tell me, how many people would you convince to take a rock to another country, which fills most of your suitcase and carry it thousands of miles away?

That's what I meant when I said there is NOTHING we could do about those characteristics we "inherited" from our relatives, like big ears, for example... **In my case, I *inherited* the Priest's love of the sounds from the rocks.**

---

[14] You can read interpretation about this at the end of the book in scientific section.

YOUR ETERNAL HOLOGRAM

This rock produces sounds, which I made and heard in my past life, thousands of years ago as a Priest... My Spirit remembers it and when I play again, it opens the door to my past life and the magic energy of the pyramid for me. (see photo of that rock few pages below and at the end of the book).
Many people love to travel to the same places. One of the reasons is that their DNA phantom leaves an imprint there and it is always a pleasure to restore your own energy with a fresh one, which is waiting for you to return. It works especially well with nature. It feels like that all of the trees, plants are saying "Hi" to you when you return and meet them again.

I don't like delving in the ghost subject. In those places where people see ghosts, powerful DNA phantom exists from the time when someone produced strong emotions in the past. It occurs often in prisons, hospitals, cemeteries; places where people were sick and died, or in the houses they built and in locations where they invested lots of energy. At the moment people die, their body produces the strongest DNA phantom, I guess.

7. Statue

The first day I was in Chichén Itzá, I woke up at 6 a.m. to be near the entrance at 7:45 a.m. I needed to take some photos for this book.
Everywhere there was a rope around the displays and it was impossible to take good photos. You could see the statue of Chak Mol, for example, only from far away... NO WAY to take a photo! But I needed his photo for the book for the next chapter!
The next day I woke up again at 5:30 a.m. I went to the balcony to see the sunrise and guess what I saw. I could not believe my own eyes! In front of my room, on the grass, was the statue of Chak Mol! He was lying down, looking directly at me! I was so happy that I stayed in the Chichén Itzá hotel, in Piste, in that room! What a lucky coincidence!This statue was a copy of the original, which was found a few years ago in the forest near Chichén Itzá and the only one of which it was possible to take a photo! So I did!

Chak Mol and Julia in the hotel garden

8. Feelings

When I arrived in Chichén Itzá the second time, it was after my past life hypnosis readings. I was half Priest, half myself. This was what the Priest's Spirit inside me felt like in Chichén Itzá. It was a deep, sad feeling I experienced from time to time. When I arrived, I was under a strong "Priest influence"... When I was near a pyramid, I felt as if it was my own home, *me casa*... my office...

I wanted ... I needed to go inside. I wanted to touch this wall; I wanted to run up these steps... I wanted to be near the Chak Mol's statue and I wished to burn incense on the red Jaguar's back at least once such as I did hundreds of times during my life as a Priest... I wanted to touch that altar where my son laid down for the last time... Sometimes, I had tears in my eyes... The feelings near the pyramid were impossibly strong. As soon as I was near the pyramid, I had visions from my past life – real and bright...
At some point, I looked at tourists around through the Priest's eyes and I was glad that "ordinary people" did not walk in the sacred temple. Yes, the pyramid had been closed to the tourists for almost a year then. Yet, I felt that it was unfair: I was a Priest before and I lived and worked in this pyramid and now, I was reborn as a tourist and I just could not visit my own home.

"By the way, the body would die and the liberated soul (spirit) would set off the old ancestor, to get its new assignment at the right moment. Thus, together with a soul, a newborn baby inherits the social status, physical appearance and ancestral name of his (her) predecessor. ("Ancient America: flight in time and prostransive. Mezoamerika" Excerpts from the book by GG Ershovoy. Uncopyrighted@Sam, 2003-2006.) [30]

I wish to visit the pyramid at least once!

Yet one thing which I enjoyed while I was a Priest and which warmed up my soul; there, I could play! I had a little, soft tennis ball in my pocket with a message, "The Priest Jaguar returns home," and I loved to spend time in the ball court ... I customized this ball to make it heavier than the normal ones. Can't tell you more. :)

9. Equinox day 2008

It was a very happy day for me! I was near the pyramid at 8:00 a.m. as usual. By the way, people who worked there asked me, "Why are you near the entrance every day at 7:45 a.m.? You are a tourist, but you're acting like you're coming here to work." It was my "office" before; my work was here and it looked like I used to wake up early to be at work on time...

During the Equinox Day, thousands of people arrived from all over the world – highly spiritual people. I was near the pyramid and this feeling of responsibility and this sense of duty just did not leave me alone... This is what I have in my mind – the Priest talked to me, "I need to be inside the temple... I need to have everything ready! Where are the gifts to the GOD? Where are the fruits, the Jewelry? How come no one will be there to meet and endorse the talk of the Spirit with the GOD when he will arrive? This is unruly... It is impossible that there will be no prayers!"

I was staying near the stairs with presents in my bag, beautiful fruits, Lindor Easter Chocolates set in gold bunny and gold, little animals and chicken eggs.
I felt really confused. Suddenly, a little Maya girl, who just started to learn to walk, took her first steps toward me! I sat down and lifted this little doll to my knees. Her parents started to take pictures.

I opened my perfume bottle; it was natural lilac oil, with a tender fragrance, and put one drop on the forehead of this little angel and one drop on each of her small, cute hands and blessed her. Next, some parents brought me a baby. After that, one parent brought to me another one... Wow! I was the happiest person in the whole of Chichén Itzá! Finally, I was in the right place!

I just stayed near the stairs of my pyramid and blessed little children on this Holy Equinox Day – the same way I did two thousand years ago, exactly on the same day and at the same place.

I was in great harmony with time and space. I was wearing a white and gold outfit for the hours of Celebration that day.

Chichén Itzá Pyramid, Julia

Later, I was walking near the pyramid when I started feeling some unusual energy at one particular place. There were beautiful tree blossoms, all of the flowers on those trees were like white lilacs, with the same fragrance I just used. I sat under those trees and waited. It was a hot day. Around me, there was something special with people, all of them wearing white clothes and sitting in total silence or talking very quietly... It was a big contrast with the loud crowds around. At some point, they all stood up, all at once and started walking toward the pyramid to see the Equinox. I felt as if these people were a flock of white birds. I also started walking.

Their spiritual teacher walked near me. His name was Julio Luis Rodriguez. He was a wise man, carrying a full face, wooden mask in his hands! Exactly the way I had dreamed, all my life! He told me that he felt a strong powerful energy emanating from me. **Next, he put the mask on his face and saw me as a Maya priest...**
Throughout the day, many people talked to me and told me that they felt a powerful energy around me.Yes, all of them felt the Priest's Spirit, I guess – difficult to hide him. I saw many spiritual people visit the site on that day, people who could feel these kinds of things. I am sure they also have some special energy; otherwise, they would not have felt the strong Spirit in me, right?

Thousands of people arrived from all over the world for the Equinox day. I was amazed how well the Mexican government organized this event. Police, ambulances, soldiers, volunteers and scouts stood by everywhere, ready to lend a hand with help and support. As you know during this day, I was in "the Priest's skin"; this event was my responsibility just a few thousand years ago. Mr. Jorge Esma Bazan, Director of Patronato Culture, State of Yucatan, Mexico and his team arrived and talked to the people from the stage.

I went directly to them and told them that I was deeply grateful for their fantastic effort to keep the architectural complex of Chichén Itzá in such an excellent shape, and I thanked them for the outstanding organization of such an important event as the Equinox day. They had no idea that this **"Thank you" was not from an ordinary tourist but from one of the previous "rulers" of Chichén Itzá, an ancient Priest.**

Mexican spiritual teacher, Julio Luis Rodriguez

Julia with Mexican artists, March 2008

10. Equinox day 2010

Two years later, when I met Don Julio again in Chichén Itzá on Equinox day, he told me that my name in ancient Maya was HIE HIOLI, which means *"child which arrived from the stars"*. When he saw me the first time in Chichén Itzá in 2008, I was wearing a white dress, but he saw me as an Ancient Maya priest, wearing a very bright outfit! And my outfit on Equinox day 2010 was very bright with amazing colors, like in the Avatar movie. It helped me explain to people that during my dreams, I travel through the universe and colors there are like those on the dress I was wearing – very bright. Yes, the Spirit world is multidimensional, full of amazing colors, lights, dynamic speed, and magic things which do not exist in our world.

I tell people that after death, everyone will live as a Spirit for some time in a Spirit's world between the previous life and the new one which they haven't started yet. And this cycle will be repeated again and again and again. So there is nothing to be afraid of. This is the nature of Spirit developing process.Don Julio told me that I come to people with an important message, and my goal in this life time is to continue passing the message to people all over the world. Yes, people have started calling me *Avatar*since I published my first book.

Maya People had this special connection with nature and Earth.The Priest said in the part you will read soon name PYRAMID:

"We lived in great Harmony with the Energy of our Planet, Space, Sound, Plants, Animals, Rocks and Ocean."

James Cameron's Avatar movie tells about this special precious connection between people and nature..., plants, animals... in Pandora. This connection was lost in our civilization and this is why we have trouble here on our planet.

YES! Finally my dreams came true these days! I talk to the people as an Ancient Maya Priest reincarnated, wearing very bright outfits, tattoos on the face and arms and peacock feathers headset. I again blessed little babies. People came to talk to me and told me that they believed that I am their real Maya Priest reincarnated. It was one of the happiest days of my life!

Photographer: Tim Orden

Ancient Maya Priest of Chichen Itza reincarnated

Photographer: Darlene Laurel SV

11. Predictions about comet

On Equinox day March 2010, around 7.30 p.m., during production of the documentary movie, astonishing things happened: two events from this dream below, which I predicted 18 years ago, came true!

Dream # 14
The grain of divinity, January 4, 1992

We knew the day, the hour and the place, where it would happen. And we were going there. Everything was prepared for this event. We calculated what day it should be. Pyramid... When we came to the place, there were already thousands and thousands of people. We arrived just at the very beginning. But not one of them knew what was going on.

At this moment, something came down from the sky. The Divinity. People were excited, scared of the strangeness of what was going on. The Divinity was somehow coming through the layers (of the atmosphere), became visible, but immediately, it fell apart into numerous pieces. But we knew what to do. We needed just one particle among them all. It was like a grain, like a sprout. The most important thing was in it. I knew, that we should take it and put it inside of what we already had, already prepared. Then our model would be complete and the pyramid would start working, would "wake up".

We were already assigned our responsibilities. First, you did something, and then I did it. I was transforming something into something else, which was becoming light and shining. And I also could name this grain. We knew exactly what to do, and we were doing it at the same time and in the same order as it was done far away in space. The specific outcome was the same. The same action at the same moment – simultaneously – we had to do it here, and them, there.

People around us were panicking; they did not understand what was happening. We were doing everything clearly, with a cold, calculating mind – we took the thing that approached us and did what we had to do. At this hour, this minute, this moment everything would change here, would be transformed. A fresh, new cycle would start. It would be the best possible outcome for all people. Suddenly, a wonderful, beautiful energy erupted in a burst of stars, like a huge energy fountain, came through the whole pyramid and went up to the sky, sending out Holy, glowing rays to all these people... They all saw it.

COMET

It happened few hours after Don Julio conducted his interview for the documentary movie. At twilight, he went to the pyramid and asked Spirits to give us a sign: I*s all what he said to me is correct? Are Spirits around and do they support me with this important mission?*
Instantlyat sunset a twin COMET with 2 tails appeared in the sky!
(See below on YOUTUBE)**Here part from my dream 18 years ago:**
"At this moment, something came down from the sky. The Divinity. People were excited, scared of the strangeness of what was going on."

YES! arrival of the comet supported that my name is right, I arrived from the stars and I am two in one – a human and multidimensional an Ancient Spirit Being,who is located in the eye of the

pyramid of the Sun and moves the stars.
YOUTUBE: AVATAR SVADI 2, KUKULCAN, AVATAR SVADI 3, ANGELS & GIANT

Here photo of my rock from the past from Coba pyramid. During movie production we visit again Coba pyramid with Don Julio. It was Big Celebration time. Spirits of ancient Maya was waiting for us all the way near the road of ancient Coba town. It was hundreds of them, all bending to us and scared to look direct at us, there Highest Priests.

Youtube, Eternal hologram (Eng)

https://www.youtube.com/watch?v=_F97riCL_JM

YOUR ETERNAL HOLOGRAM

*Bas relief from the oldest building at Chichén Itzá, part of the **Nunnery** complex, where Julia lived as a Maya Priest.*

This is why I had this hairstyle with two pony tails on a bas relief, similar to that of a Maya Priest. Ordinary Maya warriors had their hair done with only one pony tail.

Dream # 10. The Great Harmony of Nature: *It was a very strong and very real sensation. And so this* **<u>Sun</u>**, *the main part, saw my life with its own eyes – that is, I saw it with her eyes – that I am returning... There was neither satisfaction, nor anything else from the one, BIG part of me that I was here, only a very clear, cold observation...*
I spent the following night on the top of the pyramid alone. (See details about my adventure below in the PYRAMID section.)
The Ancient Maya purification and activation rituals were performed. I was stunned when the pyramid woke up after a thousand-year-long sleep. It was exactly how I described it in my dream. And both events happened within hours of each other.

"Suddenly, a powerful fountain of energy erupted in a burst of stars and went up to the sky, sending out Holy, glowing rays to all people... The sound was truly amazing!"

By the way my name is Svadi Hatra also connected with **Sun**.
Hatra, City of the **Sun** God, because the holy city, dedicated to the sun god. More at the end of the book.
http://www.expatica.com/nl/whats-on/event/Hatra-City-of-the-Sun-God.html

YOUTUBE:AVATAR SVADI 3, ANGELS & GIANT – See also on YOUTUBE how pyramid breezing P.1/4 (Fotografía) Rayo de luz en pirámide de KUKULKAN - Fernando Correa
VORTEX Energy Part 1 Pyramid Energy and the Earth Grid (22 parts)

About Maya Symbols

Don Julio says about eye on the Sun, which is located in the Sun pyramid.
He received his knowledge and data directly from the Spirit world, from his Angels.
You must also remember that he is Mayan priest and he can be trusted.

However, all the people out of the crowd were very surprised, they witnessed the comet and supported what he said!!

People, who read my book and watched the film, started sending me emails after viewing the information that supports the factabout spiritual pyramid that said Don Julio!

For example surprisingly, in the YOUTUBE was a video:LSC's Concave Earth,Platonic Solid Concave Universe, author think crystal twin pyramid exist! And in one more YOUTUBEvideo showed a real photo of the twin pyramid connected with the Sun!

Did you see in green color **Oktaeder,twin pyramid**from the left?On 10 .00 min of this video:
Eric Briggs akaCatfish interview - Mar 28 WSO UPDATE, Is the Earth Tilting? If so, WHY?

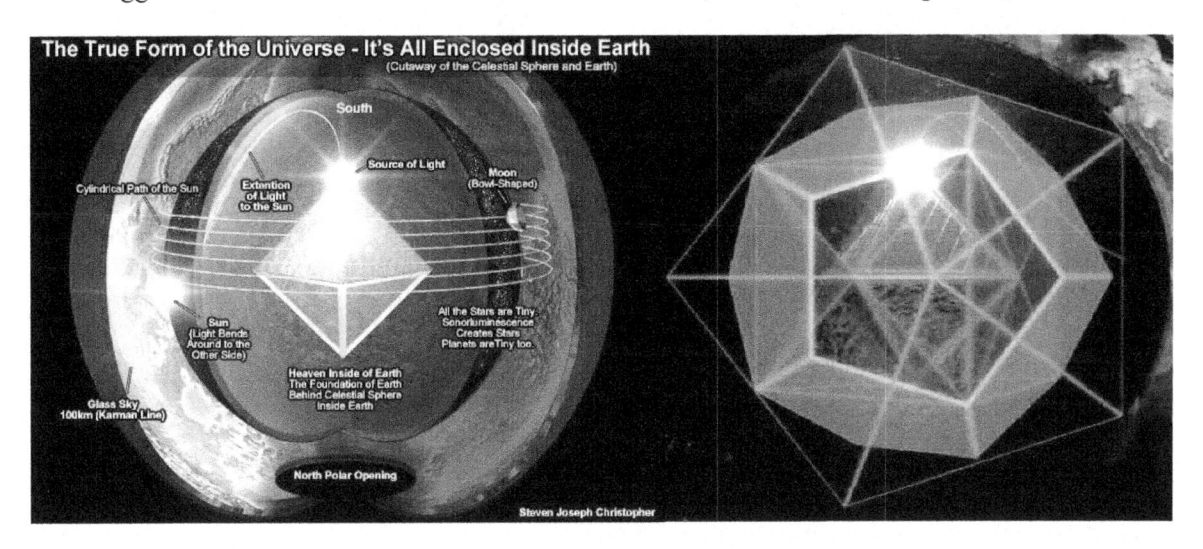

People sent to me even painting where also crystal twin pyramid in the middle of our Universe!

Do you remember crystal kingdom in my **Dream # 6? The Queen of a Crystal Kingdom, December 4, 2007**

Later in this book you will read dream, where many spheres& layers:

Dream # 25, History – Pyramid in A Pyramid (Or Maybe in the Sphere), August 30, 1994

I did described how I travel to this pyramid crossing Milky Way and throw the Black hole! You can read in this two dreams below in Chapter **5, THE VIOLET FIELD**

Dream # 35, Business in the Center of the Galaxy, July 16, 1991

"I had something to do in the center of the Milky Way Galaxy.I recalled being there. I understood that I go there quite often for business. And my goal – even if to speak about saving the whole humanity – would not be enough. Something global and serious..."

Dream # 34 Big Creature of a Holy Religion, October 31, 1993

*"It looks like I used this **Black Hole** for the travels in Space to this pyramid, when I was a Mayan Priest. "*Mayan hieroglyphs describe it as a " Hole in the Sky", cosmic womb, or " black hole" through which there wizard-king entered other dimensions, accessed sacred knowledge, or toured across vast reaches of the cosmos.

The ancient symbol as a TRIANGLE of the Sun can be seen at the entrances of many churches around the world. YOUTUBE:Triangle On The Sun, Mysterious Triangle on Sun Explained!

Eye In The Triangle Symbolism

But in reality this is not a triangle, I am sure this is about Pyramid, twin pyramid.

As well in the Maya culture, artifacts - PYRAMID of the SUN - the symbol is talking about a place of Gods, who visited our planet.

www. magic-vernisage.com, Hoteya   Sumerian God of Sun
Crystal twin pyramid in the middle of our Universe.

Numerous ancient symbols are in use in modern society and religious organizations and sometimes it adds a new opposite meaning. For example Adolf Hitler - the use of the swastika, a symbol that distributed in the temples of Asia since ancient times.

It is interesting that, for example, the number **13** is important in the ancient Mayan culture, very lucky for me, but today in some societies it is believed to be the Devil's number. The same with 2 horns - an ancient symbol of the **Sun-God** in Sumerians.

AndDon Julio says about Consciousness and Sun. **He said** *"Julia normal person, as well as a Goddess, who is multidimensional Being and this second one located on the pyramid of the Sun."*
Surprisingly, this movie on YouTube confirms this:
YOUTUBE: ANCIENT ALIEN MYSTERY OF THE ARCHONS - Invaders from Space HDstarting from 5 min.
Just like germs, animals, people our Sun, the Earth as well are all living beings, they all have a living Consciousness! Even the entire plasma of the Galaxy of the entire Universe contain living **Consciousness** that exists in it. Central Sun of our Galaxy living creature! And this Consciousness extends to the rest of the Galaxy ... it's amazing!
I guess when here said Central Sun means this crystal twin pyramid at the back of the Sun.

PYRAMID

It was a velvet-black night.

During the dream, I felt these waves of pulsating energy, this constant vibration, again and again, and again..., one after the other, until it totally woke me up and started pulling me out of bed.

The Pyramid is calling me... I opened my eyes and I knew instantly that I had to go. It was 1:08 am on the clock; good number, good sign for me.
I know that my action today can bring problems ... there can be huge consequences. Even when we obtained the permission to produce a documentary movie, yesterday afternoon there was quite a bit of trouble on the movie set. We were working on our documentary, when guards arrived. Some of the

crew members saw these guards in uniform and assumed that these were the local police and that they could end up in a Mexico jail. So they ran away to hide.

The problem was that INAH (National Institute of Anthropology and History) didn't want me to talk to the people near my pyramid as a Maya Priest reincarnated! Especially when I was dressed in a beautiful, bright outfit with ancient Maya tattoos and feathers. I told them that I was a Maya Priest from this very same pyramid, which was my home thousands of years ago. I am the one who feels and knows best what to wear for the Equinox – not the INAH workers.
It was really unfair: we had a special permit for the filming and still were not allowed to go to the territory!INAH's representative ran back many times and was forced to talk on the phone with the main office in Mexico City – until they finally agreed. In the end, I had won the long hours of intense fighting!

This was a very important first step towards the enlightenment of the whole planet and towards a change in consciousness. It will help people return to the real essence of the pyramids, perform rituals, prayers, and whatever will become necessary at the time – not just visit the pyramids like a dusty, dead part of the history museum. Yes, we filmed parts of the movie. The movie crew found me incredibly brave. Of course, no doubt the bravery was partly due to the Mayan spirit inside me.
Well, I never feared anything during my life.
I have always obeyed the laws and rules. But what I try to do now is out of line. I have no idea what sort of punishment is awaiting me in this situation! – Sadly I just don't have any other choicein the matter. I ask myself, "Will I regret this for the rest of my life if I didn't persevere and didn't do it now?"

Today, right now the only one and last possibility in this lifetime to reach my sacred goal. Goal which I had during my entire life ever since I could remember myself saying,"I wish..., I need to visit my pyramid, the place where I spend my past life long ago."
During the last two years, I made repeated requests and waited patiently for a permission to do this. And still I did not receive it! Nothing helped: my exceptional case, my books with the whole story, the hypnosis sessions, and all the evidence that have vindicated my case. In fact, I am the only one on this whole planet, who can justly claim to be an ancient Maya Priest of Chichén Itzá reincarnated.

And NO point in the rules exists for the Mexican bureaucracy clerk in INAH that in case if a Maya Priest will be reincarnated, he will be allowed to visit his home. Period.
It is a very sad situation for me, although, it may sound ridiculous to people who are unaware of what I am really doing here. I still count as a tourist! Same as all other tourists, I am not allowed to climb the pyramids because a girl had a terrible accident four years ago, and died. Since then, no one is allowed to visit the ancient pyramids.
Yesterday, during filming near the pyramid, emotions took over and I broke down in tears: "I need, I want to visit my pyramid, I want to touch the pyramid walls!" I know I will never, never forgive myself if I do not try it today.

YES! I will go for this – live or die.

I moved silently through the dark room, packing a flash light, cameras, rocks... The hotel was in deep sleep. I descended the stairs and drown into the dark night. Cold... I was glad to have taken my favorite yellow jacket with me. Fragrance of tropical fruits, flowers and leaves filled the air. I went through the alley between huge palm trees pillars toward the entrance, where the guards' house is located and stopped there, waiting for them to appear. I was hoping to talk with them as one human being to another to explain my situation, in order to receive permission to go in...

YOUR ETERNAL HOLOGRAM

Maybe a miracle will happen?

The same as it happened to Antoine de Saint-Exupery, when soldier saw through Antoine's smile that he was just another human being like he himself was, and instead of shooting him, he let him escape and gave him the opportunity to live on.
I waited, and waited, and waited... Usually a bunch of guards always roam near the gate 24/7!

Instead, someone came directly toward me through the bushes, breaking branches on the way – it was way too loud...Either it was a deer or just another tourist. If it was a deer I could not invite him to join me in my adventure. If it was a tourist, I definitely did not need such a person near me. It could have presented problems when we were walking through the territory.
No! No! No! I cannot jeopardize my life-long goal today.
I decided not to wait anymore. With that decision, I knew the responsibility of my action befell me – and me only. *"Guard dogs could rip me apart in this darkness ... maybe before the guards would arrive to stop them and it would be too late. As long as no dogs are about, I should be okay."*
Wow! What a darkness around me!
I climbed up and across the fence...
I was walking on the small path. This amazing feeling of sudden freedom was astonishing! All barriers, which had been put across me during the last two years here, suddenly vanished. I just walked easily and lightheartedly toward my sacred goal! It was such a pleasure to cross the rope that surrounds the pyramid...

I started remembering how, two years ago, I was so excited trying to take a perfect photo for the book...
> *"It was a shot of the stone snake's face – directly in front of it, but the rope was in my way, so I stepped over the rope... As soon as I did, a guard ran up to me and brought me into the office where I was told that I wouldn't be allowed to visit the ruins for a full day – what a punishment! It would be a devastating feeling for someone who came from across the world and was supposed to stay away for one day. I was lucky that this time I was here for five days."*

Now I just stepped across the rope and started climbing up, one stair after the other... It was an astonishing feeling! I was so, so very happy; this joy took my breath away! I guess my freedom had been given to me by the Maya Spirits! It was so easy to climb my pyramid... Even in full darkness. I almost flew to the top! It felt like the size of the steps was designed for my feet, the staircase made exactly for me... Wow!
I felt that I knew each of these steps! *How could I possibly fall down?*
I am the only one, who climbed this pyramid more than anyone in the world, maybe thousands and thousands of times, daily, during my previous life and, of course, my body remembered it!

Well..., when I reached the last step, I didn't know what to expect next...

I could not use my flash light; the guards below would see me instantly. It was total darkness... I stretched my hands in front of me and touched the stone wall. By touching the wall I started moving one step at a time through the tunnel to my left... Suddenly a bat flew from inside toward me and almost snapped my hair.
Strange vibrations invaded my body when I was climbing close to the top and then continued to pulsate inside me, so I decided to sit down and wait for a moment. I sat and waited for three to five minutes and this sensation dissipated as quickly as it started. The adjustment was done. The pyramid and my Spirit recognized each other. Next, I was overwhelmed by an enormous calm, a feeling of tranquility – I was in pure harmony... **Finally, I am here, I returned to my home.**

Suddenly, I could hear some strange knocking sound coming from my left. Instantly my head was full of questions. Since it was such a dark night and I could not use my flash light, it was impossible to find out who was making the sound. Maybe it was another tourist who climbed on the opposite side? And perhaps he was now sitting somewhere and playing or knocking on something in the dark? The sound continued ... and I just didn't know the source of it!

Who is producing that strange sound?

I was thinking to go and check with my flash light covered by my hands, but, if it was another tourist and I went toward him now, I might scare him to death in this darkness! And if he jumped to the side it would be a deadly move for him. The space on the edge of the pyramid is very narrow ... he would fall down.
Another possibility was that he could push me away, thinking that I was a ghost, and I would end up falling down from my own pyramid! What a shame! Of course, I could have whispered at first, but the echo from this amazing pyramid would have made the sound many times stronger and it would have reached the ground and up to 500 meters around. The guards would have known instantly that I was here.
In fact, it could have been a guard in this darkness, sitting near me and knocking – not a tourist and I could have ended up face to face with my enemy... But it could also have been an ancient Maya ghost, spirit, which was playing during the night!In the brochure for the tourists they mention that this place is full of ghosts and they even have specific names. The brochure advises tourists never to venture in the dark in this territory... I then remembered that yesterday, during the interview for our documentary movie, Don Julio, mentioned that high Maya priests are buried under the pyramid...

Well, as for me, the part about the ghosts did not worry me much. These are dead people spirits; they are my close relatives or colleagues from my past live. They would never harm me. Instead they should recognize and protect me, right?I started concentrating on the sound. The sound went from the inside out. The source of the sound was coming from somewhere deep inside. I began to analyze the sound: yes, it definitely came from deep down, maybe from the small pyramid below, this rhythmic knocking, round, sound...

Maybe it was the heart of the pyramid knocking?All of the sudden, it stopped.

Instead **soft waves of spiral** sound appeared, long and tall, like a fountain from inside the pyramid. There seemed to be some sort of barrier to the sound. Maybe I heard it with my body ... or through my Spirit and not through my ears even. Anyway, I did not feel comfortable to be on this side. I simply didn't know who created this sound and what to expect next. I walked to the right, toward the main entrance side.

I lay down on my back in front of the temple and looked up to the sky. It was black, clear and filled with millions of diamond-stars, it went on forever. The stars were so bright and big! For miles around there was no artificial light, just jungles and old buildings of this ancient Maya city. No wonder the Mayan studied astronomy and astrology.

YES, I returned to my home. I spent many, many years here during my past life. I started touching these ancient walls, so precious to me. Finally, my life-long wish was fulfilled. When I sat or stood close by, shapes and angels on the walls felt unusually comfortable. I stuck like a magnet to them – glued to them. Interesting that no matter how I stood: facing the walls or my back to them, leaning against them, it felt enormously comfortable. Somehow, it reminded me of Japanese cups, which have an imprint for the fingers to create this special comfort. How many nights I spent leaning against these walls as a Priest, during my past life, thinking about my people's needs, and watching the stars?

Once, during the hypnosis sessions, when I was asked to make myself comfortable and to find a place where I could relax, I would find myself instantly right here, in the temple on the top of this pyramid. It was the most perfect place, where I could be totally alone, isolated.
This sacred place always protected me from any visitors back in my past life and it does the same today, in this life. And here I am, now... What a pleasure!
Suddenly, I heard the screams of an exotic peacock from the hotel side and it broke the silence. Next, the rooster pronounced his independence. In total silence, a perfect echo reflected from the Ball Court site. Sky and stars began to be lighter. Forever, to the horizons, were jungles. In this early morning twilight, the Caracol observatory stood out and I began to see the contours of the Ball Court.

I checked the pyramid: I was alone, no one on the opposite side.
Time to start! Too much to do. So many thoughts and so many amazing things happened during those nights there...
I started cleaning my dear home, my magnificent pyramid – for the first time in the last few thousand years. It was very sad to see that in the most sacred temple in Mexico, this little room, closed with wooden planks was so dirty and dusty inside. I lit up some sage and walked inside, around and into the temple. My body knew what to do automatically. I only followed and observed the movements that were so much part of me. I smelled the fragrance from this sacred grass.
The Ancient Maya *purification* and *activation* rituals were performed here.
I was stunned when the pyramid woke up after thousands of years of lethargic sleep. Spiral of smoke went up. Little clouds of smoke created very unusual shapes; they followed the energy flow coming from the pyramid and then went straight up, **like a million of white glowing thinnest lines. Amazing!**

It was exactly how I saw it in my dream 18 years ago!
*"**Suddenly, a powerful fountain of energy erupted in a burst of stars and went up to the sky, sending out Holy, glowing rays to all people...**"*The sound was truly amazing!

I was very busy. We did lots during those nights ... me and the Priest. Some secret rituals must be done in some special way. There were rituals related to the pyramid re-connecting with the universe, or being grounded to the Spirit of people. I followed the lessons, which I received in my dreams as a Priest during weeks after the hypnosis sessions.

I opened my "black diamond" backpack and took out a gift for the Chichén Itzá pyramid from its sister, the Heops pyramid. It was a crystal rock from inside the tomb which was waiting this special moment, this reunion in this sacred place for thousands of years.
I heard the peacock rooster again – he was claiming his territory then. He received a number of replies from another rooster on the opposite side. The sound was amazing! The sound came from far away, strongly enhanced by the pyramid. I was proud about my pyramid! One side of the sky from the temple of Warriors started to warm up and colored the rocks of pink...

I opened the video camera and started talking. "So, here I am, on the top of the pyramid, I returned to my home. I am an Ancient Maya priest of Chichén Itzá reincarnated..." Suddenly the camera shut down... I tried again, the video camera was dead! Maybe the batteries were dead? I looked around and regretted that I could not make a video of this heavenly, beautiful view; the whole of Chichén Itzá was now draped of pink from the sun rising above the horizon.

All of a sudden, I found that I am not alone! Maybe my rituals had attracted these strange witnesses? I had been too busy with cleaning my pyramid to look around during the last few hours. From the water well, Senote side, floating in the sky, there was a huge, silver, and shiny "flying snake"! In less than a minute, the "silver snake" took off with incredible speed.

A silver-white glowing ball appeared from nowhere around the same place and almost instantly flew across the sky toward Merida. Then, I saw a second ball hanging on top of the Temple of Warriors, which continued to observe me... I wanted to start taking photos but I blacked out.

****

When I woke up, I start remember my dream...

I continued talking in some ancient language, repeating some words over and over again. A Deep Global voice was talking into my ears. My temperature rose and this was a sign of importance. My body was covered with goose bumps... I started to remember my dream...

Dream # 15
A message from the Magnificent Maya people.

I was up in the temple, standing near the entrance, and looked down. Everything was under the golden sunset light. I see the Temple of Warriors. Hundreds of warriors were standing on the bright red stairs. One by one, in total silence, all of them looking at me up here. Short skirts, belts, necklaces and spears reflected the sunset light... I saw the sunlight going through their eyes. I saw their shiny black hair, toned legs and arms' muscles... Columns made a long shadow...

I felt that my astrologers in the Caracol were also frozen in time... I saw Maya people sitting on the ground around the pyramid with their children, wives and old parents... These are all my people... I know each and every one of them. I blessed them when they were born and when they were married. Many came to me for help when they were sick, or for support and advice. This is my Big Family.

I turned back and looked inside the temple. My old teacher, the Priest, is sitting with his tortoise in his hands. All my people were around me dressed in beautiful, colorful outfits with feathers, masks and shiny, luxurious jewelry.

The Snake, the Eagle and Anubis were nearby as usual. They all looked at me very seriously – they were waiting in total silence. From the corner of my eye, **I saw long, tall figures,** watching all of us in the distance.

It felt as if TIME had stopped and they were all frozen in that moment... All these people were cut and separated from us and our time...

Something in between ... in between times ... and it was burning. I saw a big fire. I looked closely. It was literally mountains of ancient books and manuscripts burning in this fire! I saw some manuscripts that were very deep at the bottom of the dark ocean, that were covered with sand, near parts of a wooden *baroque*-styled ship.

Then I receive the message...

Now I will try to tell the message. I am not sure that people will be able to understand what this message means, especially since it was given to me in ancient Maya. I will try some simple modern way and in English – although English is not my native language...

As a High Priest of Chichén Itzá from ancient Mayan people to each human been living on Earth:

I am a re-incarnated after thousands of years to give you a message in the special time of the ending of the 13-baktun cycle.

Chichén Itzá is not just another tourist attraction. This city is where my people, my family, my friends lived beautiful, bright, happy lives. People were creative and deeply spiritual. The ancient Mayan people who built Chichén Itzá had highly developed culture, science, architecture, astronomy, most advanced astrology and were in constant connection with God and with the parallel world in space.

We lived in great Harmony with the Energy of our Planet, Space, Sound, Plants, Animals, Rocks and Ocean. Some of us had the ability to travel in time and we accumulated the most valuable information as a precious gift to the human race. What people know now about ancient Maya Wisdom and Knowledge is just the tip of the iceberg.

Curse forever those Spanish conquistadors who tried to destroy all of our books and history which belonged to the next world's generations. This information, this KNOWLEDGE exists and is available always to those who are really willing to study it.

Our life is not what you saw in the movie Apocalypse! It never had happened this way in Chichén Itzá in my lifetime. It is wrong how they portrayed us; we are noble, beautiful, kind-hearted people.

Sacrifices were very rare and in most difficult exceptional situations as a draught or epidemics. It was the way of sending our best people as a messenger to the God for help.

Jesus was brutally crucified without any special drugs and thus causing his unbearable physical suffering. Mayan people were surprised by those who did this.

Misunderstanding or lack of knowledge about our culture and history is not the way to create something from your own mind, and turn it into public display trying to make money on the energy emanating from fear, blood and suffering.

AVATAR SVADI HATRA

From My Space, Saturn Lady, artist unknown

Fears was introduced to society artificially as an instrument for the manipulations and it prevent from development of new consciousness and enlightenment. Shame on those who used our Holy pyramid for this purposes and tried to cast a shadow on my pure temple in return. They should fix this mistake to avoid karma punishment.

The Pyramid was always a very special place for the meetings with God and Spirits. It was a House of Souls. It was our Big, Perfect Crystal. It was my home and my place of work. This Pyramid is an important part of our Galactic structure as an energy and information exchange between the Earth and the Cosmos.

Creativity is the only one important product on Earth and the reason for people to be here. Those talented producer who will create a great movie about us will receive our special blessing.

Soon will be the beginning of a new Katun and Baktun time cycles.

Difficult times of changes are starting now.

YOUR ETERNAL HOLOGRAM

The planet and the world around us are overwhelmed by the side effect of huge population and in need of rest.
Please stop expanding your family by bringing new spirits to the Earth for the next seven years.
You will learn that it will help your family and you personally dramatically.
Don't let outside fear take control over your inner voice and your own spirit. Stay in Harmony. We have many lives.

The Spirit of the people is ETERNAL.

Remember that spiritual assistance is always near to support you. Creativity, Love and understanding of the Universal Principles will help your Spirit be strong and survive the Time of Big Changes and proceed to the higher stage of evolution.

PRIEST JAGUAR, MAGICIAN, HEI HIOLE
(child, which arrived from the stars)

I looked around. The sky was already bright pink. I started walking around the pyramid and took photos.From the corner of my eye, I saw a guard's car arriving and stopping in front of the steps below… Next, there was the sound of footsteps on the stairs.
I was sitting in front of the entrance of the temple, when I saw the top of his head first and then his whole body. He was a small Maya man. He smiled! (Maybe it is in the rules not to scare anyone on top of the pyramid, because tourists might run and fall to their death.) No place to run actually.
I lifted my book; "Ancient Maya Priest of Chichén Itzá reincarnated" and showed to him the back cover where there is an image of the pyramid. I told him, "I was living here a long time ago, it was my home and my office, and I am visiting today."
He looked at me and said in pure English: "Welcome home! We all know already.All local people here believe that you are our Maya Priest. You are not just another tourist. Last night we decided to watch you to make sure that you would return to the hotel – maybe you were afraid to go to Chichén Itzá at night alone. But you even went up to the pyramid and spent the whole night here!" Then he added, "Yes, you are very brave! You have a real Maya Spirit inside you."
I turned away, trying to hide my tears from him.
This was surely the best comment he could make to me. It was the most precious moment of my life! Especially coming from a guard – it meant that they accepted me, recognized me… These are my people and I am their priest. The ice was broken…
I asked him, "Can you take one photo for me?"
"Okay…," he replied, smiling. He pressed the button and we hugged each other.
I enjoyed running down to the bottom of the pyramid as fast as I could, like I never did before! Yes, literally, it never happened before in this life time – to go up and now down the pyramid was extraordinary. The second guard below was amazed. He watched me coming down and told me that he had never seen anyone running down the steps as fast as I did in all the years he had been a guard of the pyramid.
I told him, "Since I can run up and down this pyramid's steps so fast, it would be the best place to play "tag" with me, right?" We smiled.

YOUTUBE:2012 Maya Priest
Videos for Part 1 - Parallel Universes - BBC Horizon →*Matter emanating from particle strings like a million of white glowing thinnest lines.*

Julia on top of her pyramid

12. Spirit Support, Unexplained mystery

During this entire year when I worked on the book, with my editor, Roxane, my neighbors, and my friends and I felt some Spirit support, a very unusual power involvement, somebody invisible, who was watching me, guiding me, navigating and caring about the whole process with the book. Suddenly, out of nowhere, I started receiving help with information, which arrived in the strangest form, from some of the most respectable sources. People around me began to be extremely cooperative and supportive.

Who was this Spirit who wanted this book to be completed as soon as possible? Was it The Ancient Maya Spirits from Chichén Itzá? Or maybe someone from Egypt? We don't know..., but as for me I think it must have been someone from Mexico, because I have an enormous responsibility to tell the world who the Ancient Maya people really were.

Also because I really have strongest connection with them and sometimes it turns funny or even scares people! Sometimes it was hilarious!

You will find more in "**Unexplained Mysteries**" on my website www. ameliareborn.com

Two days ago, I opened my entrance door at 6:30 p.m. and found, near the door, a DELL laptop! *Someone forgot a laptop near my door! Very strange!* I put a note to the person who forgot it there: "Why is your laptop here? Call me at this phone number. Please, come and take it back."

The next day my computer crashed, the hard drive was burned. I ran and bought a new laptop, but the technician told me that he needed a few days to transfer everything onto the new computer! This happened at the same time when my daughter was finishing school – **we needed to fly to Europesoon, this book was almost done but I needed to work on it and complete it to give my editor, Roxane, for her to edit it, during the summer!**

I got a call from the next door neighbor, Tracy; he was the one who dropped the computer near the door! I asked him why? We don't know each other well enough, we only say, "Hi and Bye."

Photographer: Darlene Laurel SV

He replied, "I don't know. Something in my mind pushed me to go to my locker room, find this computer and bring it to your door. I thought that since I stopped using it, maybe someone like your daughter would like to use it!" (Well, my daughter has a good computer.)

Yet, since I just experienced unexpected delays, I guess I could use it for a few days to complete the book! Thank you Tracy!

As for me, I am thinking about this Spirit, who is really watching me and is trying to help even in situations like these. Spirits know ahead of time what will happen and they support us as much as possible. My Spirit helped me in such a way that I could complete this book as soon as possible so to make it available to people!

Here is Tracy's version of the "Laptop Mystery":

"About a week ago I decided to go to my locker room for no special reason. There, I saw my laptop and decided to give it to my neighbor's little girl. I felt that she might want it – or need it. So I dropped the laptop near the door of my neighbors, Julia and her daughter. Julia found the laptop a few hours later. However, the next morning Julia's own computer suddenly crashed! She ran to buy a new laptop, but the technician wanted to take a few days to put all the data from the old computer onto the new one and took both computers away from her.

Well, suddenly my laptop became the most important item for Julia, because she needed to finish this book before flying to Europe with her daughter for the summer! I am still not sure why I went to the locker room that day – there was no reason for me to do so.

I was watching TV after work and I just stood up, went to the storage room, took out the laptop and brought it in front of Julia's door. I acted like a robot or zombie.... It may sound funny, but this is exactly how it happened. I thought about this strange situation for a while – I guess Julia has a guardian angel which takes good care of her, helping her.

By the way, around a month ago, on our floor, there was an odd fire alarm in the hallway and it would not stop. I ran to the manager. We were ready to call for the fire truck after we checked everything and did not find any reason for the insistent ringing. Julia also went outside with her daughter and their little ferret. When I told her that we could not find any reason for the alarm, she told me that she was writing a chapter in her book right then, which was dealing with a ghost girl! She thought the ghost might have activated the alarm, trying to make her presence felt.... It sounds really weird, but after my unexplainable trip to the locker room, I started to think that everything is possible when it comes to Julia. Something special, magic exists around her. Each time I see them, my good mood returns, even when I come home and I am very tired after a long day's work.
Tracy Craig, Vancouver, Canada

****

"I didn't know Julia before I started editing her manuscript. For some reason, she insisted that I edit her book. I was swamped – I had work coming out of my ears (as the saying goes) and I had no intention to take on another project. And then it began – my other work, either fell by the wayside or no other clients came knocking. I found myself working exclusively for Julia! To date, I have only one book on the table – hers. That came as a shock – I can't survive on only one client – even one of Julia's caliber. When I told Julia about this, she said, "Don't worry, we will be soon in Mercury Retrograde, which is a great time for finishing big projects and not starting new ones – but previous clients will show up!" And yes, it happened exactly as Julia had predicted it. I got two people wanting my help with some editing as soon as I closed her book. On top of this, while we were talking about future publishing plans a car with her lucky number **085** crossed the intersection in front of us.

For all of you who read this book, let me tell you something; Julia is a true to life visionary and a superb scientist to boot. Everyone is "one of a kind" as she says, but she is the "real" thing!"
Roxane Christ, Vancouver

****

Spirits gave me a lesson...

I should mention here that I had previous experiences with Spirit support in my life. Once I bought a manuscript from China about the ancient Chi Gong form of exercises. In that book I found some "well-guarded" secrets, giving the reader guidance in order to put you into a trance so that your body would start moving by itself, which, in turn, could also produce some powerful healing. It is all about how the body wishes to move, and not how our brain decides to move our body. I was planning to publish this book and decided to try the exercises myself first. It did not go the way it should have done – my body movements were still guided by my will, I just couldn't grasp the process. Later, visited my business partner, C.P., in San Diego. He has a beautiful private Buddhist temple with a golden Buddha and ancient statues on his property. It was a rare opportunity for me to meditate in the temple alone. I asked him if I could spend the night there. He told me that there were some spirits who lived in the temple and that no one had expressed the wish to be there alone before that day – people were generally afraid, he said. I asked, "What kind of Spirit?"

C.P. told me that monks had meditated all their lives in the temple and their brain created a strong electromagnetic energy flow within it. It had built-up over the years in the "salige" (another name *"pearl relict")*– little white bones in their brain, which normal, ordinary people never have! The monks collect the "salige" after the cremation.In the Buddhist temples, it is a tradition to put the saliges of the deceased monks in a special type of containers. When many monks prayed near the little waterfall in one of the temples, C.P. saw a special, white sand, some kind of substance on the rocks around this waterfall. They explained to him that it was because of the constant meditations performed by the monks in that place over the years.

So, in his private temple, C.P. had the "salige" from a high ranking monk who lived a very long life – as I remember, around 123 years. Apparently, this Spirit came from time to time for a visit, because his "salige" was located in that private temple. He showed it to me, in a little silver container. The shape of the container was very familiar to me. I had seen the same in Tibet in my childhood. While C.P. was talking to me, suddenly his eyes began to focus on something in front of him, his head started to move very fast, and I saw something really strange and unusual in the air between us. It looked like a cloud of bees or black dots, of about a meter in length. This cloud was moving back and forth at great speed for some time, and suddenly it disappeared. He told me that the monk's Spirit had been near us.

I woke up in the early morning hours before sunrise in that temple – no one had bothered me during the night – and I started meditating. After my meditation, I remembered the Chi Gong exercises and decided to try it this time. Nothing good came from this idea again, and I almost gave up. Then, I decided to call on someone "in the know" – I called on the Spirit of the monk and asked him to help. Since this ancient exercise was originally from Tibet, I figured that he would have known how to perform these exercises during his lifetime. Suddenly, a voice came to my mind: "Hold on. Let's try it again," he said. It was an astonishing experience! I returned to reality maybe 40 minutes later. During this time I only felt that my spine turned into a powerful energy flow, like a thick glowing rope, which was going through me and I felt the dynamic, electric movement of it. What I felt was incredible – both during and after the exercise. Since then, from time to time, I call on this Spirit, when I need him. Every time, I can feel his presence strongly, no matter in which part of the world I happen to be.

Spirit safe my live, when I was the object of a sacrifice.

On that particular evening, I was walking through a district amid crowds of people. I felt happy and wonderful about myself. The spring had made its appearance and it was the first warm days. I was wearing a new outfit: white, and quite in fashion at the time. I was a very naive young girl, who was just beginning to make her entrance in the world of adults. Suddenly, out of nowhere, a man appeared near me and he began following me. I tried everything possible and impossible, but I just couldn't get rid of him. At one point, he stopped right in front of me, and I didn't have any way to escape. Then, I saw a woman near her car on the side of the road, waving to me. I don't remember exactly what she screamed to me, but it was something like, "Step here, on the other side and you will be rid of him; he will go on his way."

I took a few steps towards her and that car... and as soon as I was near, a hand from inside the car pulled me with powerful force into it! The door was slammed and the car left at great speed. I felt a knife touching my ribs and then one of these two men put some cuffs on my ankles. Meanwhile, the car kept going and I could see that we were going out of town. At one point, the car stopped and the man who had put the cuffs on my ankles got out and went into another car and left. I was left alone with the driver. I asked him, "Where are we going?" – It was dark outside and I could only see the forest... He did not answer. He continued driving silently.

Finally we arrived. We had been driving along a highway – not much traffic. He pulled into a small crossroad and drove perhaps 50 meters onto that road. We stopped and waited. Suddenly, he started talking. He told me that today was a very special day for him, because he was part of what I call now an "association". (I don't want to say where it happened, what country and what year, because this story is too terrible to tell.) Once a year there was a big celebration with a sacrifice! For this sacrifice it was necessary to have a young, beautiful woman... And I was the one who had been chosen for the sacrifice on that day!

It was a special day for him personally, because by participating in my kidnapping, he would be lifted to the next rung on the step ladder in that "association". He told me that I should not be scared; instead I should be very proud to be part of it! Because I was to see elite people from high society, and some I would recognize: politicians, business people, celebrities and even top level religious figures from two different organizations ... and that my body was to be used for such an important ritual...

Can you believe it? At first, I was sure that he was a schizophrenic or a paranoiac..., because he was obviously under stress and I saw that his hands were shaking... But after he started showing me a huge size white candle, I knew he was serious. He repeated again that today he would be "endorsed" and would attain a new status in that "association" and this day was very important for him.

Well, it sounded as if his job also consisted in preparing the victim emotionally. I asked him if they use something to sedate their victim to keep it calm and cooperative. He was amazed that I, instead of screaming and crying, was talking to him about the details of this procedure. He asked me why I was like this.

As for me, I thought it was better to spend time before my death thinking about my life, the results I had achieved, and maybe say goodbye to my relatives than losing my mind and screaming. People who scream in such stressful situations always create chaos and the situation can get easily out of control. These people can be killed first and fast, simply in order to shut them up.

I continued talking to him. I asked him if he had any family. He told me that he had only a three-year-old daughter – no mother. He then told me how much he loved her and showed me her photo. I smiled at that point, which had a strange effect on him – his facial expression changed and he went out of the car to smoke a cigarette. He went and opened the trunk of the car looking for something. I was sitting in the car alone. When I saw him opening the trunk, and before he closed it, I threw the big candle out of the window as far as I could into the brush nearby. **To date I have no explanation as to why I did this. It was like someone took my hand and moved it, as if I was a puppet. Very mechanical move...**

He returned inside and checked his watch. He told me that soon a car will arrive to pick me up for the preparation – "it will be time for us to go," he said. At that point, he started looking for the candle and of course he couldn't find it! He looked everywhere – he turned the whole car upside down... Nothing...

He then turn to me and said, "Why youdid not ask me about my wife, my daughter's mother?

"My wife was killed one year ago by the car on the road exactly at the same street where we caught you today, around the same place! And when you started smiling while I was talking about my daughter I saw that you have exactly the same smile as my wife had! And now the candle disappeared... this is a really bad sign..." "Emotionally I tried to be prepared for my participation in the sacrifices for a long time. I was told that I just need to go through it... But after all that happened tonight and no candle... I am not sure that I am doing the right thing!"

He was under so much stress that his hands were shaking and he even started smoking again inside the car...Suddenly he pointed to the road ahead. I saw a long, black limo coming on the main road towards us. He had already shut down all the lights in and outside our car before then, and now he whispered, "I will not give you up to them to be killed. I made my decision. They should not see us."

The limo waited for about 20 or 30 minutes and then left. When we were sure that the limo was totally out of sight, he asked me, "Where do you live?" I didn't want to tell him, instead I asked him to drop me off downtown.

I never saw him again. But **I know that that strange, unexpected movement of my hand, which threw the candle into the darkness, saved my life. Who was it?** My guardian angel? Or maybe the Priest in me knew exactly what to do and that this candle was the key to my freedom? I still don't know. This Spirit saved my life. By the way, when I told this story in detail to my cousin, the next day, a stripe of white hair appeared on this boy's head by the end of my account. I have never seen such a thing in my life – someone's body reacted so strongly and visibly to shock!

****

I am a professional journalist and writer in the genre of science fiction. I have known Julia for many years. As our relationship formed and grew, Julia confided in me and she began to tell me her own dreams. I listened to these dreams and was very puzzled by them. They were always very detailed, and it was impossible to imagine them coming from events of a regular, normal life. These dreams were always new and unusual, and there was the impression that they have a deep reason, with a certain inexhaustible source of information.

As a journalist, I use the technique of quick record, with elements of shorthand. I had a professional interest, as I thought that I would be able to use this in my future books. This was of great interest to me and I thought my readers would find them to be very interesting as well. The intensive handwriting, about an hour a day, was a rather grueling procedure. Her dreams were vast and full of details. It didn't take long for me to realize the difficulty of this process as it went from day to day, (every morning, soon after she woke up, and also sometimes after her usual middle-day nap) into months and over many years. As a result I presently have several handwritten folios filled with notes and drawings. In these dreams there were a lot of repeated events. They included such things as pyramids, crystals, unusually large people, and ceremonies with large crowds of people participating, strange energy rituals, stairways, person with unusual tattoos, hands with mandala-like tattoos, snow-white beaches, turquoise water, beautiful palaces with spherical roofs, and even strange energy essences. The general intonation of these dreams, and the events described in them, brought me to believe that all this is about cultures of ancient Greece, ancient Egypt or something even much more ancient like Atlantis or Sumerian.
Julia sometimes when awake, she repeated words in strange languages.*No one knows the meanings or has any idea as to the kind of language it is. The word "equinox" is often repeated after her dreams. There was the sense that some parts of her lives were in another, as if in a parallel life. These images were so bright, alive and realistic.*

Recently she has visited Mexico. At the architectural complex in Chichén Itzá, Julia suddenly began to recognize the surrounding structures. They all seemed very familiar to her-pyramids, stairways, details and the general atmosphere of this place. On her return to Canada, Julia went to a specialist on regressive hypnosis. It was here that all the pieces fell into place, like small parts of a puzzle.
Today, speculating recorded dreams, information received during hypnosis, as well as the events of her present life, I understand that they are all interconnected. Many belongings of the past life are unconsciously repeated in her present. In her dress, in appearance she unconsciously had the habits to past life: being High Priest, she carried the long cape from the skin and mask of the jaguar. Presently she loves color and patterns, drawing of the skin of the jaguar, she adores masks, as well as embellishment "accustomed" on past life: jewelry from sinks, big stones, chosen bone, seeds, feathers, heavy bracelets on her hands and legs, heavy rings on her fingers, etc. As if she is in the costume of the previous life.
In her past life, as a High Priest and Astrologer, she was also in charge of agricultural science. In her present life she became a biologist, specializing in agricultural science.

*She is also presently very interested in astrology, which has become more than a hobby. In the former Soviet Union, during "Perestroika" she put a lot of her efforts and energy into the legalization of astrology, which was previously forbidden in USSR. One of the first astrology books in USSR was released with her help. Interestingly, in the list of authors, Julia's name is not used, but instead, as we now know, the name used was that of the High Maya Priest, Magician. At the time she did not have any idea what **Magician** meant, from where this word came from, she just created this word because she said she felt harmony with it. 20 years later she found that Pyramid of Magician exist in Mexico!*

Mayan people were a great mathematicians and astrologers, they extensively used calculations. In Julia's present life, numbers play an enormous and mystical role for her, just as if they "talk" to her in some way. There are certain numerals, some of which serve as warning signs about problems lying ahead, or provide negative answers to given questions. The other numerals correspond to the favorable answers or indicate successful outcomes. These numerals can be anywhere, commencing from license plates of passing vehicles, commercial banners, phone numbers or addresses. ***The most amazing part is that when questioned, numbers suddenly show up not just one or two, but repeatedly in much larger amounts than in normal, possible situations. For example, it can be 5 or up to 10 cars with the same number around at the same time.***

YOUTUBE: AVATAR SVADI 6, Treasure from Ancient civilizations
PS: When I heard her repeating the words, when she woke up, I tried to type them, but they were incomprehensible to both of us.[15]

Tim, writer
*****

I sent letter to leaders of the Mayan Council Elder, Don Alejandro Cirilo Perez Oxlaj about the following subject

YOUTUBE: The Maya of Eternal Time – Drunvalo Melchizedek – 2009 – 1 to 14

When I saw this video I felt that I found my family and I was now returning to my roots.
It was interesting that everything I mentioned in my first books, two years ago, was also mentioned in this video:

1. **Fibonacci numbers (it was even encoded in my birthday, in the ISBN of my book Maya Priest).**
2. When I was in Egypt in 2008, I had an amazing dream, ancient and modern world met each other and I got four lessons (please see the Egypt chapter).

---

[15] You will find scientific Interpretation about this at the end of the book.

3. There was also mention made about fears, which prevented the development of new consciousness and enlightenment. (YOUTUBE – 2012 Maya Priest.)

4. **"Who am I?"** I asked in the book.

As I said, everything referred to in the video can be read in my books. Everything I have written came from my conscious knowledge of the universe and is now supported by this priceless collection of facts from the many Maya tribes. Maybe Don Alejandro and other Maya chiefs will be surprised that I know all of this from myself. But this is just further proof that I am part of them, that I am a real Ancient Maya Priest, reincarnated at this important time. I am a Messenger from the Invisible Spirit world. A Higher Power sent me to help people.

Don Alejandro and other Maya chiefs are planning to receive answers through the ancient Maya crystals scalps. 11 of them exist. I found the 12th one during the summer of 2010. This information is also locked in my inner knowledge. Because I amAncient Maya Priest reborn. YES, I am "Skull number 13" and it will complete the set.Soon atthe end of the '13th Baktun cycle. (Everything coded around me with #13. See #13 in the Unexplained Mystery on my website, www. ameliareborn.com)

Photographer: Darlene Laurel SV

Julia and the Crystal Skull – a reading.

It would be good to put me through some hypnosis sessions again or induce me into a trance and ask me what information I possess or what message I need to impart.

I am rare, because I have this ancient Spirit inside of me and Mayan chiefs could make this Spirit talk and understand if I will start talk in ancient Maya Instead of trying to receive information from the Crystal skulls – on an emotional level – and translate it into modern words.

So I wish to participate in this ceremony and help people with the knowledge that resides in me.
BUT I really mean it.

YOUTUBE:
AVATAR SVADI, part 8, Maya crystal skull # 12 found! part 9, I am #13, part 10
Remember my dream?Dream # 11 – Luminous Bodies of Plants, January 8, 1992

"In this book, the knowledge comes to the surface, which was unknown to people until now. This book was a revelation. People did not even suspect it – it opened up, revealing itself like an old secret, a treasure, as if someone dug it out of the earth. A very rare animal, a diamond animal was buried there thousands and thousands of years ago."

I am sure if the Maya Chiefs and the Maya elders and any other people or scientists, who are interested to talk with a REAL Ancient Maya Priest, a Magician from Chichén Itzá, would make a list of questions that I would answer them all. I only cannot tell if I would talk in Maya or in English for example...

I am real **"time bullet"** and will also remember this present life and will tell people in far future about our civilization.

WHO AM I?

I asked myself "WHO AM I?" a few months ago. You just finished reading who emerged from this question during the hypnosis sessions. First the Priest came out, and now see who else will come in the next chapters.... I am planning to check some more dreams with Di Cherry's help and see who else I was in my past lives.

I guess I could be a good Buddhist if I continued to follow this road of self-development properly. Buddha always asked to look at yourself and to study yourself first. Also the Buddhists say that those who achieve enlightenment can choose their new life.

According only to the numbers when I was born, the Priest, for sure, achieved enlightenment in his life time.

I just returned from the beautiful Stanley Park, everything is blooming there! And again I was talking to the animals today. I caught myself talking to a raccoon – after I heard my voice: "So how are you today? What do you do? What do you eat?" It just came automatically – this contact, this instant connection – as soon as I saw the raccoon, I talked to him.

"Oh, hi, Doc, what a cute baby you have! And you are such a gorgeous swan! I love those shiny diamond drops of water on your back!" Suddenly, a huge carp jumped out of the water, so high that I could see its full size with its yellow tummy and belly. "Bravo! Bravo! Bravo carp!" I clapped my hands. *Am I crazy?*

These animals saw me from far away and started running toward me – all of them – and they followed me; the squirrel and geese, the swan, the raccoon. I was running then, down one of my favorite trails in the park. This time I had my camera with me. When we stopped, I told the squirrel: "Just stay this way; I will do your profile. You will be a movie star!" She sat, didn't move and I took her photo. Then I came closer and closer, and she still sat and didn't move – she stayed in the same position for a long while – "Good squirrel!" I said. But something was wrong! After a few minutes she was still sitting in the same position... She was literally frozen. I ended up touching her with the camera lens, but she just continued to sit! What a strange squirrel!

By this time I was near the lake, named The Lost Lagoon, and I saw him – my cute raccoon, walking softly near the water. I continued playing the same game. I told him, "Now your turn. You stay in profile and I will take your portrait." The raccoon stopped, turned his profile towards me... "And don't move... Very nice!" I got many photos with my camera... This camera is not a fast kind of camera; by the way, it's just a normal Canon camera – after each shot you need to wait a little bit...

But the raccoon still didn't move! He stayed in the same position!
All of a sudden, I heard a man's voice behind me, saying, "Look, the raccoon is posing for this girl, can you believe it?" "Look! He is frozen!" he added.
Yes. He was frozen! Like the squirrel before him, and I just didn't know what was going on. Almost five minutes had passed since I took his photo – according to the camera time – and he stayed like this... Well..., this is kind of strange, very strange. "Bye, raccoon! See you next time," I said, walking away.

After that I called the swan – same story!!! I returned home and started taking pictures of my neighbor's cat, exactly the same thing occurred ... AGAIN!
All of these animals were frozen on the spot after I took their pictures. All of these animals understood what I told them to do and just did it!

When I started showing the photos to an old professional photographer, who always hung out around this lake, he just could not believe his own eyes! He told me that these are wild animals, "this is impossible ... no one could train them to do this." We both didn't know what to think of it. I guess the Priest knew what this was all about. He had a close connection with nature, animals, plants, birds; he was part of all this!

****

"I was jogging in the forest when I saw on the trail ahead of me a large coyote. I stopped and waited for him to clear the way. Another man approached and also waited. Just last week, that coyote attacked a woman with a baby and killed some raccoons in this area. As soon as the coyote walked away from the trail we tried to go through as fast as possible. When I turned back I saw a girl behind me – she was going directly to the coyote and even called him! The coyote started walking toward her and they stood close, almost touching each other! After that she started walking in our direction... When I asked her if she was totally out of her mind, she smiled and told us that she found the coyote very beautiful, especially his eyes.... I was surprised how confident and calm she was. I was shivering. She told me that she had a good connection with animals because her great-grandfather was a Maya Priest. She said that I could send her a note about this incident for her book. Well... she has long blond hair and obviously, she is European... But anyway, here is my report about this odd case...

Henry M."

Squirrel posing *Raccoon posing*

This wild cat only approached Julia and touched her hand.

YOUR ETERNAL HOLOGRAM

Natalia Nazarova http://500px.com/NataNaz/photos, http://nanaz555.ya.ru/e-mail:nanaz@mail.ru

The wild animals: cheetah and Siberian cat talking to Julia…

Since I connected with the Priest, I feel that his qualities add to those I had already or mostly likeactivation take place of the qualities of my Spirit during last 2 thousands years.

It feels like somebody inside me turns on a computer and I know instantly what to do, where to go and what I can expect there. I am doing things now before thinking about them. And I don't make any mistakes – Not One.

It reminds me very much of those robot with sharp ears from the "Terminator" movie. My thoughts and movements of the body are honed to a fine point, they are clear and focused. My ability to make a fast, instant and correct decision amazes normal people. I am starting to have much stronger intuition. My survival instinct is extremely high. I am very well organized and I have a cool mind in stressful or dangerous situations.

I know the source of it all now. I had the opportunity to exercise all of this in my past lives. Now and after establishing a connection with my past, all these extra skills and abilities are activated, start working inside me. It's like I have three brains in one now: mine, the Priest's and the one from the Atlantean woman. It's good that I started controlling my mind since I was very young to keep a clear head and away from the society stereotypes while saving space to add another two brains.

All of the people around me noticed these changes. But they don't know what it is.

In Mexico I saw a blanket with a picture of my pyramid and Tzolkin, Maya calendar in the middle. I ran into the shop and bought it – without thinking. An hour later I decided to move to another hotel on the Rivera Maya, located on the white beach near Tulum – a beautiful place! BUT the wind picked up and I needed my new blanket more than anything in the world that night. Since I sleep in Canada covered with huge Maya Calendar and often in tee shirt with the Chichén Itzá pyramid and all kind of Maya symbols on it.

The artist just called me while I was typing about the cover for this book. I picked up the phone and told him his name – even before he said "Hello". I just knew it was him on the line. He was surprised – me too – this was our first talk, at least in this lifetime.

Yesterday evening, I was walking down the street when suddenly, out of nowhere, two teenagers jumped in front of me and started screaming, trying to impress a bunch of teenage girls nearby. I felt this movement before it happened. I lifted my hand to stop them and to show them that I was aware of their intention. I told them, smiling, "No way! You can't scare me, Never! It was good for nothing!" They were surprised, and decided that I was "cool".

Yes, I agree, this Priest is really cool! I continue to be surprised by his abilities every day.

Now, when I walk in the park every day, my body moves like that of the Priest – adopting a kind of animal, soft, rounded walk. This is how energy flows through my body now. No straight legs, artificial, human walk anymore. I am part of nature now. I see the road far ahead and I know, ahead of time, who will come out of the bushes, who will cross the road: raccoon or people or ... spirits...

Two days ago I walked near the golf course; suddenly I lifted my hand automatically without thinking, and caught the ball that was heading for my face! Balls fly over the fence through the bushes all the time but this time it was aimed at my head! The astonishing thing was that it was not I who moved my hand – I didn't have time to realize that a ball was going to hit me. It was a very unusual kind of movement, like a pray-mantis does. Yes, this Priest is pretty cool; otherwise I would have ended up with blue bruises on my cheek, or a black eye!

Today I started thinking about the parameters of the wisdom, which I mention throughout the book, and which comes to me at the appropriate moment.

It feels as if I do not belong to some particular society, nationality, country or race anymore. Instead, I feel an attachment to the whole Universe and humanity with the warmest feelings toward nature: plants, animals, birds, insects and even crystals, or rocks. It gives me an incredible sense of harmony and comfort to feel that I am a little part of the living space around me – mountains, ocean, and valleys. Usually people think before they speak. Right?

However now, I can instantly express my thoughts in words without aforethought. It means that I often speak with synchronic thinking – my thoughts and speech are synchronized – no prior thinking. I also write at the same speed as my thoughts come to mind, and I talk without spending time choosing the words. It seems that the frequency of the working brain and the speaking channels are in great harmony. I think this is what I experienced at the Buddhist temple, when the monks were playing the drums. They have the same perfect correlation, and coordination between their brains and hand movements.

Three years ago, while I was at the temple, I remember the top monk mentioning the rare possibility of Chi energy residing in our brain. Perhaps the vibrations of my body reach the same level as that of the vibrations of my Spirit. I experienced the same thing in my dreams – Spirit is in incredible harmony with all that I just mentioned. Now, in real life, I am beginning to experience the same astonishing moments such as I only experienced in my dreams before.

A few days ago, I started paying attention, analyzing and comparing myself with people around me, on TV, and on the street. I found that in my thoughts and actions, in my emotions or in those minute wishes, personal likes or dislikes never rule or affect the situation in which I may be at the time. The feelings or apprehensive worries just no longer exist.However, I still say what I feel, directly and instantly, about things I don't like.
I noticed that I enjoy life much more now, yet, in a different way than the way millions of people do. In most cases, their activities seem flat and empty to me, if they are not connected with nature and internal Spirit life. As for my lifestyle, people may think that my life is boring. I can compare this opinion with the life of an uneducated person – a person who never realized how empty and boring his life is without knowledge. Or with the life of those poor kids in Africa, who are eating only one kind of food during their entire life. They never had the possibility to taste something else. They are living in little mud shacks in the desert – no fun, no trees, no water to swim or play, no knowledge, no sharing of information. Everything around them is only one grey, yellow, muddy landscape. They are lucky of just one thing: they will never know how bad their life actually is, because they will never have the possibility to compare their life with anything else.

For me, those moments of enlightenment and connection with the Universe are astonishingly beautiful, deep, valuable, multidimensional and priceless. I cannot compare these moments with any kind of entertainment or pleasure people enjoy here on Earth. It is free, open, and it can be reachable. Everyone, including these poor children, can attain this state of inner happiness.

Once, many years ago, during a "charity week" at Christmas time, I was visiting gifted people, kids, who were sick and poor people in Moscow. I shared some precious moments with them and donated my own money. I was a successful and wealthy entrepreneur at the time, and a pioneer in charity organization – no one was doing this sort of thing in Russia then. Newspapers even wrote articles about this new "invention". I remember meeting a talented boy who was paralyzed. He was spending his life in bed, at home. He had no friends, no fun. I brought him lots of spiritual books, and at the moment I was about to say goodbye, suddenly, I told him one sentence, "Your body is stuck, frozen here on Earth, but your Spirit is *Free* and you can travel in your dream far, far away." A few weeks later, his mother called me and asked me to visit him again. Amazingly, he had changed – he was transformed! His face glowed with happiness and excitement; he smiled and started describing to me his visits to different planets and stars! He easily described the atmospheric pressure, the minerals, some circles, and all kinds of physical characteristics that this planet displayed, in infinite details! I understood then, that in his unique situation, being excluded from all activities, which ordinary people have in their daily routine, he could afford to spend days, months of training, and focus his mind on only one goal: travel the Universe. He attained incredible results and most importantly, he now felt extremely happy and complete!

I asked myself **"WHO AM I?"** a few months ago. It may be a good idea for you to ask the same question of yourself. What you will discover may be very intriguing!

Who am I?

Photo by Tim Orden www.timorden.com

"Julia has been to Mexico and now she blossomed spiritually since she returned! Her enthusiasm soars like a beautiful bird! Some magic occurred between her and this pyramid! - You can feel the difference and hear it in her voice. **You can see that even animals understand and follow her now!** Her intelligence is beyond belief and she must be an old soul as she knows more than most people could comprehend. She strongly connected with the Energy from the Universe. But now she is full of Wisdom." Carol, Edmonton

****

"Got this weekend Julia's book in the hand. Even touching the book gave me already trills.
I have been reading several parts of it. It is more than amazing. Your statement that 'spirit is eternal' is well emphasized and believable. Your contribution to testify from the invisible world will bring back a lot of people to live a sound faith driven live. You know that you are abundantly blessed, set-apart and might fully used to serve as a priest.
It was already written by the prophet Hosea: (free quote) 'My people (says Yahweh) are destroyed for lack of knowledge.' He blames the priests for it as it is their task to instruct the people and that during that period priests neglected that and lived a shameful decadent live, not caring for the common man. Now you are here, bringing the knowledge that can save the people from destruction. That's exactly why your speech, book(s) and video (s) should be spread rapidly all over the world in many languages. Sure a giant enterprise and of course you will persevere.

Reading your book my reverence is increasing strongly for you being out there as a living testimonial of the Spirit world. Many mediums, psychics etc., tried to approach me in vain the last 20-yrs, as none *of them were pure and badly wired with the parallel world. Now finally there is you! The living model of faith, hope, love, creativity and beauty. Blessed are you that brings peace of mind instead of fear. I will order 10 copies of the book to hand over to friends. Also to my granddaughter, whom was trilled after reading the back cover."*

Alfons Ven

EVOLUTION VISION foundation
Deviser of the 28-day cure.
www.slideshare.net/alfonsven

Julia– The "Good" Priest Photographer:Darlene Laurel SV

Chapter 2

The Dreams of an Atlantean Queen

Chak Mol, Giant Atlantean man in Chichén Itzá

During one of the hypnosis readings about the Priest, I saw suddenly that the Maya people were talking to a **huge, giant man!**

It was a big shock for me and I just didn't know what to think!
The hypnosis readings' process was really new to me, and when I saw, for example, big, round, white earrings on the man's ears, I was sure this was my imagination. The same thing happened when I thought about this enormous, huge man that I saw during the reading. But when I traveled to Chichén Itzá, after the first readings regarding the Priest, suddenly, to my big surprise, I saw men wearing these white, big, round button-earrings everywhere on the walls of the sites, and I decided to go again to Di Cherry to find out who this giant man among the Maya people was.

I asked Di Cherry during the reading to pay attention and ask me questions: what the small Maya people were doing, how they lived, and I told her that maybe I would see the giant again among them. As soon as the reading started I saw him again! Well, he was way too big not to see him!

YOUTUBE: AVATAR SVADI 3, ANGELS, AVATAR SVADI **4, GIANT in CHICHÉN ITZÁ**
Here is a short version of the reading. The full reading is available on CD at www.ameliareborn.com

Reading; February 20, 2008

(Note: This reading, same as the others, is a literal transcription of the taped session – no editing.)

What do you feel, experience right now – tell me?
I saw this big man again, it's near the entrance! But he cannot go in, he so big, he staying near entrance. His eyes blue and his hair white. I see his legs, his feet very big, it is very big feet

Tell me what they call that man?
He is so big and strong – his voice, cause it's so loud. It's like a Thunder, yes.
Yea... he needs to lie down to talk, because when he sits he's also too high.
He could not see your expression if he's way up there.
You said before that he looks more like a European man than a Mayan.
Tell me, could you ask him if he was born here somewhere in this area?

(Suddenly my voice changes dramatically, it starts sounding like many voices speaking at once, talking at the same time, with an echo...)

(Note: You should hear it! I am amazed when I hear it myself! It sounds like the voice I had during my first reading. But we did not record it. This sound feels as if it came through a time-tunnel between the past and future, through the great distance separating us from thousands of years back, and affected by TIME'S vibration; one voice split into many voices with an echo.)

No, he's born far away, he was born far away.

Okay. Across the water?
Yes, he was born across the water. He was born in BIG pyramid, in big pyramid, pyramid. Turquoise color shiny big pyramid.

And..., and the other people with him were as tall as he is?
Like his mother, yes. His mother has gold hair, very tall... I saw her now, beautiful. This is his mother.
When you see his mother, is she holding him or is she talking to him? What are you experiencing? (Pause...)
Do you know if you've been in this country, this country from where he comes from? Did you ever live in this country, too?

At first when you start talking, when I talk about his mother ... you start asking me. I was sure that I am his mother... I am his mother as well. **I was his mother.**[16](Start crying)

I see... No wonder, if he can live up to 800 years old, I see how it's possible. So, tell me about this pyramid.
I think it very big sphere, it huge sphere, maybe kind of 1/3 of the round big huge sphere, it like biggest hall. This is big hall, hall as a big space, very big space, huge space.
Right.
And they have big crystal inside, very big huge crystal inside.
And I know how operate this crystal, I know.

Good, is that your job? Is that things that you do?

It is very serious, it is not job and it's not responsibility. It is a necessity. It is necessary ... to operate this crystal. Once, we have problem with small pyramid and I will need to fix it, so I work with big crystal and it some very strong power together create lighting and this electricity blow up effect and sound, strongest sound, but it may work out and I fix the problem. But my palace ... this sphere goes down on the top, start kind of flat on the top ... and people worry ... so worried ... but it is okay. This one, it is okay, it is not important, we can fix it later. Most important, I did my job and we have another seven, and we have big one.
This knowledge very powerful and very dangerous to know for everybody and it's a big responsibility to operate with this, because it can destroy so much if operated the wrong way.

And does this crystal bring water? The rain?

(My voice changes again, it sounds as if there are many voices speaking at once, with an echo...)

---

[16] According to many psychics before we are born, we establish some kind of program for the next life. The program contains goals that will assist us in the development of our Soul and Spirit, as much as possible. We sign a contract with some High Spiritual Authorities on the "Other side". We choose gender, parents, family, country, set of qualities, and the time and place of our birth, which will help in the realization of the contract. The person does not remember this contract when he or she is born, but if the person lives the right way he or she will be lucky, lead a happy life and feel the support from the High Power. It looks like Chak Mol's mother, a woman from Atlantis, chose to be born as a Priest to be close to her son, for them to be together, and to work with him, to help him and to complete her own program at the same time.

I think I know ... I know now why they call him Thunder Paw. Because he remembers this knowledge from his mother, and I think he can create rain. He can create rain and when he doing this, this is what will be it will be this horrible sound, you know ... horrible sound, which he makes with space and energy and crystal.

When you were in Atlantis and the mother of this man with the voice of Thunder, you must be nearly 12 feet tall then, is that right?

Yes. And near me another two also very tall, another two women. Very, very white everything, beautiful and white around them and they wearing something really white ... and two of them coming outside and its big stairs and very, very big white temple and white pillars.

****

Dream # 16
Destruction of the Crystal Sphere, February 19, 1992

I had not slept all night. I dozed for 5 minutes around 8:00 a.m. My electronic clock was still working, when I fell asleep, and when I woke up, it had stopped, although it worked during the night.[17] I think this was because of my dream.

I don't remember my entire dream. I was in a big building with a huge, endless hall. At the beginning, I was standing above this area, in the other premises of the building. Some girl approached me. She started saying something, something very important. It was not a warning about danger, it was some problem. I let her know that I would do it, and went on doing what I was supposed to do. **I ran over "it" with my hand, or with my mind, but it was very important.** It looked like a spiral Galaxy. I started making similar, circular movements with my right hand.[18] It was very much like another time, when I was sleeping once in 1988, and I woke up and saw how something (a Galaxy), a condensed energy, was buzzing with deep sound high over my bed, it was blue in color and it flashed.

I said to that girl – "I can do this, much stronger than it can be imagined". And I ran over it with my hand and it started buzzing, and after that, it started buzzing with a high frequency sound, like when you run with your finger around the rim of a wine glass. The sound became so hard, as if it was about to pierce your eardrums. In this "galaxy" – in this space – there were sparks of bright white color, like sparks from the trolleybus wires, with a tint of electric blue. Such sparks dropped down like snowflakes, or firework sparks. And this thing, itself – this kind of galaxy – was blinking. The thing consisted of sparks and the buzzing sound went up and down, unbearable. The lighting was like a flashing light – and when it flashed, it turned into colors of light – electric purple, then red, then electric green... Such colors are usually called acid colors. And the sparks were falling out of it. And when it was flashing, there were flashes of purple, lilac colors. It was beautiful. But then it was not about beauty, it was monstrous.
The "Galaxy" was to the left of me. On the right, at about a half a meter, there was a wall. But this thing was moving through it – as if there was no wall at all. You could see it, and everything around was unimportant.

---

[17] Electric clocks, watches stopped. It was the same, as it happened before, after this kind of dream.
[18] This very unusual movement of the hand repeated itself in many places, in many dreams and I even drew how the hand moved. In this dream, the movement of the hand connects with materialization, (see the *Atlantean abilities*).

YOUR ETERNAL HOLOGRAM

Then there was a cracking sound, higher and higher, electric, clear, and it stopped.

I went out, got downstairs, there is a huge hall. There was a sphere in this hall – not hemisphere, but 1/3 of a sphere, it was in the middle, rising from the walls, up, as high as the skyscrapers of Vancouver. It was a crystal, and it consisted of some sort of thin hollow glass tubes, connected together like in a beehive, quite thin. Under the sphere there were people walking, the sphere was for them a kind of a roof – same as the conservatory in Queen Elizabeth Park in Vancouver. The sphere was of a very elaborate design, there were many strange pieces, and they were hanging down. For example, as if the *Zurvan tracings* were hanging down. Different forms, colors, long and short.

Anyway, when I was in that room upstairs, I was amazed, that I could do even more, than I assumed. When I was going down the white stairs into the hall, I saw a group of people, about 7 to 10 people. In the middle, or on the side, there is nothing there, no furniture, only a smooth, mirror-like floor. And I saw, that because I did that thing upstairs, the sphere started to fall down, soften on one side. It cannot collapse, it is indivisible, and it started to move down – because of what I had done. And they all were looking at it, agitated, talking among themselves. But I didn't move a muscle. I did not feel myself a destructor. I remembered, what was supposed to happen. Everything was in order now. I had a feeling that I am a queen, and this sphere did not matter much to me. I knew much higher values. Let's assume that there were another seven of such spheres, and one more, a huge one – the main, the largest pyramid. What I had done was necessary. I had the feeling that I knew, but forgot about my capacities, but then I began to remember. I had a feeling that an important task had been fulfilled. Calm indifference.
****
Now I know how to control myself and the energy in these kinds of dreams, but years ago, I didn't. Usually, elevator, or phones are out of order and often, fire alarms start ringing in cases like these, and the fire trucks arrive right after that. My friend even wrote a song for his band, which is popular now, about a fire truck coming and "nothing to do here for us now."

I don't like shopping, because some days the electric buzzer near the entrance door of the store will start making this ringing sound. Even if I walk outside on Robson Street, where the stores are all in a row, one after another, the moment I pass near the open doors, this buzzer is activated and the sound follows me from one store to the next. The last time it happened, it had a stronger effect. It happened twice in the spring of 2004 in a period of two weeks, when I saw the same kind of dreams where I was experimenting with electricity and crystals. At first, the fire alarm went on in the whole of this nine-stores building.
I felt guilty when the people ended up on the street at 3:30 a.m. with little sleepy kids in their arms or holding cages with cats and dogs. We had to stay there and wait for the fire trucks to arrive to check the building. There was no electricity in our block until the afternoon of that day. The next time, it was much more serious. My friend, Marina – a psychic – called me from New York in the morning and told me that she saw a powerful electrical station blow up in her dream, which was connected with me. She asked if I was okay. I was..., but from the moment I woke up from this dream, until the middle of the following night there was no electricity for the entire day in 5-7 blocks and all the stores on Davie Street, up to Burrard str, were closed on that day.

The elevator and car incident

Since Julia's limo driver mixed the day when he was to meet her when she returned to Canada from Europe, she called me and I met her at the airport. I did not see her for a long time. So, on the way back to town, I started sharing my problems with the manager of the building, where I live. I was extremely angry at him. Because of him, my locker room was opened a few times and lots of valuable stuff was stolen. I talked about it all the way into town. Julia warned me that she just had a dream about crystal pyramids in Atlantis and asked me to stop being angry, because she didn't want to be involved with my angry talk. She said she was very tired after a long flight and maybe it would be difficult for her to control her "electrical energy." I was sure she was kidding and didn't pay attention to what she said. I continued to express my anger. What happened next was unbelievable; the alternator and an axel in the car broke down as we arrived! Lucky it did not happen on the way...

It was silly for me to spend so much energy trying to remember bad things... I got a good lesson. However, it Looked like my negative energy influence was still around Julia, it continued to have an electrical effect on things, because when we arrived with her suitcases in front of the elevator at her home (and after I needed to return to my building), the elevators stopped working! I am lucky I was not inside! I walked down the 19 flights of stairs. Yes, her peaceful nature was disturbed by my negativity. You need to be positive when you are with her, you will be happier and maybe you will be blessed. If you are negative or rude it could mean punishment for you in some little or bigger ways, such as it happened with my car.

William, Julia's neighbor
June 6, 2008

As always I try to control my thoughts. The problem is that when I think about somebody, those people feel it and try to contact me instantly with a story similar like this one below. This letter is from a man in Australia, to whom I sent my book for free as a gift, just as I have to many, hundreds of other people. He is a very spiritual man, handicapped and hoping that he will start walking one day again. It was flooding in Australia and I start remember him wondering how he is doing?

"Hi Julia, I have not written in a while... And not really sure you will remember me... The reason I write today is, I am sitting at my computer finalizing some arrangements for my afternoon and out of the blue my computer starts from sleep mode and displays website with your photo without me touching a thing... I looked up and there you were... It freaked me out a bit with shivers down my spine... I certainly felt your spirit come... It was quite funny because I had my head down writing and something made me look up... And I was surprised to see you there on my screen... Took me by surprise... A very happy one at that :-) I have had many feelings about you not being the average human...So I thought I would say hi and ask if you needed anything? ... It would seem something is going on... Hope you're doing well and look forward to hearing from you...Love and Blessings to you...
" **Rick, March 2011, Australia**

****

We live in Belgium and in the Netherlands, and once we mentioned about Julia's abilities to our friend, who is psychic. **When she started thinking about Julia, suddenly the electricity at her place began acting up.** *Her TV-set was turned on, and even after she pulled the plug out, it was still switched on! This scared her and she waited a week before she dared tell us about it. We then told her that Julia lived across the ocean in Canada. When we told Julia about this, she explained it as, "Easy. When we have day here in Europe, in Canada it's nighttime." During her night-dream, her Spirit may have felt this psychic attention and maybe electricity in the house started reacting to Julia's Spirit presence.*

A few weeks later, Julia was coming to visit my nephew and his wife in Australia. I sent him a note (as a joke) saying, "A storm is coming," because my memory was fresh of our experiences with our psychic friend. They live on the top of a huge old volcano crater, below which there is a large valley. During the first night when Julia slept in the house, strange electricity problems occurred in town, they blew up the station in two places and there was no electricity from 11 p.m. until the next day (in a town of 75,000 people). That night, on the first of January 2009, Julia saw some global flooding in her dream; with waves two-third the height of the snow-capped mountains. That huge ocean wave inundated this valley and she tried to do something about it. I guess she saw fragments of her past life and flooding in Atlantis. The next evening an enormous storm and rain started, which beat all Australian records with a huge amount of lightning. There were some 80,000 lightning strikes recorded that night! The entire valley was under constant, bright, electricity light.

These two cases are, by some coincidence, connected with Julia, and all related to her presence in each area. There is already a list of the cases and witnesses, and it forms a pattern of occurrences. **It looks like her ability from her past life as a queen in Atlantis is still a strong part of her Spirit even now."**

Wim, Holland http://www.akaija.com/

I try my best to control myself in my dreams. Since 2004 it never happened again, except in these few instances and I am really glad! It was very disturbing to me, and I even had a dream about it. This second dream occurred 8 months later, during the same year when I had most of the dreams about sphere palaces and working with pyramid energy.

Dream # 17
Elevators Were Ringing Because of Me, September 12, 1992

I was walking down the street, it was getting dark. A man and a woman were walking arm in arm. She said to him, "I will invite 7 women to put my flat in order." They had already passed me; I ran after them and said, "Take me, right now." The man left and she turned back to her house. She said, "OK, but why do you want it?"
I said, "I have everything, I don't care about anything." Something like – I want to turn off my life, to have a respite from myself, to take care of somebody else's problems.
We entered a hotel. A doorman was near the door behind the front desk. I managed to pass somehow. Then we approached the big elevators. I said, "They torment me, always watch me. Everywhere, wherever I go, there is some kind of electricity, which reacts to me. They can trace me easily – in elevators, entrance doors, in a subway, shops, etc. They always know where I am, this secretive team of people. I am always asked, stopped in the most inappropriate places, they lead me there; maybe they are attuned to my moods in order to recognize me. They cannot kill me; they don't want to shake me or torment me. They even cannot interrogate me seriously. Everything is done in a friendly tone. They cannot overdo it, maybe because they don't want my mechanism to be broken."

In this instance, when I wanted I went and visited "the others" – not people – but this secretive team of people, some wanted to know everything about the others. When I came to them, they asked me who the others were, what kind of weapons they had. **I could transcend to the other world in a moment, by my own wish, like going one-step up.** I had just one impression – our world was unpleasant, gray, and empty – the Stone Age – compared to another more dimensional one. There were others – very different from where we were here, very light, just like angels. It seemed strange to me, that the ones here were hostile to the others and sneaking about to learn about them. They didn't need to know about "the others". They could not even imagine – just a little bit – grasping the reverberation, the reflection in the mirror of those kinds of angels. But they would not mind trying to eliminate them. They were just like thickheaded ants, who wanted to clutch, to *press* down and to destroy.
There was a trick. When many people entered the elevator, it started ringing because it was overloaded, but it also rang because of me. I knew exactly how many people would create the ringing. So I waited with this woman, then we entered the elevator again, but the ringing continued – I had caused it and it was mixed with the passenger overload. One of the men left the elevator and we went

up. We entered her flat. It was semicircular. At the window, which was supposed to look over the street, I saw the window of the other flat through it. It was like an anthill. I saw how the light went on in that other room, how the woman entered. I said, "Close the curtains, they will see us!" (I was afraid of being chased, somehow). Maybe it was the reason why I went to strangers, just not to be watched and have a little rest from it. And here – a glass looking into the other glass! But that woman seemed not to see us. My woman told me, "Calm down. They don't see you. You see them but they don't."Her furniture was very strange – small – up to your knees. The ceiling was just head-high. Everything in the room was up to your knees. I sat down – with difficulty – everything was so low. **The wall was transparent from bottom to ceiling. It felt as if I was about 3 or 4 meters tall.**[19]

Reading; March 25, 2008

(Note: This reading, same as the others, is a literal transcription of the taped session – no editing.)

I see again this big man. He sit right now in front of pyramid from right side
(Pause...)*And I see his face very good right now. He has blue eyes and he has dark skin, skin tone skin. And he has long this chin. And yes, he have nose little bit up on it. And he has wrinkles near the eyes and he try to close his eyes from this sunshine...*

Di Cherry: So he squints. As I understand it, Thunder Paw can activate clouds, he can activate the clouds, and he can cause the rain. When you stand beside Thunder Paw could he put his hand on your head?
(Worry voice...really worry)

His hand so big and heavy! So big... heavy...

What he can do to you?

We are good friends ... and when I talk with him... He lies down...
I walk to him now ... and he sit and I look at him up and even when he sit he too high and now he lie down to his elbow and I see his face so close now, right in front of . And he looks at me and he talk with me and he turns his head toward me now.

Is he wearing something behind his ears today?

He has hat ... it's hot and his hat near him now on the land.
And this hat ... very kind of complicated looks, it just hat on top, and on the top its same and it kind of strange ... he has same like we have when we listen music now! It's like a head phone, like this shape but its big and thick, and it like button on the top. And it closes his ears when he wearing this...
I see it, and it's near him, he don't wearing this all the time, but just when it necessary...

Yes...

His name Thunder Paw, Thunder Paw. When he starts talk it's so strong and loud, so I step back, because it so crazy loud when he talking.He asks me talk with him very loud also.

And since you are so close to Thunder Paw, tell me does he have blue eyes?

---

[19] It looks like I was an Atlantean in this dream – very tall. This woman in the dream saw me but other people didn't or I just followed her. I wonder how I even fit in the apartment. I guess I touched the ceiling with my head. Number 7 again, it is the number of pyramids that were in Atlantis.

YOUR ETERNAL HOLOGRAM

Yes, you don't even ask I already feel that you will ask about blue eyes.
Because I look right to his eyes now and its blue turquoise eyes, blue eyes.

Turquoise blue?

Blue, blue eyes. Yes.

If I will look in your eyes, you must see your eyes.

I have dark deep blue eyes ... he has light eyes.

Yes, I have seen these dark, deep blue eyes.

(Pause. Suddenly I start crying...)

His eyes he has same like his mother has. His mother has blue eyes...same eyes.

You knew his mother?

Yea, it's beautiful mother, he have beautiful mother...
(I continue crying)
Big mother, she so tall this woman, slim and very tall mother and he loved his mother. He misses his mother ... very much he miss mother ... and he cry about his mother ... his mother so far, so far away. He will never see his mother again ... she so far away. I was his mother...

Does Thunder Paw ever tell you about his father? You ever speak of his father?

I see his father, his father have curly blond, dark blond hair. I see his father. His father have nose like him, with little bump ... and up at the end. His father have same nose.

Okay.

Yes and his father and his mother they king and queen of beautiful kingdom, they live in beautiful white palace, big palace...

I see...

This Kingdom ... they have many big palace, but they looks like a sphere, they 1/3 of sphere ... they not like a palaces we know, they sphere's palaces
And under so many crystals, big crystals and statues and some crystals so big!!!

Perhaps it was once a part of Atlantis.

Yea...When he uses this crystal, he makes thunder, he makes real thunder!It was lightning it was crazy strong lighting and it's very big loud sound, very big sound. And when he using this, he has his hat.

When you see pictures of him as a Chak Mol and see him lie down.
It's the famous carving of him where he lies down on his back...

120

Thunder Paw and Chak Mol it is the same person.
 (Start crying)

I feel him like my close friend. My close dear friend ... I had so much time with him. And I now I want just hug this statue ... this is my friend.

What he has got in his hand? Did he have a crystal when they made the carving of him? Was this a golden disk?

He has disk, very sharp slim disk, made from some strange metal, it's very thick and its very sharp like things, but it heavy ... yes. Yes, very powerful things he has...It's rigid, it's strong. And flexible. He likes to play, he likes to run, he likes running.

And playing ball? Did you watch him play ball?
He have in his bag ball, yes, he have rubber ball in his bag.

Is this ball too big for you, too heavy for you?

Yes, it's big ball and...

And? And now?

They build a walls and they put on top for him ring. And he play with this He play same when I was in school and it was fashion between children to play with fuzzy things, but heavy with their legs and with legs and they kick with legs and with knee ... and he play same way...

So we need to come back to this day, when you're waiting for rain, you're waiting for a cloud. All the people who came here are waiting to hear you speak, waiting for you to do something, so they can have rain and plant their crops.

YES...
This is another day, this is another day...

Then tell me about another day.

This day was later ... it was when Chak Mol left, he left us and he not near anymore ... and he cannot help me, he cannot help us ... he left ... we have drought ... we have ... and people need water, people can give anything for this water. And this day so important, it's very important. We pray God to help us. And when Chak Mol left, Thunder Paw ... we make statue of him. I miss him ... and in my kind of office with jaguar, near jaguar we put his statue ... I ask ... case I miss him ... I want him near...

****

I had numerous hypnosis sessions. Di Cherry told me that after each session during the next 2 or 3 weeks, I would be in this special state of mind where I would continue to see more and more. It was a real shock for me during the first reading when I saw for the first time this huge giant, a real live mar sitting near his platform between small Maya people!
Literally, I just couldn't believe my eyes! It was impossible to understand who this man was. ʼ was he so big and how could he possibly exist, because he was such a real huge human! On ʻ this, I did not see it as we see things at the movie theater, for example. I was suddenly right ne

And when, during the reading, Di Cherry asked: "What will happen if he puts his hand on your head?"
"I was scared!" My voice dropped... "I was worried because his hand was too big and heavy!"
Chak Mol was very tall, but at the same time extremely thin, skinny, light. Maybe the big steps on the pyramid were made for him to climb to the top?

He always wore an outfit similar to what our warriors wore – (except that he had some big shiny jewelry made of some white and silver metal around his neck and I think the bracelet or maybe the ring on his finger were made of the same metal. I am sure about the jewelry around his neck, because it reflected the sun when I looked at him during one of my hypnosis sessions.)
A month ago, I was in Acumal, Mexico on the Maya Riviera. I visited the Yal Ku Park there. This park is amazing! It is filled with beautiful statues made by different artists. Some of the statues are located on a small island surrounded by the ocean lagoon. There, I saw a very unusual kind of statue made by the same artist - CHARLOTTE YAZBEC.
I think this woman, in her vision, saw Atlantean people, how they look – very tall and very slim. I am glad that the Avatar movie came to the screen and it's easy for me now to explain what Atlantis people looked like. The proportion between the woman and the unicorn are about the same proportion I saw in Thunder Paw – she is his size and the horse is the size of a normal horse.

Yal Ku Park, (Statue by CHARLOTTE YAZBEC)

Below, I describe what came to me in my visions and dreams regarding Thunder Paw – Chak Mol.

For many years, we had a happy life in Chichén Itzá with many rituals and celebrations. In my vision and dreams, I saw lots of joy.

The **drought** came and the problems started. Thunder Paw, who is Chak Mol, left and I was grieving because of my son.

It was a very emotional day when Thunder Paw left us. It was a farewell day with all kinds of rituals and long discussions. We never saw him again. He never returned...

I remember how we sat with him the last time at sunset near the water well ("senote") on the big flat rocks, looking to the water. It was our favorite spot. We often sat there and talked. In those days I had an enormous, sad, heavy feeling...

We had droughts for a long time already. It was impossibly hard to collect food for Thunder Paw – he was so big – there was never enough food for him. People brought what they could to him on his platform but there wasn't enough. Yet, most important we, the leaders, couldn't do anything about weather like we did before – the climate conditions had changed dramatically.

He left with a few warriors to the faraway temple where we hoped there were no droughts and where there would be food for him.

Later, I think people decided that he went to the sky and started calling him the GOD of Rain.

Because he had an unusually shaped nose compared with the local people, long and turned up at the end, with a bump at eye-level, people began to consider such a feature as the "trademark", the symbol of the GOD of RAIN. According to the hypnosis sessions, he also had blue eyes, white curly hair, long strong chin and straight forehead. I remember that in my dream I always called him: Father. People around me also called him Father, perhaps because he was our noble leader and a teacher. People adored and loved him. I remember feeling this deep emptiness in my heart for a very long time after he left. It was impossibly hard, he was always near me for many, many years, maybe generations, I guess longer than my whole life. I remember sitting in his huge empty house on the way to the sauna and talking to him in my meditation.

It was time when I experience powerlessness. It was a feeling of having reached a dead end. I could not do ANYTHING to change the dry weather to help my people. It was a time when we, nobles, saw and experienced the first breach in people's trust in our Great power. It was a time *Drought dictated our lives – not Man.*

I had a dream, which reminded me of one of the days when we sat with Chak Mol near the water well (senote). I seem to remember that at the time, the senote was full of pure water – filled to the rim – without green algae so that I could see his reflection in the water. I make the name for this dream ZARATUSTRA, but really, I don't have any idea who it was...

Dream # 18
Zaratustra in Water, September 6, 1993

It was a dream at night, but it was like a vision. I have a feeling that I was not sleeping. I was standing on the shore of a little round lake, near a high bluff. I was looking at the reflection in the water. The surface reflected a person of huge size. His reflection was on the surface, but it partially went under water, it was three-dimensional, and I could see him. I was conversing before that about astrology, or just contemplating. I wanted to see him. He was either high in the clouds or standing up on the hill. I thought that, in fact, he was in the clouds, but in order to make it seem real, he offered a conventional way, as if he was standing on the top of the hill and was reflected in the water, in order to calm my imagination down. *I knew that I could not; I was unable to look straight at him. But he wanted to show himself to me – at least as a reflection in the water.* [22]

Zoroaster *(Latinized from Greek variants) or* Zarathushtra *(from* Avestan *Zaraθuštra), also referred to as* Zartosht, *was an* ancient Iranian *prophet and religious poet. The hymns attributed to him, the* Gathas, *are at the liturgical core of* Zoroastrianism.
Although a few recent depictions of Zoroaster show the prophet performing some deed of legend, in general the portrayals merely present him in white vestments (which are also worn by present-day ***Zoroastrian priests****).*

Part 2

Giants, Chak Mol

Here are some facts, which prove that what I saw during the hypnosis sessions about giant men in Chichén Itzá are real! Yes, he did exist there a long time ago! It also means that all the other things I saw during my hypnosis sessions were real and did occur a long time ago as well! Amazing!

© Josephine Wall. All Rights Reserved. www.josephinewall.com

The current name **Chacmool** *is derived from the name "Chaacmol", which* Augustus Le Plongeon *gave to a sculpture he and his wife* Alice Dixon Le Plongeon *excavated from within the Temple of the*

Eagles and Jaguars at Chichén Itzá in 1875. He translated "Chaacmol" from Yucatecan Maya as the ***"paw swift like thunder"*** *(Le Plongeon 1896:157 – Wikipedia, the free encyclopedia).*

Why did people call him "Paw swift like thunder"?

According to my PLR (Past Life Regression) sessions and dreams, people called him "Paw swift like thunder", maybe because the Chak Mol statue is the statue of an Atlantean – a man from Atlantis. People from Atlantis were very tall like many other ancient, giant human races.

"Most all ancient civilizations believed in the Titans, the race of giant humans that inhabited Earth long ago. Different races knew them by different names. These 7 to 12 foot humanoids were thought to be legendary until the excavation of over a dozen skeletons 8 to 12 feet tall, around the world, shocked archaeologists. The Spanish Conquistadors left diaries of wild blond-haired, blue eyed 8 to 12 foot high men running around in the Andes during the conquest of the Incas" (Wikipedia, the free encyclopedia).

Giants on the USA territory:

1. In 1833, soldiers digging at Lompock Rancho, California, discovered a male skeleton 12 feet tall. The skeleton had double rows of upper and lower teeth.
2. A giant found off the California Coast on Santa Rosa Island in the 1800s was distinguished by its double rows of teeth.
3. A 9-foot, 8-inch skeleton was excavated from a mount near Brewersville, Indiana, in 1879.
4. Skeletons of "enormous dimensions" were found in mounds near Zanesville, Ohio, and Warren, Minnesota, in the 1880s.
5. In Clearwater Minnesota, the skeletons of seven giants were found in mounds. These had receding foreheads and complete double dentition.
6. At LeCrescent, Minnesota, mounds were found to contain giant bones. Five miles north, near Dresbach, the bones of people over 8 feet tall were found.
7. Near Toledo, Ohio, 20 skeletons were discovered with jaws and teeth "twice as large as those of present day people." The account also noted that odd hieroglyphics were found with the bodies.
8. Miners in Lovelock Cave, California, discovered a very tall, red-haired mummy in 1911. This mummy eventually went to a fraternal lodge where it was used for "initiation purposes."
9. In 1931, skeletons from 8.5 to 10 feet long were found in the Humboldt lakebed in California.
10. In 1947 a local newspaper reported the discovery of nine-foot-tall skeletons by amateur archeologists working in Death Valley.
11. One of the latest accounts of a race of giants that occupied Europe comes from the Middle Ages and involves a surprising figure: Saint Christopher. Jacques de Voragine in The Golden Legend, wrote of St. Christopher: "He was of gigantic stature, had a terrifying mien, was twelve coudees tall." (A coudee is an antique measurement equal to or larger than the English linear measurement of a foot. According to this ancient account, St. Christopher stood from 12 to 18 feet tall (a fact that has become hidden in or even erased from church history). [21]

In other words, according to the contemporary accounts of his day, St. Christopher was the product of a spiritual being that mated with a human woman. And once again the result of this union was a creature that matched the descriptions of the Nephilim.

GENESIS 6:4 *There were GIANTS on Earth in those days; and after that, when the SONS OF GOD (Fallen Angels) came in unto the daughters of men, and they bear children to them, the same became mighty men, which were of old, men of renown.*

YOUTUBE: Giants and Ancient History Hidden Proofs Of A Giant Race [32]
Interesting that right now on Solomon Islands exist this kind of Giants.

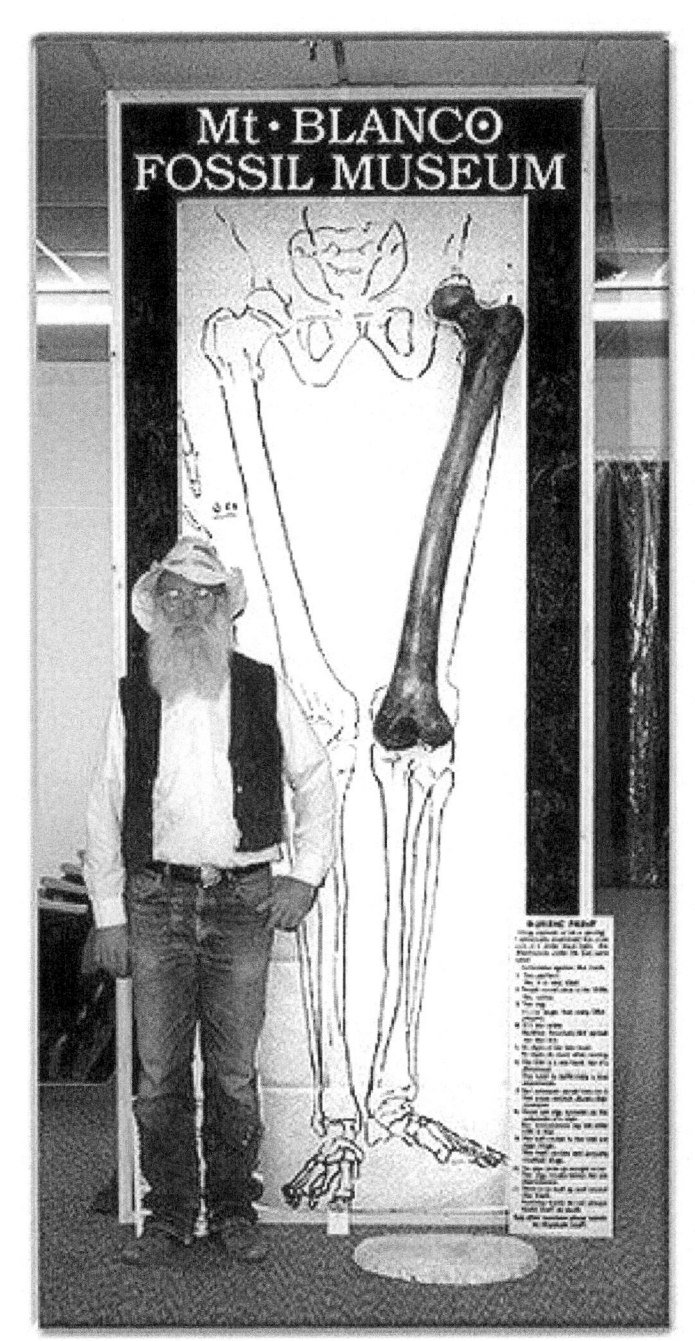

47 inch Human Femur

In the late 1950s, during road construction in south-east Turkey in the Euphrates Valley, many tombs containing the remains of Giants were uncovered. At two sites the leg bones were measured to be about 120 cms "47.24 inches". Joe Taylor, Director of the Mt. BLANCO FOSSIL MUSEUM in Crosbyton, Texas, was commissioned to sculpt this anatomically correct, and to scale, human femur. This "Giant" stood some 14-16 feet tall, and had 20-22 inch long feet. His or Her finger tips, with arms to their sides, would be about 6 feet above the ground. The Biblical record, in Deuteronomy 3:11 states that the Iron Bed of Og, King of Bashan was 9 cubits by 4 cubits or approximately 14 feet long by 6 feet wide!

GENESIS 6:4 —
There were Nephilim (Giants) in the earth in those days; and also after that when the sons of God (Angels?) came in unto the daughters of men, and they bare children to them, the same became mighty men which were of old, men of renown.

More Info & Replicas available at mtblanco1@aol.com or www.mtblanco.com
Mt. Blanco Fossil Museum • P.O. Box 559, Crosbyton, TX 79322 • 1-800-367-7454

YOUR ETERNAL HOLOGRAM

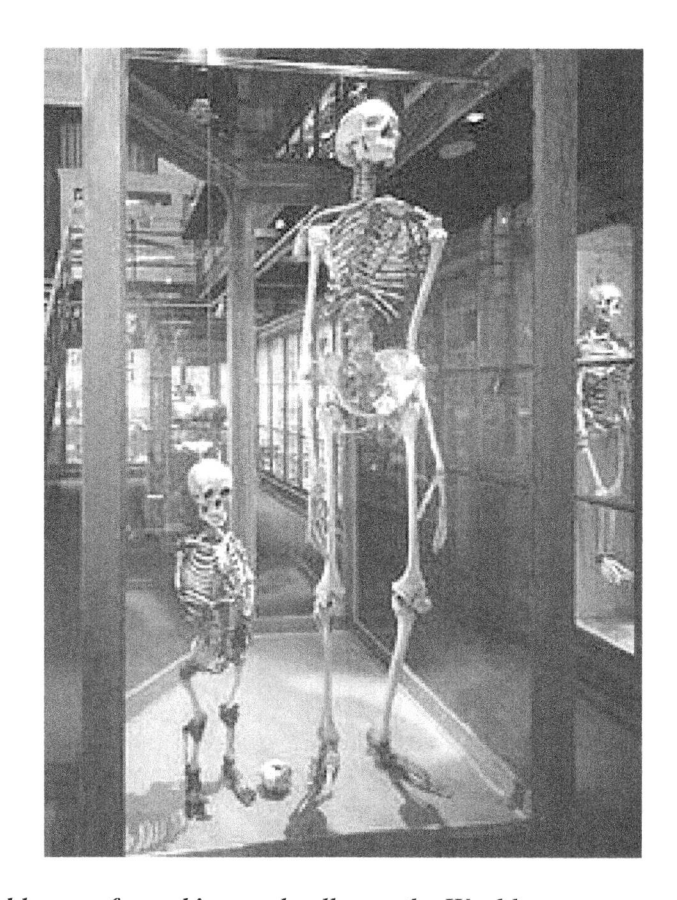

Scientists have found bones of very big people all over the World.

Giants near Mexico

"It has been over 10 years now since Patrick Quirk and I traveled with another 10 more people the back roads of Aztlan searching out the Ancient Halls of Record. We come across nearly 150 mummies and skeletal remains as we searching out the possible locations according the old Spanish Manuscripts that told the tale of the Ancient ancestors of the Azteca. The archaeological specimens shown here were found in the Southwestern portion of the United States bordering the Western Rocky Mountains.
 Spiral, conical tombs was found. It feels that this is Hybrid Annunaki offspring. Some 14 feet when standing. Female 8 and 9 feet. The big lady was buried along with some rather unusual metal objects, they were not terrestrial in origin. Symbols and script tell of a sophisticated civilization. Perhaps the survivors of great cataclysms children of Sun and Moon.

There mostly the goddess, the Matriarchal nature of their society, her priest and priestess. They described great devastation, volcanic eruptions, floods. They seem to be telling us about a previous knowledge, in their home land, they include charts, and many examples of mathematics and sacred geometry, from the occult sciences such as there below. So they weren't aboriginals running around eating bugs. The carved inscriptions represent ancient astrological and high occult symbols. This type of script is Pre-Egyptian and could date as far as 8,000 BCE. In the Sumerian culture this was the secret language of the priests. These symbols are rare, although we have at least 7 or more locations from Central Mexico up the Pacific Coast and well into B.C. Canada.
The code is 'written' in sacred geometry for Jupiter Square and ancient Sumerian Occult symbol. We have found the writing of 11 different languages in the area from various Euro-Mediterranean which

indicate that there was in fact extensive "Global" trade and interaction going on with the people of this area at list 5,000 BCE. Thus this extensive trade and interaction could well have been going on longer than 8,000 years ago.

There was found burial robe made from Camel hair, which had pre-ice age characteristics. Examined under an electronic microscope the weave proved so intricate and complex, that the only way we could reproduce it today, would be by computer, using finest silk. Also found sort of netting from Lama hair with technique is that common to proto-Egyptian civilizations in the Mediterranean regions around 3,500 BCE but what is it doing in America?

http://www.robertghostwolf.com/Aztlan/outheretv.htm

ROBERT GHOST WOLF, http://www.lightstreamers.com/ghostwolf.htm

Maybe among them were Chak Mol's relatives?

Because of the location and also because in this amazing website, the author described Atlantis people as "Hybrid Annunaki offspring", because in his opinion Atlantean people are descendants from those who came from space and who were named Annunaki.

So they were part Angels from the cosmos and part humans. You will feel how fragile they felt and being so distant from real people, who are down on Earth, in the next chapter Atlantis in Dream # 23, The City Of Crystal Pyramids, June 13, 1993.

"Dear Julia, I found your book and this website interesting. It reminded me of the caves at what we call "Four corners" in South West America. I saw many writings and symbols very similar to the ones on this web site. You may find it interesting that the Cherokee have been studied for years trying to figure out where we came from? The Mormon's think we are the ones that had the golden tablets that became their bible or Book of Mormon. DNA tests was done on the Cherokee and found out that we are not Jewish, and we are not Vikings either, both of which were theories about us. Many historians believe we are the survivors from Atlantis because we are very tall, we have facial hair, and our skin is whiter than all the other tribes around us. We have our own written language and we have a calendar similar to the Maya, the only difference is our calendar ends on Oct. 29th, 2011. We do know exactly where we come from: our planet Alcey One in the Plaieties star system which is close to Orion's belt. My Grandfather always said we are half Star Man and half human so I know we came from the stars in the first place. My great-grandfather is Arron, Seven Eagles and he was just over 7 ft. tall. Everyone called him a mountain of a man because he was so strong and powerful."

Marc Eagle Eyes, from the Eagle Clan of the Eastern Band of the Cherokee
http://www.burlingtonnews.net/pleiadians.html

Alcyone is the brightest star in the Pleiades star system. The names of 2 more stars in the Pleiades system are included: Maya, Atlas. ThePalladian's are a very ancient race of humanoids. They have kept a record of the complete history of Earth's human evolution from the very beginning to our present time. The Pleiadians stayed with humans on Earth until 10 A.D. trying to help develop various civilizations such as Lemuria, Maya, Inca and a civilization at Machu Picchu. They also were trying to guide humans toward a more spiritual path.

Thunder Paw - Chak Mol:

a. He was very big and tall and because of this, he had a very strong voice compared to the small Maya people.

b. He also produced a strong loud sound when he used the crystal device to make electricity – electrical lightning bolt – and as a result, it created thunder and rain in the clouds around him. It looks like because of this sound people called him *Thunder* Paw.

YOUR ETERNAL HOLOGRAM

This photo depicts a copy of the statue of Chak Mol, which was excavated few years ago around the Chichén Itzá area. The original of this statue is located now in the Merida City Museum. I was very lucky to find this copy in the Chichén Itzá hotel at Piste.

No one knows why, in his statues he is always in the same position, why he lies down and always turns his head to one side.

Chac-Mool is the name given to a type of Pre-ColumbianMesoamerican *stone statue. The Chac-Mool depicts a human figure in a position of reclining with the head up and turned to one side, holding a tray over the stomach (Wikipedia Encyclopedia).*

According to my PLR and dreams, it supports Augustus and Alice Le Plongeon correct translation of his name:

1. Chak Mol and Thunder Paw is one and the same person.
2. Chak Mol was a very tall, real giant person, possibly an Atlantean. I saw Thunder Paw as a very big, maybe a 16 to 18 foot tall man.
3. He needs to lie down each time he talks to people. He also needs to turn his head to one side, because this is the only way he can see people and the expression on their faces. This is the best way to talk and listen to them.
4. On the bas-relief all around the rim of the Platform of Eagles and Jaguars, all around the top of the temple, a man lies down on his back and turns his head to the opposite side of a long tool he holds in his hands. Possibly, this bas-relief shows how Chak Mol tries to activate rain because I saw him often lie down on this platform: he lies down on his back, points his tool toward the clouds, sending rows of lasers toward the clouds.

This man has **round glasses** on his eyes maybe for protection from electrical sparks.[20]

---

[20] This kind of glasses is found on this ancient carving as well as in another places in Chichén Itzá.

1. Chak Mol – Thunder Paw was a leader and a great teacher. According to the Indian spiritual beliefs, "Nagval" is the name for a teacher who always lies down. So maybe the ancient Maya decided that the big teacher, Chak Mol, should be shown in the sculptures always in a lying-down position. He is very big, so he was posing in a lying-down position – the only way to see him close-up for those who sculpted the statues.

Men with goggleson the bas-relief of the temple of Platform of Eagles and Jaguars   *Chak Mol is obviously wearing goggles*

2. Is Chak Mol an ancient, powerful warrior prince?
The name, he said, was given by the ancient Maya to a powerful warrior prince who had once ruled Chichén Itzá, and was represented by the sculpture (Wikipedia Encyclopedia).
I agree. Yes, according to my PLR he was a Prince, because his mother was a Queen of Atlantis.
His real name is Thunder Paw. Why did they call him "powerful"; because he was powerful. He was simply big and had much more power than the ordinary person. Mentally, he was also powerful as an Atlantean, who brought his special knowledge to the Maya people. It looks like he came from some island, which was originally part of Atlantis.
The statue of Chak Mol is a statue of an Atlantean. He was named "Paw swift like thunder" because he was very tall and had a very strong voice compared to the small Mayan people.

How many and how far away are each statue of Chak Mol located?
Twelve chacmools have been located at the Toltec city of Tula, fourteen at Maya Cheche'n Itza', one without provenance is stylistically Aztec, and two are from the Aztec Templo Mayor in Mexico City. Other chacmools have been found at the archaeological site of Cempoala, in the states of Michoacan and Tlaxcala, and at the Maya site of Quirigua' in Guatemala.
If Chak Mol was just a normal human, he would have lived for a maximum of 100 years. How come all other people who lived so far away in different places and maybe hundreds of years apart knew about him, adored him and made his statue? He was an Atlantean, who lived up to 800 years and maybe much longer. He may have lived in Chichén Itzá for a few hundred years and traveled to other places and continued to live there for the rest of his life.

Chac-Mool should not be confused with Chaac?
Chac-Mool should not be confused with Chaac, *one of the leading deities in* Maya mythology *associated primarily with the phenomena of rain and thunder, and with whom they are not associated (Wikipedia Encyclopedia). As well as: Chak was the Mayan God of thunder, lightning, rain, and crops.* I do not agree with this. YES, they are associated. No doubt.
According to the encyclopedia, my PLR, my dreams, the statues of Chak Mol, many drawings and the bas-relief depicting Chaak, the God of Rain, all over the Chichén Itzá site:

YOUR ETERNAL HOLOGRAM

1. The ChacMool name came from Chaacmol. The name of the GOD of rain is Chaak.
2. At first, people called him ChacMool or Chak Mol & Thunder Paw and considered him as a normal human, except that he was as tall as an Atlantean who knew how to operate crystals, to create loud sounds, electric lightning bolts and to create thunder with rain from the clouds.
3. For this reason, people made him the GOD of RAIN and continued to call him CHAAK.
4. If you look at the profile you can obviously see the European features of the man's face. This face also reminds me of a kind of noble Texas man's profile – with a strong chin. The mask of the God of Rain, CHAAK, looks exactly like the face I saw – that of Thunder Paw and Chak Mol.

1. Each corner of Nunnery Complex building inChichén Itzá decorated with the masks of the God Chaak, God of Rain.
2. Chak Mol with European face, Tulum.

YOUTUBE: **New Giant Skulls Found!**
Here, in this film can be seen about Kukulcan. White man with a long skull on 1:55 min.
This image supports what I see in my hypnotic session.
KUKULCAN at 2:48 min. white, blonde - giant, who lived 2,000 years ago, found in Peru.
5:06 min. K.N.Makarov explains that people with long skulls may have additional intuitive abilities such as weather prediction ....this is only tip of the iceberg, please see Chapter "Egypt"

****

I was walking in Amsterdam near some souvenir shops when, suddenly, I stopped – literally frozen on the spot!I saw a boy from my own book! He had exactly the same as Chak Mol. He was a very tall and very slim man – a Nordic type of man, with blond hair and this characteristic profile.
Back to the real boy; his name is Henk. He was wearing a T-shirt with my luckiest numbers (**5 and 8**) on it!When I began talking to him, I was even more surprised.I told him that these were my lucky numbers, and he replied that it was the same for him, but that **7** and **13** were also very special numbers for him!
(Do you remember the most important Maya numbers?)Next, I said something that brought me another amazing reply.

Henk's "baby face"

"Your face looks like a baby face!" I said. He smiled and replied, "I wish you were my **mother**! Please, be my mother!" (Remember? I was the **mother of Chak Mol,** Thunder Paw in Atlantis!)

Now about his profile! His nose has a little bump on the top, it lifts slightly at the end and it's a little long! And his chin and straight forehead are the same as those of Chak Mol! Amazing! Henk's features are exactly the same as those of Chak Mol and those of his father in Atlantis! His profile is also identical to the one carved on the bas-relief in Chichén Itzá. He also looks exactly like the God of Rain! On top of this, I call him "boy" here, but he was actually 34 years old. However, he looked way too young for his age – that's how Chak Mol looked. On the photo you can see that he had a real baby face!
We liked each other from the first moment we met. He probably had different ideas, but for me it was the feeling that I had met the real Chak Mol that was important.
Well..., his looks, his youthful appearance, his numbers and his instant wish to call me "mother" made me think that maybe he was the real Chak Mol, Thunder Paw, an Atlantean man, a long time ago, in another past life. Moreover, he lives in Amsterdam, the city of crystals, diamonds, and diamond factories... Maybe Atlanteans come from Amsterdam, or some of them came to live in this part of Europe after Atlantis sank. Roads and palaces, deep in the ocean, exist near Portugal, not far from the coastline.

If I met him again, I would ask him to go to a past life regression specialist. Maybe he would go, maybe not. For me, as you remember, it was a struggle when my friend mentioned it the first time.
When I was in Chichén Itzá during the Equinox, I met a Maya man who had curly hair and blue eyes like this boy fromAmsterdam. He showed me a photo of his two daughters who had white-blond hair and blue eyes! Wow, maybe Chak Mol is the ancestor of many Maya people who live today in the Chichén Itzáarea?

Where did Chak Mol - Thunder Paw live in Chichén Itzá?

In my hypnosis session, I saw him in his big, spacious home in the area near the steam bath, which is located near the "Thousand Columns". I remember itwas a tall, high, columned house, which supported a large Maya-style roof. There was a high entrance and maybe it was the only building in the whole of Chichén Itzá city where he could go through the door. When I was in Chichén Itzá, I only saw one place that would have been suitable, which the guide called the "market", but had no roof – only big columns. I think this was his home, which later, after he left, was used as a meeting place, for meditation or maybe became a market at one point.
"Marketplace and consists of a long, stepped platform giving access to an enclosed, square patio with a central depression surrounded by tall, thin columns (supposedly the highest Mayan columns anywhere). The title Marketplace is purely hypothetical. "
http://www.geocities.com/atlantis01mx/yucatan_north/chichen_itza.htm

The "Market" or what I feel was Chak Mol's home in Chichén Itzá

Where did Chak Mol - Thunder Paw play in Chichén Itzá?

During the hypnosis sessions and in my dream I saw him playing with the warriors in the ball court. There was a ring on a wall located 8 meters from the ground, which would have been extremely high for the Maya people to reach, but just perfect for Thunder Paw.
It is known, that the ball was supposed to be driven into the rings, situated on the side panels of the stadium. Although the probability of the four kilogram ball coming into a ring situated at eight meters height seems doubtful. ("Ancient America: flight in time and prostransive. Mezoamerika" Excerpts from the book by GG Ershovoy. Un-copyrighted@Sam, 2003-2006.) [30]

The Ball Court (Juego de Pelota) - From the Pyramid of Kukulcan, head north-east to the Great Ball Court, the largest of its kind in the Maya world. There are eight other much smaller ball courts at Chichén Itzá and more in other Maya cities, but this one was deliberately built on a much grander scale than any others. The length of the playing field here is 40 feet (135m) and two 25 feet (8 m) high walls run alongside the field. Imagine, then, the significance of this giant court, where the goals are 20 feet (66m) high and the court is longer than a football pitch (Wikipedia Encyclopedia).

The Great Ball Court itself is the largest not only in Mexico, but in all of Mesoamerica.

YOUTUBE: AVATAR SVADI 4, GIANT in Chichén Itzá

****

After Chak Mol left Chichén Itzá – out of desperation – the people offered in sacrifice the best person among them – the one who won the game. His Spirit would be sent to Chak Mol, the God of Rain to ask for rain.

(This part was hard for me to type, even now – it has been months since I had my past life sessions. I found out it was my own son that had been sacrificed on that particular day. It was a very hard feeling. I remember the event very clearly. I am seeing his face right now – my tall boy with curly, black hair, dark blue eyes and a fancy tattoo on his high cheekbone.)

Group of people which stay exactly near the ring

How can it be possible that Atlanteans lived in Mexico before?

Retrieved from:http://en.wikipedia.org/wiki/Gene_Matlock

More than 25,000 books, plus countless other articles have been written about a fabled confederation of city-states known as Atlantis. If it really did exist, where was it located? Does anyone have valid evidence of its existence, artifacts and other remnants? According to historian, archaeologist, educator and **linguist Gene D. Matlock***, both questions can easily be answered: Only Mexico is*

named Atlan; Itlan; Otlan; Tlan; Tollan, etc. No other nation on earth can make that claim. Since this is the case and every nation on earth is what it is, Atlantis is Atlantis! [4]
He might be quite convinced that ancient cities from the Mexican gulf to Tenochtitlan are related to some Atl'epec, Tolan, A-tolan and other TLAN like cities.
Quote: "Should we continue our fun guessing games about Atlantis for another few millenniums? Or should we confidently begin our search for the submerged half of Atlantis from Atl'epec's (Mexico's) southeast coast? Will the ruins that we'll surely find be those of the real Atlantis?" He believes we should be conducting the search for Atlantis in the **Yucatan region of Mexico.**

This is the exact place where I found Chak Mol!
Chichén Itzá is located in Yucatan! When I sent a letter to Gene Matlock about my discovery regarding Chak Mol, an Atlantean man, he was very happy that it supported his theory absolutely!

Gene D. Matlock cites place names as one of the compelling proofs.
He also cites an ancient, spiral-shaped harbor with high banks or dikes lining the channels that once existed near San Lorenzo Tenochtitl' Mexico. This layout is very much like that described by Plato for Atlantis's great port city.

****

Part 3

Atlantis

Archeology, history or linguistics is not my profession or interest in life.

What happened during my first reading was suddenly and absolutely unpredictable. Nor me, nor Di Cherry, no one expected such a deep, serious development from just one dream and from the chain of past life regression sessions. After many advices, I agreed to write this book. I never wrote a book before, and English is not my first language. So I tried to do this as concisely as possible, just to deliver the main information I got to people. Because all of this happened so suddenly, it put a hold on my life right now...
For the first few months, I tried, with purpose, to keep my channel free of any information about ancient Mexico, to avoid interrupting or influencing the information stream I received directly through the hypnosis sessions.
I don't have a goal to start studying Atlantis either. Hundreds of books were written about it already. If you will start read about Atlantis from Wikipedia, you will find that all of the facts you read there exist in my dreams and PLR as a reflection of my past life in Atlantis. I guess I don't need to study Atlantis, this was my previous life, it was lived, and I need to concentrate now on this present life and on my future. http://en.wikipedia.org/wiki/Atlantis

The things I have experienced in thousands of dreams are very clear, with many details. I understand now that my dreams "are not fairy-tales". They are real. And there are items which Atlantis people had, like TV screens, the size of an entire wall, modern technology, and so on. Someone just told me that this is not a dream, but an astral projection (or astral travel). I don't know the terms people use to describe this kind of things in English.
Anyway, according to these dreams, I was like all Atlanteans, very tall, living in a big, spherical palace, in a huge crystal pyramid, using crystal energy for many purposes, including healing, meditation, psychic development or increasing mental capacity.

Astral Voyage

As she sleeps, she dreams she's floating among the stars.
Her silken sheets become clouds, and the clouds contain the spirits of the heavens.
Below her, great galleons sail majestically on the currents of space to explore the universe.[21]

I saw examples of dematerialization and transport of objects, transformation pictures and something allowed us to see movies like on a real TV. I had devices, which allowed me to see far away and into the near future, travel in space at very high speeds, impossible for us to reach with today's technology. It was communication with non-human intelligences and all kinds of spirits and mind-travels to other dimensions. All of this was thousands of years ago in my past life as an Atlantean.

As a scientist myself, I will be happy to help those scientists who try to solve the puzzle about ancient Mexico and Atlantis. I am willing to continue my hypnosis sessions and answer any questions they would have for me.

So who were the Atlanteans and how did they live?

The following information has been gathered from various sources for a very brief introduction. I recommend that you read the original documents for more in-depth information (linked at the end of the book).

---

[21] © Josephine Wall. All Rights Reserved www.josephinewall.com

The original Atlanteans were of extra-terrestrial origin and came to earth over 50 thousand years ago. They were of human shape, but not modern earth humans as we are. They were very tall and fair skinned* and probably originated from the Lyrian star system. They are also known as the Elohim or Annunaki and their story is hidden in the texts of Genesis. They had life spans of around 800 years and are known in some texts as 'the tall ones'. Most all ancient civilizations believed in the Titans, the race of giant humans that inhabited Earth long ago. Different races knew them by different names. These 7 to 12 foot humanoids were thought to be legendary until the excavation of over a dozen skeletons 8 to 12 feet tall, around the world, shocked archaeologists.

The early Atlanteans were peaceful people. As they developed more physical material bodies, they used the crystal to rejuvenate their bodies and were able to live hundreds of years while maintaining a youthful appearance.

Here little bit about Atlantean crystals

Atlantean crystals were natural forms, but their growths were speeded up. Some specimens of clear quartz were produced to almost 25 feet high and 10 feet in diameter, had 12 sides and were used for storing and transmitting power. Small crystals, four to five feet high were infused with different colors, and had a varied number of facets, to be used for different purposes, such as healing, meditation, psychic development, increasing mental capacity, communications, powering generators, dematerialization, and transport of objects, magnetic force fields, and travel at speeds undreamed of by our culture today.
A number of crystals were shaped into inverted pyramids, with four to six sides, were infused with various shades of pink or rose, which created a light beam for surgery, by changing molecular structure, and for soothing pain, particularly in the delicate areas of the brain, the eyes, the heart and reproductive organs. Gold or yellow crystals changed colors to deeper hues in the presence of disease or bodily vibrational disorders. Ruby and purple stones helped cure emotional and spiritual problems; and black crystals, no longer in existence, were powerful protectors.

For general rejuvenation and a return of vitality the ancient Atlanteans periodically meditated 15 to 20 minutes inside a circle of 6, 11, 22 or 24 stones of different types, holding a clear quartz in their hands, which acted as a control and focalized.

All these various crystals received their power from a variety of sources, including the Sun, the Earth's energy grid system, or from each other. The larger stones, called Fire Crystals, were the central receiving and broadcasting stations, while others acted as receivers for individual cities, buildings, vehicles and homes. On a higher spiritual level, rooms made of crystals were places where the Initiates left their bodies in the Final Transcendence, often never to return.

In the modern Bermuda Triangle, on the ocean bottom where the ruins of Atlantis now exist, the energy build-up in the sunken and damaged Fire Crystals can periodically trigger dematerializations of anything in the area. One of the most detailed descriptions of the Atlantean use of a mysterious instrument called the Great Crystal was given by Edgar Cayce, who mentioned it many times. The crystal, he said was housed in a special building oval in shape, with a dome that could be rolled back, exposing the Crystal to the light of the sun, moon and stars at the most favorable time. The Crystal itself, which Cayce also called the Tuaoi Stone, or Firestone, was huge in size, cylindrical in length, and prismatic in shape, cut with six sides. Atop the crystal was a moveable capstone, used to both concentrate incoming rays of energy, and to direct currents to various parts of the Atlantean countryside.

Later the Crystal was put to other uses. Currents of energy were transmitted throughout the land, like radio waves, and powered by these, crafts and vehicles traversed the land, through the sky and under the sea at the speed of sound. By utilization of other currents originating from the Crystal, the Atlanteans were also able to transmit over great distances the human voice, and pictures, like modern television. In the same manner, even heat and light could be directed to specific buildings or open arenas, giving illumination and warmth by seemingly invisible means.

The word pyramid is derived from the Greek words PYRAMIS and PYRAMIDOS. The word Pyramidos has been translated as "Fire In The Middle"...ancient Khemitians used the term PR.NTR, Per-Neter, for pyramid. In alignment with the indigenous tradition, we use the interpretation "House of Nature, House of Energy" for Per-Neter. One of the main purposes of the Great Per-Neter was to generate, transform, and transmit energy. The Indigenous Wisdom Keepers of Egypt have provided us a concrete paradigm to support the power plant theory of Christopher Dunn. Indeed, if we support Dunn's ideas that the energy reactions in the Great Pyramid took place in the so-called Queen's and King's Chambers, then certainly it was Fire In The Middle.

Dream # 19
Ruby Emerald, February 11, 1988

I remember now the other thing... There is a huge living space. I saw something like that in some Hollywood-shooting sets. And in this space, there is a huge ruby crystal, and she is standing on top – this woman... It is like a cathedral and a hall with the wall which repeated the form of a crystal. There was an enormous big crystal in the middle of a circle. And this crystal was surrounded with a liquid, but this is not water. The walls are black (dark) inside; there is nothing there, not a thing, no entrance or exit. In the middle, there is a huge circle, surrounded by high molded, synthetic barrier (colloid), quite accurately placed. Inside, there is a cave with water, but it is not water, and on it, there is a Bordeaux-red, huge, precious stone, floating, very bright, succulent. "Emerald" – the pronouncing of the word becomes this stone. Bright, cherry color. Deep, bright edges. The woman is standing on the top of the stone. **I look from above, like a huge person. The woman is standing like little Thumbelina**, dressed in white. The fabric of her dress runs down in waves, and it seems there is a shining pattern... It is not water, not steam... It is a pool filled with some substance. It is thick like quicksilver, light as steam, heavy – everything is covered with it, the pool is full, a lot of it. But the crystal is not covered, all its facets meet on top, and there is this beauty, the one that gave away the belt and the sheath in my other dream, and she looks up, she aims from the top of her head, like a ray – up, everything in her is aiming just there. The strange substance around her, not water, it slightly reminds me of slime, when some energy was coiling around my arms, and something was humming, I remember now! I know – it was the product of those creatures. There was a lot of it then! I know this strange substance... It is something in between, colloid... It is one of the components....

Dream # 20
Woman on a Red Crystal, September 25, 1994

I had another dream about the same big, red crystal.

At the beginning, I saw a huge hall. There was a mount at the bottom, like a sphere. It was a hemisphere, and the rays were coming out of it in all directions. The top is cut off. On the top of it, there was a woman standing. From above she looked like a dot from far away, but I knew it was a woman. The surface of this mount was changing – it became like Science World building in Vancouver, rising up in some places, bending inside in others, and it was opening. It turned into a red crystal. The red crystal came out and the light began to grow. The entire floor was flooded with gold.

YOUR ETERNAL HOLOGRAM

© Josephine Wall. All Rights Reserved. www.josephinewall.com

Dream # 21
The Lilac World, March 4, 2001

I saw a big crystal, and right after that, a big opened book, its pages were flickering, on one of them there were fragments of the future, which already happened now. On the side of the book there was a long dark hose, like on the paintings of Brueghel (or Bosch), like a tunnel.[22] I was flying through it for a long time, swaying like seaweeds. Then I saw something – it is very, very far from here. The lilac Sun, twisted protuberances, it looked like what we see during an eclipse, when one disc covers another light disc. But here the covering disc was also of lilac color, darker. On the left there was a crystal pyramid, with ledges, but the top was sharp as a pin. Later on, I saw it from above – all of the pyramids were sitting on a big crystal cupola, like a hemisphere. And above this cupola – there were blue and yellow colors. Very strong blue... There was also an emerald, but it was transparent, crystal-like. It was called AIUM ... OUM.

In this dream "book", there was a device, a real mirror to see the future. It was like the one in the children's fairy-tale, the queen who looks into her magic mirror, which tells her the future. And this "long dark hose, like on the paintings of Brueghel (or Bosch), like a tunnel" is a real STARGATE

[22] This is worm-hole, through which I am traveling in the Universe.

through which I always travel far away to the Universe. Very fast – almost instantly. In this dream I visited again the same planet, which I visited many times in my other dreams and where I met the man-lizard numerous times. (Dream # 50 Kukulcan (Human-Lizard), September 19, 1991)

Dream # 22
The Woman-Double and a Wise Man, July 8, 1994

At the beginning I was with this person – a wise man. I had a talk with him, and I went out. He was a wise man. He was as wise as eternity. I lived with him. There was nobody else, only inconspicuous servants.
In front of me, on the table probably, was a little dancing dragon. He was about 12 to 13 cm high, bright green, standing on his hind legs, like a little person. His miniscule wings were open, his arms had outgrowing, membranous wings that were raised (like a bird flapping its wings) and his legs were like the Indian figure of the six-armed Shiva, with a leg raised to the knee. He was dancing and singing with a human voice, "Where is my *van*? Where is my *van*? Where is it, my *van*?!" I was feeling excited, in a ritualistic way toward him, but it seemed to be a normal everyday thing – like the queen in the children's fairy-tale, who looks into her magic mirror, which tells her the future, but she uses it very often. On the other hand, a part of my current reality was reasoning – theoretically a lizard can't have wings. According to Darwin's theory, at the beginning it came from water, then turned into a lizard, then it climbed a tree, and got his wings later. Yet, when it was dancing, you could see every little green scale, very beautiful. Then I made an interesting move, like a figure eight with my hand, and a cup and ketchup appeared. I took the bottle and poured the tomato-bright ketchup into the cup...
(That's an example of materialization, I guess. This unusual move occurs very often in the dreams of Atlantis. I even draw how I move my hand.)

I looked directly in front of me – outside the building they are moving towards us – I don't know how to call them – maybe students, listeners, or colleagues – I don't know how to describe them... This was some kind of a chamber, a house, cool and dim inside. One part of it led onto a semi-circular veranda. The wise man was sitting in the center, in a hollow. These students came in and sat down in a semi-circle (the wise man was sitting in one part of the circle, and they were sitting in the other part – in a semicircle, so the crystals were around them at the back). I saw one of them – I recognized him immediately. He was clean-shaven; he had a strong face with regular features, a round skull, with beautiful ears – all strong and healthy, much like Buddha – everything roundish and pleasant. He came in and sat down with the others. The wise man, my host, started to say something. And I knew that it was time for me to go. I took a wide ribbon of red and white stripes on the left of me.
It seemed that there were **even three ribbons, red on the sides and white inside***. I was carrying it with stretched-out arms – I did not touch it with my fingers or palms – it was lying on my wrists, straightened. I brought it to him, came behind him and started to tie it up around his head in the same rigid way. In the first moment, when I started doing it – some part of him, which was not accepting it, resisted – like hot fudge poured on ice-cream – it was resisting, and then it broke, fell apart. You could not see it.
And the internal content, which was under this shell, accepted it with gratitude; it was like an honor for him. I wrapped it around his head, and it stuck to his head by itself. Then I went around these chambers, not the outside, not in the house – I came into a big hall. The hall was huge, like a cathedral, maybe the whole city could be placed within it. Above it, there was a cupola – also huge (a SPHERE). Inside the hall there was a gallery, like in China in the Princess Tsi-Si garden.

© Josephine Wall. All Rights Reserved. www.josephinewall.com

There were tombstones in the gallery – one after another, I think there were five of them. I remember how I was standing in the center of the circular hall and I was looking at the gallery. A crowd of women was walking towards me, wearing some Greek-like robes – with many folds, even their faces seemed to be covered with folds. I knew that they were weepers. They were standing near the last burial place. I knew that there was a teenage girl buried there, she died at the age of 14. She did not die from some disease or violence, but by the law of the cosmos. And they knew it – those priests, or magicians. Everything was happening without any sound. In that dream only the dragon was saying something – and just this one phrase. *They* rarely speak in my dreams. I went behind them. **I was walking in a spiral, snail-like. But when I got behind them, I was my double, I saw myself, the other one, who stayed in the same place, and the other one saw this one, too.** It was similar to the situation when I was wrapping the ribbon on that student. There was a feeling that my ancestors – my lineage – were lying in those tombs. Or that I was there myself, as if I was dead and then being born again. These magicians knew that the same spirit is born and dies, and it comes to them. Right after this, the action moved into another hall. There were enormous tables; full of sweet and beautiful, refined and decorated ice-cream, cakes, creams, fruit, peaches, grapes. These tables replicated the shape of the rooms within this big hall. They were semi-circular, following the curves of the walls. And I knew that it took the whole day to put all this here, to lay the tables, and the feast was going to start soon. In one place, I noticed some lit candles – 25 of them, I inhaled and blew them out. Then I went through all of these halls – the last servants were leaving already. All this happened before dawn. When I was leaving the last hall, on the steps of the last hall, the ageing one gave me a cup, in which there was something lumpy – it looked golden, whipped, like a big gold nugget, I could hardly hold it...

*" **three ribbons, red on the sides and white inside**" repeated in my next 2 lives, as an Amelia and Julia, see next Chapter Amelia return.

In this next dream you can see how fragile this Atlantis people, who come to the Earth from Heaven were. They were like angels – very clean, pure, tall and slim. Their body was not yet really developed physically, material. There was an extremely big distance between them and the people on Earth. Atlantis people had very light spirit, very Peaceful – it was human-angel kind of spirit – which, I guess, arrived from Heaven.

Dream # 23
The City Of Crystal Pyramids, June 13, 1993

I lived in some town, in a place with pyramids – such splendid houses, like crystal pyramids. I lived in a very high pyramid; all of them were like the pyramids in Egypt. There were two more pyramids side by side with it. In my pyramid there was a woman, Nelia, she was noble, with ruffles, laces all over, white, soft, lacy, sublime. And there was another white woman with very fine features, white, light hair, thin. She was also wearing laces, some flowers. All this was very beautiful, noble, and they all were representing purity. And they all were dazzling, radiating light. In one such day, I went to visit my friends. My friends were Japanese; they also lived in such pyramids, but theirs was smaller, and there were only Japanese people there. My friend, a Japanese, and I had a feeling that I knew him for a long-long time, somehow, although I saw him for the first time in my dream. And everything in their place was like the Virgo sign – clean, modest, and very correct. Every movement, every look, even walking, every object, everything was based on some kind of ritual, some order, conditionality – sparkling, light and serene. I was visiting this Japanese, entered some room, and had a kind of vision – as if you turn on a TV crystal and watch what is happening to these pyramids, where we lived (if it was a town, then there should have been other pyramids). It was not the city exactly; there was nothing between the pyramids, no cars, no ground, no top or bottom, as if they were hanging in mid-air. And I don't remember seeing the sky there either. And now this vision... I meditated from time to time in there, in a pyramid; maybe meditating in this Japanese room was best since it was so impeccably clean and orderly, or quiet. I knew that it was my room, in their home. And so, one room turned into a screen, like in a cinema – every wall turned into a screen. I saw a prairie-like desert, and huge crowds of horrible people coming from there, a terrible number of people, like a herd of sheep, head to head. It looked like termites running in the prairies, eating everything on their way. They ate all the animals, insects, grass – or maybe like locusts. And they were approaching, approaching... I told them, that they are coming for us, "they will be here soon..."

The crystal town was separated from the prairies by a road, and I saw how they were approaching the place where these pyramids were standing, from far in the distance. I saw them from where I was standing in the Japanese pyramid. Our town was separated by this road from the prairies, and there was a feeling, that they would never be able to cross this road, never, ever. But they were coming from this large steppe in a bug-like, black crowd, thick as foam. But they were very close to the road and just near the base of the pyramids.[23] There are only bases of pyramids, and they are mounting very high... I woke up from this vision and told them all about it. Then I went back to my pyramid, maybe by crystal passing, or through a tube. I told them, that "they" will come for us soon, something very horrible. And we started preparing for it. But preparing did not mean doing something, just understanding with our minds, why this is happening, why this herd is moving, and what will happen

---

[23] I decided to click on "*Japan pyramid*" on Google – what I found was astonishing! "One of the greatest discoveries in the history of archaeology was made last summer, off Japan. The monument is 600ft wide and 90ft high and has been dated to at least 8,000 BC. The oldest pyramid in Egypt, the Step Pyramid at Saqqara, was constructed more than 5,000 years later.
Robert Schoch, professor of geology at Boston University, dived at the site last month. "It basically looks like a series of huge steps, each about a meter high." And I know why these steps are so big! Because according to this dream, we were 8 meters tall!

to it afterwards. Actually, it could not harm or damage any of the pyramids – nothing. But it was very unpleasant.

When the morning came, we went to meet this crazy crowd. We descended to the ground, stood up in a row, on the steps, like in the amphitheater in Roman cities, like in a circus. Everybody came out from different pyramids and everyone stood on their terraces. And then I came out from far, far away, down the crystal steps. They all turned their heads and were looking at me. I was descending the steps, and two of them followed me, her, and the other one. All those around me, they were not people, not humans. In these pyramids everything was sublime, pure and beautiful, majestic, crystal-clear, unusual, pure, pure. Not just cloudless, but airless, lighter than air. Such lightness – even the air was heavier than everything there. On the other hand, it was such horror – the enormous number of people that came together, were crowding near this road, and they were arguing with each other, I saw all their faces. The moment I came down, when all of them approached this road, they stopped. They could not cross it. But everyone around me started to tell me... They were whispering to me, strange, right in my ear I heard whispers from one, from the other; from my ... colleagues ... servants ... I don't know how to define them. But could they be court servants? It looked like that.

And they were saying, "Look, look, what a horror, what they are doing." It was such a crystal-clear whispering – like the little bells ringing, such strange voices – at that moment I heard their voices, all of them, so unusual, like little bells, or crystals, as if a crowd of elves with toy-like unspecific voices was babbling in my ears. "Look, what a horrible thing," they were describing what the others were doing, but could not pronounce the words. I see – the horror, just at the very edge there, in the crowd, there is an orgy, right on the street, among other people, on the ground, on the other side of the road, where the ground is dirty, dusty, right there. And there is a barren steppe, no grass, no birds, only yellow-gray dust. They are doing it just on the roadside, where everyone could see them, how they are doing it, the terrible ones. They are all so rude, disgusting, and odious. They scream, yell, and squeal. The orgy was started by black people, but there were people of all nationalities. In our life we watch horrors on TV sometimes... But here they all came together only to demonstrate their atrocities all at once. **They stopped near the road, but there is a feeling, that a transparent wall had been erected in front of them, and they could not get through it.** Even their screams could not be heard. We just saw it. They are not ashamed of each other. It was like they were victimizing, killing each other, swearing... I don't remember. It seems that something happened in the end, I don't remember what followed... It was disastrous, horrible, an outrageous impression.

All my life I lived in this world and learned about it gradually, one thing after another. I met bad people in life, in the movies. And I learned about it slowly, got used to it; I did not look at it from the outside, and today it was such a strong contrast between good and bad, like black and white, Earth and Heaven. I can't find a comparison. It was just wild. In this crystal city we were not just humans, but god-like people and the others were – it feels wrong to call them animals – something like devils, there is no name for them...

Dream # 24
I was Very Thin and Extremely Tall, February 11, 1997

In my dream you hold me. I was the size of a little baby, such a small size, fitting in your hands. But I am very, very tall... I see myself from the side. I am very thin, legs stretching far to the ground, wearing a white, transparent dress... It was my real appearance, the way I looked at that time. I am with you; we are in the big hall somewhere far, far in the Universe. And there, different Spirits have gathered. It was an enormous huge hall, a ball-room. I am a tall, thin figure dressed in white. If I were a person, a human being, I would be probably three-meters tall or more which made me look even thinner than I was. And I did not have weight. Weight did not exist – it looked like we were only souls in that dream, at that moment.

However, this was not a dream. It was some kind of special, very real – another reality – a special condition. It felt as if I was going through deep water; if you try to talk, for example, it is very difficult.
We went there from time to time. We know this place and what it is all about. I go there often while I am sleeping, in this strange condition. And *you* were in the middle of a hall. *You* held me. I was very, very light and very-very tall.
I cannot see these *Spirits* directly. They speak about me, discuss my snow-white clothes. It was multilayered, made of the thinnest possible fabric, pure, shimmering fabric. I cannot hear what they say. They are all around me, looking at me and talking about me. I can see only myself from the side. It's a double sensation. The first sensation; I see you and me from the side, and at the same time, I feel myself in *your* hands and how I hold your hand, I even feel the softness of your skin on your neck.

This is all so real... Then you left, and carried me out of that room and out of that space. I asked you,

"What did they spoke about?" You told me that they spoke about my dress. Somehow, I was sleeping there.

When I was there I felt everything, but I did not understand anything, nothing made sense. We came out and into another space. There I could understand and talk to you already, no more of that influence. We were in such a strange magic world!
*"**layers of fabric**" in Spirit world was structure of my Spirit...

I was very thin and extremely tall

Dream # 25
History – Pyramid in A Pyramid (Or Maybe in the Sphere), August 30, 1994

It is the beginning of a school year now. I always liked it – the beginning of classes, I would like to start learning something somewhere. I see some uncertain crowd. They are waiting for something. They are standing in front of a strange building. I am among them. I know that now there will be information of the past of humanity in the different cells of this construction (building), all divided in time periods. In every cell, there is a piece of information for a certain period of time. I knew approximately what I wanted – I had some expectations – what period of time I needed. But before everything started, I decided very quickly to capture all this construction with my eyes. It was important to understand it as a whole – as usual when you study something as a whole – you look at it in general, and then it is easier to understand the details, particularities – like a tree, the trunk, the branches, etc. The entrance of the building was an archway, and then dark corridors, where you should choose your particular space, the cell, using your sense of smell, like a dog – using your instincts. But I did not go inside, I ran around the building. When I had gone around in one direction I retraced my steps in the other direction – I was really surprised, shaken.

THERE WERE HUGE SPHERES – LIKE HEMISPHERES – ONE WITHIN ANOTHER. They were just huge. And I had to race around them very rapidly. They were on the side, and when I was rushing by, I wanted to see what was inside them. I had special eyesight. The walls became transparent – **I was really surprised. Inside of this construction made of spheres – there were similar construction of spheres, only of smaller size, like a pyramid in a pyramid, like matryoshka dolls. They were put one inside the other and matched each other. You cannot imagine this – it was an endless construction.** Then I returned. I entered the building. Intuitively, I got into that same space, in the time period I needed. Inside, there was some sort of teacher, even several of them. I asked a question. But there was a feeling, they reminded me somehow of the things I knew myself some time ago, maybe even better than the teachers did. And I started to recollect things gradually, and even said something that was interesting to them...

**Dream # 26
Hundreds of Followers. Rubies, November 8, 2003**

There were different dreams, but there was something similar in each dream. All the air, all the space surrounding me – as far as I could see – was made of the **finest gold threads.** One moment I was in the mountains. But sometimes these threads, like seaweed, were loose, feeling free; they did not cross each other, like cobwebs, they shone, but did not entangle. In one of the fragments of my dream, in those threads, there were bundles of them, thin, star-shaped, but still there was no entangling. They were arranged in a beautiful way, equidistant from each other and from me.[24] I was walking, surrounded by followers. At one moment it seemed to me, that the followers disappeared, and I was surrounded by these little stars. Once I was walking in the mountains, in a valley, by a wide road. I could see the valleys down there from above, the followers were walking behind me – they were many – a hundred, two hundred, three... Usually when people, a crowd, follow you, it is hard to focus, or even understand where you are going – it is overwhelming. But this crowd was light, like specks of dust flying behind a bird captured by the wind. They reacted to my every word, my thoughts. It also looked like the fish in water – all of them turned at the same time. These people were very light. You could not hear them – how they walked, talked, how they thought. As if they were flying one meter above the ground. Floating.

Once we approached a place, where there had to be a bathyscaphe, shaped like a rugby ball, but the size of a huge trolleybus. We were walking by this place. On our way a construction emerged, made of thin wooden sticks, like bamboo scaffolding, or a huge warehouse made of freshly whittled sticks, which were all around; it smelled good, but we could not pass through. There were very many of them, like matches. But we knew that this was the place where the bathyscaphe should be. When we entered the warehouse, I knew, from where the bathyscaphe would emerge, through which wall it

---

[24]   It looks like the Maya Priest and the Queen of Atlantis had the ability to see these "gold strings" which was created by particles! This occurrence was repeated in my many dreams. In this book, you will find few more. Please see YouTube.

would enter. In the middle there were some strange constructions, very fine, and there were others; something like chairs. And I thought that they should be put away along the walls. It came to me instantly. My followers, like little fish, put everything in place in one moment; they flew to the walls. It was very strange, very swiftly done, like a school of fish moving effortlessly through the water. I saw the owner of this thing; he shook his head and expressed surprise at the superb cohesion of our team. He was a strange, tall, old man, like the ones we see on icons in a church, with a halo, a long face, a thin mouth and nose, like an iconic, perfect image. After that, I made an effort of some sort, and the bathyscaphe began to appear – not inside, but in front of the entrance of the warehouse (the entrance on the other side), in order not to break anything.

Probably we flew a bit farther in the bathyscaphe. It was a big tube. We entered it and did not see the view. Then we turned up in a strange place. It was a room, where there was a woman; she was selling odd things, rubies. My followers stood up along the walls in one line in the direction of the entrance. I passed them by. I entered the place and saw the rubies lying there, big stones, egg-shaped, flat, the size and form of those found by Indiana Jones (when they were shining together). I stopped, surprised. It was as thick as honey, red wine, dark, and in the inside there was a deep cherry light. It was of a tremendously rich color. There were about eight of them, and I needed them desperately – we came just for them. In real life the surface of a ruby is like glass, but in this case, the surface was lusterless (the glass was cheap!).

I think that all the polished stones lack something. The stone develops as it should be! I feel that crystals are like animals. Faceting them is like performing surgery on a newborn baby. It is best never to touch a gemstone. The surface of the stone protects its qualities. They should never be polished! (There is a connection between the shape, texture and energy of a crystal, same with strange square-round shape.)

There was a feeling that this woman looked like the huge one, who was standing in the other dream, the natural one, in national clothes, and like Montaha in "The Music of Andes". Such a woman will always look as a naïve, awkward person among people ... She was standing and waiting for me, in order to give me the necklace made of these stones. This necklace – as they would say here – an antique one – was very well structured, double layered. The stones were hanging down to my navel, and the second layer was made of metal and between the layers there was a connection – a very complex design, like letters, or signs. At breast level, there was a huge crescent of stones and signs. I took it and said that I also needed the stones that were lying there. And she said that I should not refuse me those stones, that I should take them (usually I take just one thing). The stones in the necklace were smaller, but there were more of them and they were facetted. But the other ones were huge... They put the necklace on me. But I also took the other stones. I wanted them. I saw those golden threads everywhere. At the same time I had a feeling of bliss. We were in the mountains. It was a bivouac.
My child appeared near me. He approached me, stopped, and stood erect. I asked him something, he answered. It was absolutely incomprehensible. I had a feeling that he was answering with his mind and I asked the question with my mind. And he was answering like an adult, clever person, as an equal. And this contradiction gave me a feeling that he could do everything and would do it. And he fell down flat, and I realized that I was silly, that he was still small in real life. He hurt his forehead a little. But he did not cry – no sound at all. Then I understood that it was my fault that he fell down, that I expected him to be an adult. And I took his little feet and started putting on sandals on his plump feet. I still have the feel of his skin. I put the sandals on him, and he started walking... In the end – I have a cup and a saucer in my hands (the cup seemed to be stuck to the saucer). It's made of very thin china, fine design and form. I remembered that at one point, all my followers received similar finest crystal cups, as thin as eggshells, as a result of our quest. I remembered that during our quest everyone was drinking from these cups – something like golden, transparent dew...

One scene was repeated several times. I opened the door from the room to the street. And some wild creatures, like wet, little dogs wanted to rush into the place where we were sitting. I allowed one of them to enter. The door was transparent. Behind it there were several of those frenzied, fluffy and incomprehensible creatures. I separated this one. The wet, screaming and wild one, I left behind the door, and let the amorphous one in. Then something transparent, quiet, came out of him, floated out... First, it hit me on the right hip when it wanted to rush in.

Yesterday, when we were at the beach and we were talking about my talents, which should be developed, I felt like this **creature** plopped into me; it was running wild like unbridled passion **with wet black fluffy fur...** And I thought that if I should develop my talents, then I would know how to describe it.

*All the air, all the space surrounding me – as far as I could see – was made of the finest gold threads. YOUTUBE: Parallel Universes [1/5] → *Matter emanating from particle strings discovered recently, but I saw it since I was little child.*

****

Bruce Moen describes "heaven" in his book as a place where people go after death. There, non-human intelligences from other areas of our physical universe, other universes and other dimensions can be found, and communication with them is possible. By Bruce Moen © 1999 www.afterlife-knowledge.com [3] According to my dreams during my life as an Atlantean, I traveled to the Universe and meet these spirits. (See Chapter: Kukulcan).

****

If I were to interpret the word "**Crystal**", to me it would mean a "pyramid with fire inside". I know; I always feel this power. In my present life it is like an echo from the past: From my past life in Atlantis I felt the importance of crystals with energy inside them.

1. I was working with a team of scientists who made numerous patterns with laser technology. I have a patent in X-ray technology.

2. From a young age I was attracted to crystals. I started to "grow" them often while I was of school, age from 12 to 16 years old. They were turquoise, orange, green colors crystals from 10 to 14 cm in diameter. I gave them to people and, at the time, I felt that those crystals were the best possible presents. Kids in school called me "Diamond" because I always said that diamonds were the most perfect, organized crystals.

3. My first part-time babysitter was a woman, who was living at the Tsar's palace during her youth. She was issued from a rich, high society family, part German and part Russian. She was a "demoiselle de compagnie" (a young lady keeping company) to the tsar's daughters. Her name was Barbara Semeonovna. She told me many interesting stories about the daily life of the Russian Emperor's family, especially about his daughters and what kind of entertainment they had. Most memorable for me was her story of a presentation of fakirs and magicians from India who showed many amazing tricks of prestidigitation. She had an astonishing and very valuable collection of stones from her family. She managed to save it during the communist era and through her life, until an advanced age. In her collection, there were big ruby crystals, emeralds, opals and many others, including diamonds. My favorites were two of them: one huge, blue sapphire, which had a star inside it from the reflection of shiny rays, and a large alexandrite, which changed color during the day from light-green, blue in the morning to pink at noon, and was always dark violet

with purple flashes at night under artificial lights. I could spend hours listening to her stories about each of these stones, holding them in my hands.

4. For years now, I have been in "close relationship" with my top-quality, huge, quartz crystal, which cost me a fortune. It is a big, round ball.

5. The name of my company is "Diamond Star" and it bears the symbol of a diamond with rays going through it.

6. With the help of the most advanced latest technology I can createabsolutely unique, astonishing plants. It can be a collection of the 30 most common plants people used in agriculture on our planet today. First, their seeds can be saved, kept alive, in perfect condition and ready to start growing after 5 and even 8 or 10 years! Second, all of these plants can grow in a totally new environment; for example in sudden droughts, or much higher temperature, chemical problems, or nutrition deficit or different soil or something else.With this technology possible send a signal to the plants and teach them what to do, when their environment will change. With climate-changing problems on our planet, this technology is priceless. This can really save the world and in case of sudden climate hazard we will have strong plants on which we will survive and will reap great harvest.

"On the approach of a dire winter, which is to destroy every living creature, Yima, being advised by Ahura, builds a Vara to keep there the seeds of every kind of animals and plants, and the blessed live there a most happy life under his rule.Thither thou shalt bring the seeds of every kind of tree, of the greatest, best, and finest kinds on this earth; thither thou shalt bring the seeds of every kind of fruit, the fullest of food and sweetest of odour. All those seeds shalt thou bring, two of every kind, to be kept inexhaustible there, so long as those men shall stay in the Vara." Excerpt from Zend Avesta, Iranian Bible. http://en.wikipedia.org/wiki/Avesta

7. When I was a Maya Priest, I studied the sounds of the rocks. The rocks from the underground caves were made of stalactites and had an inner crystal structure. This is why they make this amazing sound. Maybe when I found my rock, which also has an inner crystal structure my Spirit felt and read information, which was written in it a long time ago, and recognized this rock through these characteristics.

8. It was astonishing to me to see the diamond collection named the "Almaz fund" at the Kremlin in the diamond museum. There were some of the biggest, best quality diamonds in the world in the collection. I befriended the director and always gave him a little present just to have the possibility to go inside, near these perfect, fabulous, rare stones. It was like a magnet to me. I was always there, until the last minute, until the exhibition closed. I feel this special energy from them and I talk to them in my dreams. It was the most important place in the whole universe for me in those years.

You could not just buy a ticket and go to see the exhibit; you had to wait a long time to receive a special permit to enter the museum. Only a very small number of people were allowed to be inside at once. I remember, near each window, there were guards in black suits watching the displays and the visitors.

9. I studied everything possible (and impossible) about diamonds. I started working with diamond-cutting factories, stores and even spent a few years preparing a diamond company for the stock market in London. Doctor in geology, Bakirov A.G. studied healing and the protecting ability at the cell level of minerals, crystals and rocks. He found the existence of strong energy information-connection between human and minerals. According to his research, rocks have

some form of consciousness. Just the fact that the life-span of the rocks is much longer than that of humans and their evolution was complete before ours, gives the possibility of effective communication between minerals and bio-organism.

Crystals grow like a tree, but much slower. They have a life span of thousands of years. How crystals are born, and start forming, is still a mystery to the scientists. They have an external energy cover, same amount of aura layers as all living organisms on Earth. In a crystal structure there are slow waves of atoms, running electrons, and ions, if another element is included. They display inside "movements" of life such as breathing in and out. Scientists find that just one breath is necessary over a few days to a few weeks for the crystal to survive. Each beat of its "heart" lasts for one day. Scientists found that smaller quartz crystals breathe faster than bigger ones. Rubies, for example, send "bursts" of energy from the center of the crystal to its perimeter and once the energy trade-flow is complete, the beams return to the center. Diamonds have two flows of energy: one is similar to a breath intake of energy, which comes from outside, and the second one, which flows from the center, looks like a "bouquet" of solid strong light-beams.

For Maya people, quartz and amethysts were symbols of creation and cosmos; they saw the reflection of the Universe in them with all its amazing events. In Yucatan, the modern shaman still uses the "*san tun*"("shiny priceless stone")for healing and prediction purposes. The ancient shaman used crystals as a door into another reality world. Through this door, the shaman went to the God of the Moon or to the God of Jaguar and asked information about the past and the future, or even returned his Soul to a sick, dying patient. They also used mountain quartz for diagnostic purposes, as a healing power, to gain wisdom, and some say, to have the magic power of flying through the air.

According to Edgar Cayce, my dreams, and hypnosis sessions, the Atlantis people lived long lives, up to 800 or 1000 years. Maybe it was because of their relationship with crystal energy? Perhaps it was because they used crystals, the rocks of longevity to restore health and solve emotional problems that they were able to live hundreds of years while maintaining a youthful appearance.

YOUTUBE:
Spontaneous DNA, The Rapture, and The Rise to Fourth Density
Vortex Energy Part 2 of 22 Vibration and the Secret of Healing
Vortex Energy Part3 How the Human TACHION light field works - 22 part series

"I have known Julia all my life. What strikes me in the strangest way is that she is not aging. She has always looked like a young girl with her young and beautiful body, the longest, fullest, thick blond hair, beautiful skin and teeth. She is always full of energy and one of the healthiest persons I have known. I don't understand how this could be possible. She looks like someone has preserved her as she looks 25 years younger than her actual age!! I am so envious. I think gerontologists or genetics should study her to find out the secret to youth - maybe something special about her genes.
Luba Alecksandra

This is the funny part, but YES, people think I am 20 years younger when they meet me and never believe when I tell them my age. I guess my Spirit remembers my time on Atlantis and that Atlanteans live up to 800 years

Back of the CD cover, **year 2000, Canada**
(Photo by Bryan Ward)

Teleportation, materialization

Two months after I finished writing this book, I am still surprised by what's happening to me and around me. I just don't have words to describe my feelings after what happened and continues to happen from moment to moment in my present life. I was not sure that I should write this in this book, but since I don't intend to hide anything, and, on the contrary, open the doors to many secrets, it would have been unfair to keep those amazing events from my readers now. At least one person on the planet, somewhere, may have had the same experience as I did...

First, I want to tell everyone that if you have a WISH and really want that WISH to come true, I mean very strongly want it – it will come true. NO matter how unusual this WISH is and no matter how absolutely impossible it looks for it to come true, I, for one, have *no doubts* that it will happen. I guarantee you this after what happened to me. But be careful what you WISH for, as well. The results can be outstanding, or devastating...

When I finished writing this book at the end of June 2008, I wrote my wish: *"**I also wish to have another hypnosis reading to return to Atlantis, to start remembering how I performed the teleportation, materialization, and so on.**"*

Now see where it brought me just a few weeks later.

Okay, here we go... No matter WHAT, this is what happened. I actually wish to share these events in the hope of receiving the support of someone else who had similar experiences to mine. I am still a scientist at heart and can't believe that it all happened.

1. I asked my daughter, "Did you remember what happened in the Japanese restaurant?"

She replied instantly, "If you put that in the book, no one would believe it! I saw it and still can't believe it!"

On the 6th of July we celebrated Dee finishing elementary school and her up-coming birthday. Soon she would be leaving to Europe with her mother for the summer vacation, and to visit relatives. We went out to Robson Street for Sushi for lunch. While we were eating, Dee pointed out to a tea cup on the table, saying, "Did you see, it moved!" Julia looked at the cup, checked the table, it was dry so the cup was not sliding along, and it was three-quarters full of water. As we continued to eat, another cup moved again, between her and Kristy. The first time the cup moved, only Dee saw it, however the second time we all saw it. When the waitress returned, we asked her if there were ghosts in the restaurant as a joke, but she laughed and walked away. So other than ghosts, we didn't have any other explanation. It was strange but it did happen. **Shawn, D. Lauren, Kristy**

Kristy.

Yes, Kristy and Shawn were sitting across from us. Suddenly, my daughter saw a white cup, between her and Shawn, move. At that moment, I was talking to him and looked in his direction. Dee started screaming, "Did you see the cup? It moved!" YES, I thought I saw it move a little from the corner of my eye, since the cup was in my line of vision. I checked it; it was a tall cup and more than half full of water. We thought that some water had spilled over, and I checked the table under the cup – it was dry. Paying no mind to the incident, we continued talking, when suddenly, a few minutes later, a second cup, in front of me, moved! This time it wasn't just a fleeting glance – I saw it move! I mean I was looking at the cup when it was just standing in one place and then move to another spot... This cup was exactly the same as the first one, except for the fact that it was full of water and quite heavy.

When the waitress came to the table, I asked her, "Do you have ghosts here?" She replied, "Why?" We told her that the cups had moved... She then added with no uncertainty, "No, we don't!"

At the time, I had just finished writing this book and the ghosts' stories were still fresh in my mind, so I was sure that they had at least one ghost in the restaurant...I then asked everyone at the table, "How about if I called this ghost to come, and if he is here, I'll ask him to move something else?" At that point I could see that Dee was getting scared, so I stopped and we returned to our little celebration.

Between us, during the last four and half months since my few readings about Atlantis, I noticed small objects moving in front of me on my desk numerous times. I tried not to pay attention to it, though.

2. Next, something happened in Amsterdam on September 9. The hotel was near a diamond factory, from where a "hop on – hop off" bus took us on a sight-seeing tour of the city. At the last stop, the tour guide advised me to cross the road to the office and get some coupons for FREE DVDs

about Amsterdam, the diamond factory tour and a canal cruise. The last two items sounded very attractive to me, so I took his advice and went inside the agency.

Now, please follow carefully what happened:

The front part of the office was a rectangular room, stretching to some steps, which led to a counter along the far wall. There was no one inside except for a couple of agents at the far end desk where I went. I opened my small RED bag, pulled out a ticket and asked for the coupons. I put the two coupons into the RED bag, which I put inside my backpack. I turned to walk toward the exit.

The store was still empty. I look *ahead* of me, stopped and stared in utter disbelief. My RED bag was lying on the floor about eight meters *in front of me* near the entrance! The girl who was minding the souvenir store near the entrance, she pointed at the bag and asked, "Is this your bag?" I told her automatically, "I guess so...

I crossed the road, sat in the bus and ask my daughter opened the bag...I stopped breathing when I saw that inside nothing had "moved" or "disappeared" – the money, ticket and coupons were all in there! That store is maybe 12 meters long; I didn't lose consciousness, and I don't remember throwing my bag across the store. Even if I tried to do this now it would still not "fly" that far away. I checked it when I came home and threw it casually; it landed about four meters in front of me.

I remember very clearly how I opened the bag, pulled out the ticket near the desk, and gave it to the agent to receive three papers back – a ticket and two coupons, which I put inside the red bag, and closed it.

When I walked towards the entrance, I saw the bag, it was at least eight meters away from me – how did it happen? I took a photo of the store the next day when I was there with my daughter.

Inside the agency office and RED bag.

But this is not the end of the story that day!

3. 20 minutes later, I arrived with the bus to my stop near the Gassan Diamond factory and decided to walk to the flea market nearby. It was a few minutes after 6:00 p.m. and most of the tents with souvenirs had already been taken down for the night. Some people were still in the process of closing down their shops. I was walking in the same direction as a man who was walking slowly towards a tent. I looked up thinking that it wouldn't be much fun to open and close these tents every day. I remember looking at the long piece of wood lying down on top of the steel frame. Then it happened. All of a sudden, the piece of wood moved and fell a few inches from this man's head! He screamed at me, "You looked at that wood and it fell down! I saw it! You moved it!" He continued repeating this a few times, "This is impossible!" Lucky for him he had not been hit by the piece of wood – it could have harmed him. He seemed to be a very friendly,

polite and positive man. I guess he was dealing with tourists every day and his attitude had become part of his demeanor towards foreigners. I was very surprised to say the least. Actually, I was still in shock after what just happened with the RED bag... and now things seemed to continue to happen. After he calmed down, and told him how sorry I was but that I had nothing to do with this incident; I asked him to write it down for me. He had been quite surprised of what happened because he was very sure that the big piece of wood was firmly fixed on top of the frame of his tent. He was no less surprised when I asked him to write the incident down for me. He asked, "Why?"

"It's just odd that it happened, that's all," I said. "And because maybe tomorrow, I'll wake up and think this was all a dream. I want it for the memory."

Here is what he wrote.

"This girl with long blond hair passed my tent at 6:10 p.m. I was closed for the day. All souvenirs were already in the boxes. She walked by and I followed her in the same direction to talk with my friend at the next tent. **Suddenly she looked up and a long heavy wood stick moved and fell down right where I was. Thank God I am okay and no scratches!** *This is what happened – really, weird... and I hope she is not a witch from Canada... no this is a joke. She is an attractive girl and her hair is very rare."* **Barent**

Cases like these start happening again and again. Now I try to study my ability and find out how I could possibly control it. I also began remembering that similar things happened to me in the past as well. It actually happened many times in **Hawaii.**

I arrived in Kauai in July 2008 and went immediately to the Kalapaki beach. Suddenly, I realized that in my rush I forgot my **sun glasses and hair clips**. I cannot swim without those clips since I have very long hair. It would take hours to wash it and dry... *I wish very much to have them right now*, I thought. In the middle of the beach there were black, volcanic lava rocks. I walked towards them with my daughter, since I couldn't do anything else on the beach. On this black rock, in front of me, I saw a pair of sun glasses and hair clip! I just could not believe my eyes! I stood in shock. My daughter picked them up and gave them to me.

"See, now you can swim!" she said with a broad smile on her face.

The most amazing part was that both items were brand new with the plastic tag still on them! And I love and still use these glasses each time I swim! It was like someone knew my preferences and chose them for me. There was only one store nearby which sold sun glasses. I checked with them and they didn't carry the same type. The name of this one pair is *Argon Serengeti*.

Now when I think about these things, I remember another case that happened in Maui, when my daughter was 5 years old. Every day we walked to the beach, which was about a half-a-mile away. I loved it, because, on the way, there was a private house with a large front-lawn. On the lawn, there were two enormous live Galapagos tortoises! And I loved watching them. I always carry a very small (6 cm) turtle with me.

On that day my 5 years old daughter lost her sandals on the beach. It was a very hot day, and it would have been impossible for her to walk without shoes anywhere – the hot sand would have burned her feet. Also, there were little, sharp rocks everywhere. I am a very slim woman and even being fit, I couldn't have carried my daughter for half-a-mile in my arms. I really didn't know what to do. Suddenly, two pairs of sandals appeared before us in the sand. One was her size and one was my size! Both pairs were brand new. Obviously, no one had ever used them, since the tag between the two shoes was not cut.

I looked around. All morning we were alone on this beach. We waited for some time to see if someone would come and pick them up. No one showed up. So we went home as fast as we could and I ran back to put the two pairs of shoes where we found them, with a "thank you" note. During the next three weeks the sandals remained in the same spot. No one showed up to pick them up!

****

When we just arrived in Maui, our friend and owner of the house, June, decided to pay a visit to her friends nearby. They had a big house for sale, located right on the beach. June's friends invited us to come in.My daughter had never seen a real palm tree with coconuts before. She pointed to the tree and said, "I want those coconuts!"June replied, "We will go to the farm market on Saturday and we will buy some good coconut for you."
As stubborn as a child could be, my daughter said, "No, I want that yellow one right now!"
My daughter just continued to insist that we gave her that coconut.
I remember looking at the coconut; it was very high in the palm tree.
Meanwhile June's friends had come out of the house and were watching us, waiting for us to go inside.My daughter still didn't want to go anywhere. She just wanted that yellow coconut.
Suddenly, that coconut fell down! She ran to it, picked it up, and happily carried it in the house asking to open it!Well, everybody was more than surprised, and stood in silence looking at the coconut. Unripe coconuts do not fall from the tree before their time – unless there is a storm or something that would dislodge them.
Today I talked to friend of mine, my dentist Serge and he told me that a Brazilian man can do this! Objects can appear from nowhere and group of people witnessed it! Maybe it is the same man who is a healer in Brazil and which I mentioned earlier in this book? We all know that he is working with 33 Spirits; if they can do internal surgeries in a split second without instruments,they could bring him anything, I suppose.
Good to know that he have the ability to perform teleportation and this is his "daily routine".
And now I found on YOUTUBE a real example of how it works!
YOUTUBE: **Teleportation Tutorial: Tesla's Magnetic Wall**

****

I received numerous letters from readers where they asking if any new cases of teleportation was recorded?In 2011 most amazing was this one:
It was a very hot day in September on the **Black Sea** and I was walking for a maybe 2-3 hours and just dreaming about water.When I returned to my hotel, a girl named Veronica finished cleaning my room and was near my door washing floor in the hallway. I stopped in front of her and at this moment suddenly **cup appeared in the air between us!** I caught it automatically and put this cup on top of the refrigerator near me...and don't know what to think about it ...the cup was full of water....! I realized what just happened but cannot understand it.
I ask Veronica: Did you bring this cup? She say: No, I did not. We don't have cups like this one.
I went down and ask manager of this little hotel. He told me that in this place they don't have any cups with this design...Veronica told to manager that will she never will go again upstairs to clean that room.On the cup was picture of the girl and boy in Ukrainian costumes. I photographed the cup and sent e-mails about this strange case to my relatives to Moscow.

Suddenly one relative recognize the cup! He told me that he bought this cup years ago and it is in the room upstairs in there summer house, which located few miles away! I did stay in that room last time in 2009, 2 years ago. This house was all locked up because the summer season had finished, everybody left a month ago before I arrived from Canada.

How did this cup arrive at the hotel through closed doors? Who sent to me a cup with water in it when I needed this so badly? Cup which I maybe use 2 years ago (I don't remember) and Spirit choose exact this one from all area around.

****

*This happened during documentary movie production in Vancouver, **Canada**
"After we finished filming part for the movie, we went outside the building with Julia and other members. Suddenly I saw little things which fell down around Julia! It came from nowhere; I mean literary from the air! It was hard to understand from which material it was made. But most amazing was that all 5 colours on each of this little pieces was the exact the same colour as the outfit Julia was wearing, including her bag and bracelet! But not only the colour; it was the exact, precise shade & tone of these colours! How can this be possible? And from where did it come from? I was amazed, so I took the photo."

**Andreas Kerlie,
camera man**

*Next day it happened again in a department store of the **Pacific Centre shopping mall** in front of the girls...they was really amazed :) Colorful pieces fell down like a rain all around me... :)

*During last few years people pick up little pure crystals which appear around me from nowhere...I guess crystals because past life in Atlantis.
I think my body doing this the same way like in this video on YOUTUBE. My Spirit in great harmony and for fun just find somewhere on the planet this particles, which fit precise this exact combination of the colors on my outfits. Or maybe Spirit "simply" created them?

And...YES, I did it again! In **Australia**

It happened today, the whole family were witnesses to a funny teleportation & materialization story. I sent a bantam egg from a cage outside, in the garden into the house! A distance around 50 meters. The egg landed safely on the bed of their beautiful 13 years old girl with black hair and blue eyes, name Leno. She was writing for a long time a boring letter and as soon as I start to know this, I guess my Spirit decided to amuse her... :). It was in an instant and in a split second. On the photo normal chicken eggs and those which smaller sized **bantam egg** was teleported.

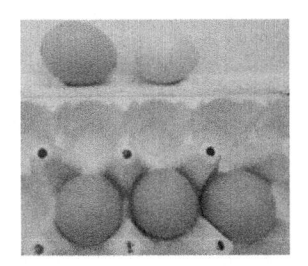

Valeria

Olga, a neighbor of Julia and her aunt Mery:

"I went home with Julia after the massage. My daughter Valeria phoned me from Astana, **Kazakhstan** and announced the good news that it has received a marriage proposal from her boyfriend. I was very happy and decided to celebrate this littleevent. We went to the grocery store to buy a good bottle of red wine and chocolate. At the supermarket, I wanted bananas and my daughter loves them. I mentioned this to Julia, but for them it was necessary to go to the other end of the store, and Julia hurried to the conference call with a publishing house in New York via Skype and we went straight to the checkout.   Almost no people were in the shop.

On reaching home, I began to pull out bags of groceries from his car and was greatly surprised to see a package with bananas.

At home, I checked the bill, but there were no bananas!

I asked Julie that if she bought bananas? She said no.

In fact, it was a shock when I realized that we were always together there in the store. Who sent the bananas? I spoke with Julia in the store, my daughter loves bananas, and Julia was very happy with the news of her impending marriage.

This is the real magic! And no explanation! How did this happened?? "

March 1, 2016, Olga Petrova. Almaty

YOUR ETERNAL HOLOGRAM

Chapter 3

Amelia Return?

"Amelia Earhart came perhaps before her time ... the smiling, confident, capable, yet compassionate human being, is one of which we can all be proud." (Walter J Boyne.)

Julia, Hawaii 2010, Photographer*:Darlene Laurel SV*

I have an enormous amount of amazing facts in this Chapter, which I collected during the two years of my research. I decided to put them here in response to questions which were asked during a TV show. It should help people in understanding and assimilating the information contained in this chapter.

So, are you Amelia Earhart being born again?

YES, I am. I was Amelia Earhart in my past life and I was born again.

Everything you will hear today may surprise you. As a scientist, I NEVER believed in past lives. After thorough, careful research, rebirth was the only explanation for the endless similarities that Amelia and I, Julia both share.

Nostradamus wrote quatrains about Amelia Earhart's re-birth?

Yes! You can find it in the interpretation in "The Strange Disappearance of Amelia Earhart, Nostradamus and the New Prophecy Almanacs Michael McClellan". www.newprophecy.net/pastceleb.htm [11]

Quatrain 10.84
The natural girl so high, high, not low,
The late return will bring grief to the contented,
The long journey will not be without debates
In employing and losing all of her life.

Yes, he was right, lots of debates and yes, employing company like TIGHAR and many other.

Quatrain 2.45
Too much the heavens weep at the birth of **Androgyn**,
Near the heavens human blood is spilled:
Through death too late a great people renewed,
Late and soon comes the awaited assistance.

By the way, on that website discussions refer to the reasons Nostradamus called Amelia an **Androgyn**.

I think Nostradamus wished to point out that Amelia was doing a man's job. She was a leader of the feminist movement, and she was wearing men's clothes: leather jacket, pants. She was extremely brave, concentrated on her goal with persistence, which helped her to fly solo across the world. Maybe Nostradamus also felt that Amelia was a Priest, in her past life and that she carried this man's quality: "tomboy", hunting?
Maybe when he called Amelia Androgen he mean her Goddess side? This what was saw in our Spirit with Amelia, Don Julio and Supreme monk Wondam? There were quite a lot of Goddess that were Androgynous…

Michael McClellan: *Still, line 3 Quatrain 2.45 remains a mystery. Through death too late a great people renewed, its meaning does not seem applicable to Earhart's final adventure, raising the possibility that this quatrain may be a repetitive one. Thus, we see both the Amelia Earhart of the past and a futuristic entity, yet to be conceived or created perhaps, who will truly be biologically sexless.*

It makes me smile... I am here called a **"futuristic entity"**, which will truly be biologically sexless. I should tell Michael McClellan that I am reborn and I am a mother in this life and a normal woman, not an Androgyn and, by the way, people think that I am pretty feminine and sexy. So Amelia was a normal woman as well, not an Androgyn, such as people described her in this article. It is important to understand that the Spirit is built as a hologram – a multi-layered structure. This unique crystal, which everyone has, collects memory of both characteristics: male and female, and all of the past lives they had. In Amelia's case it included the Priest and now this Spirit is added to all of my characteristics as well.

So, when Nostradamus said, "Through death too late a great people renewed," he talked about re-incarnation and here I am, Amelia re-born!

How long have you known this?

I have known this since April 29th, 2008.

On April 29th and I had a new past life regression reading. While I was checking my dreams about Atlantis, I suddenly found one dream which occurred 16 years ago and I found another two dreams which connected with this one. I started remembering that these dreams repeated themselves from time to time during my life. In one of the dreams, I saw the same thing at least 5 or 6 times. That's when I decided to visit Di Cherry again to try to understand what it was all about.
It was interesting that on the way to Di Cherry and on the way back, good numbers showed up all the time! They were on each license plate in front of me. Any car near me had a good number; 085, 058. I think something really special happened today, very good and important.

Reading # 4, April 29th 2008

As we started the session, I said to Di, "I come today because I have had this dream a long time ago and I will read it to you now. Since then, I have had a few dreams similar to this one – they kind of continue." I started reading the dream:

Dream # 27

Woman pilot disappeared, dream on June 22, 1992

Time is mixed between past and present. I was dreaming of an old documentary movie, newspapers and this paperboy selling them on the street. In all of these, there is only one subject (Waves of goose bumps go up to my cheeks!) There was a woman, young, maybe 30 or 40 years old. This was before the Second World War. She was wearing a helmet everywhere, like the ones pilots or people in tanks wore. She was inside in the cockpit of an airplane. I looked at all of this and then I began recognizing it... I recognized everything! I remember it in all of the little details, even feeling and touching the control-panel.

I said to my guide, "This is me!"

"YES, this is you!" he replied. No one understood what happened to her – she and her airplane disappeared. This goes on for a long time like in a movie. She spoke English and her story was connected to the USA and Canada. I was looking at the screen at first. After I recognized her, and after that, I was inside the cockpit. I touched everything, operated the controls automatically. I know everything without seeing it; it was not necessary for me to see it, I could do this! Half of me was in those times! Lights were burning, flashing, flickering and running... Everything was real!

I said to Di, "The reason I wanted to do this hypnosis reading is because she is desperate and nobody knows what happened to her. Maybe I carried a heavy emotional luggage in my Spirit. And if we go through this hypnosis session it may be like a treatment, to help me open the door to all these emotions she had when she died or what happened to her, and she could be relieved of the burden, and this won't sit on my Karma – or I don't know how to say this – on my Spirit. This is what I think."

By the way, something very interesting happened when I was at University, there was a boy – a student in our class...

This boy, his name was Oleg, could look at somebody and say something about the person and sometimes he was even rude about it, but what "he predicted" always happened. One time he said to another boy, "Stop eating, you're eating too much; your stomach already needs surgery" or something like that. It was uncomfortable for everybody especially for this boy. This happened around January or February, but when the summer came – I think it was June – this boy went to the hospital to have surgery. He had numerous surgeries. He spent 3 or 4 months in hospital to regain his strength but he was fine in the end.

I remembered the day of the biochemistry exam – the most difficult part of all of what I studied in biology at University – the teacher opened the door, came out in the hallway and invited somebody to come in for the test, and then the next one... and people began running away from the door, because they were afraid. We needed to know all about these molecules, all of these processes – everything in the human body from beginning to end.

I was standing in front of the door and the teacher said, "So you're next?"

"YES, I am next," I replied.
"So you're not running?" the teacher asked.
"NO."
This student was near me and he suddenly said, "She is not afraid of anything. If you put her in an airplane, she would operate this airplane with her eyes closed. She knows everything about airplanes from beginning to end." It was all very sudden. I looked at him, the teacher looked at him but everybody knew about his strange kind of behavior. So, I just went for the exam and everything was fine, but I remember this moment. (Later on in my life I was an agent for an airline.)

I said to Di, "Maybe for now we can try to do this. We'll see what happened. The main question we could ask is what happened to her? And maybe we will find an answer. But the main thing for me is that I don't want this heavy emotional burden – if it is still there, I want it to come out."

Di Cherry then put me into a deep hypnosis state and started reading the dream. I always start to envision the dream when she reads it word for word to me – literally how I wrote the dream many years ago. It feels as if some kind of dream-energy is encoded in the words and how they were organized and I start to envision the events when the dream is activated by reading it.

When she finished I started talking:

(Note: The text below is a literal transcription of this session, but short version. Full version you can find on www.ameliareborn.com*)*

When you read this, I see water in front of me and I see myself in the airplane. We are flying and the sound of this motor is very strong. I hear this sound, it is so strong.

When you start saying that it connected with the USA, I see myself with a President, I see a President right near me, and a flag, an American flag and I think...it's inside...

I remember my yellow, bright yellow airplane, very bright... Canary color. This is Canary color.

Yes. This one I remember, I love this airplane very much, it's my toy.

This being the day, the day of your flight. Tell me, are you taking this yellow airplane this time, for your long journey?

No, No, I have another one. I have beautiful airplane, this one best! This one best in the world. I am so proud. Very powerful. I am very proud to have it. They make it especially for me, it's for us to fly...Lockheed ...Lockheed... I am very proud.

So let's go to the most important event in that life time. See where it takes us. Please go to that most important event in that life time.

I remember my grandmother now and big tree near the house. I remember my grandmother. I love my grandmother. I like to climb to this tree. I remember I like to climb this tree very much. Maybe when I was 8 or 9, I climbed high, too high, my grandmother not happy. She worries that I will fall down.

****

I see myself talking to one club. It's... (Oh, I have goose bumps now! I am covered with goose bumps.) *It's club I have and my members in this club and I have meeting. I have meeting for preparation for something and I am talking. It is very happy time, very happy time and I need to go to another city and after to another small city and also talk with people there.*

****

I see myself in some hospital, I am working with some people...like I am doctor or nurse...

Are you a patient there?

No, no I work there and I have this outfit, strange outfit they have those time. They have white apron. And this is how they look in those days. Around me nurses... I think I am nurse, I think I am nurse...

****

I see old buildings, bricks buildings, like 3 or 4 floors ... buildings all the same looks, red bricks color. I work in some office; I see office, people coming for help. And I see line. I see line in the hallway.

Line of people or line on the floor?

It's line of people sitting on the chair from this side, from left side. I open door and I invite next one and right now it was mother with two children and she left...

If you look at those papers, in what language are they written? I'd like you to look at these papers and tell me what you think, in which language they're written?

English, all English. I see on the wall English. Beautiful hand writing, people don't make like this hand writing right now. It's beautiful how people write before. No computer by the way in this office. Across another girl she is writing something. It is lots of papers that time...

****

One man talking to me... And he makes for me kind of proposal, kind of business proposal. Now he is telling me and it suddenly, strange, unpredictable ... what he telling...

He says, "You will just sit, you don't need to operate right now, and you just sit and fly this time."

And I say, "Okay!" I am very proud, I am very, very proud. Something really special, very special...

What does he call you? Does he call you ma'am; does he call you by your first name? Listen, listen to him.

He has voice, bright, kind of low men voice. I like his voice; I like how he talks. He says something... Oh, I have goose bump now so strong like a wave...
He says, "Miss, Miss Amelia you are part of the crew now..." It is so special for me, so special; I am part of team of pilots. I am part, I am passenger, but I am still flying with them ... it's like a dream come true... I will fly with team of pilot.

A photographer come and this camera, his camera, he makes crazy flash to the eyes, just crazy flash, right to my eyes. It's hard to keep eyes open, because flash all the time. He asks me to stay near this big motor and he makes pictures right now, I see it... It is okay to take pictures, but this light killing, just very bright.
 So bright, his camera huge big, heavy...

It is so strange, today, when I am talking, I am using muscles I never used before. I kind of press my nose from both sides. I never did this before in my life, very strange ... never used this muscle before ... I am pressing my nose like this now, all the time, from time to time ... When I am shy or I worry. I am pressing my nose like this ... at the end kind of press it on both side, very interesting; strange for me... You see it.

It is not easy, when you find yourself in a different body... Yes.

YOUR ETERNAL HOLOGRAM

I never knew that these muscles exist, I never use them ... but now it is strange...

****

I like name Surinam, Surinam something really special and beautiful... I was there very short moment ... Surinam it is nice name for anything, people or animals. I like Brazil also, Brazil was nice... People are very nice. All smiles. I am for them so special. And now we fly and they stay and wave, all of them wave, so many, many people, I see they wave...

****

I am amazed sometimes. I am flying and by the moment I arrive already so many people waiting and so many people waiting and wave to us ... they probably wait for long time.

They support for me, their support, it's very important, because when we flying, it so, so long and its sometimes like forever long ... ocean, stars and I know that far away, far, far away hundreds of people waiting for me to come ... hundreds of them waiting; they will all come to meet us. It such a big support for me and for Fred ... we're very tired ... we hardly walk from airplane when we land ... our legs can't move ... stuck ... and ... back ... we tired so much ... so many people waiting...

Yes, they have no idea what you feel like, how tired you are.

Yeah... And I need to look good... They take pictures ... in some places we arrive photographers running... They take pictures... We're like people on the war ... doing something very serious ... and its big responsibility, very big responsibility ... for people of America, President and all this newspapers and factory, which give me airplane ... big responsibility and we need to be best... We need to be very good; we're like a hero of some kind...

You are very good.

Because it's long way, very long way... I am glad that I have Fred with me... When I am flying alone ... totally alone ... strange feeling. Only when I am fly in airplane I am alone ... those time I think about many, many things in our life ... and it very special feeling, because you fly so high ... far from people from everything ... and I am think about stars, about future ... about past ... you kind of think global ... about all world ... our Planet so beautiful. Big.
And I remember I work in some hospital ... it was war ... it was war before ... I don't want people to have war, they injured themselves. It happening fast, but healing can take years ... and it's painful. I always care about people.

Yes, you do.

I think it is time for me to take you to the day of your death. I count one, two, and three... Now!

Through the ocean light. But I scream: "Where we are?" (O, I have now goose bumps so much! Through all my legs goose bumps.)I scream to him... I cannot find place, he cannot find place. I look all the time, every minute I look to the meter... I want see gasoline, how much left ... and it almost zero ... it almost zero ... and we lost.

We don't see island ... we lost! And it's ... it's very cold in my head one thing: "This is end, like a robot. This is end, we're lost, no gasoline."

From another side very emotional, very emotional ... how can it be now, to finished everything now? Suddenly, cut off. Everything will be cut of, all my promotions; my articles need to be in magazine next month, everything, so many things ... so many, many things. It's impossible ... it's breaking all plan, we have plan ... we fly so long ... we should finished this trip ... this island right on time, just arrive there...
I think it was mistake in navigation documents, map, which Fred received just before we fly... I think mistake there...

It's unfair, it really unfair... I am doing everything right, but this island just not exists. I don't know where we are...

I know this is end. This is end. I see myself... I watching my own lungs; I pay attention to my lungs. I cannot do nothing. I look to my lung and I know. I know: In my lung wall connected with blood vessels and with air from another side. Inside in the lungs we have air ... so when water will be inside and when it touches walls will be no more air; this is moment when I will die. This is moment when I will die.

I only watch... Can't do anything, impossible to do anything to survive... This is it. It's last day of my life, Fred life, we will drown now...

I look all the time to the meter and I look to the place where we are. Numbers, numbers, numbers... I check this numbers. I remember I scream to radio, "We cannot see you; we cannot see you..." We try going north and south, up and down, we try to find this island, now we go South, more South and straight to east direction. It very strange it should be islands around. But we lost ... our flight finished ... this is our last point, we arrive here... Lots of tears, through all this time so many tears, like rivers of tears... (Long pause.)

Strange... I am continuing to use this muscle near my nose from both side and top lip ... never used them before. Strange...
And now, it's close, it's within of a moment or two of your death... And as you go down ... feel it, experience it and breathe ... breathe comfortably, easily ... water in ... water in the cabin ... breathe comfortably and easily ... just keep breathing...

It is interesting even ghosts breathe after they die ... they continue, just as humans, to breathe comfortably and easily... From all deaths, drowning is the best.

You felt the impact of the plane on the water, it wasn't nice. But you had a good seat. Just allow yourself to go... It's peaceful. You're leaving through the top of your head; you're leaving that body...

I see inside near this navigation place something, it is right there in front of me. Shiny from left side of me, parallelogram shape ... maybe a plaque.

Yes, okay. I'd like you to leave your body behind ... leave the airplane; it's time for you to trip up, up, up. It is a feeling of being on a child slide, but going backwards. You're leaving behind this beautiful blue planet. The atmosphere looks like a halo around. You're going very, very, quickly. Your guide is there. And look at the number of people who are greeting you! Just as they met you on Earth at all of the places where your plane came down. There are even more people here in Heaven waiting for you, for your company, waiting to welcome you home, to your real life. You've accomplished really what you meant to do. You died at the height of your career. And it was a good trip for us. Very good trip.
 I see so many people! All like angels. All white kind of, many, many, many... Door open and I go there... Yes, they all you can see through, I see them through ... light, light. So many...

****

It was interesting that until the last moment, I continued seeing many people; they all have this see-through kind of looks. If you take, for example, a clear plastic bag and put one inside another maybe 5 or 7 times, this is how it will be, how people look in Heaven. Interesting that in the middle, near the entrance, at the last second, I saw someone like a priest, with the shape of the outfit they wear in the Orthodox or Catholic Churches. He also had the same quality – a see-through being – but with gold color, like gold sand on the upper part...

Wow!!! I visited real Heaven today! I loved it! I didn't want to return from there, by the way. It was such a pleasure to be there, such a light happy feeling!

I know, Heaven is only one place for everybody, but for each person the particular Priest will be near entrance, according to his or her religion, or in case the person doesn't have any, it will be according to his beliefs. (So it can be for example Buddha, Krishna or Jesus, or some shapes, images and so on)

How do you know that the woman named Amelia, which you saw during your hypnosis sessions, is Amelia Earhart?

That day, after the reading, I returned home and decided to Google: *Amelia, pilot woman* and *Fred, Pilot, disappeared*.

I was hoping that maybe something would come up. To my big surprise, there are many articles on the internet with Amelia Earhart's name!

As soon as I saw her photos, I recognized her instantly – the same woman I saw in my dream, in those long documentary movies and on the front-page of all of these old newspapers, which the paperboy was selling! I had goose bumps again, and each time I saw them. I knew everything there; I recognized all of these airplanes. I remembered the car on the photo, everything inside the car, the spacious interior, the high seating and the low front window. Fred looked very familiar to me also; it felt as if I knew how he talked, his voice, and how he walked, how he laughed.

With purpose, I avoided watching documentary movies about Amelia or read anything about her, because I tried to acquire information as to how I felt about her through the hypnosis sessions and my dreams. The book was finished when I allowed myself to look through this information.

It was very emotional, hard for me to type this last day of Amelia's life. I just can't hear this part again; I am starting to cry... It feels really unfair that I did not complete that flight to the right place and die there. It didn't finish how it should have done – all of the plans were cut short. When I flew to Japan, Korea, and Australia across the ocean, I knew that if something would happen to the airplane there would be no possibility of survival.

Right after the reading, that night, I saw myself again in the airplane, flying over the ocean... I was Amelia again and I was thinking only about my baby, who was not born yet. Perhaps it was my future baby ... and I started reciting a poem! I woke up with this poem on my lips, and with tears in my eyes, I started writing it. This is what I remember:

I am feeling you near,
But where are you?
For many cold years,
I am waiting for you,
My love and my diamond,
My soul and my dream,
I love you forever,
As long as I am here.

Today, November 28, 2008, a letter just arrived with my daughter's birth record. The attending nurse's name was **U. Lougheed.** The Lockheed Corporation (originally **Lougheed** Aircraft Manufacturing Company) was an American aerospace company founded in 1912.

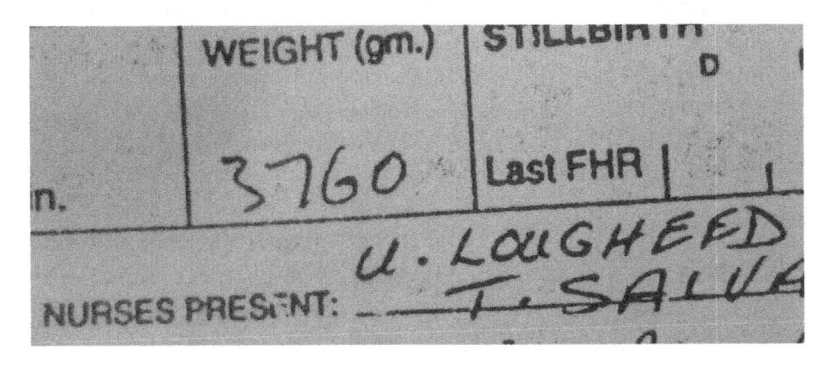

Detail of the Birth Certificate showing the nurse's signature

At the most important moment in my life, during child birth, my Spirit chose a nurse with an airplane name for support! It makes me laugh now...
I can tell you one more of Amelia's secrets; she wished to write more books... So if you were in Amelia's situation, suddenly dying and thinking that you did not finish or complete something in your life, you would like to know that you will have many lives ahead of you to do it. Well..., today I continue with the book and type the last part of Amelia's life. The reading was difficult for me again. Tears... I prefer never to listen to this CD again. It is very unfair not to complete the flight at the very end, when it was almost done!
It is like a red line around the Earth, which I can trace with a red marker – all the way around... But, it did not connect in the South Pacific part... It stopped there. However, since I lived through all of my past lives and I traveled so much in this present life, I can easily connect this RED line around, even a few times!
So, no more sad thoughts, dear Amelia, because you did not complete that trip around the world, ok? We did it together with the support of your reborn spirit – we were one Spirit.
It goes through Atlantis, Mexico, USA, Egypt, Tibet, Europe, Australia and Canada. And, by the way, this line also connects through the South Pacific, with Hawaii and Los Angeles. I know this for a fact, because I flew this same route for her from New Zealand.
It was very strange, each time I flew over the place where Amelia died, I lost consciousness! I am very healthy and never, ever have something like this happened to me in my whole life! It happened twice during a flight to New Zealand and twice on the way and back from Australia to Canada.
I simply blacked out for maybe 20 seconds. I remember they brought me a bottle of water as soon as I realized I couldn't breathe. I was literally choking for air. Yet, as soon as I drank a little, I began breathing again normally, taking a very deep breath at first, same as a new-born baby does.
The next time I would fly near that zone, I plan to leave some instruction with the flight attendant beforehand. It's a very embarrassing situation when you faint and choke for air inexplicably.

****

I had my **Second hypnosis reading regarding Amelia.**
Here are my notes right after the session:
This time Diana Cherry started the session regressing me back throughout the years. Diana started

going back with me to age 18, 12, 5, 2 years old...I started to tell her what I saw when I was 2 years old. What I remembered was... there were very bright memories and after she made me even smaller and then I saw that I was a baby and after that in my mother womb and next in the black dark tunnel, there was brightest light at the end and she start count 5, 4, 3, 2, 1, ...and !!! **Suddenly in split second I was right inside in the airplane!!!**

This means that seconds before I died as Amelia, I was in airplane. Means that Amelia Earhart and Fred Noonan was NEVER EVER been on Saipan Island.) I felt very tightly strapped to the seat, I touched the airplane panel in front of me, I felt how smooth it was...

I saw the brightest SUN light outside on the water. I saw that meter showed almost NO gasoline

I look at the panel in front, there was round meter... as if it was clock it was around noon, maybe 12:30pm ...(I guess Lae time, local will be 9.30 am ?) It was total SILENCE from FRED and Radio, I was by myself, only sound of the motor...it was a hopeless situation.

5.I look to the right and it was FRED sitting near, strapped to his chair, on his head was white blood soaked wrap with blood soaking through and on his face. Blood also on his journal and maps. He was in and out of consciousness. His left hand was also bloody, from his head I guess... hand injured near wrist and swelling and little bit scratched... swelling was not blue yet, but a pink bump there...maybe it was fracture... I look, his watch was broken, one piece of glass, triangle shape missing, the watch had stopped working... It happened with him during second part of the trip (if we will divide to 3 part distance for example) when was dark and storm. Whole airplane was shaking terribly and did hit his head and injured his hand. On top of this all the time from FRED was this smell of alcohol, he had taking I guess evening before and I opened the window try to rid from it. I was very, very tired...deadly tired... I was sleepy...I did not feel good.

I think I made a turn and the SUN started to be more from left side and I think I started feel this moment when I was in hypnoses from right side some island can be seen in the distance... but I cannot judge how far. Moment when airplane goes down I did not remember... looks like I blacked out.

At first, when I am back, I did not understand that I was dead...I just surprised that no more bright sunlight, instead gloomy dark around...BUT I saw very sure in front of me in a distance like a mount ... in front of the airplane more toward left side in the dark twilight light, like a contour of this mount.

Or like a night dark light, how it can be with light only coming from the MOON. I cannot see this mountains range on top of the water before, where did it come from? Now I understand it is located UNDER the water... (Maybe on top of the water this mount is part.... was some island)

I saw close to the airplane a long wall like a (carrier wall) which I saw on the photos, when work with diamond mine in the past. Not many but just one like this wall, one level, some underwater coral reef I guess, almost flat from the front side this wall and like a half sphere horseshoe round shape.

All of this I saw as a Spirit, with Spirit vision.

Well.... I saw from time to time during my current life this nightmare: that I am going inside of the airplane through the roof door and I am sitting there during first few seconds it strong feeling: **I know that I will never come out of the cockpit outside again**. Well this was mistake until today... after I died I did come out and left cockpit and went with the Angels... I got my freedom....and this relief in some way. I have more info. Diane Cherry as well has all the details of the hypnosis session; I have questions about Ancient EGYPT and that will be in a future session with Diane.

****

I found: In 1997 another female pilot, Linda Finch, recreated Earhart's final flight in an around the world tribute entitled "World Flight 97." The event took place on what would have been Earhart's 100th birthday. Finch successfully completed her voyage, the identical route that Earhart would have flown, around the world. http://www.worldflight.com. (July 1997).

Thank you dear Linda from both of us: Amelia and me!

What about Airplanes and Aviation?

I have a time-tested friend (or a longtime friend) in Japan. Gousaku Michihata is his name and he is a retired Major General of JASDF (Japanese Air Self-Defense Force).
He had worked as an experimental test-pilot for many years to put new aircrafts through their test-flights, and in the training of test-pilot students. "Experiment" meant no one was privy to the results of the tests, which included whether the prototype aircrafts would fly or would land safely.

It was funny; when I asked him, "What month, what day were you born?" He replied that he was born on October 8th. "8th of October?" I asked." Yes, October 8th," he repeated.

I thought that maybe he did not understand English very well and I repeated what I said. We were born on the same day, and month, and almost at the same place! He gave me good advices about airplanes.

Gousaku Michihata in the cockpit of an F-4EJ Phantom before take-off and on photo # 2beside F-10 Starfighter after landing

Years later, I was working with the Pratt & Whitney airlines in Los Angeles, CA. They had 1900 Boeings in the Mojave Desert. They have huge airplanes and they have many small aircrafts as well. I was an agent for the airline, trying to seal some deals to buy some of these aircrafts. I remember being very happy there.

I would just be running between all of these airplanes, people showing me what the insides looked like. I always ran to the cockpit to see the control panel of each of the planes. All of them were different – especially the small ones. I just loved them! I remember that once I dreamed of buying an

YOUR ETERNAL HOLOGRAM

airplane – a most high-speed jet. In that dream, **I ended up owning my own jet and I was so happy flying in it!**

Mojave Desert, California, 2004

What a luxury "toy"!

In this photo below we are discussing the plans for the re-construction of the airport. As you can see, for such an important meeting, I covered myself in **Jaguar print.** Unbeknownst to me then, the Priest and Amelia were supporting me in those days!

It was interesting that the business plan for the airline was prepared on a long sheet of paper – **opening up like an accordion.** I was so excited to see it that I even took a photo of it.

The Priest had a big book, pages of which opened exactly in the same way – **as an accordion!**

See, here again two things – the business plan about airplanes (Amelia's connection), and the Priest's book (the accordion).Bar on top of main page in my website www.ameliareborn.com also **opening to the side like an accordion!**

By the way, the man on the left of the photograph next page is a legendary man. Somehow, I meet **"extreme" people** way too often. He is the only man, in recorded history, who survived a fall from an aircraft from a height of 1500 meters. At the time, he was responsible for the training of cosmonauts in critical situation as part of the Space Program in Russia.

Jaguar outfit, airport map, California, 2004

The Business Plan – an unfolded accordion.

He was training over the Black Sea, when suddenly, his airplane experienced some malfunctions and it started spinning down. Everyone on board parachuted to safety, but since he was the head of the mission, he left the plane last, and his parachute did not open! This brave man was, at that time, teaching how to survive a fall from great heights – he taught me as well. What saved his life was the fact that he went down into the water keeping his legs straight, so there was the least surface of impact – he hit the water with the soles of his feet. Nevertheless, he suffered two broken legs; some ribs were fractured as well, and so on. But, now, years later, he is active and has almost fully recovered. When we were in Disney Land after the meeting, I noticed that it was hard for him to stand for a long time to watch the parade. His name is George **Nazarenko**. In Ukrainian, Nazarenko means "from **SUNRISE**". He is the owner of a private airline in Russia and he celebrates his second, re-born life each year and he counts each coming year as a gift from God, who helped him stay alive. I am sure that our meeting in this lifetime was not an accident. After all, I know that, in my past life as Amelia, my airplane also fell into the water... so we understand each other on some other level, pretty well, and I help his airline, as an agent, as much as I can.

I was ready to move to Brazil to start selling the Embraer in the summer of 2005. I adore my cousin, who works as a new aircraft builder in Russia. I was very happy to see, touch, and check all sorts of airplanes during the 2005 MAX Show in Moscow! Here blue dress, exact like Amelia had and right now it in her museum.

MAX Air Trade Show in Moscow, 2005

The original Amelia Earhart did some revolutionary things. How about you?

I helped millions of people change their lives on a grand scale in two countries. And what I bring right now is a new, revolutionary idea. I am a pioneer again. My goal in this life is much more difficult than Amelia's ever was. Because it will change people consciousness and open the door to the possibility of attaining wisdom and enlightenment.

I had the responsibility to invest my knowledge, abilities and skills to build a new country during perestroika in Russia, open new freedoms and new possibilities to develop the body, soul and spirit of people. During my life, I helped many talented, creative people.

For some unexplained reason, I flew to the middle of the South Pacific to a tiny island and started working there with some black pearl farmers. It is a 12-hour flight from Los Angeles to the Cook Islands, followed by a four-hour flight in a small-prop over the ocean to Manihiki Island. Now, six years later, I know exactly what attracted me to that place. Manihiki Island is located in the middle of the South Pacific Ocean close to the place where Amelia's aircraft disappeared!

I remember helping there 1200 pearl farmers in little Manihiki Island in the middle of the South Pacific Ocean. Just imagine 1200 people; they didn't have a doctor or a dentist on the island ... and the brokers kept them as slaves for many years by taking their pearl harvest and paying them little money for risking their lives every time they dove.

During the presentation on the island, I drew a pyramid representing the pearls harvested by the farmers.

I asked the farmers, "How much are you paying the technicians who place the little plastic ball inside the nucleus of the oysters?"

(The technician is a person who opens the oyster's shell and places a very small plastic ball inside its nucleus. During the next two years the oyster envelops the ball with many layers of secretion for it to become a pearl. Once the process is complete, the farmers open the shells and 'harvest' the pearls.)

I found out that some farmers paid 50% of their harvest and some even 70%!of the harvest. They thought they were paid around 30 to 50% of their harvest after the technician's visit. They had no way of knowing any better.

I marked the pyramid with the amount they were losing to the brokers and asked the next question: "How long does it take for you to reap the harvest?"

A farmer replied, "We get a harvest every two years."

I then asked, "How long does a technician work to carve a harvest?"

"Around 2 days," the man replied.

I said, "So, for two days of work you giving to him 50% of your harvest?"

The farmers nodded. "And that means that you're giving the technician one year of your labor free of charge!" They looked stunned. "Is that fair?" I asked them. "Do you know that the best technician in the world in Tahiti receive only 17%?"

I marked the pyramid with the portion representing what the farmers were giving the technicians. In fact, it showed the farmers how much they were losing to the technician.

The farmers were amazed!

When I asked the farmers how much they paid the brokers, they could not tell me, because they simply didn't know the value of their harvests. Moreover, these farmers didn't have the tools to separate the big pearls from the small ones and therefore, they could not count the value of their harvest. Then showed them that they didn't need brokers. If they were to establish a website and put photos of their pearls for the world to see, they would get the best buyers interested in what they had to sell from their harvest.

Since they don't have any doctors on the island in most cases they need to fly to New Zealand to see a physician or go to a hospital. I taught them that if each family paid only $10 they would have their own doctors on the islands. On the other hand, if they sent their own children to Tahiti to study to become technicians, in a few years, they would have their own technicians. And these children would not trick their own parents and relatives into paying 50 or 70% of their harvests for only two days' work.

It goes without saying that the brokers did not like what I did. When I arrived at the airport in Rarotonga, I received a message: "Go back to Canada or you will "feed the fish!" (Meaning that I would be killed and thrown into the ocean.)

Of course I did not fly back to Canada! I worked as much as possible to help these poor pearl farmers.

They told me that they had prayed and waited for help; for someone like me to come to their aid for many years. They were even ready to make me their representative in the New Zealand parliament...

Mr. Michihata Gousaky started working with me as an agent, representing the black pearls trade in Japan. Our company participated in the **13**th International Jewelry trade shows.*(# 13 here, my lucky Maya number!)*

I brought a couple of real pearl farmers from Manihiki Island to Tokyo, to the trade show, to teach them the business. Everyone ran to meet the "real pearl farmers" – magazines and newspapers reporters included. Usually, in this lucrative business, pearls are going through the hands of 4 or more people before they end up in the stores in Japan.

From left: Julia, a pearl farmer Trainy and Michihata in Tokyo

You mentioned many times that you visited the place where Amelia disappeared...

I visited the South Pacific many times – Cook Islands and Manihiki Island, which is close to the place where Amelia Earhart disappeared. It looks like my Spirit tries to attract me to the place where my past life ended.

I was working with pearl farmers in that area and **modeling**. (See photos www.ameliareborn.com)It is a heavenly, beautiful island in the South Pacific where pure white sandy beaches are full of amazing white corrals. The turquoise water is full of bright multicolored, tropical fish, and in the jungle, you can find blossoms, rare orchids with gardenias spreading wonderful fragrance around. People are wearing flowers and leis in their hair every day. When I was sitting for the first time on the white, sandy beach, between white corrals, I was thinking, **"If ever Heaven exists on Earth it is here"**.

I did not know then that my past life ended there and I went to Heaven from this area. On the next page book cover for the first addition of this book: "**Re-birth of an Atlantean Queen**".

It is interesting that the owner of the place, where I stayed on **Cook** Islands, was named "Aunty **NOO**". It was the name of the navigator who was with Amelia, when the airplane disappeared – his name was Fred *Noo*nan. It is also interesting to note that Fred was born in **Cook** County (Chicago).

*Modeling for a label of herbal products from Scotland,
Cook Islands, photo by Darlene Laurel SV*

Amelia launched a fashion house to manufacture and market clothing designed by her.

Amelia had a dress with a big white collar. I had exactly the same dress with a big white collar and loved it!; it had been designed by the famous Vecheslav Zaizev for an important business trip to China to sign an agreement. I drew this collar and asked him to make the dress with it. Now my favorite top by "Victoria's secret" also has this big white collar. I designed all of my dresses and even three dresses for the "Avon" company.

When I looked at the website about Amelia's home museum, I was surprised that when Amelia was small she had a swim-suit that looked like a sailor's suit.

It was interesting that I drew a picture with the little child in a SAILOR suit, years BEFORE my daughter was born. When she was two years' old, I bought **a sailor suit** for each of us. And just now,

I noticed that my mother – on a photo, in the next section of this book – was also wearing a sailor suit when she was 15 years' old.

Amelia and Julia's document photos –
Notice the similarity between the white collars.

I always love overalls and all kinds of clothes with many pockets, to put all kinds of stuff in them, like instruments or tools. I saw a photo of Amelia in a brown, leather overall and rain coat and start instantly remembered that I bought a long, **leather, brown coat** when it came in fashion (at a sky-rocketing price) of exactly the same color and quality! I remember my reaction when I saw it; I just wanted it – right there and then - I didn't think twice about buying it.

When I was small, I loved the children's fairytale entitled "The Magician of the Emerald town" (or "The Wizard of Oz"). According to the story they lived in a city named **Kansas.** Each time when my parents read me this story my heart melted... What a magic place it was, this Kansas! It was my dream town. Before I went to sleep, I often thought about this town, trying to imagine what it looked like. I never knew that this was a real place until I moved to Canada. I wished to visit this city as soon as I could, but it is too far away from Vancouver and the only slim excuse I had to go there was the fairy-tale.

Now I found out that **Amelia was born in Kansas!** My past life was there and this explains my deep attachment to the place. I still wish to visit Kansas someday and I wonder what I will experience in this place. Will it be the same as to what I experienced in Mexico in Chichén Itzá and in Egypt?

I visited London, Paris, and Rome – following exactly the same route that Amelia took in 1932. I also went to Australia, New Zealand many times, and to Japan, China, South Korea, Florida, Hawaii, Egypt and Los Angeles. I visited the Grand Canyon, the South Pacific, Caribbean islands and I wish to visit Latin America. At one point, I was ready to fly to Brazil, to become an agent for some airline company. I worked for years with a company from Abilene, Texas, where the brave Amelia experienced the **autogiro** and was almost ready to move there! It looks like my *DNA phantoms* imprint was calling me and is still strong in these places.

Perhaps the reason I moved away from Europe was that I lived in North America as an Atlantis woman, as a Priest from Mexico and as Amelia from the USA in my three past lives.

Do you like hunting like Amelia did?

Yes! I do. I was hunting all over the world.
I love the feeling of heavy rifles in my hands. I just knew exactly what to do and how when I got my hands on an air rifle for the first time. I never killed anything in my life and will never do in future ... but I love the feel of a well-made instrument of power and it is okay to use it in the shooting range.
For some reason, I just can't eat animals, for the last 25 years. And I never wanted to start. My friend, a monk, told me that this gives me the ability for intuition, predictions and it helps me to see what other people cannot see. The DNA which is found in animal protein has loads of information, which could disturb metabolism and Spirit. It also carries that fear-of-death signal which the animal produces before dying.
During my life I had all kinds of animals at home. My father was the best to provide me with a variety of them. Last year, as soon as I arrived in Kauai, Hawaii, we went with my daughter to the Kalapaki beach. It is near the Marriot hotel in Lihue and I started swimming near some big, black, lava rocks in the middle of the beach. All of a sudden, I saw this big sea **turtle** near me! First time in my life! I started "hunting" for the turtle. All I did was to navigate her, to swim toward the beach and the black rocks to a shallow place. When she was on top of the black rock, I lifted her up from the water by her front claws. I was able to do that when all of her body was out of the water and I could then show her to the children. A Japanese family from a cruise ship was watching me, they told me that it was "good luck" that I found a turtle. When I told them that I just arrived 20 minutes ago from Canada, and this was my first sea turtle and my first swim in Kauai, they said that I was blessed. I just loved this turtle! She came almost every day during the next 40 days to eat seaweed on those rocks. I easily recognized her by the little scratch on her back. I used to sit on the rocks for a long time, watching her swim around.

This funny photo was taken by a celebrity French photographer;
I am hunting here with a "photo-gun"

YOUR ETERNAL HOLOGRAM

Every day, when I went swimming in the morning, in Rarotonga, on Cook Islands, the same bright **tropical fish** followed me! Usually, I stopped near a big, round coral and she started to swim around to try to touch my legs. I instead tried to catch her, clapping my hands together. I could continue doing this forever until I would lose interest. Yet, I continued doing it every day for three months!
I flew back to Canada and returned three months later. All this time, I remember that fish and prayed that no one caught her and ate her .I returned and she was right where I left her, following me again.

Crazy fish

Two months later, I saw some fishermen who catch all kinds of fish walking on the beach with a fish that resembled my friend. I told him my story. The fisherman smiled and told me that this particular fish tried to protect her territory! Nothing more! My illusion was gone! Now I knew that this strange fish didn't play, she actually tried to attack me a little bit to show that this was her territory!
"Recently we were on vacation in the Cook Islands. Suddenly we saw on the beach a girl with longblond hair with something really weird in her hands. She came close to show us that itwas a fish that looked like a devil! We had never seen such a fish so we took somephotos.Some local fishermen passed by and told usthat this is a **Rock Fish.**VERYdangerous. It has sharp needles on the topofits body and it contains poison, neuro-toxin.

Kathleen and Jim Emory, US

An article in the "Cook Island News " a few days later confirmed that they are one of, if not the most, poisonous fish there is. A two days later that same girl was "hunting" on the beach as usual and this time she found in the ocean some really weird creature. No one knew of its origin. Very strange indeed. The following week an article came out in the local newspaper about Amelia Earhart and we learned that Julia is Amelia-reborn!! Obviously her habits from previous life for the hunting and tomboy actions follow her in this life time. As well as **Persistence and Perseverance…**"

Kathleen and Jim Emory, USA

On that day, the students and I decided to go hunting for *jerboas* in the desert. This is the cutest animal I ever saw. It is the size of a tennis ball, with a long tail and brush at the end, long ears like a rabbit, and black and white stripes! They have enormous black eyes. In the desert, the animals are mostly active at night and they need good vision. So we all climbed into the jeep and drove through the valley in the middle of the night. With the spotlights mounted on the hood of the jeep, we saw an old Muslim cemetery full of mud-houses kind of graves with moons on top instead of crosses...

Suddenly, on this dry, cracked desert soil, right in the beams of our spotlights, we saw lots of tennis balls jumping, up to a meter high. WOW!!! It was surreal ... unreal... The trick was to jump from the moving jeep, continue running to try to catch them while they were up in the air. But the most important part of this game is to jump from the jeep and continue running as soon as you touch the ground, so you won't break a leg... Only one of the students and I volunteered to do this ... and I loved it! It is lots of fun to catch this cute creature in your hands – this fuzzy, fluffy, lively ball. They are so naïve they never even think of biting you... Guess what? I collected lots of them and the next day we measure their tails, ears and we weighed them. Once we completed our observations, we brought them back to the desert and let them run and jump on their home ground. I was dealing with the cutest, adorable ones from Central Asia, Tibet.

The next day we were **hunting for scorpions.** I love this game! All you do is lift the rocks. In the desert, all living creatures hide under the rocks. So when you lift a rock, you can find anything; from scorpions to snakes, lots of insects as well, and tortoise.

But my favorite is the **pray-mantis.** I was hunting for them all over the world in different countries! I just love them. Afterwards they lived in my home. They sat in a big glass container, in the same elegant position, for hours – in front of me near my computer. Occasionally, with one perfect, fast move, they caught a drosophila. I fed them honey and fruits as well.
I remember running through the jungle in the South of Japan when I heard a cicada screaming for help. I knew that something was wrong. I always pay attention when a crow is screaming, this is an indication that something special is happening in the area. I was stunned when I saw a huge green mantis hanging upside down from the branch of a tree, holding a big, fat cicada by its front legs! I grabbed the cicada, let it go and caught that elegant, gorgeous mantis instead. I already described its future life in Tokyo in the "ghost story" of The Priest's chapter.

This **snake** comes all the time to eat eggs and little chickens... So Julia caught her and took her far away. The owner of the place tried to do the same, but the snake always returned – this was her territory.
It was great hunting for **octopuses** in the waters of the Cook Islands in the South Pacific! Some people walk on the reef in the dark with flashlights, trying to find them in the water between the rocks. People try very hard to catch them – octopuses are extremely smart. They swim very fast out of reach if you try to chase them. But I outsmarted them, I simply gave them my hand and they stuck

around the hand with their long legs, and once they had a good grip, I just carried them, swimming toward the beach. And that's it!

Hunting snakes in Australia
Photo by: David Holliday

While I was a student in University, I was high in the mountains, studying plants, animals, and insects, for two weeks. I woke up always early in the morning, at dawn, and climbed as high as I could. I am sure it comes from the Priest habits climbing the pyramid daily. I loved to look around, far down into the valley and high onto the mountains. Once, early in the morning, I found an Alpine field where only some big, blue onion-flowers grew – round-shaped, like blue balls. They stand straight and apart – a distance of 20 cm separating them – and around 1.5 meters high. In each of them was a huge white sleeping butterfly! It looked like white triangles! It was like the butterfly in one of my dreams but a real one this time ... so magic to see it. There were flowers all around, going far in the distance ... forever ... and on each of them there was a butterfly... It felt as if I were in a butterfly kingdom where these little sleeping angels were all around me... I remember I even stopped breathing... YES, it looks like I experienced this special feeling because of the Priest ... maybe he thought he was in heaven with butterflies-souls all around him! According to hieroglyphic texts, towards the end of the classical Maya period, there was a belief that right after death the deceased went down to the cave-homeland of his ancestors and went through a purification ritual. The souls of the buried ones came out of there in the form of butterflies that are called "the eyes of the buried ones". When it was time to return, I collected them easily, one by one and kept eight of them between my fingers. But it was not easy to go down the mountains without the support of my hands –

© Josephine Wall. All Rights Reserved. www.josephinewall.com

I had both hands up and to the side, like kids flying an imaginary airplane... So I started to play airplane and ran down the hill. On the way down, I catch the branches of some bushes for support with my arms, like a mantis. At one point, during this rapid descent, I almost stepped on an EFA, the most poisonous snake in the region. This snake looks like a rattle snake, with a short, piggish face and a rude attitude – it just bites – no warning, no cobra dance. BUT she is beautiful – all covered in powder-pink, innocent color! She slithered across the path and my foot stepped next to her and I felt my skin touching her but I just continued running down. It was impossible to stop anyway. From time to time you need to slow down for a bit, though, or you will turn into a ball "rolling" down the hill instead of "running". I guess the Priest's knowledge taught me how to run down from the pyramid stairs without anything to support me.

I let them go, all of them, at once. I took them while they were sleeping, dreaming, so it would have been easy to start spraying them with perfume and kill them for the collection. It was beautiful when all eight butterflies started flying from my hands! It was magic to see how they flew ... so big and slow ... it was unreal ... like planes...

Hunting wild piton snake in Thailand.

Youtube: Maya, TIME LINE,
https://www.youtube.com/watch?v=dRHGSNZDxnE

When I arrived back at the camp, the students just started waking up, coming out of their tents. They were all amazed when I showed them the butterflies. We all dream to catch at least one like these for the collection, because this is the biggest butterfly living in Tibet! It is huge, gorgeous, and all white with two big round dots on its wings!

****

Near the place where we were camping with the students was an astonishingly beautiful waterfall. Every morning all kinds of animals came to the place to drink fresh water. I always went to the foot of the fall before sunrise, hid in the bushes and watched them. It was magic to see the light dancing through the water; it looked like a million shiny diamonds dropping down ... and all kinds of birds and animals, drinking together at the same time.

Once, I decided to **climb very high**, up to the top of the waterfall to see as far as I could possibly do. I was very happy and excited, so I didn't pay attention that I was way too high already, so high, in fact, that I found myself in a silly situation – I couldn't climb down to go back to camp! I just couldn't see any possibility to go down from my perch!

I remember sitting there for a long time until I suddenly saw our teacher with a group of students, very far down below. They looked like ants to me. At that moment, I decided that if I could not turn back I would jump ahead of the fall as much as I could to make sure that I would not struck any rock on the way down. It would be best for the students to find me dead right there on the little road next to the waterfall. Otherwise, many people would spend lots of time trying to find me, and most likely, they would never do. To be listed as "lost in the mountains" would be a shame and it seemed to be much better to me, at the time, to be dead and easy to find than **"lost forever"**!

It looks like my past life's experience in Amelia's situation, when I was lost and died in the middle of the Pacific, very much affected my spirit! And my spirit, was struggling and suffering from the event.

I was in a hopeless situation... The sun was setting behind the mountains. I closed my eyes for a few minutes trying to think of what to do ... and when I opened my eyes, I saw a huge, noble deer with big antlers near me. I remember how he looked at me with his big, brown, shiny eyes. I saw his breath whiffing out of his snout – he was an impressive animal. He saw me and started running away, jumping... It was an awesome sight. I saw him literally flying with one long jump from my left to the next rock. And then, a miracle; he showed me the way to survive and I followed in his tracks. I started to move toward the place where he landed from his first jump and found a stable ledge from which I could step and start moving down ... back to life.

Persistence – Perseverance

When Amelia decided to fly around the world, she ***persisted and persevered*** with the idea, and she did it. All my life, from a young age, I have persisted *and **persevered*** with everything I do.
Here just one example.
When I was six years old, I played with other kids outside in the street near a large drain pipe. All the kids were 8 or 9 years old and they jumped from one side to the other across a big hole in the land. In the middle of this hole there was a pipe which was going across the hole to the creek, to the other side to a wall where the cigarette factory was located.

Photographer: Darlene Laurel SV

I wished to be like these big kids. But I was too small; I couldn't jump the way they did, so I decided to climb across the pipe instead. Suddenly, boiling water started flowing through the pipe. I had already put my legs on the hot metal pipe – it was too late to go back. It was pretty high. I only wished to prove to myself that I could do it – that I could go over this pipe! I wanted to show that I was no less than these kids! So I continued to go over the pipe. When I was on the other side, the leg, which had touched the pipe, was burned. My leotard was melted into the skin on the thigh. I remember how I went to my piano lesson and played, sitting at the very edge of the chair, afraid of touching this very painful spot. Afterwards, I spent the day in school – same story – I sat at the very end of the bench and lived with this, this excruciating pain throughout the day. In the evening my parents brought me to my grandmother and left for the weekend. When she called me to take a bath..., she saw what happened. My thigh was melted into the stocking, through the skin and up to the muscle... Now I have a big round "kiss" imprint from that pipe on my leg – a mark of *my persistence and perseverance.*

Has the recent Amelia movie changed anything in your life?

Amazingly, I found even more common things between Amelia and myself in the "Amelia" movie. For example, when I saw the **tiger picture** on the carpet near Amelia's bed in the movie, I literally stop breathing! All my life, at the last moment before I fall asleep, I see a tiger coming from the jungle and if someone is near I tell them that "the tiger has already come!" My parents used to know what that meant.
Also, I wrote **rules for my ex-husband**, much like how Amelia asked for freedom in marriage.
I recognized myself when Hilary Swank said: I WILL FLY, never mind how impossible the difficult situation. Yes, people have told me: "**If no one else can do this, only you can do this."** The last time someone told me this was just in March 2010 in Mexico.

Do you know why Amelia was lost?

Yes, I know why Amelia. It happened, according to her astrology.
We have 12 houses in astrology. Each represents a different sphere of life. She was a Leo. She was lost one month early, before her birthday. It was July 2; it was under the Cancer sign. For her it was the twelfth house of her horoscope.

Below are some of the meanings for the 12th house:
*Mysticism, the occult, psychic matters. Places of seclusion such as hospitals, prisons and institutions. Retreat and reflection and **self-sacrifice**. Secrets and childhood problems. The subconscious mind, hidden resources, **hidden problems**,(broken and lost antenna!)social responsibility. The Twelfth House marks where we may be required to have patience and acceptance, perhaps **sacrificing our own personal needs in order to move forward a cause greater than our self.** This is where and how we find greater acceptance and the means to embrace fully what life presents to us.* [4]

One month before their birthday, people don't have enough energy. It is the end of the energy cycle, which starts from their birth date, each year. Since they have a lack of energy, most people get sick around that time. Yes, Amelia did not feel good before her last flight. I felt it intensely during the hypnosis session; she was sick and very tired during that last flight.

She should have started that flight around the globe at a different time – just one and half to two months later – and everything would have been okay. That way she would have started her flight when her dangerous cycle was finished .If she had started to remember her past life as a Priest, and chosen the right time according to her astrology, she would have completed her adventure and would have died much later.

I read that statistically 70% of people die during the last month before their birthday – mostly due to health problems. People also get lost easily at that time, no one can find them, or they lose stuff. This is what happened to me when I had a 12th house experience – when I was in Japan. It was September, one month before my birthday. I was totally lost and didn't know how I was going to pay extra for the subway ticket, and finally, I lost control of my stuff, and **forgot** my bag with all my documents, money, and airplane ticket – everything important was in that bag – and it was stolen.

I remember another 12th house incident, when I went for an audition for a modeling contract. I sat near the door all the time, but they never called me – not until the very end of the audition. I was wondering why they always came out, called somebody else's name and these people did not come

YOUR ETERNAL HOLOGRAM

for the audition? I asked why, and we found out that my agent had put down a different name for me by **mistake.**

My business partner, Jay, from LA, California, told me, "A bunch of teens was with my son at my house playing and I **couldn't find** my digital photo camera." I told him, "It was in July, right?" He was amazed. How did I know this? Simply because I knew that he was born in August.

Once I was **lost** in China, Beijing. It was September (again a month before my birthday in the 12th house of my horoscope). I went to the park at 5:30 a.m. to see how people study martial arts, Tai Chi and Kung Fu, and lost my way back to the hotel. It was in 1988. At that time, there were only Chinese hieroglyphs around – not one English sign. For almost two hours, I tried talking to people around me in English, trying to find my way back to the hotel... No luck. I was prepared to live in the street for some time. Then suddenly an old Chinese man asked me, "Can you talk Russian, maybe?" Of course, I can! He showed me to hundreds of people around and said, "No one talks English, but each and everyone here talks Russian. They all studied Russian in school!" Wow! It was a surprise for me! I started laughing at myself!

When people are in the 12th house of their horoscopes, they could also **die** as a result of an accident. They simply did not see the car approaching or fell down or didn't pay enough attention to what they ate and ended up eating something wrong. Or they take some medicine the wrong way or something else happened to them. My mother and grandmother died a month before their birthdays, the same happened to a few other people whom I was lucky to know during their lifetime. The father of a boy who studied in my daughter's class died because he did not see some electrical wires and was killed. It happened in the last month before his birthday.

My friend, David, diedtwo weeks before his birthday because ... (this is really a terrible story, I am not sure if I should put it here, but maybe it will help people to be more careful during the month before their birthday) ... he was at home, in Toronto, with his little granddaughter, Rita, during the 12th house of his horoscope. He simply was not aware of the danger. He did not feel good, so he could not pay enough attention to the little Rita. He allowed her to play on the balcony and she fell down from the 24th floor. She had been trying to see the swimming pool below and bent down too far over the railing. She was a very bright, happy, dancing, and singing child. She, too, was in the 12th house of her horoscope cycle. A few hours later, David himself died of a heart attack. This story is heart-breaking. Yet again, it's good to know that people have many lives and maybe they are re-born already as twins, for example, and will spend a full, long life together. They loved each other deeply during their lives.

In Vancouver we have lots of benches donated by people. You find them everywhere along English Bay and in Stanley Park. I decided to check those statistics and began paying attention to the plaques on the benches. Yes, the statisticians were right! On each bench you can read when the person was born and when he or she died. In most cases the person past away during the last month before his or her birthday! Or they died at the beginning of the month of their birthday, when the cycle ends and they have no more energy left...

After I finished writing this book and my daughter's summer holiday started, we decided to visit the rest of the ancient civilizations on the planet. We flew from Canada via Paris to Rome, visited Greece, Turkey and Crimea. When we jumped from the train in Rome, my daughter suddenly realized that **she had forgotten** her small backpack, with the camera and our tickets, on the now departing train! The train was on its way to Naples. A few minutes later, we met a handsome Italian journalist, Cristiano, who was pretty tired after two interviews in Milan that day, and who had also forgotten his wallet with money and credit cards on that same train. He was gracious enough to invite us to drive with him to Naples. When we arrived at the station, everything was returned to us instantly – no harm done. But I had to ask – "What month were you born?" That man and my daughter were born just a few days apart – and he belongs to the same astrology sign as she does.

That day, when they both lost their stuff, was in the 12th house of their horoscope!

I think it is not necessary to add anything else to this subject in order to support Amelia and explain why she was lost. I read on a website:

"It might appear that whatever happened in the Central Pacific did not fit the pattern of Earhart's previous problems, but perhaps it did. The fundamental cause of the flight's failure to reach Holland seems to be Earhart's failure to adequately understand the capabilities and limitations of her radio equipment. In other words, she got in over her head, except this time the consequences were not a bent prop and a bruised ego, and this time she couldn't walk away." (http://www.tighar.org/)

I am not agreeing with this, because I know astrology. It was not her ego or whatever this Richard Gillespie think led her to her death. It was the fact that she was in the 12th house of her horoscope!
Yes, Amelia was not fully aware of the capabilities and limitations of her radio equipment, because she was in the 12th house of her horoscope at that moment, which closed all possibility for her to understand how serious the situation was. This is the same thing that happened to David and Rita. Amelia tried her best and she was very organized. It was NOT her ego.
And yes, Fred's map was not correct. Since Earth is not exact round, (in reality it ellipse shape) as people thought in the 1930s, distance on the map over ocean was shorter than in reality! I am angry at this silly Richard because of the last sentence in that paragraph in that website. He is the one who got *"a bruised ego"* in people eyes with his dishonest activities!
Knowledge of astrology is a powerful thing. Why did President Reagan meet with Gorbachev in Reykjavik in the middle of the ocean with such good results? Because his astrologer advised him to do it that way. Why was the Declaration of Independence (marking the birth of the USA) signed in the middle of the night? According to astrology, time and place to do something are very important. I am sure if we asked a professional astrologer why Amelia was lost at that particular time and place, s/he would give us a serious explanation.
As you know, after reading the chapter about The Priest, I am acting in my daily life like a priest for a few months now. I am learning some new things, which I love and I am studying from him, or I start remembering things from my past life and continue to cultivate them, trying to develop them.
It is interesting that the same happened after the reading about my past life as Amelia.

During the hypnosis session about Amelia, I developed new habits; I started using muscles I never used before! I always press my nostrils together, for example. The next day, I walked down the street and noticed that I walked differently! I tried to be taller, more straightening my back, (Amelia was little bit taller than me).

Was Amelia MEANT TO DIE?

Today is the 28th of September. I finished writing this book in the summer. Now my editor, Roxane, has finished editing it and will complete the formatting and photo insertions today. The book will be ready to go to the publisher early next week... BUT, I woke up this morning and remembered that I was just talking, in my dream, to my guide, my guardian Angel, about Amelia! We were in some city park, sitting on the ground and I leaned against something at my back. It was dusk.
During that dream, my guide told me that Amelia was MEANT TO DIE according to the plan! And the name for the book should be *Amelia Return?!* This was terrible to hear after all the emotional suffering I had to endure during the hypnosis session about Amelia. These last minutes before her death make me cry each time I start reading about it again!

I asked him: *"What plan? Who makes this plan?" Her death was extremely unfair!*
Here is what he told me:
My life, priest life, hers and this book were planned even before we were born! The Spirit planned a few lives ahead to ensure the best outcome for the planet from the next few lives. Well..., even for me

who wrote this book about it, it was a shocking thing to hear – and way too much for me to handle at once!

To plan the next few lives?

He told me that before the **Spirit was born as Amelia, Spirit made a plan where to be born, who to be, what to do and how to die!**

The plan was...

1. To be a **famous person** in the era of aviation in order to have all the data of her life available for me to insert in the book, to compare her life with mine and possibly with other people's lives in this chain such as that of the Priest.

2. **To disappear in this mysterious way** in order to become an even more renowned person, attract attention and keep this interest alive for many years, long enough for her to be reborn and complete the goal and write the book.

3. To disappear in order **to create mystery for me.** To have this dream for years in my mind, ultimately to push me to go to a past life regression specialist; at first, thinking about my "little self" as a person, just wishing to achieve some level of emotional comfort while trying to get "rid of the heavy emotional burden" of a past life.

4. And afterwards find out a much bigger, serious level, and real purpose to what happened to Amelia and the reasons for her and me to be born.

Last, what my guide told me is this, *"In reality, the life of just one person is not so important... The kind of impact his or her life has on the well-being of the whole planet is what is important, not only for the people, but also for nature, plants and animals."*

I woke up then and started thinking about it...

And I remembered this sentence:

*Ironically Amelia Earhart has become more famous for disappearing than for her many real aviation achievements*http://www.acepilots.com/earhart.html

Yes, if Amelia did not die in this mysterious fashion, perhaps she would have been one among many other popular, pioneering aviators and live a long and happy life. However, it was her final flight that made her life a legacy.

I would not have had repeating dreams for years about a woman disappearing before the Second World War started. My guardian angel would never have shown me, in my dream, this "documentary movie about this woman-pilot's life" and I would never have remembered that, in the dream, I recognized the aircraft, how to operate it and screamed, "This is me!" or afterwards ask myself, "What happened with me then?" I would never have gone and asked a hypnosis specialist, Di Cherry, for help to understand what this was all about? If I would have only one past life as a Priest, it would have been a *nice* book, but fewer people would have paid attention to it, found it and read it!

Lots of spiritual books are available. But putting Amelia's life in front of millions of people interested in what happened to her will attract their attention to this book and they will read it.

It will be a key word, like a password, for people to open the door to find, to study and to acquire serious fundamental knowledge about their own chain of lives and to start thinking about their own Spirit development. It will be useful, important and priceless for each and everyone in the world to know.

What is the nature of YOUR Soul or Spirit? What happens to YOUR SOUL after death? When this life is finished, will it be the end of everything? Or is it only one little step among many that a person has taken already – walking through the chain of lives, still having many to walk in the future? The Devil, the prince of destruction, of darkness and ugliness is not the one who created people   God created people to **be Creative,** pure of heart and thoughts and to try to do the best they can to make this world, happier, brighter, cleaner and more beautiful by their mere presence (EXISTENCE).

There will be a time when each and every one of us will die and will go to the Spirit world and reap the "harvest" of this life which has just passed. What did he gain? Maybe lots of new knowledge, new abilities, skills, appreciation from the people around him for the gift of love and happiness he imparted to them? It will be an astonishingly sad moment for someone who will deeply regret that he did something wrong during his life for his family and the people around him. Or maybe with his power and intellect, he initiated the huge destruction of a society, country, or nature on the planet!

Maybe someone tried to make money and acquired fame and fortune – an "image" – during his life, while destroying forests or oceans, or a whole country, and killing many people. However, then, he will be sitting in line waiting for his judgment with empty hands, because he just couldn't bring with him money or anything from his life to that place. Perhaps he will feel that he was sadly misinformed! The devil simply tricked him, attracted him to money and material possessions which became a "big thing" during his life. He spent all of his energy working on it very hard, but the real "gold" is now in someone else's hands – in the hands of those who were creative and improved their Spirit positive quality ... how unfair, he will say!
 "What goes round comes round..."
Now I understand the enormous responsibility that has been bestowed upon me to try to bring this book to the people. And I cry for Amelia who lost her life so young in order to help millions of people understand and prove that our Spirit does not die after death and to demonstrate it through her own example. My guide told me that I should study Amelia's life and that I will find much more common between the two of us than I first observed!
By the way, when I said, "I leaned against something at my back" at the beginning of my dream, the "something" was Amelia's bronze statue! I didn't even know that such a statue existed. And I full in love with that statue in N. Hollywood instantly!

About Hollywood. As for me I believe **Jessica Biel** will be the best actress to play role of the Amelia Earhart in the movie. Her facial most close to Amelia's looks. Even nose on the Amelia's statue and hers nose similar shape and I love this shape!
While I was writing an email to Roxane, I checked Amelia's website to find out what this statue looks like, and I ended up in her museum, the house where she was born. I clicked **FUN Facts** about Amelia.http://www.ameliaearhartmuseum.org/AmeliaEarhart/AEFunFacts.htm
Well.., my guide was right as usual.

I added these facts in the part called, **What about your family?** Discussed below.

The most important thing is that you got the idea why *Amelia was meant to die* ... and now I can say it easily, without stopping to take a breath, as I did when I heard it for the first time from my guide in my dream today.

You have a new theory about Amelia's disappearance?

After this dream, I can add one more version to the collection of Disappearance Speculations of Amelia Earhart. It may sound really strange, but as for me after the crazy things which happened during the production of this book, I think it is possible. Remember the unexplained force which lifted a man from his chair, sent him to his locker room, and pushed him to bring his laptop to my door hours before my laptop burned out so that I could continue writing this book on his computer? And many other cases... It looks like a "team" of Spirits is involved and supports me in writing this book.
Do you remember the story of the "The Miracle Man" who lives in Brazil? He incorporated 33 Spirits entities into his body. There were doctors among them, and he, in a split second, performed invisible surgeries through these entities and treated up to 600 people a day! (*The Miracle Man: The Life Story of João de Deus, by Robert Pellegrino-Ostrich. Extracted from his book Published in 1997, ©1997/1998. All rights reserved.*) [5] See how
If it was the Spirit's goal to make Amelia disappear mysteriously, in order to give people knowledge that the Spirit is eternal and never dies, it is very important to live a creative spiritual life.

The Spirit manages to do this perfectly: "*The mysterious fate of the larger than life woman flyer tugged at the public's consciousness. No trace of the craft was ever found – although an extensive coordinated search was carried out by the Navy and Coast Guard. Despite the efforts of 66 aircraft and 9 ships and an expenditure of an estimated 4 million dollars, authorized by President Franklin D. Roosevelt, their fate remained a mystery.*"

A few hours after the reading, I found out, on the internet, who Amelia was and that her airplane is still missing. I called the TIGHAR Company which tried to find her and which was preparing for their next voyage. I told the director that I just found out that I was Amelia in my past life, that I knew the location of the airplane and that I wished to divulge it to him. I told him that I am very happy about their efforts in trying to find her aircraft and that I am ready to help as much as I could. If they wanted, I said, I could even fly with them to the place and invest my feelings into this, which would point us and navigate us in the right direction. It was nice to hear that they already had a plan where to search this time, "but please also check the location I have," I said. "Because I can tell you the exact place!" I also mentioned that with the goose bump sensation I experienced this spring, while visiting places where I was in my past lives; maybe, they could monitor my skin reaction to give them direction and help navigate the search.
The problem was that he simply didn't believe that it could be possible; that people have many lives and he couldn't see any value in past life regression. Me too! I was exactly the same just five months ago. I didn't believe it. I am a scientist. I didn't even want to go to any of these sessions. I told him about my experience and proposed to put me into a deep hypnosis state with some specialists of his choosing to ask Amelia directly, one more time, the exact location of her aircraft: "Where is the airplane right now?" He didn't want to do the session, even with his own hypnosis specialists. He had nothing to lose – he could only gain popularity when he would finally solve the mystery, right?

I start even think: **maybe for some reason Richard Gillespie did not want really to find Amelia's airplane so fast? I know it sound weird, but this is was my impression after talking with him numerous time later when we was meet in Washington.** From another side maybe it is good? He did his job very well: he did kept Amelia's popularity high all this years, right? And finally when airplane will be found when my book will be ready?

So, I just went for a tomato juice refill and started playing my Priest's rock from Mexico. Believe me, perhaps more than anyone on the planet, I wish to find her airplane, solve the mystery. Maybe this is one of the reasons why I was re-born. It is strange that this man dedicated maybe all of his life in the search for Amelia's airplane; that he made a wonderful website with Amelia's biography, but that he did not want to deal with the person who was the real Amelia in her past life.

I just laughed when he closed his eyes trying to avoid seeing the real person. But, YES, I could understand his point of view, too. This subject dealing with past lives is unusual and strange.

But that aircraft... I wish to find it and lift it from the ocean... It is still in my mind like a dream toy. I have this enormous attachment to that airplane, deep in my heart and Spirit. I think if Amelia loved airplanes so much it is a great honor for her to have it as a coffin.

I saw in *http://www.tighar.org/TTracks/14_2/14-2Bones.html* that bones were found in the Nikumaroro Islands by a British colonial administrator of Irish descent, Gerald B. Gallagher, whose nickname was in fact, "Irish."

"When only about 24 hours out of Suva, he died. The natives are superstitious as the devil and the next night ... they threw the gunnysack full of bones overboard". Actually this person: *"Gallagher did not die in a boat 24 hours out of Fiji, but he did die on Nikumaroro about 24 hours after returning from leave in Fiji."*

So he did bring bones to Fiji for forensic examination. **This incident with its CURSE can be one of the extra proofs that Amelia's Spirit was involved!** YES, it sounds weird, but this is exactly what it is! Hers and my past lives were Ancient Maya Priest and Egyptian Royal Priestess. The Spirit was not happy with this man, Gerald. **I guess the Spirit didn't plan on someone finding Amelia's bones or anyone else's which may look like they belonged to her, so soon.**

And, by the way I found out recently that this island is full of ghosts and they don't like foreign people! The locals teach the "Tighar" team, who is searching for Amelia's airplane to cover their faces and body with sand to try pretending that they are locals and to "trick" the Spirits, to avoid danger. Everyone follows this advice!

So from another side maybe Gallagher's death doesn't have any connection with Amelia's case? **Spirit's plan was to disappear in this mysterious way in order to become an even more renowned person, attract attention and keep this interest alive for many years, long enough to be reborn and complete the goal, and write the book...**

Thomas E Devine wrote a number of books saying that Amelia was killed by Japanese on Saipan and he died. R. Wallack pretends that he saw her briefcase on Saipan and died **from throat** cancer. He was cursed as well!! There was NO Japanese around. Only bones of native people were found on that island. It is a shame that people play games around Amelia's death. It is impossible – NO WAY – that Amelia was kidnapped or immigrated to Japan under somebody's name. Please read the book and the hypnosis sessions. It is not her, and my character is not to hide and run. What reason would she have to do this?

During my present life, people around me have lots of luck, gain prosperity, and some win the lottery. (On my website www.ameliareborn.com at "**Unexplained mystery**«part examples about luck and Blessing for the people who around me).But 6 people were punished! They were **CURSED** in some strange way when they did something really bad for people or community around them!

YOUTUBE: Amelia's mystery

Yes, Spirits can do amazing things even over the internet! Remember how Spirit produce 3 ISBN numbers for 3 books with numbers 5 and 8? Here is one more example of what Spirits can do. After experiencing many instances like these, I am sure this is not just a coincidence, but a game played by the Spirit, who tries to show me his ability to give more time and supplementary proofs that the Spirit of people lives after death and that people should be "mindful" of this!

We were in Hawaii in the car with a teenager named Lauren, and Dawne, who is the manager of the hotel we were staying in. www.gardenislandinn.com
Dawne tried to park her car in the parking lot when I pointed right in front of us to the car with the **number 085**. I told that this is my lucky number and mentioned that Spirits talking with me throw the numbers to guide me and protect me... Lauren replied: "I don't believe in it and lucky numbers is not exist."Dawne replied: "I like # 777. This is my special number. What if this number will appear? So maybe I will also start believe in it..."
That moment she turned the car with intention drive further and try to find available spot near shopping mall. As soon as she pronounced this sentence car right near her, from her side was with this number 777! We all were very surprised! **Well... some High power or some Spirits decided to prove to us that in fact they can communicate with the numbers and this time, when 777 appeared... it is not by some coincidence, but by this Spirits involvement!** See what happened next!
About a week later in Canada I was talking on the internet on messenger (MSN) with Shawn, who is now in Hong Kong about this case and I mentioned to him that stories with the numbers continued to happen in Hawaii... Shawn had witnessed similar situations already like these occurring around me and saved my life. (His testimonial is on the chapter PRIEST of this book.)
As soon as I finished talking with him, suddenly a story arrived to my inbox with the same words!

These are the kinds of messages that people forward to each other in a chain mail. There was a story about girl **LAUREN**. She was in the **car**; driving and she had a problem and phoned **#77** to call for **help**. If anyone dials a sentence on Google.com that starts with #77 you will read this full message: ***77 It was about 1:00 p.m. In the afternoon, and Lauren was driving to visit a friend, to be safe she need to call *77**. (#77 is a protection in this case and was a direct link to State trooper info)

I sent the message to Shawn and Dawne:

From:julia **To:**ShawnS **Cc:**dawneM
Sent: Saturday, September 26, 2009 9:19 AM
Subject: THIS IS CRAZY!!!!!!Fw: Larry G- Do you know about #77

SHAWN, this is ASTONISHING! We stop talking about those case with **777** and that **Lauren** did not believe in numbers and that we were in the **car driving** and I told you that **Spirits with numbers warned me and protect me, right?**

And I saw that some kind of spam story to arrive from Steve K. from Florida and wish to delete it, BUT there was:***77 It was about 1:00 p.m. In the afternoon, and Lauren was driving to visit a friend, safe place.** So amazingly Spirit found this message on internet and managed to send it to me!

To prove that YES Spirits with the numbers protected me and cared and warned me!!!
77–protection in this case below!!!On top of that there was the number **777**, a girl who did not believe in numbers' relationships and who sat in the same **car** as a girl named **Laura**!

So, Spirit managed to find the story on the internet which included all 3 things: **777, car, Laura, safe.**

However, and most importantly, it supports the main idea of my book: **People after death, continue living in the Spirit world as Spirits, "mindful" of who they are and what they do. As you saw, they can even do tricks like these!**

It looks like that after death the Spirit of people is highly organized and much smarter with many more abilities in this multidimensional outer Space. Remember that João-in-entity, the Spirits of 33

Doctors, who can heal people in split-seconds after they enter the body of the "Miracle man" from Brazil?

NaturalNews Insider Alert (www.NaturalNews.com)

Dear NaturalNews readers,
A "science skeptic" neurosurgeon named Dr. Eben Alexander had his brain partially eaten by an aggressive E.coli infection. He lapsed into a coma, and for seven days, his consciousness was completely untethered to his mortal brain. During that time, he experienced a **"hyper-realistic" journey into the afterlife**, complete with contact from God, angelic beings, a view of the multiverse and intelligent life in our known universe. Thanks to a healing miracle that defies the limited knowledge of modern-day science, he returned to consciousness and was able to write a book describing his experience: **"Proof of Heaven."**

As you'll see in my review of the book and the exploration of his experience, what happened to the consciousness of Dr. Alexander is a crucial and timely message for us all: There is LIFE after LIFE, and our souls survive human death.

Last summer in Hawaii I met a healer, Howard Wills, with astonishing powers. With a snap of the fingers he healed people through instant connections with God and Angels. His little adorable son, Romana also inherited this rare gift from him. He, himself looks like a little angel.
http://www.howardwills.com

I am really amazed about my Spirit, which created a plan of succession with chains of lives. At first he entered two powerful individuals like the Maya Priest and Amelia Earhart and now me as a scientist, who is currently collecting facts and already proved to the world that Spirit is Eternal.
But most amazing, of course, for me was that Spirit counted and arranged for Amelia to be born in a family where there were so many common things – too many to count.

So you have many things that prove you are Amelia reborn?

Please see below a list of the common life traits, characteristics, habits, appearances, interests, and activities between myself and Amelia.

I am lucky that I can compare my life with my previous life, because of Amelia's popularity.
I put **Amelia-Julia** together for easy comparison.
I discovered that I am exactly the same as Amelia Earhart – just 75 years later!
Plus, information that was restricted in the 1930s that Amelia was forced to hide has now been unwrapped and unfolded.

From: webmaster@near-death.com:

"JULIA look exactly like Amelia - especially her eyes.

It is said the eyes are the "window to the soul" and she definitely have Amelia's eyes and soul. "

Peace and Light,
Kevin Williams

YOUR ETERNAL HOLOGRAM

Here list of some of them and below more details about it.

Now, let's begin with common things between Julia and Amelia:

- Both have the same facial features.
- Open to new freedoms and new possibilities.
- Both have had lots of followers.
- Both are pioneers
- Both adore Asia.
- Are pacifists.
- Workers in charge of children, teaching.
- Clothing designs, models (we wear similar clothing, are both attracted to the color yellow. Amelia even had yellow airplane and yellow car).
- Both even share being named for a flower: Amelia- and Julia's nickname is Jasminrose.
- Ear**hart**, Svadi **hatra.**
- The same hand writing
- **YOUTUBE: Amelia Earhart: Seen Through Her Handwriting**
- **Julia studied piano for eight years. At the age of six, she began attending ballet classes.**

(Since Julia was five years old, she had a private teacher who taught her how to play the piano. At the age of six, she began attending **ballet classes**. From the age of seven, and for the next seven years she went to **music school**. She enjoy studying music and the biography of the famous classical composers. Her favorite music, which she loved to play, was Mozart's bright and happy music and that of the wise John Sebastian Bach.)

From Julia's past life as Amelia Earhart, the pilot, she have similar interest for **music, poetry,** as well as **fine arts, drawing, clothes design, modeling,** and **aviation,** in this life.

Julia studied also the same things that Amelia also studied: **biology, zoology, plants, chemistry, biochemistry, agriculture, physics.**
Amelia was very good in **math**; Julia also finished special math school. This helped Julia understand multidimensional world much easier. (See Violet field chapter.)

Julia's **essays, poetry, and stories** were the best in my school. Principal collected them and not only read them to the pupils in her own class but also continued to do this even after she left the school. (After the hypnosis session Julia started to write poems in English and you can see her drawings on my website www.ameliareborn.com and in the book.)

Julia also studied **photography.** Amelia had her own photo studio and studied all of these areas above.

Julia addicted to the color yellow ... like Amelia did.

Amelia had a red and white scarf. I have a skirt and scarf which was also red and white, and I love to wear them!

YouTube: Amelia Earhart: Soaring, on min 3.15
The Final Hours Amelia Earhart's Last Flight - 2000 Documentary Part (¼) 5.17 min here

When it was time to go to university, Julia tried to decide whether she wanted to be a doctor like her

mother or study plants and be a scientist like her father?
Yes, I wish to be a doctor and a scientist at the same time. By the age of 14, I had read all of the medicine books my mother had in the house. They were big, heavy books, encyclopedias about internal medicine, microbiology, gynecology, skin disease, biochemistry and so on and so on. I loved it and it was like a food for me, to which I was addicted. It was impossible for me to stop devouring the knowledge contained in these books – until I would come to the end of each one. I guess I chose my parents before I was born. I decided to study plants only because I worried that I would make a mistake as a doctor. Amelia loved **biology, science** and spent lots of time with **medicine,** working in hospitals and studying. I have a state-of-the-art diagnostic **medicine machine** and I am checking everyone's health trying to help my friends – I do this as a hobby.
In University Julia was top-of-the-class in **physics and chemistry** and graduated with honors. She was the only one, from hundreds of students, who got a "RED diploma" (meaning she was the best from the best).
Julia finished university with a **teaching degree** in biology and chemistry. After that, she took post-graduate courses in horticulture physiology, biochemistry, and radiology.
Amelia was a "**Worker in charge of children** ranging from toddlers to teens". (This is what I saw during the hypnosis sessions, when a mother comes to Amelia in some office with 2 children!)

My daughter asked me a few days ago: "Why you always in this **pilot shirt** at home, when you have so many beautiful things to wear?" Interesting... I had never paid attention to this; that I typed all this book often wearing a T-shirt with a **map** of the Caribbean Islands (the Atlantis place – I prefer T-shirts with maps) underneath my favorite shirt. I looked down at this khaki, light green color shirt and wow! She was right! It is a pilot shirt, from L'Aero-Club de France, "Flying with the best" and with the logo of a small propeller airplane on the front pocket... I think I know now why I was deeply attached to this shirt for the last 10 years... I wish to have Amelia's "99 Club" shirt one day, if they exist. No doubt I would live in those shirts 24/7...

By the way, I read them all; I mean every book we had in our school library.
My aunt, Merry, always sent me **science fiction** books; I read them during math classes, because I always had time to read after I finished the assignments quickly. More than once, our math teacher took the book I was reading and punished me by withholding the book until the end of the year. In the end, she had a good collection of science fiction books, maybe around 12 or 14 of them.

I loved books about **fine arts.** I can stare at paintings for hours. I loved to visit the Hermitage and spent days there, and I am planning to visit the Louvre in Paris this summer. I always envy the people who live in St. Petersburg or Paris. They can go any day and see the many paintings displayed in the museums! You can see examples of my owndrawings in this book. Thanks to Amelia; I gained from her, as an inheritance, her **drawing skills**, which she developed during her life.

Interesting! I found out that "Amelia Earhart was a known devout **pacifist,** was a 'world humanitarian. She was also deeply spiritual, an artistic thinker, and she commanded a supreme intellectual quality. This is exactly the description of who I am now in this life! I am against war and violence. I just can't watch movies about war or violence.
Amelia also very much **adored the cultures of the Orient**, and the social and religious philosophies inherent to the countries of China and Japan".
I visited Japan, China and South Korea during the last 18 years at least 20 times and was even told bya Highest Monk that one of my past lives was spent in Asia. It looks like this is the reason why Amelia and I were attracted to Asia. Even my e-mail name: **enjoyjapan**!

"As well, she always had trouble with limelight living, and a marriage prone to expect almost anything but **true love** from her person." I had marriage proposals from famous people, celebrities and rich tycoons during the last few years, since I am single again, but true love is the most important factor for me. Well, maybe all men will now be scared to death to deal with me after reading this book and I will not find any brave one left!

In a past life, I was **Amelia**. This is the name of a flower – the big Lily kind. The Lily is my favorite flower. I always wish to have a flower name. I picked the name **Jasmine Rose** for myself and I have been using it everywhere since 2000. And I still wish to change my name for Jasmine Rose Lily! It sounds funny, too many flowers, right? But this is what I really want.

Perhaps another few people among the billions living on the planet may have the similarities you mentioned with Amelia, right?

Right, I have thought about this possibility as well.
BUT – what about the ***black, fuzzy, hairy creatures*** that followed Amelia?
This is funny! Can you imagine the same black creatures following both Amelia and myself in her and my own life?
*"During her childhood, Amelia invented a tribe of imaginary, **small, black creatures** she called "Dee-Jays". Described as a cross between a Crazy Kat cartoon and a **jabberwocky**, the creatures were often blamed for Amelia's own irresponsible behavior, such as: talking out of turn, eating the last piece of candy, or when something turned up lost."*

*Now, do you remember how Dream # 5 starts – The Upper Kingdom, October 24, 1993? *"It was some terrible, **black, big and hairy creature.**"*

*And in Dream # 26 – Hundreds of Followers – Rubies, November 8, 2003; do you remember the wet hairy creature at the end of the dream?
*"One scene was repeated several times. I opened the door from the room to the street. And **some wild creatures, like wet, little dogs** wanted to rush into the place where we were sitting."*

*Dream # 37 A Man of the Forest – His Name, December 13, 1991
*But it was not from our life. This reminds me of something like **jabberwocky**, in Lewis Carroll. I understood, they understood. But here I cannot understand at all. In Jabberwocky there is a substantive and adjective. But here there were neither of them. It was an event from my other life.*

Can you believe it? I even tell in my dream that this was an event from my other life! This dream was in 1991, when I didn't have any idea that we have many lives and this at a time when I was living another life, when I was living as Amelia, her life!

"I've never seen Julia in person and communicated with her only by Skype. Julia lived in Canada, and I'm in Russia. One day after our talks - I went to bed, and between sleeping and waking, opened a space through which came the **black round shaggy creature**. The creature was not friendly, it attacked me! Horrified, I jumped out of bed and pushed him away with great force. It is not clear why and for what purpose it appeared at my house, from somewhere in a parallel world?
It appeared several times after. When I told Julia about the black shaggy creature turned out that she also know him. It came to her in dreams and she described it in her book. I think that during my sleep I started to know about them and now I can see them and protect myself. This is very important."
Elena from Saint Petersburg

Surprisingly, I **saw this black round object** as a Maya priest!!!
*in a Dream "Upper KINGDOM" October 24, 1993
*as well as the Queen of Atlantis "Hundreds of followers. Rubies"

Yes, Amelia, in accordance was told to her relatives as well. http://www.ameliaearhartmuseum.org

And now in this life intuitive people like Elena from Saint Petersburg see them again around me! When I met Russian top psychic, he told that this Black hairy round Entity, which Amelia called D-Jay is protecting me, through all my previous lives including little Amelia down through the ages. Suddenly I found answer about this black creature in the YOUTUBE video below! It is creature which coming from 4th dimension in to the our 3rd dimension but not fully, so it did not reflect light from our 3rd dimension and this is why it looks like a black hole, **black fuzzy** contour around body. They can be dangerous for the people.

So Amelia and me, we both had ability to see it, and as a Maya priest I even was fighting with one of them...When Elena talked with me I activated in her this abilities, and as a result she starting see black creature as well. Yes, since that day, when that creature comes she can see it and can protect herself, which is very important. I am thinking about this situation. Maybe sometimes some people die during dream from heart attack, because this type of creatures attack them and since they not aware about there existence, they die without protecting themselves?

YOUTUBE: The Alien Agenda - Conspiracy Documentary Simon Parkes 2015, start from 39.27 min

How about detail of my daughter's birth certificate showing the attending nurse's signature as U. Lougheed. The airplane flown by Amelia Earhart on her last flight was a Lockheed L10 Electra.

Here are some **Habits,** which we have in common with Amelia: (Richard E. Gillespie, Amelia Earhart.) .Thanks Ric!

http://www.tighar.org/Projects/Earhart/ResearchPapers/Earhart.html#2

What about **tea and coffee,** which Amelia and I cannot drink, and tomato juice which we both love?

"Amelia does not drink coffee or tea, she takes tomato juice instead."

I can't drink tea, especially dark or strong, for as far as I can remember. I drink herbal tea sometimes – always very light. And I just cannot drink coffee.

*She loved **tomato juice.***

I arrived a few days ago from Egypt and I am still on European time, now in Canada. I woke up at 3:15 a.m. this morning and started working on the book. I have been typing for the last 16 hours – it is now 7:20 p.m. – already. I only took a few short trips to the kitchen to refill my glass of **tomato juice** I prefer the Extra Spicy Tomato-Clam cocktail, when I am working on the computer. Since I can't drink coffee or real tea, the spices in this juice keep me in great shape to type for a long time and ... I didn't fall asleep while flying my airplane in my past life...

I love and drink tomato juice every single day with all kinds of spices. My grandmother knew about my love for tomato juice. For many years in the fall she used to buy boxes of tomatoes and made juice, and some with little tomatoes inside it. I remember the three- and five-liter-jars at her place.

When I go to an Italian restaurant these days, I usually order the smallest plate possible with noodles, sometimes even from the kids menu, but I ask them to bring me cups and cups of tomato sauce! I love Italian restaurants! :)

Yes, it is strange but for some reason, I just **can't drink tea, coffee.** Everybody in my family drinks all kinds of teas. So it is not genetic. I was wondering, how come with my perfect health, I have a problem with this. When I read that Amelia also did not drink tea, I was very surprised. Our bodies, hers and mine, can't accept tea! Please tell me how it could be possible that this characteristic transferred with the Spirit into a new body?

I even decided to check one more time and I agreed to drink one cup of tea with my aunt Mary, during my visit this summer. I felt so, so bad, I lost a whole day because I couldn't do anything with this terrible, sickening feeling. I counted the hours, waiting for my body to get rid of it.

I wonder if Amelia loved **sour cherries**, the same as I do. I know that Amelia with her friends named an imaginary city, Cherryville.

AVATAR SVADI HATRA

Since I found that I was Amelia in my past life, it helps me explain many things in my present life. For example, for the last 20 years every day I go to Stanley Park, to the same place, to the rose garden and I sit there on the same bench.

*Now I know why! I always see **small airplanes land** every 10 to 15 minutes, flying through, very low on top of my head! Because the lagoon is near the landing area. Right across from the rose garden, I always look at the strange row of pine trees, maybe a dozen of them... I just found out that one of these airplanes, with people from Japan, landed in this **lagoon and sunk with** all its passengers still aboard. These pine trees were planted in their memory, standing in rows of two, like people sitting in an airplane. Well... Amelia also drowned and did not arrive on the island...

*And this is what attracts my Spirit to this place, the same as it did on Kalapaki beach in Kauai, Hawaii. I really love these beaches and now I know why! Near the Lihue airport, I can see **airplanes arriving** during the day non-stop over this **small island in the Pacific.** Amelia was unable to reach and land on Howard Island, and watching the arriving airplanes on Kauai islands provides great joy to the Spirit!

* It was interesting that at the end of the movie, "**Night at the Museum: Battle of the Smithsonian**" (2009) they showed a girl with long, blond hair with Amelia's face visiting a museum... I have long blond hair... Maybe the screen writer felt there was an Amelia with long, blond hair somewhere reborn...?

*Interesting that when I was in school near our street was **air club,** and there was part of the real airplane, but without wings...I remember that after school, evening time, when no one there, I often climbed inside and sit there, it was during at least 7 years.

I kept this picture in front of my eyes for many years... Now I know WHY!
Because, as Amelia, I received this medal in my past life with similar image.

Once in my dream I saw man, we was talking with him about serious problems American people experiencing with banks, it was something about loosing there houses. I was very worry and try to help. Few days later I saw documentary movie and recognized this man! It was **President Franklin D. Roosevelt**. I open Google and suddenly saw on the photo woman near him. She was very much familiar to me! Goose bumps starting all over my body and after tears start running from my eyes! It was **Eleanour Roosevelt**, Amelia's dearest friend, with who she shared common ideas about Woman Status in society and Human right. Eleanor was 1st Chair of the Presidential Commission on the Status of Women, 1st United States Representative to the United Nations Commission on Human Rights. This explained why from the moment when I was baby I start walking and talking I started ask my parents why I don't have sister Elena? I was repeated this over and over again until at age of 5, I finally got what I wished for, my sister was born and of course her name was **Elena** & my **Elean**or !

Eleanour Roosevelt   **President Franklin D. Roosevelt**

What about your family and Amelia?

Amelia's spirit chose to be reborn in Julia's family:

*Julia's father is a scientist who studied everything that Amelia also loved throughout her life: **Biology, chemistry,** and so on.

*Julia's mother was a **doctor** like Amelia; she also flew in small **airplanes** and did parachuting and skydiving. She also looks like Amelia. You can see her photo on next page.

*Julia's grandmother's second husband was a **lawyer and drinker** – exactly the same as Amelia's father.

*Like Amelia, Julia also has a **younger sister.**

*Amelia had lots of imaginary friends, playmates, horses... Well..., that's only because she saw them, in the same way Julia see them. There were always **Spirits** around Amelia as there are around Julia, both of them.

*Julia's best friend at school was **Laura** – just like Amelia's playmates was named *Laura* – in school.

*Julia even had the same **angry black dog** that Amelia did. He had the same nature as Amelia's dog had; he was very protective, angry and ferocious! His name was Black Ball.

*Amelia had the middle name **Mary**. Julia's aunt was named **Mary.** She is living in Russia and bears an English name – because her father read an English book once and he liked the name. My aunt told me that there was a problem with her birth certificate 65 years ago in Russia – an English name for a Russian girl was not acceptable in those days. But he wanted it no matter what and got it for her.

*Amelia named the twin maple *trees* in her grandparent's Atchison front yard Philemon and Baucus after a **husband and wife** in Greek mythology." This was astonishing to me! I named two huge trees here in English Bay which grow from the same roots with my husband's and my name. One tree blossomed with white flowers – mine, the second one never had flowers but had a luxuriant crown of leaves. When my ex-husband needed to move definitively to Europe, years ago, his tree suddenly died, and soon afterwards, it was cut down by the city's garden maintenance department!

Julia's father looks exactly like Amelia's mother!

They also both have " Pinocchio nose"

Amelia's parents

3 scientist TV show, 3 academicians, Julia's father, Vladimir, first from the left.

YOUR ETERNAL HOLOGRAM

This bust, statue of Julia's father, was gift for him at his 80 years old celebration from University, where he worked during last 50 years. **Photo of him at the moment of opening obelisk.**

Did you see **Pinocchio** on the photo of father with the Julia's sister?
I am sure this is not happened accidently.
This is Spirit's plan to prove to people that people born again and again and again...with many similar details and astonishing similarities.

Julia and Amelia both had special love for their **grandmothers** and spent the better part of their younger years with them.

When I saw Amelia's photo for the first time, it reminded me instantly of my own mother! They looked like twin sisters! Someone told me that before we are born we choose our parents. She chose a woman who looked like her! **My mother had the same as Amelia, high cheekbones, beautiful straight teeth, a small nose, and the same shape of eyelids.**

This is hilarious!

When my father saw Amelia's photo on the cover of the book, "Amelia Reborn" he was sure that this is photograph of my mother! He asked, "Why did you use such an old black & white photo? Why didn't you use some of the more recent color photos of your mother?"

In this photo below, I am near my mother. I am maybe around 2.5 or 3 years old. That day I **drowned** in the lake. I remember that I was looking around me under water and I was surprised that the sun, the beach and people had suddenly disappeared and I wondered... I didn't know what to do next and how to get back. My Aunt Mary saved my life that day.

Well... I **drowned as Amelia** and I drowned again in this lifetime, but this time at least I was lucky.

AVATAR SVADI HATRA

Julia's mother *Amelia Earhart*

Julia's mother at age 15 years old *Amelia Earhart* *Julia's mother*

But my mother, who was the mother of the future Amelia reborn spirit, also studied medicine at the medical institute to become a doctor, worked as a doctor and attended flying school to **fly small aircrafts and to jump with a parachute!**

(**Please** pay attention to the parachute few page below here!)

I remember that I was **addicted to the sky.** I love Leonardo Da Vinci's paintings because of their spaces displaying the sky. As soon as I watched the first movie on YouTube, I saw that Amelia wrote: *"The **stars** seemed near enough to touch and never before have I seen so many."*

Now I know why I ran with little kids trying to touch the **STARS!**
Here is the story: I remember that the sky was like a magnet for me, from an early age, calling me ... talking in my dreams ... I felt that something was there. I always wished to know what was there; I wished to touch the sky. I am sure it came from the Mayan priest and Amelia, who both were studying the sky and stars for astrology and navigation. Maybe. But also from Atlantean queen. She understand how important to keep in perfect shape sphere on the sky, very high above the pyramids.
Once I talked about the sky with my grandmother, I was three years old. I asked her, "What is the sky made of?" She told me "from the air which we have around us." It was astonishing to me! I was so shocked that the same day I wished to touch the stars, and share this joy with my friends! So I called all the little children around to go with me, "I will tell you about the sky and you even can touch it," I said. Wow! So it was a secret adventure. I organized a team of 10 to 12 kids, 4 to 6 years old. We took some little pillows and pretended that they were our backpacks. We had to cross the street where there was a deep creek, which was dry in the summer, and go down the gully. We continued going and kept on going and on talking ... and I told them what I knew about the sky... It was a long walk because we were hoping to touch the stars, but we needed the night sky for that, right? No one saw us, because we were all small, our heads didn't go above the edge of this creek. At some point, we just sat on our pillows and stared at the night sky.
Our poor parents...! Suddenly all the small children who lived in this building had disappeared! At that time children played free around the houses and no one needed to watch them. It was a happy time... There were no kidnappers around. As an organizer and leader of this trip, I was punished. My parents skipped the reading of my favorite fairy-tale and I had to stay home the next day...Yes, I was *addicted* to the sky and **high places.**

Julia's niece, Susanne.

Not only Julia, but her sister, Lena and her daughter Susanne look alike, like Amelia: almost no eyebrow, little nose, full lips, same smile and bone structure...I guess that's enough comparisons...
We could continue to discuss the similarities endlessly ... the same, the same, and the same again! It looks like the Spirit found the perfect configuration in which to be reborn.

You just mentioned that in Amelia's past life she was a Mayan Priest? Can you tell us more about this?
YES! This is most amazing – Similarities also exist with the Mayan Priest! When I started reading about Amelia I was surprised how many similarities there are between the two of us. Yet, there was

something even more amazing to me about her; she had so much in common with the Priest from Chichén Itzá! I wondered if she had a déjà-vu feeling while she visited Mexico. It is three people – three lives of one Spirit. Yes, all of them had the same consciousness, thoughts and actions. Let continue, but I would also like to add here facts about the Mayan Priest just for fun! It is most amazing that the Mayan Priest shares the same similarities ... again supporting the idea of rebirth!

So Amelia, Julia, and the Mayan Priest: What do all three have in common?

- Leadership, responsibility for the well-being of people, society, the community.
- Maps of the earth and maps of the sky, stars.
- Healing, medicine.
- Basketball, (Amelia played, Julia was very good of it, and the Mayan Priest played in his ball court)

I did not exercise or play basketball, but this skill, which they both developed and gave to me as an inheritance, helped me to "survive" when I tried to avoid gymnastics in school and instead threw balls into the hoop without mistakes, precisely, and gained good points this way. See, The Priest chapter.

- Martial arts, hunting. This is why people called Amelia a tomboy. I was president of a martial arts association.

- Intuition. Many of my predictions come true. Amelia inherited this from the Priest. This is why Amelia said before she flew on her last journey that she would not return – not because she had planned to run to Japan – just because she predicted it. (By the way, Amelia should have said: I will be back in 70 years!)

- Biology, herbal plants, agriculture. The main responsibility of the Priest, my profession, and Amelia's interest.

- Ghosts. It is also interesting to note that the town where Amelia was born, Atchison, is the "Most **Ghostly Town**" in USA. Probably, there is some special electromagnetic field surrounding the area. Amelia Earhart often spent her holidays in Kirwin, a Mining **Ghost Town** in Colorado with her husband, George Putnam and asked to build a cabin for her nearby. This makes me think that perhaps the Priest was close to these **Spirits subjects** during his life and it attracted Amelia to be born in such a place as well. In Julia's book, you will find stories about ghosts that contacted her for months!

- Curse (Connected with Amelia's disappearance and her past lives).
- Airplanes, aviation, travel in space, and the pilot shirt which I wear all the time.
- Addiction to masks, goggles.
- Addiction to sky, high places, climbing up to the tree, pyramid or TV towers.
- *Math (Julia finished a special math school, the Mayan Priest would use math daily, Amelia was great in math as well).
- Music, sounds (remember mystery, secrets about coding sounds of the Chichén Itzá in Mexico)

- Inventions, patents; Amelia had numerous inventions and Julia had 3 patents, and Priest studied and wrote manuscripts about sounds.

- Persistence and perseverance

- The Priest, during my past life regression, was continuing to perform the sacrifice rituals, even when Di Cherry offered him to stop it and to change the subject... No matter how hard it was for him personally to perform these sacrifices, he *persisted and persevered* with them, because he felt responsible...

What happened to me you already read in the section dedicated to **Persistence – Perseverance**

(Remember burned leg?)It is interesting that I did **X-ray studies with seeds**. X-rays came from my living in Atlantis and my interest in the seeds, I guess, came to me from the Priest and Amelia's sides...?

"She was a tomboy – climbing trees, sledding in the snow, and hunting" (Richard E. Gillespie, Amelia Earhart)

*By the way, why was Amelia a tomboy and climbed trees all the time? Why was she addicted to the sky, maps, the same as she was to hunting and wanted to fly? Because she was a Maya Priest in her past live!

The Priest climbed his pyramid every day, studied martial arts, astrology, sky map and stars and hunting.

Amelia used to see everything from a bird's eye view as a Mayan Priest from the top of his pyramid! I guess I inherited my love for adventure from Amelia, to be a tomboy like she was. I always envy the workers at the Marriot hotel on Kalapaki beach in Kauai, who climbed coconut trees with special shoes and cut coconuts. I wished I could climb these coconut trees, too! And I asked them, but their insurance policy did not allow the tourist to do this!

As you already know, I was *addicted* to the sky and **high places.** When I started traveling, the first thing I wished to see was a TV station. I arrived for the first time in Moscow at the age of 11, and the most important event was when I went to the Ostankino TV station with my mother, and sat in the restaurant and observed Moscow "from the sky above". YES, As a Maya Priest and Amelia, I also loved to be very high, to see everything from a birds-eye-view either from airplane or high rise buildings or TV towers.

When I was in Japan, for the first time, I ran to the TV station in Tokyo as soon as I could. I wished to see the place where I was, all at once, from sky level. After I spent the night on top of the Chichén Itzá pyramid, I understand why I am addicted to high places.

Now I know for sure that Amelia and I got this love for the **sky** from the Priest, which he studied constantly – the firmament during the day and the night sky with the stars. The same as Amelia,

Priest worked with **maps.** She had maps of the Earth; he had **maps of the sky**, the stars, and the galaxy, all full of numbers. Amelia use stars for the navigation.

Amelia built a slide near her grandmother's house, which looked like the side stairs of the Chichén Itzá pyramid!

Table of Common Characteristics

Common things in life: characters, habits, looks, interests, activities in the lives of the four people, who lived from 70 years, to 2 thousand and 10 thousand years apart from each other.

CHARACTERISTICS	AMELIA EARHART	SVADI HATRA	MAYA PRIEST	QUEEN OF ATLANTIS
Healing & Medicine	Yes	Yes	Yes	Yes
Basketball	Yes	Yes	Yes	
Biology, agriculture, herbal plants	Yes	Yes	Yes	
Math	Yes	Yes	Yes	Yes
Maps; land & sky	Yes	Yes	Yes	Yes
Airplanes, aviation, travel in space	Yes	Yes	Yes	Yes
Black hairy creatures "Jabberwocky"	Yes	Yes	Yes	
Love stars, addiction to the sky	Yes	Yes	Yes	Yes
Can't drink tea, coffee	Yes	Yes		
Tomato Juice	Yes	Yes		Yes
Lougheed as an airplane & nurse's last name	Yes	Yes		
Hart and Hatra	Yes	Yes		
Flower named Amelia Jasmine Rose Lily	Yes	Yes		Possible
Twin trees with couples' names	Yes	Yes		
Leadership	Yes	Yes	Yes	Yes
High responsibility	Yes	Yes	Yes	Yes
Strength of character, brave nature	Yes	Yes	Yes	Yes
Responsible for the well-being of her people, society community	Yes	Yes	Yes	Yes
Hunting	Yes	Yes	Yes	
Ghost, Atchison "Most Ghostly Town in USA"	Yes	Yes	Yes	
Curse	Yes	Yes	Yes	
Importance of numbers	Yes	Yes	Yes	Yes
Inventions, patents	Yes	Yes	Yes	
Persistence and perseverance	Yes	Yes	Yes	Yes
Lots of followers, pioneers	Yes	Yes	Yes	Yes
Studying, sciences	Yes	Yes	Yes	Yes
Open new freedom and new possibilities	Yes	Yes		
Drowning	Yes	Yes		Yes
Problems with own children	Yes	Yes	Yes	Yes
Worker in charge of children,	Yes	Yes	Yes	

teaching				
Big "ego"	Yes	No	Yes	No
Adoring Asia – Japan, China	Yes	Yes		Yes
Fine Arts	Yes	Yes	Yes	Yes
Physics, studies the sounds of the rocks, energy, transportation	Yes	Yes	Yes	Yes
Music, sounds	Yes	Yes	Yes	Unknown
Poetry, the same hand writing	Yes	Yes	Unknown	
Chemistry	Yes	Yes	Yes	
Zoology	Yes	Yes	Yes	
Pacifist	Yes	Yes	Unknown	Yes
Supreme intelligence	Yes	Yes	Yes	Yes
Same facial features, lines on the hand, same voice	Yes	Yes	No	
Deeply spiritual	Yes	Yes	Yes	Yes
Creativity	Yes	Yes	Yes	Yes
True love	Yes	Yes	Possible	Yes
Thick hair	Yes	Yes	Yes	Yes
Extensive travel	Yes	Yes	Possible	Possible
Martial Arts, tom-boy	Yes	Yes	Yes	NO
Fear of "lost forever"	Yes	Yes		
Younger sister	Yes	Yes		
Angry black dog	Yes	Yes		
Someone named Mary	Yes	Yes		
Girlfriends named Laura in school	Yes	Yes		
"Extreme" people in extreme situations	Yes	Yes	Yes	Yes
Pilot shirt, similar clothing	Yes	Yes		
Astrology		Yes	Yes	Yes
Jaguar skin, or print clothes		Yes	Yes	
Tortoise (turtle)		Yes	Yes	
White jaguar		Yes	Yes	
Connection with the Goddess, meeting with God		Yes	Yes	Yes
Word Caracol		Yes	Yes	
Word *Equinox* talking in ancient Maya.		Yes	Yes	
Priesthood, priest's connection		Yes	Yes	Yes
Intuition, predictions	Yes	Yes	Yes	Yes
Masks, pilot goggles	Yes	Yes	Yes	
Sacrifices	Yes	Yes	Yes	
Aztec God Xochipilli		Yes	Yes	
Addiction to crystals, growing crystals, diamonds, museums, factories.		Yes	Yes	Yes
Playing the same "Rock from the past"		Yes	Yes	

Laser, X-ray, technology, studied, seeds.	Yes	Yes	Yes	Yes
Book opening up like an accordion, website moving bar, bus. plan		Yes	Yes	
Spirit support		Yes	Yes	
Big, tall people		Yes	Yes	Yes
Materialization, teleportation, moving objects.		Yes	Possible	Yes

My whole room is painted white, with white corals, white sand from the Caribbean and the South Pacific, with the white, big, musical limestone from Mexico, the limestone pyramid, a souvenir from Chichén Itzá and the white limestone pyramid from Giza, Egypt. The furniture is white with gold trimming, and many turquoise-color accessories accent the décor – a huge painting with the ocean of turquoise water (the same as Atlantis, in the Caribbean), and another painting with turquoise colors. My bedding set, my robe, and many of my outfits are turquoise. The entire room is decorated in white and turquoise, like a white sand beach with the turquoise water of the Caribbean, or Atlantis and Mexico. It looks like I used to live in white palaces in Atlantis, and in white carved buildings in Chichén Itzá and it had an influence on my current environment and that for many years, for as long as I can remember, in fact.

As you already know I sleep for years with white cat and a turtle! But now I have a full set! I sleep in a tee-shirt from Chichén Itzá with the Mayan Calendar and my pyramid imprinted in the front of it, and with a blanket from Mexico with pyramids and all kinds of Mayan symbols, including both Maya and Aztec Calendars.

I am lucky that I can compare the Priest's life and mine, with Amelia's life, because so many facts about her life are available on the internet. It helps me and my readers understand how Spirit continues his life through the centuries and exists in the next and the next human life.
YOUTUBE: Amelia Earhart was Maya Priest and reborn as Julia

I recognize now that I am also lucky in this life, because I had the rare possibility to see the chain of my past lives, the echoes from my past, and make adjustments to my future spiritual development. For example, I inherited a big "ego" from the Priest via Amelia and was finally able to shut it down in this life. As a result, I am wise now.

It is like an award door opened for me that allowed me to make the connections with a Higher Power, Goddesses and Spirits, to experience the possibility to receive lessons, rare knowledge from them and improve myself.

Conclusion

These four people had the same Spirit, which was transferred from the life of one person to the next and to the next. Skills, habits, experience, and knowledge accumulated in the Spirit holographic crystal are transferred with the Spirit to the next newborn person as an inheritance from all of his past lives. This is the chain of lives of people who carried the same Spirit. The Spirit of the people is ETERNAL.

Joan of Arc

YOUR ETERNAL HOLOGRAM

When I was at the Louvre Museum in Paris, I suddenly stopped in one place and my whole body went to goose bumps ... I look around and I saw across of the room, a crowd of people with the guide.

When I got closer, I saw the statue of Joan of Arc... and all kind of things about her.

Reaction of my body was as strong as if I was near the pyramid.
For example, when I visit the place where I used to live, this skin sensation with the goose bumps is a sign for me to pay attention.
It started to worry me...I returned to Canada, but memories about this day have returned to me over and over again...I decided to visit Di Cherry to gain peace of mind. I hope very much that I was not Joan of Arc in my past live.
But as a result, under hypnosis, we find a new past life: I was Joan of Arc!

Personally, I find it hard to admit to myself that it was my past life.

Even now I still hope that this is mistake...After hypnosis I was relieved in some way, but I was upset.... I did not want to know that I was burned at the stake, even if it happened in my past life...

The problem is that I had in this my present life, a really bad painful experience with the fire and burning.
About one case I already covered in this book. I had burnt skin on the legs at age of 6 years old, when I started burn my own leg to prove to myself that I am strong, not scared and not less than the big kids. The second time was during the terrible fire in Australia in 2012. During a house fire my daughter and I lost all that we owned.
We are lucky to be alive after that nightmare. We ran outside with only laptops in our hands, bare feet...I also managed to grab a little bag with the my documentary movie files on tapes. All files which were on DVDs was lost in the fire.

****

The hypnosis session is recorded. It was a very emotional experience with visions holding many details and the secret of her death. During hypnosis, we found that Joan was not burned alive!!!
People loved her, and at last moment they wrapped her neck with the cloth that fits snugly against her neck. Before the fire start she was already unconscious. This part make me enormously happy. What a relief!

It's interesting that Jeanne played a **game throwing the ball into the ring** very well, although nobody taught it to her. I'm sure it comes from the skills of playing basketball from the Maya Priest. The same skills of playing basketball were inherited by Amelia and myself Julia from the Maya Priest.

"In Chinon, Jeanne astonished Charles V with his mastery of riding
Riding, hers impeccable knowledge of games, common among the nobility: kentno (Fr quintaine.)
[5], ***a game in the ring*** *- demanding perfect possession of weapons. Alain Chartier, secretary of the*

kings of Charles VI and Charles VII, said: "It seemed that this girl was brought up not in the fields, but in schools, in close contact with the sciences."

On the name of Joan of Arc.

"In different documents and chronicles of that time there are different versions of writing the desired name - Dark, Tark, Dar, and so on - due to their origin of the Lorraine dialect, in which the" p "practically disappears, and the recording of the surname by ear In any case, choosing the only "right" option is not possible. "(Wikipedia material.)

I'm sure that her name was **"Dar"**. Because I chose a name for my daughter who also begins with Dar.

Also, **DAR (Direct Air Resource)** was proposed by me for the name of the company in California, USA in 2004. The company produced direct supplies of aircraft parts.

Surprisingly, Joan fits into the list of people from all my past lives... It seems the Spirit has made the order and experience of transition of the hologram from one person to another to prove to people that reincarnation really exists. It looks like Spirit wishes to show how the Human Hologram transfers from one incarnation to the next.

Joan of Arc:

*"The messenger of God."
* Legendary woman, 16th century
* Fame
* Army, use men's clothing for fighting
* Very brave
* Spirit, Holy people, Angels, God
* extrasensory abilities.
* Women, which acts like a men
* accepted by the Church as a Holy woman
* injustice of the sentence
* injustice of death at a young age

Amelia

YOUR ETERNAL HOLOGRAM

* Pioneer, a legendary man of the 20th century,
* Fame
* Very brave
* Hunting, use men's clothing for flights
* extrasensory abilities
* Spirit, ghosts
* Women act as men (called Nostradamus Androgen)
* Injustice of death at a young age

Julia

*Pioneer
* The Messenger
* Martial art association, hunting
* brave
* extrasensory abilities
* Spirits, Ghosts, Holy people, Angels, God

Maya PRIEST

* army, hunting
* very brave (to sacrifice his own son in order to safe life of his community members)
* Spirit, ghosts, God, Angels
* extrasensory abilities

The Spiritual Court of France condemned Joan de Ark for words she did not say, for whose deeds she did not.

This process - an eternal disgrace to the barbarism of the French clergy, the process was a mockery of justice and human rights.The French people's faith in the divine mission of the Virgin of Orleans did not waver from the verdict. Jeanne did forgive her enemies. In 1456, Jeanne was acquitted, was rehabilitated and in 1920 was canonised - ranked by the Catholic Church to the rank of saints.But this did not help Catholic Church to clean blood on there hands, which killed holy person. This explained why my Spirit still don't trust
Catholic Church and can not stand that reincarnation became an enemy concept and was declared heresy for the Catholic Church.

I am back, i am re-born and I did proved with this book that reincarnation exist 100%.

WHAT DOES SPIRIT LOOK LIKE?

I often see vision the Spirit body looks like a 3-D hologram, with some sort of crystal-like appearance. For some reason, I always see my Spirit as a perfect, strong crystal, as perfect as a diamond.

Our body is covered with an energy field, which is actually a matrix, a plan of the body structure. Inside our body there are over a million biochemical changes occurring every second. Our body is in constant changes. This plan around the body controls its functions and re-builds everything according to that plan. Maybe this energy field structure is responsible for our thinking process and consciousness. The thinking brain can only exist on biochemical or at the molecular and atom levels, where the possibility of "containers" for the consciousness on the level of elemental particles and their fields may exist.

The **Biofield** is an ideal environment for *fluctuation*, which are holograms. It is possible to say that the biofield is actually a multi-component hologram. This way all of the person's life experiences – all his words, thoughts, words he ever said or someone said to him, what he saw, what he felt, all of his emotions – everything is preserved in that biofield in the form of holograms. These sets of holograms together form a kind of crystal, which we could name Soul or Spirit. [10]

In addition, I am sure the energy crystals' structure of the Spirit is the best to collect and save information from one lifetime to the next.

The same as with any kind of information, to preserve it on the real crystals is much better than using something like CDs, DVDs or paper.

I am amazed and proud how unique and strong our Human Hologram is!

It survives, when people's bodies are destroyed in fire or melted in volcano lava flow! People, who died in the nuclear explosion in Nagasaki and Hiroshima in Japan remember their past lives, when their body literary melted or evaporated from enormously high temperature...

This is astonishing! **The Human Hologram is stronger than any one object, any material on the planet!** It has an everlasting life and immortality! This is our precious **ETERNAL HOLOGRAM**. It was mystery, "terra incognita" to genetics about DNA for years for what responsible 90% of the DNA genome? After my research I believe it belong to unique magnificent Hologram of Eternity!

I am thinking now that when people travel through the Universe in their dreams, what we call here, an "astral body" is actually this energy crystal made from sets of many hologram components. It is interesting that the body of the person, who left with visitors from another planet to see their world, did not exist in time and space. Maybe it is transformed into the field structure because this is the only of entering the world of the field forms[25].

In that dream below, I tried to describe the crystallization process of my body as a preparation for space travel.

Dream # 40 A Gray Dumb-Bell in the Head, September 4, 1991.

I had not fallen asleep deeply yet, I still remember myself, when some substance of gray color entered my head from both sides and started to crystallize inside it. It was not a pipe, the whole thing was filled in, crystallized all at once, and it was fitting very well...

However, when a person returns to our reality, to our world, that "plan structure around the body" shows amazing capabilities for analyzing and collecting components and for regeneration; returning these components into their previous structure, not only at the body level, but also at the level of consciousness and emotions.

Maybe while we are here on Earth, in the form of physical bodies, we are collecting some experiences into this energy field, crystal structure, named Soul or Spirit. After the biological body dies, we fly

---

[25] Please see the "Violet field" chapter where I described Invisible Spirit world in my many dreams, my connection with creatures from the Universe, and while I am myself, my body turns into the wave-field structure.

toward the Universe Consciousness with all of these new qualities that we accumulated during our life as a human in the physical, materialistic world, where the field-form from Space just cannot develop at all.

"Captured humans are often brought to play with the children of the visitors, who are described as melancholic and lethargic. The Gray children play with the blocks, which do not have letters or numbers on them--- instead, they emit different emotions when they are turned. The toys seem to indicate, that they are trying to learn how to feel. Could it be that this yearning for effect is one reason the visitors seek human contacts" (Daniel Pinchbeck, 2012 The return of Quetzalcoatl, 2006)

Here is how I found what the SPIRIT looks like:

Dream # 28
Rays Coming From the Eyes, April 1994

It was as if the earth started trembling under my feet. A strange noise was pulling me out of this dream. There were waves of vibrations in the air, throughout the whole space. The intervals between the waves were getting shorter and shorter, and the power of the waves was becoming stronger. It mounted to a physical sensation in my ears, like when blood rushes back and you hear noises in your ears. I was still sleeping, but I thought in my dream that they told me that I should let it go, let it open, "do not stop it." As soon as I thought about it, I could not bear it anymore, because it became many times stronger. But I was sleeping with some ear plugs and I felt all their roughness, so I pulled them out when I woke up. It was absolutely dark. But the sound filled the entire room; it was in different places – in the wardrobe, in the middle of the room, but everywhere at the same time. It was not just the sound, but a strong wave of sensation. I was scanning the space of the room as if I were using a laser – it was near the wardrobe at one moment, then it came together near the bed, then near my head. But this was not just the sound. It was the strongest sensation; I don't know how to describe it. It was something that entered the room. As if all of the objects melted, turned into jelly and started trembling. The sound turned into a crash. I wasn't even frightened, I was just a witness, and there could not be any fear, any interest. Perhaps it captured all of the nervous points of a person. It was a strange experience, revealing the life around me in a totally different shape. It was in our life, filling the mind and memory. At the same time, I felt a point of energy between my shoulder blades very strongly – where the blades meet. It was the only parallel sensation. Then, in a second, like an explosion, I saw, in front of me, near me – I saw, something that fits the description of "emanation". I knew clearly, that it was an emanation – of the best, of the most refined, spiritual, and light – the outburst of the soul, the ringing in my ears.

It was a live hologram with crystalloid structure, where all memories about the person life, many events down to little details, were stored.

I saw immediately many sights before my face.
In fact, this noise and waves burst out, they exploded with "emanations" of my mother. Suddenly, one by one, I was shown some facial expressions, different ones, quickly – but all of the expressions were the ones she had during her life, when sparks of the Holy Ghost were coming out of her. They were very short, similar to flashes, just in front of my face, as if in a movie. Parallel to this, I could see her different hairstyles, at various times of her life – like a backdrop to the "emanation" scene – were changing continually. And all the while these sparks, drops of light continued to burst about the room. It was amazing. At the same time, I had a feeling that this was happening for about an hour. Then everything stopped abruptly and I thought – it is strange, that such a person is dead. Perhaps it is the only thing that stays after death. Everything else is unimportant.

AVATAR SVADI HATRA

(This dream occurred a few weeks before my mother died. I start remember that I saw before many times when someone dies, their hologram in my dreams, where preserve history of their lives).

I got frightened, because I moved in my bed and there were some sounds, maybe just common squeaking of the mattress springs. I was taken a back and sat up in bed. Then it started to squeal even more. I even jumped off the bed. I thought that something was wrong with me – that I should go, but this woman started walking upstairs. Her every step was like thunder; something cracked in the corner, such as it always does in my room. It was exactly 4:00 a.m. on my clock. Before, there were different events happening to me in dreams at 3:00 a.m., but now time had been moved to the daylight saving time, an hour later...

After I published my first book with *What the Spirit looks like?* This video was uploaded onto the internet. It fully supports how I described it. **Human_holograms_extraterrestres**

"As I read Julia's book, "Your Eternal Hologram" I was amazed by her remarkable abilities. She can see things that for normal people, are impossible to see. We are a group of scientists that have witnessed that when aliens meet a person, they take information from that individual. This hologram, which each human has, contains information about the person's past, present and possibly its future..." V. Uvarov.

From My Space, Dharma omniyogi, artist unknown

Dream # 29
Bifurcation similar to a "vibrating" ruler, May 13, 1991

YOUR ETERNAL HOLOGRAM

In a dream, I bifurcated. Such as when you shake a ruler vigorously, it becomes two before your eyes – it "bifurcates" and both parts are viewed separately. In the summer of 1991, I had this dream many times in which I bifurcated and once even divided into three parts. Sometimes the dream started only after and from the point where I saw myself bifurcate. For example it was the same as in the dream of Atharvan. There were two of me at once, one was of a normal size and the other one was an enormous, big, huge-size person. After I woke up from that dream, I saw this huge man, Atharvan.

"The Trinity": Father, Son, and Holy Spirit

The projection of our Eternal Hologram or I will say our Spirit, at various times and in different conditions, will appear in slightly different forms. In my case, for example, here on Earth, it was the same Hologram that projected itself through the body of a Maya priest, the Queen of Atlantis, the pilot Amelia and the scientist Julia. Through different times, it just used, occupied a new body. But the original Hologram-Matrix still carried exactly the same, unique quality for each person in all of his past lives. Our Hologram is a storage of accumulated information, memories, emotions, experiences, habits and knowledge, our Spirit gains through all of his past lives since the beginning of time. This Hologram has a huge spectral of activities, it is also a control system for the human body and it occupies 90% of our DNA code. In other words I can say that 90% of our DNA information describes this Hologram's characteristics and abilities.

Now let's think together with me.

1. You already know that we, humans, have a personal, unique ETERNAL hologram, right?
2. Each human has a second one, Higher Self. It can be somewhere in Space, in another dimension.
3. Both of them, Human and Higher Self are in constant connection with our Eternal Hologram and with each other through this Hologram.
4. This way, each Human is a reflection form of his Eternal Hologram on the Earth level and in many parallel realities at the same time.

And his Higher Self is a reflection form of his Eternal Hologram in outer Space.

Suddenly I began remembering "**The Trinity**" and searched GOOGLE.
 http://www.forerunner.com/orthodoxy/X0005_4._Trinity.html
I began reading... At first it sounded far too complicated. But, it began to sound extremely logical and easy to understand when taken in the context of what I just described.

So what is "The Trinity": Father, Son, and Holy Spirit here on Earth for each human personally?

The **Holy Spirit** is a Hologram, which I call Spirit throughout this book as well.
Father is our Higher Self and
Son --> we are Humans (which I prefer to call Soul) here on Earth and in parallel realities.
So what did I see when I was "bifurcated" in two of me in the dream?

When I was in this special condition during the dream and have this, I actually could see what this REALITY is all about: I began by seeing this second one, my Higher Self!

© Josephine Wall. All Rights Reserved. www.josephinewall.com

And when it started to be three 'beings' at the same time, I also saw my Hologram. It was the full package – completed: The Trinity! http://www.forerunner.com/orthodoxy/X0005_4._Trinity.html

Now let's read the references below. They sound so simple and easy and understandable now.
* "To the apostolic mind there is also the simplistic insight that one God is revealed and expressed to men as three persons: "the Father and the Son and the Holy Spirit". (Matthew 28:19)

* "To them that are sanctified by God the Father, and preserved in Jesus Christ ... praying in the Holy Ghost, keep yourselves in the love of God, looking for the mercy of our Lord Jesus Christ unto eternal life". (Jude 1: 20, 21)

* "For there are three that bear record in heaven, the Father, the Word, (John refers to Jesus as the Word - the LOGOS; John 1: 1) and the Holy Ghost, and these three are one". (1 John 5: 7)

I saw this for the first time and just enjoyed reading it! It was an astonishing feeling to be able to understand EXACTLY what the Bible is talking about! It was like a de-coding for people today. The Bible and my book are speaking the same language: "... eternal life, three are one, Holy Spirit"!
Yes, the Bible, the most precious book on Earth, is in great harmony with my book!
Now I ask myself: **Who Wrote the Bible?** And go to Google:
http://www.allabouttruth.org/Who-Wrote-The-Bible.htm

"Who wrote the Bible?" is a question that can be definitively answered by examining the biblical texts in light of the external evidences that supports its claims. 2 Timothy 3:16 states that "All scripture is inspired by God..." In 2 Peter 1:20-21, Peter reminds the reader to "know this first of all, that no prophecy of scripture is a matter of one's own interpretation ... but men moved by the Holy Spirit spoke from God." The Bible itself tells us that it is God who is the author of His book."
And now we try to understand what God said in the Bible text ... not easy, right? So I am helping by sharing my own experience with you, which come from my unique abilities in my dreams. I mean we all HUMAN, we can imagine how God, Trinity looks like according ONLY to our own possibility to imagine. Because it in another dimension. (For example, fish only can describe WATER life. Fish cannot imagine life without water, where there's only AIR, right? Tell me how for example insect ant can describe the computer?)

Fully understanding what GOD looks like still goes beyond our human understanding.

Here the proof: **YOUTUBE:** Physics-Evidence of God.
Nothing to lose by trying to understand more, but everything to gain!
Let's continue... Read the chapter "Violet field". By using my extraordinary abilities, I will show you much more sophisticated world – an invisible magic world.

Why do you always refer to some Royal Priest and Priestess – celebrities anyway – why not just some peasant?

Good question! **Skills which we developed in previous lives are available for us in our present lives and when we use these skills we add more and more qualities to them.**
Some kids are born very talented. They developed these skills during their previous lives and continue their development in their present lives. Many creative people were artists, musicians, scientists, architects, builders or good cooks, for example, during their numerous past lives. Their Spirits try to polish some particular skills in their new lives.

I was a Maya Priest, a Queen of Atlantis, who was also a High Priestess, a royal priestess in Egypt; these were people who drove and organized large population. There were either Associations or Kingdoms to direct, to organize and counsel; to give people the knowledge they needed to thrive or even survive. YES, in most of my previous lives I was a Priest or a Priestess!
Amelia was a pilot and it was the Spirit's "trick" to attract people's attention to the subject of reincarnation due to her popularity, and I was born as a scientist who collected all the facts to prove it. What am I doing now, in this lifetime? I was a scientist at first and a doctor, and now I am like a priestess again, giving people knowledge, which will be very important in next years and beyond. It is my goal to maintain my Spirit's support, in order to help people in their Spiritual lives.
It is interesting that when I published my first book, **I was sure that I had reached my goal in this life time and that I could die in peace.**

Soon after this, one amazing Spirit from the other side found me and started giving me some readings through the psychic and gifted singer, **Zzak,** from New York. Zzak's channeling, powerful Spirits, Oversoul Seven, advised me wisely as to what to do and what not to do, who to avoid and who to embrace. They mentioned to me names, places, events' dates, people I will meet, and all of this happened precisely.

Zzak gave me a message from the Invisible World. He said that I only accomplished 50% of my goal in this lifetime! And that the other 50% will be the process of passing on this knowledge to people using the media of radio, TV shows, internet and documentary movies. This is what I am doing now.

Also Spirit told: *Energy will change, new religion will come, death of all old consciousness and new will come, new consciousness. You, Julia, will be highly involved in this. I see you on the top of the pyramid...* (This was predicted 6 months before I visited the pyramid!)

My dear "Guardian Angel" highly spiritual singer Zzak (Irving) Grinwald, from New Jersey, NY

The predictions described below were given to me by him before I fought for two years to access the pyramid and to be able to talk to people as an Ancient Maya Priest reincarnated – in a Maya outfit;

I was on the right track.

"Pyramids were built a long time ago with the help of another civilization. Soon these pyramids will be re-activated and people will return to the pyramids for the rituals. Pyramids will be the key monuments to affect the human consciousness.

"When people will start freeing themselves from FEAR, it will help them to be free from the old consciousness and accept new consciousness and to proceed through the difficult time much easier."

On YOUTUBE, you can find people who are channeling Spirits daily from another dimension... These Spirits were people who died a long time ago. For example one Spirit's name is Ramtha.

These Spirits are channeling the higher knowledge to the needy ones. They are logged on the infinite, universal knowledge which has answers for every situation and "problem" (there is no problem, only experience).Just dial YOUTUBE: Ramtha on Emotional Addictions 1 of 3, for example.

I wish to tell you one important thing which I understood and learned for myself during the last five months, since I started studying my past lives. What people see from a distance of famous, royal people is just a flash, a glimpse of what their life is really about. I experienced the kind of life they really have, their personal feelings from inside, and it is a hard life, not an easy one as many people would think.

All of my past lives were full of responsibilities, intense and at the edge of most possible human capabilities. I feel uncomfortable when I hear people around me talking about meaningless things for hours. They communicate on a shallow, surface level, but with great emotions, though... That's a waste of time. They are losing their valuable energy this way.

Each person from my past life cares about people deeply.

The **Queen** from Atlantis had the responsibility for the well-being of her people. She was responsible for one most important part of their lives; the Energy of the Crystals. This energy supported all and each part of their activities in Atlantis.

The **Priest** had lots of onerous responsibilities – for the harvest, the health of his people, astronomy... He was also teaching astrology; performing rituals and dealing with droughts, dry land and worrying about future harvests and his hungry people. It was overwhelming for him to sacrifice the people he knew and loved...

Amelia had the responsibility to do her best in order to prove to the world that there were new, wonderful possibilities for everyone to travel by airplanes for long distances.
Secondly, she wished to prove that women can do very well, that they were no less than men (especially if some of them were men in their past lives. I can assure you that each man on the planet was a woman in his previous life, at least once.)
By the way, Amelia lived at a time when most women on the planet were housewives and this inspiration from Amelia was priceless for them. Now, 70 years later, according to statistics, up to 60% of workplaces are filled with women!

The Economist magazine, cover

And she did not aware that her another responsibility: to be very popular. This way all facts about her life will be preserved and she can use them in her future life as a scientist in order tocomplete another very important goal: to tell the world this knowledge that the Spirit has no death and is eternal, that only the physical form dies.

I had the responsibility to invest my knowledge, abilities and skills to build a new country during perestroika, open new freedoms and new possibilities to develop the body, soul and spirit of people. During my life, I helped many talented, creative people. I helped millions of people change their lives on a grand scale in two countries. And now I try to help people all over the world.
I had a dream where I was an angel myself with two real pure-white wings and my guide, in my dream, told me that he and other Spirits called me DIAMOND. I ask him, "Why diamond?" He told me that when I try to help talented and creative people, I try to cut off the problems from around them which liberate them from the frictions of their everyday life and make them more productive. It is interesting that kids in school also called me by that name. Kids often see things adult can't see.

All of the people from my past lives had painful problems with children. The Atlantis woman was separated from her son forever. The Priest sacrificed his son's life trying to save the lives of the people in his community. Amelia sacrificed her personal life and delayed the birth of her child for years... I am glad that I fulfilled Amelia's wish and that I am a writer and also a mother in this life; never mind, it almost cost me my life.

Amelia died by **drowning**. I hope my Priest's bones were laid amid the seven graves of the other High Priests I saw in Chichén Itzá. I know how the life of the Atlantis Queen ended with the catastrophe they experienced, she did not left her people and have been with them until the end.

I got letter from Douglas Settles, past life specialist:

"Remember the past life I did between you and me? You were the Atlantean Queen. I was the Spiritual Leader. You were supposed to be teleported to another country along with a small group of other survivors to start a new civilization ... that never happened and you went down with Atlantis, you drowned."

Douglas understands how important it is for people all over the world to access precious knowledge about the HUMAN ETERNAL HOLOGRAM. His generous, enormous donation covered the full production of the documentary movie in Chichén Itzá, Mexico. He is also a noble, caring and kind-hearted person.

I hope this is my last life on this planet. It looks like there is not much luck in my coming back – not too much fun or joy down here... Or perhaps I will be re-born and just study and experience pleasure next time... Most likely, I will be reborn again, and if not I will always help people as a Spirit, a Guardian Angel like those 33 Spirits which heal people in Brazil.

My friend, Marianne, who was with me in my past lives, told me that she had a vision around year 3000 in Tibet. In that vision had lived enough, I was simply tired to live, and I gave my body to her. It means that my Spirit will go out of my body to the Spiritual world and her Spirit will enter my body and will continue to live on. This is possible. (See the case below – how it already happened!)

YOUTUBE: We met in a dream, together in Atlantis and we are reunited in real life now!

I wish that, when I die to have an epitaph on my tombstone that reads: **"Here lies to rest the latest reincarnation of the Spirit of the Mexican Priest Jaguar, the pilot Amelia from USA, and the Queen from Atlantis kingdom..."** What a team! I imagine what it would be like if they were alive and together, they would be like twins – triplets actually – different on the outside but exactly the same on the inside. But the best part about this epitaph is that it will teach people even after my death about reincarnation and it will support them! (See **Power of Reincarnation** at the end of the book.)

"In 2008 I met Julia via Internet and we have been sending each other many emails ever since. As a professional past life/regression therapist, with my own practice in the Netherlands, I have done thousands of sessions with clients to their past lives over the last twenty years and I've read Julia's book and was impressed by the many details she had produced in proving that we, human beings, do not need fear death because our spirit is eternal. She did this by unraveling her own dreams, deep investigation, visiting countries and comparing information out of 4 of her different past lives. Julia was definitively **an Atlantean queen** (I would rather call that some sort of an Atlantean high priestess) in one of her past lives. She has vivid memories of me being her sister in that lifetime. I only have vague recollections about that specific past life, but I am pretty sure that she is correct about that. Not all persons remember the same way, one in colours, images, another in feelings, emotions, knowing. Once I did a past life consult with a friend of her, Simon D., and he also stated during his regression that he knew her from that past life as a queen in Atlantis.

In another life time Julia was a **Maya priest.** No doubt she had lived many other lives as well. I have had vivid images of a lifetime in which Julia and I were travelling in space together in a strange grey vessel. Lucky, that this lifetime Julia is a **scientific investigator,** so she is able to proof things.

I found many little details in the book that made me able to say: yes, Julia was once Amelia Earhart,

or even better: the **soul in Julia's body now, was in Amelia's body** the last time. But besides that, it's a lovely book to read. I do hope that Julia's book will reach many readers so that people everywhere will learn that indeed our soul goes on..."
Marianne Notschaele-den Boer, (January 2016) Past life therapist/writer, author of books, article about past life. www.vorigelevens.nl **(in Dutch)**

YOUTUBE: Amelia Earhart reborn as Julia, Maya Priest reincarnated as Julia?
By the way Marianne just published a book about people, who were together in their past lives and met in this lifetime again!

The book is written in Dutch, with a foreword by a famous Flemish female cabaret performer, Els de Schepper. For more information: www.vorigelevens.nl

You know some truly amazing cases about Reincarnation?

YouTube and the internet are filled with examples of reincarnation cases. The difference in my case is that I proved it scientifically with cold facts. So there can be no more doubt whether reincarnation exists or not.

For the people who do not use the internet, here are some examples of very special reincarnation cases, when governments, police and scientists studied it and accepted it, according to the facts, without knowing the mechanism which actually underlies the process.

However, it must be said that through the work of quantum physics a certain notion of reincarnation has been re-introduced over the past few years. Today many experiments have sought to prove re-incarnation and these experiments have been greatly supported by the reports of spontaneous past life regressions which have occurred to people in various states of altered consciousness.

I remember a few years ago I saw a story on TV about reincarnation. It was about **a little girl in India.** From an early age she began to tell her parents that she lived before in a town nearby and that she was married and that her husband, a doctor, had an affair with his nurse and they killed her and dropped her near a railway, near some river. Her parents decided to go to that city and check her story. They made a documentary movie and showed how they arrived with their car to that city, how this girl pointed to the parents' house and her previous parents waiting for them on the balcony. She ran inside the house and showed everyone where her toys and books were – which her past-life father had kept for some reason.
It is the only case in history where a person, her husband, from her previous life was charged and is now in jail!

****
Another case I saw in a documentary movie; **an old lama died.** Before his death he made a promise to his students that he would be reincarnated. Years later, a student had a dream where he saw the old lama's body step out and into a little baby boy's body. The student began searching for the new born lama. He used his lama's pink crystal necklace, which lamas use all the time, to find the boy. Many toddlers saw this necklace, but didn't pay attention to it. But, one little boy wanted it as soon as he saw it. He instantly put it around his neck and did not want to give it back to the student. This little boy was then brought to the Buddhist temple and was asked to undergo a test. The monks placed all kinds of ritual things which the lamas usually use, in front of him. The boy needed to choose the right items, the items which the old lama used during his life.

For example, the boy had to choose one of the many bells that had been placed in front of him. The boy didn't hesitate; he chose the exact bell which belonged to the old lama. The same happened with all of the other items. In fact, this little boy was the reincarnated lama and was recognized as such by the Dalai Lama.
****

The case below is absolutely amazing! I read about it in a newspaper, it filled two pages, (no kidding!) Everybody in this story are real people, with their names, last names, photos and many details regarding the places they were born, worked and so on.

During the Second World War a boy and **a girl** were in the Russian army. They deeply love each other and were always together for four years. At the very end of the war, the blond girl was killed. The war ended. The broken-hearted boy returned to Leningrad and continued to work at the factory, where he worked before the war started.

A few years later, in a small Russian town, a young boy and a girl were on a scooter and had an accident. The boy died as a result, and the girl was in a coma for a month. When she woke up from her coma she did not recognize anyone from her life. No one. She only talked about the war, about some man she loved and missed, and she wished to find him. She cut her hair, adopted a different hairstyle and colored it blond. She arrived at the factory in Leningrad where the man worked. He said that she was taller and looked different than the other girl he loved and lost. But everything else was exactly the same! How she talked, how she laughed, all of her habits and so on were the same. Only she and he knew many things which no one else knew. They got married, had a daughter and spent 20 happy years together until she died as a result of the onset of complications after the motorcycle accident. A group of Russian scientists studied and monitored her case until she passed away. They proved absolutely that this girl is the same one which died during the Second World War. However, they could not explain how it could have been possible.

I guess the Spirit of the first girl wished to return to her boyfriend, the man she loved and perhaps made a deal with the Spirit of the girl which was in the scooter accident, or most likely, it just took over her body without asking her. But I think it happened with God's help and his personal approval. The power of love was stronger than death and won this game!

And one more:

Michael Jackson was a Pharaoh woman in his past life. With the help of plastic surgeries he tried to return to his previous, more comfortable image of himself – the face he had as a pharaoh woman. This is also why he was attracted to Egypt. Egypt was the subject of a video he produced, and that's also the reason for which he always talked in such a soft voice.

YOUTUBE: Michael Jackson – The Pharaoh of Pop? Slower Version
Ancient Egyptian Bust Resembles Michael Jackson

YOUR ETERNAL HOLOGRAM

Michael Jackson – the reincarnation of an Egyptian Pharaoh woman

While I am writing this book, I am thinking about all of these re-born situations and always come back to one question, which has been in my mind for years. Are people who died, often re-born in the same family or in a nearby place? Yes. I got this positive answer already from a different sources.

My mother died from sickness at the age of 59 – way too early and suddenly. She came in my dream three months after her death. She stood in front of me and smiled. I don't know why but I asked her, "Maybe it is time to be re-born?" She continued to smile, didn't say anything. Kind of, "I don't know... I will think about it..." Soon after that, I was pregnant – at the most uncomfortable moment of my modeling career, when I got a very lucrative contract!

As soon as the child started to walk and talk everything she did reminded me of my mother. First, she **wanted to be a doctor**, like my mother was, since she was two years old. She was always wearing a doctor's hat with a cross and a white lab-coat which I made for her. She drew cats with a doctor's hat in a situation where another cat visits the doctor.Now at age 12 her favorite books is about **Anatomy and Health**, she truly enjoy visited the unique exhibition of "Body World" by the talented Dr. Gunther von Hagens, as well as Leonardo De Vinci exhibition where was display of his famous drawings with anatomy of human body.

The first time we visited my mother's sister, my aunt, Merry, when my daughter was 2.5 years old, she found many of my aunt's necklaces on the dresser. She was particularly attracted to the **white pearl necklace** and put it around her neck immediately.

I asked her to give it back, worried that she would break it and all the pearls would fall everywhere on the floor. (This is what a little baby does usually.) But she didn't want to give it back! She repeated, "This is mine! This is mine! This is mine!" Years before, I had brought to my mother and my aunt exactly the same pearl necklace from China. Secondly, she suddenly started asking about her potty! She stopped using it a long time ago already, in Canada! Since my aunt never had any children of her own, there was no way she would have one. But my daughter was adamant: "Give me my **potty!**"

Finally, my aunt heard that we were fighting and came to the living room. She told me that there was no need to fuss about this, that she indeed had a potty! And she brought a brand new one out of the cupboard. I was very surprised and asked my aunt, "Why have you got a potty? For what?"

She then told me that my mother brought this potty to my grandmother one day and after she died, when my grandmother moved to my aunt's place, to another city, the movers put this potty with everything else. I was even more surprised then. I asked, "Why did mother buy this potty in the first place?"

My grandmother said that my mother told her that she was walking once in the street and saw store selling it, and she started to think that maybe one day she would need it, and she bought it! Well, she was a doctor, maybe she was thinking that one day she would be very sick in bed and would need a potty. Anyway, my daughter got what she was asking for and she was very happy! She played with it for the next few days. Two days later we arrived at my father's home, in another city.

Patient visiting the Doctor with the cross on the hat

Is this 'baby' my mother reborn?

My father remarried another woman after my mother died. We went to visit him and his new wife then, and we stayed there for five days. During all this time my child did not eat any food there! My daughter refused to touch anything that his new wife brought her on a tray to her room. She would take the tray and throw it out into the hallway and shut the door of the room! This behavior was unexplained. I was very worried. She was **hungry** and I had to change our tickets to fly home earlier than anticipated. All this baby ate, during the five days we were there, were cookies which my aunt had made and which she gave to her in a big bag. If she is my mother reborn maybe she couldn't forgive my father for re-marrying so soon after she passed away? Or perhaps she was jealous of this other woman? But the next thing that happened really made me think that she was my mother in her past life. One morning she closed the **door** of her bedroom (where she used to live) from the inside. My father and his wife were very worried. I didn't understand why. They told me that a child would never be able to open this door and it may be necessary to call a locksmith and break it down in order to open it!

My father said that only my mother knew how to close this door from inside the room. He tried to close it many times – to no avail. We then all started asking the baby to open the door but she ignored us and continued to play. Suddenly, when we were about to call the locksmith, she ran to the door and opened it without any problems!

The next day we needed to fly home and my father had organized a farewell party for that evening. The guests were having a good time when a young man, who had visibly too much to drink, started following me. So I went to another room to sleep. I tried to close that door for at least half an hour, worried that the man would follow me and wake me up and the baby! And I couldn't close this damn door! I tried everything possible... So I ended up sitting in the chair, shut off the light near the baby and waited until all the guests had left.

I have a list of the common things between my mother and my daughter ... not genetic ones, by the way. For example, for a long time, she searched for another name for herself. She played around the name Laura for a while and finally created the name: **Lu**rr. My mother's name was **Lu**dmila.

I started paying attention to all of the above after the day my baby daughter jumped on the kitchen counter and suddenly stopped, and without turning or looking at me, she told me: everybody called me **Lu**... before! Wow! "**Lu**....." was the nick name of my mother! NO way for her to know this, we never even mentioned it: according to superstition it is not good to call person by name after the person died, in order to keep Spirit of this person in peace... so my aunt called her : "my sister", and I always called her: "my mother"...

A few years later, my father gave me the jewelry that my mother loved to wear. Among the pieces, there was also a pretty pair of gold **earrings**. They were designed in the shapes of flowers with a bright, blue sapphire at the center of each earring. As soon as I showed them to my daughter, she immediately wanted to wear them and told me that they were hers and she would never, ever take them off! Well..., she chose them in the store herself during her past life! When I saw my mother for the last time before I moved to Canada, she gave me a **blue stone necklace.** My daughter wears it all the time and lately I noticed her many paintings – all with **blue colors.** She told me that, yes, blue color is her favorite color.

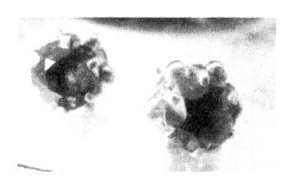

Once I went with her to the jewelry store. As soon as my daugter saw one **bracelet**, she asked me to buy it for her. The owner of the store pulled out the Buddhist bracelet and showed us that it had been made in Tibet. Anyway, I bought the **bracelet** for her birthday.

It was the same bracelet with only one difference; this one was made of amber. When we were in Australia, two years ago, my daughter wished to buy some souvenir gifts about Australia. Instead of a kangaroo or a koala, like all the tourists bought, she bought the softest bird she could find – a **KUKABARA** – the size of a real grown chicken. Ever since, she's been sleeping with the toy, the same as she had as a pet in her past life. My grandmother told me that before the Second World War there weren't many toys for children, so she gave my three-year old mother a baby chicken to play with. The little girl loved her new pet and it grew to a mature hen very quickly. My mother had fed this hen way too much and, as a result, the **chicken** became so fat that it could hardly walk.

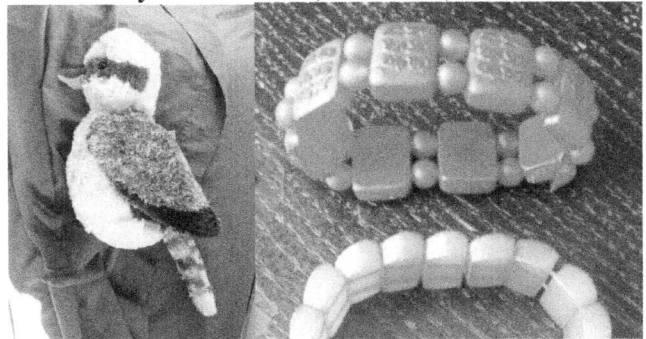

On one occasion, and to my big surprise, I found a big book about the **Second World War** in my daughter's room. She was reading it. She was revisiting a difficult part of her childhood in her past life during the war...
She saw my father, her grandfather, only twice. Each time she spent a week with him when she was two-and-a-half years old and when she was about six years old. When he sent me his book with his

Memoirs, my daughter is the one, who was glued to it, like a magnet. For days she looked at the photos of my young mother (her past life) and photos of my father (her husband in her past life) and photos of other events from her past life. Today my daughter keeps this book on her bedside table. It

was difficult for her to read Russian, but finally she managed it, too!
In 2011 they met again and my daughter told to her grandfather things which did happened at his years when he study in post-graduation, and which only he and my mother knew!
And Yes! She loves **parachutes** again in this lifetime! **Lurr, 2014, Antalya, Turkey**

It looks like this girl is the result of my unique capability to talk/deal with dead people, to direct them to another world and guide them to doing things I want them to do. Is this my heritage from the Priest? My daughter ... is my mother. It also makes me think that maybe Spirits had her re-born to show me further proof that reincarnation exists!

By the way, it was impossibly hard for Amelia's Spirit to be reborn as me, Julia. I believe dark forces tried everything possible and impossible to prevent people from receiving proof that reincarnation is real and that it exists, while I begin the development of new consciousness on the planet.

Just see for yourself how many obstacles there were…My grandmother, Valentina, was three-and-a-half years old. Her father was a Russian doctor, missionary in Asia, near the Chinese border. Suddenly some local Muslim people started killing Christians. They came to his house – never mind that he healed them and their families for years! Luckily the little girl hid at the back of the big Russian stove, which people used in those days. Valentina witnessed the merciless killing of her parents and her four siblings. She told me that she saw how they lifted the one-year old baby and cut him in half with a long sword. Next, they killed her brother, with whom she played all the time. When they left, she could not stay in this house of horror with dead family members lying around in their blood. The poor child ran as far away as possible to the forest.

Later on, Russian soldiers on horses came to protect Christian people. When they were crossing the forest – five days later – they found the little, poor child alone, scared, hungry and cold. She was lucky that a wolf, a bear or a mountain lion had not attacked her.

And this is not the end of the story!

Valentina grew up in her aunt's family. She got married young and her first baby was still born, unfortunately. Her second baby died soon after birth, her third baby was still born, and her fourth child also died at birth. Can you imagine? Yet, she did not give up! Finally, she gave birth to her fifth child, my mother, successfully. She was born a healthy, beautiful girl. She was a gift from God to Valentine after she had suffered the death of four children. Soon after, Valentina's husband, who was also a doctor, died from cholera. She and baby were very lucky not to have contracted the disease and to be alive.

If Valentina had been killed during the raid, if she had not hidden in the forest, and if she didn't have the fortitude to give birth to a fifth child after losing four babies, I would never have been born. And Amelia's spirit would never have been reincarnated in my body as Julia. And no one knows where Spirit would have found such a perfect configuration again.

By the way, my mother finished medical college and studied child-birth problems, to become a gynecologist. I am sure this is because she was miracle baby # 5 and because her mother had so many problems during child-birth. But later my mother decided to be a doctor like her father, whom she never knew, since he had died during the cholera epidemic when she was very young. She completed the medical institute program successfully and concluded her post graduate courses as a microbiologist.

REINCARNATION AS A GROUP!

During writing this book, I was in contact over internet with **Kevin Williams**, who lives in the United States, Oregon. He created a very good website: **http://www.near-death.com**
There he published articles by many scientists researching the life and death. They are very supportive of my book! After death Spirits of the people in "full mind" can do, for example, healing (story of John of God in Chapter Priest) and other amazing creative things.
We are very good friends with Kevin and he kindly gave me advise me to add to the book this astonishing info, which he prepared.

I wish to tell here about 2 American presidents, who carry the same Spirit.

http://www.near-death.com/experiences/reincarnation08.html

First, this Spirit lived in the body of President Abraham Lincoln, and then reborn in the body of John F. Kennedy. These were the 2 most democratic President of America.

The most amazing thing is that a large group of people around them reincarnated all together as well!
This was the case of their wives, children, business partners, astrologers and even those who'll killed them! For example, Spirit of that woman who was the wife of Abraham Lincoln was the in the body of the wife of John F. Kennedy. The same with the rest. If you open this link, you can see that they have similar facial features and the names! It seems that all of them were in the Heavens and made the decision to get back together: "Let us be born again all together and do something good for the American people" For me as a scientist, it is interesting to know: **"How to they found each other again and formed this group?"** I did find answer to this question and you can read in part: "Mind over Matter"at the end of the book. As you will see on this photos evidence is incredible.

Here you can see the two presidents and also their fathers, mothers, wives, sons, friends, teachers, assistants, and even their favorite poets! Surprisingly, they looking the same! Some of these people have the same first or last name, as in a previous

YOUR ETERNAL HOLOGRAM

The Presidents: Abraham Lincoln, John F. Kennedy
Their Fathers: Thomas Lincoln, Joseph Kennedy
Their Mothers: Nancy Hanks, Rose Kennedy
Their Wives: Mary Todd Lincoln, Jackie Kennedy
Their Son/Brother: ROBERT Lincoln, ROBERT Kennedy
Their Friends: ADLAI E. STEVENSON, ADLAI E. STEVENSON
Their Teachers: William GRAHAM, Billy GRAHAM
Their Assistants: CHARLES S. TAFT, CHARLES P. TAFT
Their Favorite Poets: Robert BURNS, Robert FROST

Here their Vice Presidents, Secretaries of State, Successors.

Their Vice Presidents: Andrew JOHNSON, Lyndon JOHNSON
The Vice Presidents' Vice Presidents: Hannibal Hamlin, Hubert Humphrey
Their Secretaries of State: William Seward, Dean Rusk
Johnson's Successor:
Johnson's Successor's Cabinet Member:
Grant & Nixon's Successors:

AVATAR SVADI HATRA

Here they are killers, murderers of the killers, helpers of the killers.

YOUR ETERNAL HOLOGRAM

Comparison of faces of both presidents.

Comparison of faces of Andrew Johnson and Lyndon Johnson.

Chapter 4

Egypt

During my life – in the last 18 years at least – I had many dreams about ancient Egypt. To make the story complete, I decided to visit Egypt. Some amazing things happened to me while I was there and these events solved the mystery which I carried for years, it shows one more Amelia's past life experience and me, Julia.

Heopse pyramid, Egypt

> *"I was Julia's private tour guide and driver in Giza, Egypt. The first morning we arrived at the pyramid's site, I started to tell her about the history of the Cheops pyramid.*
>
> *During my talk I asked her if she felt something from the pyramid, maybe some special energy or something like this. Instead of answering, she pointed to her legs and to my surprise; I saw big goose bumps covering all of her legs! It continued with her getting these goose bumps from time to time during my talk. Obviously, she did feel something really strong!*
>
> *At the moment, when I started to mention to her that the mummies were removed from the pyramids and were now in a museum, she changed dramatically. Suddenly, without any explanation, she started to be extremely angry about it! I was very surprised... She started talking very emotionally, with gesticulations and loudly... It felt like her own body was removed!*
>
> *I am glad that there is a big space around the pyramids and we were far away from the other tourists, because suddenly from a very polite, dignified, courteous, quiet, Canadian girl, she changed into some angry, real ancient person! Julia just changed completely! I never experienced something like this in my life before. It was obvious that she tried to stop herself to behave in a normal way, but she just couldn't!*

I felt that it was much easier for her to go with this strange "flow" than to keep it inside... This energy or I don't know even how to name it – it was coming from her independently from her own will. And it surprised her not less than me. At some point I was even scared...
She had a clear experience of déjà-vu and felt that she lived here a long time ago. There was a very strange feeling about her. I was her personal guide during 4 days and this feeling never left me. It felt like two people lived inside her and she switched from one to the other without warning. As soon as we talked about ancient subjects or we were near the pyramids, ***she instantly turned to that other ancient side of hers ... her voice, face and the way she talked and acted changed instantly at the same time!*** *I can tell you: I meet all kinds of tourists every day – for many years, but she is the only one who was like this. From my point of viewand maybe it sounds unusual, in some way she belongs to this ancient people or this family or was in touch with these ancient rituals and she knew the way it should be performed immediately. And when the rules were broken it upset her deeply. Those first hours when I witnessed this unusual behavior of hers, I decided to bring her to my spiritual teacher, Samir, who is working at the "Atlantis" oils, healing and well-being centre.*
His place is near the pyramid site. It was the right decision. He explained to her and me what this was all about." **Mohamed Abas Fattah, tour guide, Egypt, Cairo**

Yes, Mohamed had his opinion. I suddenly completely changed near the pyramid. It was interesting that I never paid attention to Egypt history during my life.... (The following paragraphs will show you the extent of my ignorance in this regard.)

Yes, I was extremely upset that the mummies were removed from the pyramids and sarcophaguses. Since the trip, this feeling is still there; it never left me. I continue to feel guilty and ashamed for the people who did this.

On my last day in Egypt, on the way to the airport, I visited the Cairo museum. I bought a ticket to see the golden Tutankhamen mask and Mother golden treasures, but instead, by mistake, I ended up in the mummies' room! When I saw them, I changed instantly again! Lucky I was totally alone there. The problem was that I wanted and I began talking to the mummies with my full voice..., with a totally clear mind. I repeated to them again and again, "I am very sorry, I am very sorry, I am very sorry.

I feel very sorry for the people who did this serious mistake and took you from your sarcophaguses and pyramids." There were 13 mummies there, mostly Egyptian kings and princesses, all gathered in one room, laid on tables, like in a morgue, side by side.

I stayed near the wise, the greatest – King Ramses II. He ruled Egypt for 65 years! And now, without the simple respect due to the common man, his body has been laid down in this glass box like an exhibit – without a coffin even! And everyone going near him looks and points at him! How humiliating!

He ended up without his own place in the cemetery! How unfair! Any ordinary human being has a place of final rest. I am sure his spirit is extremely angry! I felt this huge spirit-tension atmosphere in that room. I could almost hear how they all started screaming and complaining to me!

YES, it was a big, shameful mistake on the part of that archeologist and for the government of Egypt to follow the archeologist's decision! As for me, it is okay that they took all this gold and treasures for themselves or brought them to the museum. I agree, "Just take it!" Even though I know all of these special tools, these precious objects, played a very important part in the rituals during and after the burial of the mummies. I am still okay that these

treasures ended up in the museum. BUT why pulling the mummies out of their sarcophaguses and pyramids?
49 Why did you put them in these damn glass boxes? WHY?
Someone simply tried to make some extra money by taking US$18 from the tourists to show the mummies of the great Egyptian kings to everyone – when they already took their priceless, golden treasures and made a fortune from these artifacts. It was still not enough. What a bunch of greedy people they were! Where was their pride of their great history and culture? There should not be any acceptable apology or forgiveness for this! These people deserve punishment and they got it! I am still angry about it and it looks like it will never change unless the mummies are placed back where they were meant to be.In modern law terms I can say, "Their tombs were private property and no one's business or right to enter their mausoleums and do what they did." I am almost ready to sue all of them, to drag them through the courts on behalf of the ancient people in order to protect their privacy. These kings do not have any relatives who could protect and support them....
It is interesting that I am a Libra, the most peaceful sign of all zodiac signs. The Libra sign is very calm, quiet and private, until someone disturb his or her privacy. If a Libra starts a fight, it will be only for one important reason: to restore peace.
Two of the mummies had flowers around their bodies and I felt that I knew these flowers. I know their fragrance; I even started seeing those ancient times, the blue sky, the white limestone around us, and how these flowers grew in the desert…. For some reason, I felt myself very close to these people, who now lay as mummies in these glass boxes. I felt that I knew some of them personally. I was grieving and felt deep sorrow for them....
When I packed in Canada to go to Europe and I knew that there was a possibility for me to visit Egypt, I put my golden outfit – golden pants, top and jacket – with gold jewelry in my bags. I also added some deep blue pieces. I knew these clothes were going to be in great harmony with Egypt.
So, I wanted to wear my golden outfit when I went to the Egyptian museum. I felt it was the outfit I needed to wear in this instance. But the tour guide stopped me and said that it would attract a lot of attention in the museum, because I am an attractive European girl, a model with very long golden hair... and we already had problems with the local people following us in Giza all the time.
I didn't care if I drew attention on me. But my tour guide persisted and advised me not to go to the museum in this outfit because it would be a problem for him to try to keep me safe. (I was never afraid of people. I talked to anyone at any level – from presidents to homeless people in the street. People from villages are my favorite kind; they are closest to nature and very spiritual.) Anyway, he told me that he would not drive me to the museum if I wore the golden outfit. That day was a unique opportunity for me to visit the museum and maybe seeing the mummies. I thought there would only be one or two.... So I ended up wearing my best dress for meeting kings and queens and to pay them my respects.

Yes, he was right; my presence in that museum drew a lot of attention.
Everyone who worked there waved to me and tried talking to me until, finally, all of them followed me to the exit and outside on the street. They even took me everywhere – free of charge – to another room where the Tutankhamen treasures were displayed. By the way, I didn't wear anything short or sexy; I was in my favorite, long, silk dress from Saint Barth Island in the Caribbean.

Last year, after I visited the unique exhibition of "Body World" by the talented Dr. Gunther von Hagens, I even thought of donating my body for "plastination" in order to preserve it, (www.bodyworlds.com). [27] But the fact that I would be another exhibit in a glass box for the viewing of crowds of people like King Ramses II stopped me from carrying out with this idea. For some reason, I was attracted to this king more than to the others. I saw a few dreams about him during my life.

A few years ago, I visited a Russian monastery which is in the middle of Moscow. In a beautiful silver coffin, with lots of fresh flowers around it, there were the remains of a holy woman named Matrona. I was envious. I wished I could be lying there instead of her.... For some reason, I feel that it is very important to preserve the body after death. I suspect I know now why I cared about all this..., after I visited Egypt and I knew that I was a Priest in Chichen Itza in my past life.

My tour guide, Mohamed Abas, brought me to see the Light and Sound Show.

It was interesting that when I was in the plane on the way to Egypt, I started thinking about the pyramids. In my vision, I saw a round shape with turquoise, blue color, and near it, there was another round shape with pink and green colors. Very unusual colors. I didn't have any idea what these colors meant until I was near the pyramids the next morning.

They were lights placed in a row, facing the pyramids, which were used for this Light and Sound Show.

Round shaped lights – turquoise-blue, violet-pink, and yellow.

It was a spectacular show with great sound and superb laser effects. It was an enchanting display of music and colors on the Pyramids and Sphinx. Everyone enjoyed it very much! It was a little bit cold with the wind blowing through the night in the desert. But they had warm blankets available for everyone.

During that show it was said how great and special each of the three pharaohs was and in which pyramid they were located. Also, they said that we should respect the enormous effort on the part of 100,000 people who worked very hard to build the great pyramids. It was mentioned that a special rock covered the entrance of the pyramid to hide the real entranceway to the place where the sarcophagus was located. It was made in order to confuse the intruders when they would try to go in. Yet, after all this, amazingly enough, it seemed absolutely normal to everyone who saw the show and the people of Egypt that the bodies of those pharaohs were ultimately removed from the pyramids! Impossible!

Can you imagine yourself in the pharaoh's situation, when for many years you had your pyramid planned and built with great purpose and huge effort by devoted people, it is broken into, and without any respect for the sanctity of your final resting place, your dead body is pulled out and put in a glass box, on display, for your people to come and stare at your mummy for small change? How would you feel about it?

YOUR ETERNAL HOLOGRAM

Here is a letter from **Mr. Samir, director of the "Atlantis oil healing centre", Egypt.**

When Julia arrived to my healing centre, "Atlantis", I was not surprised. I was waiting for her. I saw a dream during the night that someone from the royal Pharaohs' family would visit me in the morning and would bring some special gift to Egypt. I felt the unusual energy from this gift. She did bring a gift for the Big Pyramid. It was a special rock from Chichén Itzá, from the famous Mexican pyramid!
Julia told me that for years in her dreams some ancient person, a priest or pharaoh talked to her from Egypt. She described this person in detail and the animal which accompanied him, and she told me that they have a very special relationship. I know instantly that this animal was Anubis. I explained to her that this was a mixed breed of dog and fox in Egypt, and each pharaoh had his own animal which lived with him during his lifetime, and followed him after death to the other side to protect him there. The Man with a very long head was possibly Akhenanten, Nephertiti's husband.
I felt that she had a very unusual, powerful energy within her. She mentioned that the next day she was going inside the big Cheops pyramid. I instantly felt responsible for her preparation to this event. I felt it was necessary to have her undergo "an oil session" according to the ancient Egyptian tradition. It felt that some High Power or God sent me to help her to make the necessary adjustments for the special meeting with the Spirits of Ancient Egypt. So I had an "oil session" numerous times with her. The result was astonishing!
The next day and the following day she told me in details what happened to her after my sessions. She also started asking me about a very magic, unusual cat, which was visiting her! A blue-colored cat. I knew instantly that this was the Holy Spirit of Bast, the Royal Cat Goddess, which visits only very highly spiritual people. And maybe only once in a life time! This is a very rare gift. Julia was very lucky. And I am proud of my involvement to this story.

Samir Ali Baba, Egyptian healer, "Atlantis centre", Giza, Egypt [19]

Yes, an ancient EGYPTIAN PRIEST or Pharaoh contacted me from time to time in my dreams for the last 18 years... Here is a very short part from the dream.

Dream # 30
The Blue Vessel of an Egyptian Priest & Pharaoh, January 10, 1992

There is a large, blue vessel, high above me, like a mirror, but situated a bit higher – since I cannot see my reflection in it. And from it – there is a way out to the other side of the Earth ... or another planet, a galaxy. There is the face of a person, looking at me from that side. He looks straight ahead, but it is not a face; it is some kind of mask...

I see him not for the first time, I knew him, and he knows me. He is a friend. He is astrologer. He is very clever, and he is the main figure there. His main purpose – not the Pharaoh problems or the construction – is to pass his knowledge onto his successor. It is the most important thing for him, he is thinking about it all the time. Everything should be reflected, like in a mirror; everything should be polished. The rest is trifle. Only one per cent of his knowledge is used in life. That is why all of the problems of the Empire are all mere trifles. It is like a gem which is passed from one generation onto the next. In this state, the most important thing is not a Pharaoh, but this knowledge. This is the most valuable thing in the Empire.

His knowledge comes from strange people. They are wearing white, silvery clothes. Like that snake in the desert – as if made of aluminum. They are dressed in some sort of spacesuit of a square shape, like truncated pyramids. There are squares on their heads. And around the neck there are some lines, similar to those of the pharaohs. They look like pharaohs. But they are similar to a dragon-fly shedding its skin... The Pharaohs started copying them and painted such long eyes on their drawings because of that. These people gave this knowledge, and afterwards it was passed on during the life of a man. Besides the main Priest, there were some others, less significant. Each of them had just one part ... but everything he was giving, he gave only to one person. He is like a queen bee; everybody valued the knowledge he passed on. But if something had happened to him, the others probably could restore it part by part.

His head is of a strange shape – a long skull. The head is bald; probably under it, all of it is artificial. It is long and flat, squeezed on both sides. And in the place where the fontanel is, there is something that was inserted – some sort of lens. When he was a baby – something round was inserted in his skull – it was stuck between the bones. *The skull was growing, and the bones in the fontanel did not knit.* The ray *(from the crystal)* would get in and the brain would not be able to endure the influence. However, the bigger the lens, the more the power the person had. The width of the lens was very important. This thing is right at the crossing with the third eye. With the lens it can be done four times a year, at the change of seasons. It is better when there are two dates – the Equinox – on the equinoxes, they do some corrections.

There is a strange animal beside him. It has stripes all over its body, and the face is narrow, like that of a dog. It is about the size of a medium-sized dog, bigger than a cat. Its ears are sticking up like those of a fox. It has almost no fur. It senses everything. On its neck, there is a golden hoop and stripes and two or three stripes on its back. Those pharaohs were from some other planets, maybe, and they drew these stripes on their heads to imitate those of an animal.

These animals could talk to the Priests. They could prompt the solutions. They put a similar crystal on their heads. Between their ears, there was something the shape of an olive – like an eye looking from a crystal, a lens. Maybe they used it for meditation.

He may have felt that this little creature (animal) knew where the truth was, and could correct it. It perceived the intentions, color, planets, and influences. There were eight or nine senses besides the common ones. Here there were two of them – him and the animal. They had a question. They had some sort of *aquarium*, where the liquids merged together (90% of it). Now they were merging, but they did not merge as such. A man (a human being) had a set of senses to feel things. This animal also had it. When there were intentions – the feelings came alive. And the animal felt the range of it, fed it, rectified it, and helped identify the positions, like on a map. The animals didn't have words, nor logic, no abstract mind, the things humans invented in their world and ultimately blocked out. That is why the animals can feel and sense things better than humans do. It perceives a man and helps him. The main thing for the animal is those ten senses from the *aquarium*. The animal senses a human, and the human being does not need to feel an animal. For the animal, the person is like a father, mother and for his part, the animal is a tamed one.

Who is he connected with?
The Priest is connected with me. This connection is very important for him. Maybe in the future, through generations, I must become his student, and the generations were interrupted. He knew that the following should have been this creature, but he saw later, that between them there is a generation gap. And he transcends his knowledge through his mind to him, and the other one absorbs it in his dream, but he does not realize it. But maybe he sees a chain of people. He values the diapason of life, the chain of people, from one to another via this tube, going through centuries. They could find with their minds the time period of humanity. And to define those who will be born in the future, they put together these people in one line and transfer them through the tube. This is their duty, obligation – this channel is supposed to be eternal. At any moment there could be a necessity for this channel to ring a bell, and then the person will come out. *Nobody knew that there was this sprout in the earth – but it is growing.*[26] It is right. And it is an axiom.

YOUR ETERNAL HOLOGRAM

Does he have enemies?
The Priest did not have enemies – only in time, only in the future. There could be others who would want to acquire this knowledge – but without initiation. They were imposing themselves from the outside. It is unnatural – they are enemies. If he chooses a successor – the one could be any person, but he sees and knows whether the one is capable to be that successor. But from the early babyhood – even before birth – they predict when the time of conception should take place and they know then when the infant will be born. It is very important – when the sun goes down, in the first month after the birth – it is important to insert the lens. The lens is replaced by another when the child is 5 or 6 years old. After that, once again, it is replaced at the age of 12 or 13, and for the last time, at the age of 19 or 20.

What does Devil think of it?
He does not envisage the depth and enormity of all this He only suspects all this; the knowledge, abilities, and capacities. But he does not know the reasons and roots, and does not even know what we were just talking about. He knows that there is a very strong, white knowledge. It is very easy for him, like champagne bubbles; he does not have ability to capture them, to feel them. It is like a metal that could not understand (or become) a soap bubble.
He turns from black into white when he flares up. His anger is the only expression of his creativity, the only possible one. He is like a metal, which is white hot. He could melt, disappear. He could transcend into the light substance. He is dark, but he also can produce light. Creative energy destroys him.

Where do the enemies come from?
He is not an enemy of the Priest All the enemies appeared and stopped the normal development on the Earth in 2341. (Perhaps this figure is from the Mayan Calendar...?)

The destruction came much later – normal people with normal brains became sick. It was like an infection, a virus. They stopped everybody, turned them back. *People lost their connection with the parallel worlds, lost the integrity of development. Before, they were walking in step, in one stream with their teachers. But they stopped, dropped back, lost the sense of knowledge.*

****

There is information about the ritual of drilling the skull in Tibetan tradition – in order to "open the third eye".
In the spring of 1943, the US military started building landing strips for their aircrafts on the small island of Schemia, located in the Pacific Ocean. Twelve feet beneath the surface, they found a cemetery **of giants.** They found the bones of giant people – six to eight meters tall – together with the bones of mammoths and giant rhinoceroses.
They were all found in the sand stratum which was at ground level during their existence. All human skulls which, by the way, were 60 cm. long, had a high, straight forehead – the same features and shape as people have right now. The most interesting find for me was that each skull had a hole 2 inches wide in it which looked like it had been covered only with skin. No one knows how or why this hole was made, or what sort of ritual the person underwent before its death to get this hole in its skull.

Some think that maybe it helped their Spirits to escape freely after death. I guess, these people were "relatives" or in the same "business" as my friends, the Pharaoh – the Priest, who had the same kind

---

[26] I just found out that it is the symbol of reincarnation, or new life, in Maya.

of hole in their skulls, and who made another one in their animals' heads, using this process during their lives successfully. The Editor of "Fate" magazine has contact information for three witnesses who were on Schemia Island at the time of the excavation.

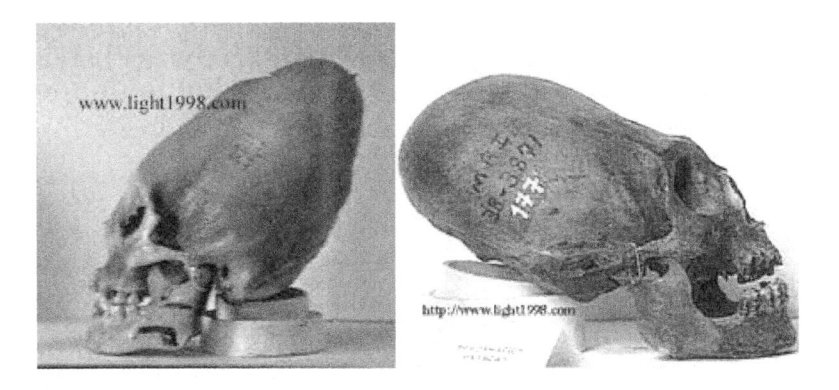

Long human skulls
(*Coneheads*. Researcher Robert Connolly photographed this strange elongated skull in 1995. It was found in South America and is estimated to be tens of thousands of years old. http://www.light1998.com/Weird-Skeletons/Weird-Skeletons.htm). [25]

YOUTUBE:Massive Skulls of the Nephilim
On the first two photos you will notice the holes in the middle of the skulls.
Alien Annunaki Illuminati who gave us Science, Language, Mathematics, etc.

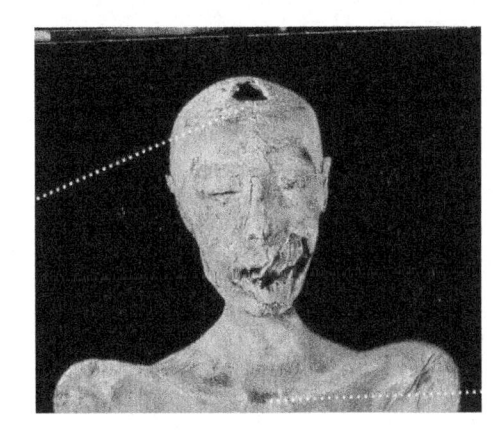

Egyptians removed the brain through the nostrils. Why there is a hole on the top of the head, no one knows. (Discovery Magazine, April 2009)

Here is what the Priest-pharaoh, his animal and Maya have in common: Arguelles was exploring the Maya conception of time, energy and consciousness. The Mayas actually possessed a more advance science than we do: What distinguishes Mayan science from present day science is it is a system operating within a galactic frame." With this synthesizing and holistic worldview, based on mind as the foundation of the universe, inseparable from time and space, "not only do the Mayas challenge our science, but they play with our myths". The basic goal of Mayan civilization, underlying their obsession with astronomical orbits and vast cycles of time, was synchronicity, synchro-astronization, or what Arguelles calls "harmonic resonance". Their "exquisitely proportioned" numbers' system was not primarily

a counting code, but "a means for recording harmonic calibrations that relate not just to space-time positioning, but to resonant qualities of being and experience.
Maya intentionally left behind a trove of secret knowledge, hidden teaching on the nature of time and being. This information was not just some quantity of statistic or facts, but a new pattern that had to be sensed and felt as well as logically grasped. To receive a new pattern, one must be open to it. The essence of information...is not its content but its resonance", he wrote, "This is why feeling or sensing things is so important. To sense the resonance of incoming information co-create a resonant field"

****

Mr. Samir and his staff kindly offered to me an oil chakras' massage. He has a big collection of organic oils with wonderful fragrances made from all kinds of plants, flowers and seeds.

His place looks like a crystal kingdom with thousands of oil canisters and containers. The containers were of all sizes and colors and some looked like Christmas tree ornaments. When I saw all these treasures, I started remembering my childhood.
I ended up swimming in these oils! I was covered from head to toe, totally submerged in fragrant oils. It was an absolutely fabulous feeling bathing in this oil bath!
I returned to the hotel in my Japanese kimono smelling like a bunch of exotic flowers with the aura of this luxury fragrance surrounding me.
I was delayed to go to bed, almost until midnight. It was the end of my first day in Egypt. I had arrived very late the night before and got up early in the morning to see the pyramids, so now I was trying to organize my stuff and thoughts a little bit....

When I turned off the light I found that my room was overcrowded with all these Egyptian "papyrus animals"! It was very sudden and unexpected... I was scared, maybe for the first time in my whole life! I turned the light on instantly and closed my eyes. But I continued seeing them! So I tried to keep my eyes open..., but I was very sleepy. So I repeated the exercise – closed and opened, closed and opened, like in a hide-and-seek game... They were real live Spirits! They were a little bit shorter than normal people. All of them wore masks! All of them were in my room! A full set of Egyptian "papyrus drawings" were standing in my hotel room! They seemed to be saying, "Finally she is going to bed and our time has started!"
At one point one of them stood very close to me. That was Anubis – and he bent down over my face. Another one touched the big toe of each of my feet, pinching it slightly, very fast and at the same moment, he touched the place where the third eye should be – in the middle of the forehead. This

creature, Spirit..., stayed near the end of the bed where my feet were. How it can be possible that I started feeling my third eye at the same time? I just couldn't explain it... [24] It looked like this Spirit was trying to make some adjustments; activate my energy flow through the channels and my third eye vision. Nonetheless, I soon fell asleep with the little light near my bed and the red, elegant lamp in the corner on.

Mohamed Abas (my guide) and Mr. Samir

In my dream, I saw myself sitting in a big chair – a throne – with all these animals down and around me.... They were talking to me in this unusual, bird-like voices..., kind of asking how I had been all these years?... As if I was meeting them again after a very long absence while traveling far away....

I know now, without any doubt, that this oil massage, this fragrant oil bath was the key! It was a very important and necessary step for these spirits to recognize me and accept me as part of their environment. It was important also that it happened before I visited the tomb the following day.

I knew then that the oil bath was an important ritual.

Plants play a very important role here. Time goes on, but exactly the same kind of plants grows around here, the same kinds that grew in Egypt thousands of years ago. These oils from the Egyptian plants helped my spirit reconnect with the Egyptian spirits and with my past! Maybe it was also an ancient tradition to be soaked in this oil. Maybe this way, the oils penetrated the skin very deeply and influenced the chakras, aura, spirit level..., or I don't know how to name all of this – which we cannot see or touch, but is still a part of us.

There was something else that became part of the ritual – and which is part of us. During the oil sessions, Mr. Samir sang some ancient Egyptian song and prayed with a low vibrato in his voice. I started seeing myself inside some room with huge solid walls and because of the very long, but not wide window that was very deep, I could feel the heat from outside and I saw the white desert sand in the distance. I saw him talking to me that time in a room and I understood what he said, and I caught myself talking back to him in this ancient Egyptian language....

*In my second dream, I saw myself sitting inside some big, golden box near the pyramid. The pyramid was two-third complete; only the last third part on the top was still unfinished.

YOUR ETERNAL HOLOGRAM

There was a big fan, slowly moving round and round, on my right side and I saw people working on huge rocks on the left side of me. A man with long painted eyes was sitting next to me on my left and talking slowly.... He had black hair, cut straight across the forehead, tanned skin, and he wore some unusual, shiny, blue and gold striped fabric covering his head and both sides of it. I saw that his hand was covered with some symbols, drawings....
*My next dream was a global dream where past and present societies meet in the desert near the pyramids in that area. Someone teaches me in my dream and I received four lessons.
Close to the morning, I saw something extremely magic! I am not sure that I was still asleep or already awake; it was in between, because I heard the sounds of the birds outside on that big tree, full of orange flowers near my patio...

Bast, the Royal Cat Goddess

The **"Cat"** stood on the floor in the middle of my bathroom! It pushed the bathroom door with his paw and opened it, but I remained inside and it looked at me with his round, shiny, huge eyes. He had the smoothest, silkiest fur I could ever imagine. I am not sure about his color, maybe it was black or very dark blue, but his fur was very shiny with bright blue, turquoise intense reflection in it. It was astonishingly beautiful!

I woke up that morning with a strong feeling. I felt one point at the back of my head, where the crown chakra and pineal gland are located, and I am sure this was also influenced by those oils, or maybe the pyramids, which were very close to the hotel.

I remember when I lived in the Korean Buddhist temple, a few years ago, I had the same feeling of this point; I could feel it continually when I was there. I also felt the place between the eyebrows – the third eye chakra – at the back of the eyes, located near hypothalamus and pituitary glands. In the Korean temple; I also felt that point between the upper lip and the nose.
I know now, without any doubt, that this oil massage, this fragrant oil bath was the key! It was a very important and necessary step for these spirits to recognize me and accept me as part of their environment. It was important also that it happened before I visited the tomb the following day. I knew then that the oil bath was an important ritual. On the way to breakfast I stopped near the window of a papyrus store in the hotel lobby. This little store was not open yet. But to my big surprise, I saw my night-guest on display! Exactly the same, a beautiful, blue cat! It was a drawing on a papyrus! On the opposite wall, I saw some drawing representing a scene with all of these Egyptian

Goddesses and animals, the same personages which visited me in my room and in my dream the previous night!
Later that day, I asked Mr. Samir about the cat. He told me that I was very lucky that this cat visited me. Her name is Bast, the Royal Cat Goddess, a royal cat, which visits very spiritual people sometimes. He told me that the cat will come again and will be closer each time. He was absolutely right.(Read below what happened the next day, in the afternoon!)

"Judgment day" with all Egyptian animal Goddesses

As for me, I know for sure that I was not asleep yet when I started seeing all of these Egyptian Spirit animals. I also heard the birds chirping in the morning when I saw the cat. Mr. Samir told me that this Spirit cat lives around the pyramids and visits people from time to time. Now I am really confused – He is a Spirit, right? He is not a real live cat.... I am still a scientist and I wish to have some explanation of this mystery.
I thought about it during the next few days and even now this cat still comes to my mind from time to time. I bought a little statue of him and he is right in front of me, right now, watching....
I know when people think about ghosts; these entities feed on people's energy, especially on their fear. Fear makes the ghosts stronger and they can even start moving objects or harm people.... Maybe it's the same story with this cat? Maybe it was the spirit of an ordinary cat a long time ago walking around, but people's thoughts are material and ultimately they created this beautiful blue-color cat in their imagination? And now this image, this phantom DNA, is moving around and some spiritual people who can see energy see him as well? The problem was that I never knew this cat existed until I saw it with my own eyes or perhaps, I should say, I saw him with my feelings....
Maybe it was the same story with this Egyptian Goddess and animals? A long time ago they were real people with masks; later people reproduced their images in paintings, on papyruses, and in the statues. So they always had these people in mind and it continued for thousands of years....

Ultimately, their images became strong enough that ordinary people, like me, could see them in profile, or feel them at the stage when they're about to fall asleep or were not fully awake yet.51
This twilight zone, by the way, this in-between stage of not being asleep and being asleep always brought me many visions during my life.

And now back to the cat subject. I remember that last year, in August, I was sitting silently with my daughter on the porch at the back of the house in Kauai. We returned from the beach and we were very relaxed. Suddenly she asked me, "Did you see that cat?" I replied instantly, "Of course I saw him!" But when I turned to the side and looked at the place where the cat had been sitting, it was no longer there! It did not exist! I could continue seeing it from the corner of my eye, but could not see it

if I looked straight at it! It was the spirit of the cat, which may have lived there at one time and was now visiting this place.
Anyway, let's return to Egypt and the days I spent there.

****

It was a very special and important morning for me next day. My goal was to be the first person to visit the tomb inside the pyramid! I ran directly to the entrance. The guards called me Shakira and started telling me not to be afraid, because I was going first and that I would be totally alone inside...

I just shoved my way passed them and I didn't pay any attention to their words. At first, it was a solid entrance leading into a wide corridor. All of the walls were made of strong, giant, granite rocks, but soon it turned into a very narrow corridor, a small tunnel like a square mouse hole. This corridor went up and up, and up and I couldn't see or know what I would find at the end of it, in the dark!

It was so narrow that two people abreast could not move through it – I think. I was glad that there were some electrical lights in there... I could imagine how difficult and uncomfortable it would have been for someone in ancient times to move through this narrow hole with a torch in one hand and carrying all these ritual tools in the other....
There would not be much oxygen to breathe with the torches burning – because there are no windows; it is deep inside the pyramid. In order to go through, you have to climb and crawl through this tunnel. Instead of steps there are just metal staples.... You cannot stand straight; you need to move up by climbing in a bent or sitting position with a very narrow, rocky ceiling extending above you. I advise people, who have claustrophobia, never, ever to go there; you would be scared to death.

Well..., I was glad when it was over and I could stand straight and walk again....

Finally, I was inside this big room with a high ceiling. It was dark in there; you could hardly see the sarcophagus near the opposite wall. But for some reason I was very excited and happy to be there alone! No word to describe it! It was like a dream come true and here I was!

First, I gave a **present to the Great Cheops pyramid**; my special present from my precious crystal, my Mexican Chichén Itzá pyramid. I hid it in the most important place and far from the guard's eye, the one who would come, and clean the place. I felt strongly about the importance of this, it was like a ritual and now it was done, completed. Next, I did what doctor Alfons taught me. I said aloud to the top of my voice: "I am not more than somebody else, I am not less than somebody else, I am myself." And then I pronounced all my reincarnations one by one: Queen from Atlantis, woman with a crown from Egypt, Priest Jaguar, Magician from Chichén Itzá, pilot Amelia from USA, T. from Tibet, and Julia & Jasmine Rose from Canada, Svadi Hatra, a human from the future".
The sound was extremely strong, bright and very loud. Each word continued to echo many, many times... It was like a symphony orchestra with drums and gongs. Wow! I loved it! This sound was great! Wow! Wow! Wow!

Suddenly something changed... At first, for a second, I was frozen and silent. Next, **I started talking in some unusual language!** I just talked quietly, as if I was praying. I didn't have any control over what was going on with me... I did not feel my body, my muscles or bones; there was just one pillar of energy going up through my body. I finished with some strange movement, as if I was performing some rite, with strange bends; up and down and to the side. It felt the same as if Chi Gong energy was pulling me in different directions. I was like a toy, a puppet in someone's invisible hands.

I felt as if I were in heaven with this carrying, cuddling energy within and around me. I ended up leaning with my back toward the sarcophagus and both arms spread wide to the sides of the top of the sarcophagus's wall. I was facing the entrance on the opposite side, in total silence, when I started hearing an echo from down below; up through the corridor, and moments later, three Japanese tourists entered the room. One of the women was suddenly scared to death. She was screaming, literally jumped, and ran to her husband. I guess she saw someone (me) – a dark human shape – near the sarcophagus and decided that I was a ghost...

It was a problem to return outside, by the way. As usual, I took control of the situation. First, I asked the Japanese tourists who already came up to the room to wait until the second group would come up, through the narrow corridor, so that we could have a free passage to return one by one down the staples, down the corridor and out of the pyramid. Then, I sent this first group of tourists through this corridor and stopped to wait for the next group down below to arrive until the corridor was cleared out. I was glad that they were Japanese tourists because they fully cooperated and did exactly what I asked them to do. I am not sure what it would have been if instead of Japanese I would have been faced with a bunch of spoiled American teens, for example. I think it would have been a nightmare and we would have all been "entombed" there forever....

****

After the pyramid, I went to visit the Sphinx that morning. By the way, at the Sphinx, I experienced the strongest sensation I had while visiting Egypt. I felt waves of goose bumps going up and down my body continually. One local boy ran to me and offered to show me an ancient wall with real Egyptian hieroglyphs, the statue of King Ramses II and so on. I ran with him through the desert and to the ruins. My driver was waiting in the car far away where the first street into town starts.

When I ran back, passing the Sphinx I found myself face to face with that Japanese family. The man told me, "It was a good idea for you to bring a flash light!"

I looked at him and just didn't understand what he meant. I asked him to repeat, "What did you say?"

He then told me that when they entered the room, at the back of me and around me, there was a glowing light, like an aura from the flashlight which I kept at my back... and when I left it was gone! How could that be? I did not have any flash light! And I remember that my hands were spread on both sides of the sarcophagus... When I told him that I didn't have any flashlight, he instantly began to step away from me – walking backwards...he seemed in shock when he realized that I didn't carry a flashlight...and stepped away from me – in broad daylight... I guess they were exhausted after climbing that scary corridor. Anyway, he gave me a good idea – next time I will take a flashlight with me.

The next morning I became aware of "new" muscles in my legs – the muscles in front of my legs from my knees upward. I think people never use these muscles in their entire life! I found out, the hard way, that I have them when I could hardly stand up or try to walk – I was in great pain. It continued to be painful for more than a week. Even when I left Egypt and I was back in Canada, my legs continued aching. I walked like a handicapped person or a very old grandmother....

It is interesting that I always loved the desert. I often drew pictures of deserts, palm trees, camels. In Egypt, near the pyramids I saw exactly the same shapes with my own eyes – for real! I was very happy and excited! I remember giving one of my paintings for an exhibition; it was at the time I was at the university. I received many compliments...but my painting was stolen! It looks like someone liked it way too much. I should have made a scan from it, but who could expect that a painting would disappear from a university exhibition?

****

That day, I had a second oil bath, and the Spirits visited me again! This time, I was in bed, ready to take an afternoon nap, not under the influence of the oils, like the first time, not in the darken room, only the curtains were drawn to shade the room from the sunlight. It was the middle of the day!

This part is very interesting...

I was again in the "twilight zone", right before I fell asleep. I was lying down on my back, in my comfy "5-star-bed", sinking into the softest pillows with my hands lying on my tummy. Suddenly, I saw the blue cat on the floor near my bed! He jumped up and landed softly on top of my hands. I stopped breathing... It was the softest, warmest ball of energy. The cat was sitting and looking directly into my face. I could see his eyes, with the lines across the eyes – in detail! It was hilarious... The cat continued to sit for the next two or three minutes, when, from the corner of my eye, I saw this Anubis, the Spirit animal, which stood near the next empty bed! He stood like a human at first, in his Fox and Dog mask... but, as soon as I saw him, **he bent slowly and slid instantly from a standing position to a lying down one on top of that bed!** He lay down as dogs usually lie down and looked the way he does in many of his statues. It was truly amazing; it was a wave of pure energy! I saw something like this in a movie, in a computer animation maybe – when robots turn from one configuration into another. Or when the Chi Gong master moves like a wave... I fell asleep instantly after this, and I don't remember anything else.

BUT this "movement" got top points in my book of all the magic things I experienced in this truly Mysterious Egypt. Egypt is now like a jewelry box for me which if you would open it, you would be astonished seeing the flush of rare, magic multicolored stones inside it.

This animal Anubis, I saw it twice in Chichén Itzá in the temple on the top of the pyramid during my past life reading. It was during the sacrifice scene. Then I saw him the first evening when all these Egyptian animal Goddesses visited me. He was always near me that night and now he showed up again!
When I woke up that afternoon, I continued lying down with closed eyes for a few seconds, and suddenly, I had a vision. It was very fast, like a flash, like in the blink of an eye, but I remember it.

I saw two giants with crowds of normal size people around them. There were about 40 or 50 people there, the top of their heads only reaching the hips of the giants. All of them, including the giants, were wearing luxurious, beautiful, very ornate outfits. This crowd was standing where today the road from the Cheops pyramid to the second big pyramid crosses the road going to the Sphinx...

Anubis standing   *Anubis lying down* [23]

For some reason, each time we drove through this area, I always found an excuse to ask the driver to stop the car at that place – to take a photo or to see a policeman on the camel or something else. I always wanted to stop there and step outside the car for a little bit; something invisible attracted me to that spot. I felt something really unusual there. I saw this place in my vision, but at a different angle. Maybe this place marked our Stargate to the past? Or another timeline crossing there?

People who read this passage may say: "At first she saw a big man in Mexico, now she sees giant people in Egypt!" Yes, I saw a huge man in Mexico with many little details of his daily life and he was a dear friend of mine. And yes, I saw these two giants for a short moment in that area at the crossroads from the pyramids to the Sphinx. What can I do about it?
Yes, I saw them and I trust my vision very much, since throughout my life what I saw and felt has come true and happened.
I saw, in my vision, a blue, pink, and yellow round sphere near the pyramids while I was in the plane, even before I arrived in Egypt. I wrote it in my little book in the plane to check my record later, and I saw them right there, on the first morning I arrived, right near the pyramid!

While I am typing this, I am thinking now about these two giants... maybe they were Atlantis people, too? And I remember that the tour guide mentioned that near the Sphinx they found the Hall of Records which Atlantis people left ... and that Edgar Cayce mentioned this in his predictions.

Edgar Cayce - Atlantean Hall of Records

Edgar Cayce predicted the discovery of an Atlantean "Hall of Records" between the Sphinx and the Nile with a connecting entrance under the right, front paw of the Sphinx.
The following segment was taken from Cayce, Edgar "On Atlantis" New York: Warner Books, 1968.

"...It would be well if this entity were to seek either of the three phases of the ways and means in which those records of the activities of individuals were preserved -- the one in the Atlantean land, that sank, which will rise and is rising again; another in the place of the records that lead from the Sphinx to the hall of records, in the Egyptian land; and another in the Aryan or Yucatan land, where the temple there is overshadowing same, (2012-1; Sep 25, 1939).
"...the entity joined with those who were active in putting the records in forms that were partially of the old characters of the ancient or early Egyptian, and part in the newer form of the Atlanteans. These may be found, especially when the house or tomb of records is opened, in a few years from now," (2537-1; Jul 17, 1941).
[The entity] was among the first to set the records that are yet to be discovered or yet to be had of those activities in the Atlantean land, and for the preservation of data that is yet to be found from the chambers of the way between the Sphinx and the pyramid of records, (3575-2; Jan 20, 1944. p.147

A record of Atlantis from the beginning of those periods when the Spirit took form, or began the encasements in that land; and the developments of the peoples throughout their sojourn; together with the record of the first destruction, and the changes that took place in the land; with the record of the sojourning of the peoples and their varied activities in other lands, and a record of the meetings of all the nations or lands, for the activities in the destruction of Atlantis; and the building of the pyramid of initiation, together with whom, what, and where the opening of the records would come, that are as copies from the sunken Atlantis. For with the change, it [Atlantis] must rise again. In position, this lies -- as the sun rises from the waters – as the line of the shadows (or light) falls between the paws of the Sphinx; that was set later as the sentinel or guard and which may not be entered from the connecting chambers from the Sphinx's right paw until the time has been fulfilled when the changes must be active in this sphere of man's experience. Then [it lies] between the Sphinx and the river (378-16; Oct 29, *1933*) - *P.147-8 (On Atlantis – New York: Warner Books, 1968).*

I know exactly where this place!!!! They start digging to the wrong direction!
WOW! Today, June 22, 2008 – 3:45 p.m. when I almost finished the book and I was only checking pictures; I suddenly found a website about Giants in Egypt!!Giant-Titan Pharaoh! You cannot compare the brilliant Edgar Cayce's predictions and feelings about the tall Atlanteans when you can see them in your own eyes on the real ancient picture!
 And it is exactly what I saw in my vision!

Egyptian Giant-Titan Pharaoh

The above shows a Titan Pharaoh of Egypt with typical red-ochre skin paint. The Titans were the Adanyas, and settled in the British Isles and the Americas. They and others were called them 'Red Men' because of their red-ochre painted skin.

What really struck me: this is extra proof that I can go back to 2,000 years in Mexico or 7,000 years in Egypt and see, really see, how people lived in those times. And it is obvious to me that during those times giant people were living and walking this Earth amid normal-size people.

But it is also an additional proof that the **Cat and Anubis** were real "spirits" which I could see (and feel) in my vision. It shows amazing possibilities to us "mere human beings"! It feels as if there is a storage of information somewhere – a library of lives.

****

I am very excited right now and overwhelmed. I even allowed myself to visit the kitchen and eat cherries and ginger in chocolate, right before dinner. I love sour cherries very much! I wonder if Amelia loved them as well?

The black Golden Cat Bastet and Anubis are hiding and staring at me through the jasmine and roses on my desk. The nearby vase is full of white, naive daisies. At this moment, I am in Heaven!
I sent this letter to Egypt yesterday…

"Happy to hear from you, dear Samir!

Magic things continue to happen to me in Canada.

AVATAR SVADI HATRA

The **Spirit Cat** visited me again during my dream. It was right after I returned home. I was tired after the flight and I was deep asleep for a long time, so I don't remember the details.
But what happened today was really amazing. Today is June 12 – 5:30p.m. I decided to take a nap for an hour. I asked my daughter to wake me up at 6:30p.m. I lay down in bed, closed my eyes and as soon as I did, I saw a girl right near me. Her face was very close to me. I wasn't even asleep yet.

While I continued looking at this face, I heard my daughter opening the entrance door and taking her bike outside. This girl has the face of a doll, with big eyes, full lips and full cheeks – kind of a baby look, puffy. She has an ebony face with a very smooth skin. A powder or sand-spray of bright, lapis-lazuli color seemed to be sprayed over her ebony face! She was too perfect to be human. She was a Spirit – or I don't know how to name it. At first, I thought that maybe she was the Spirit Cat who decided to show himself as a girl – or maybe the opposite – maybe she showed herself as a cat to people, but she was really the Spirit of a girl, because she had this neon-blue color powder covering this smoothest ebony skin.
She continued to peer down at me with this very serious look in her eye. I just didn't know what to do! For a moment, I thought that even she has this black face, she is not a person from Africa, although this black color was not painted on her face. I know that she is from Egypt, but she has also a kind of Persian look.... When I was thinking about her looks, it reminded me of the Tutankhamen mask. It had the same features – of the same nationality. I thought that maybe she is not even a girl – maybe she is a boy.
Perhaps, I brought her spirit from Egypt with me and now she lives here? Or maybe, while I was in Egypt, the Spirits began to know that I could see them and now they visit me and show themselves to me! I continued looking at her and she continued staring at me – I just didn't know what to do next. I decided to check if it was my imagination or if I was seeing a real Spirit. I decided to ask her some questions; suddenly I had so many things to ask. So I stood up and went to my desk, took a pen and paper to write down the answers. While I was preparing myself for this "interview", she disappeared. So, I went back to bed and fell asleep. When my daughter woke me up, I thought that maybe this was one of my dreams. How can it be possible? Yet, when I looked near me, I saw the pen and paper, which I brought to bed when I saw her before I fell asleep!
It looks like after your amazing oil baths, I saw Spirits in Egypt many times, so many times in fact, that I started getting used to them as if it was normal – part of my daily routine! So today, instead of being surprised, I just enjoyed looking at her and maybe asked something simple – I am already way too practical! I am sure that she is still here and that I would see her as soon as I closed my eyes. I am sure she is not the ghost of some dead person.
She looked very radiant, healthy and beautiful and way too perfect to be human. She was astonishingly beautiful! Who is she? Do you know maybe?
Sincerely, Julia "

Anyway, I ran trying to find a container, some vase, or an amphora to accommodate her Spirit. Somehow, I knew instantly what to do since I have a connection with the Priest! Lucky that I found a brand new, fine quality "porcelain" vase from China.

From Samir:
"You should know that you have with you good spirits from Egypt and you should have more of my oils to keep you communicating with them, it is very important. I know you are a very good and highly spiritual person."
Then I started to study this **mystic cat and girl.** Here is what I found.
Bastet
Responsible For: Joy, Music, and Dancing! Also Health and Healing. She also protected humans against contagious diseases and evil spirits. Her cult can be traced back to about 3200 BC, and she became a national deity when Bubastis became the capital of Egypt in about 950 BC. If you plan to

do a portrayal of Bastet, consider wearing a red costume – a priestess of Bastet, like the goddess herself, was known as "the Lady with the Red Clothes" http://www.shira.net/egypt-goddess.htm.

By the way, it was said that this priestess of Bastet was like the goddess herself and was known as "the Lady with the Red Clothes". For some unexplained reason I brought a red dress with gold ornament with me to Egypt and started wearing this red dress during the next two days after I saw the Bastet Cat, when I visited the pyramid and the Sphinx and until I left Egypt.

Now I know why! It was my intuition in the first place that told me take this dress, and after I met the cat I started wearing that dress because it suited this situation perfectly, according to ancient Egyptian rules! When I read this, I understand who this extremely beautiful girl was. She is the Goddess, the Spirit that came to me in the middle of the day and showed herself as soon as I closed my eyes! She is the Goddess priestess of Bastet!
I was not sleeping; I was 100% awake! She appeared immediately after I close my eyes. Moreover, she was not a ghost. She is a real live Goddess in Spirit world and comes in our world since I saw her. I found more about Bast and now I know why this is all connected with the perfume oils! Wow!

Bast, Perfumed Protector, Cat Goddess

Her name has the hieroglyph of a 'bas'-jar with the feminine ending of 't'.
These jars were heavy perfume jars, often filled with expensive perfumes - *they were very valuable in Egypt, considering the Egyptian need (with the hot weather) of makeup, bathing, hygiene and (of course) perfume.*
Bast, by her name, seems to be related to perfumes in some way. Her son Nefertem, a solar god, was a god of perfumes and alchemy, which supports the theory. http://www.crystalinks.com/bast.html

It is an endless pleasure to look at her beauty! On top of an absolutely black skin, she has a dark, very bright, blue color – something like the "neon fish" I saw in a pet store. It is exactly the same as the Cat had on top of his black-colored fur – this bright, neon blue color! This is why I was sure that they were connected somehow.
Now I know that these are actually **T**wo **Spirits in one** – such as I saw myself many times, in my dreams, as a **twin.**
So this Anubis, which came to me and slid down from one position to another, and the Cat, which came already three times, and this Goddess girl – all of them are REAL and exist in our world! And I will be very happy to meet them again!
It is interesting to note that all of them are as black as ebony and that their statues are all sprayed with gold. Maybe 7,000 years ago the sun emitted very strong radiation, or for some other reason, people and animals at the time were black.
From another side, totally black color will not have any reflection and it will be impossible to see it! Wow! Maybe this is the way how this goddess is hiding in our world between us? So we can see them only in special condition. Those scientists, who will create this kind of fabric, will be geniuses!

I can tell you a secret that may help you to see them. First, you need to divest yourself from stress, get out from a negative environment and away from negative people. Since they are never happy with themselves, they will always try to control you, ensuring that your door to happiness is locked as well. The problem with people is that they don't like and don't want you to change. They will try to shut you down. It is also best to disconnect your TV, where they always show negative news, and all your wireless equipment, which kills your psychic ability and may ruin your health. Instead, spend time with plants and nature. Eat only when you're hungry and just a little amount to give your body a rest from toxins and the possibility to return to health fast while being in excellent shape physically and mentally. Meditate. Forgive to yourself and other.

YES! But you should already have a happy disposition, be optimistic, and spiritual with only very positive, kindest, pure, direct from the heart, loving the whole world kind of thoughts. Some "oil sessions" with someone like Samir would help. Soon this effort will pay off. It will open doors for you to see amazing dreams, to connect with wise Spirits and receive lessons from powerful giant Gods and Goddesses.

****

Regarding wireless equipment – since the fall of 2007 bees have begun to die in great numbers in the USA and Europe. In the western US states, 60%, and in the eastern states 70% of bees have disappeared. In Europe it also happened in Germany, Spain, Portugal, Switzerland, Italy, and Greece. Scientists from Landau University in Germany found that in most cases the electromagnetic waves of the wireless phones and antennas destroyed the mechanism of the orientation in the bee's body, and the bees simply couldn't find their way home! No bees, no harvest. Most of the people whoare using cell phones don't know that they are not only killing bees, they are killing themselves as well – and fast. Soon there will be NO food. Many people will then start remembering that Albert Einstein told us that people could only survive for a few years after the bees will have disappeared. It is my most sincere wish that people who read this book would stop using their cell phones, except in case of emergency. By the way, cell phones can also cook brain cells in the same way as if you were to put your brain in a microwave.

Dream # 31
CROWN, September 6, 1991

Maybe there were many people; maybe the Lord was speaking. It was a very long and serious dream. Something was going to happen to me, something they were all waiting for. Everybody stood in their places, each in his or her own alcove – designed for just one person. There were men to the one side of me and women to the other. I started to wave my hands, like a butterfly. Then I looked at myself from above, as if a huge creature was looking down onto little ants – The Power! Two girls took me by the arms. They came to stand at my side at once. Some wave-like process started – very energetic, very dense – maybe it was a cloud. It seemed I had seen it in my dream already. I was entering this wave, and someone was moving my body, as if in the wind, very powerfully, without my participation. It was becoming stronger. The girls were holding my upper arms with one hand and joined their other hand to form a circle.
I remember hanging my head downward. I saw my hair, very thick, ash-blond, running in a wave motion down to the floor. Their hair was also very long – chestnut or black – touching the ground. It was waving in the same rhythm. I don't remember what happened afterwards.
I felt like a caterpillar turning into a butterfly. I understood that it had happened, and then they seated me on something and carried me somewhere. I was sitting at level with their heads. Then I lay down in a recumbent position. I saw a sign written above someone's head – something most important – the goal. The man was sitting on an eminence's throne – five steps up from the floor of the hall. This hall was made of marble surrounded by columns. He had a beard and long hair. He was performing some enchanting, powerful acts, ignoring the others. He looked very noble, dressed in white, pleated robes like a God... I saw a sign in the space.

It was very important; this was the most important thing in my dream – like hieroglyphs, in which the Chinese see a lot of meaning. It was a complex sign, a round sphere, and inside it, some inscription which reflected all of the essence of the disciples as a whole. Any person, who does not know anything, after looking at this sign, could have understood everything, not through their intellect but through their "perception". Then there was a chasm... There were high columns which were dividing the space into segments. Men were on the left of me; women on the right. The left side was more

YOUR ETERNAL HOLOGRAM

important. I was in the center. Something was happening... When I remember this later on, I had seen a sphere in front of me, then I had seen myself from above, and on my head there was an **oval-shaped, very clear cut hole** – straight through the occipital membrane – **ready to insert the crystal.** Inside – the eternity, like in space. It was much unexpected. I raised my eyes and saw another hemisphere. Later, I saw a red cap of the same form as the **concave shape** in front of me and I wanted very much to put it on. I was impatient, but they gave it to me instantly and I put it on. It was covered with **crystals, large stones...** One of the girls, when she noticed my impatience, giggled, as if saying,

"You'll get it anyway!" It was incredibly comfortable and it fitted exactly, although there were no strings or laces, but it fitted tightly.

The hemisphere was round at the base, but on the top, it turned into a pyramid with a square-cut top. Next they placed the **second, spherical hat on top of the conical.**

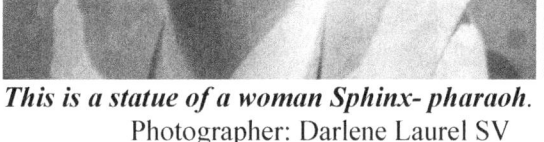

This is a statue of a woman Sphinx- pharaoh.
Photographer: Darlene Laurel SV

Amelia Earhart.

Do you see on the photo a resemblance in pharaoh girl features with those of Amelia's?

I was attracted to her and could not stop staring at her. It was my past life!

I had exactly the same Brazilian leather coat, like Amelia wearing here on photo!

Conical hats – bas-relief

Nephertiti

What is in her head? It looks like a cut pyramid, square at the bottom, but round at the base, exactly like what I saw in my dream.

MY SPACE – Dharma to DREAM

It was question for me what is in Nefertiti head?
It looks like a cut pyramid, square at the bottom, like what I saw in my dream.

The mystery was solved **17** years later when I visited the Cairo museum in May 2008. I found, among many others, two sarcophagi which had exactly the same "crown" on their heads that I saw and put on my own head in my dream after this special ritual! It was the shape of a cut pyramid with a square bottom which is the same shape as the Chichén Itzá pyramid, by the way. I asked the opinion of three representatives in the museum and they all went with me to see these "crowns". They all told me that this is the symbol of royalty; it is a queen's crown! What an unusual shape!

It looks like, **in my dream, I was the subject of a royal initiation ritual**. This could explain why I was so attached to the mummies in the Cairo museum, why I had goose bumps, why I was looking for the house where I lived before, and why I was so angry that the mummies had been removed from the pyramids. Maybe, in my past life, I was one of the royalties who later was entombed and removed to the museum room. For all these answers I need to visit the wise Di Cherry again and ask her to read these dreams...
When I walk in Sakkara (located about 30 miles from Giza) in 2008 I feel like I have been in this "cemetery" many, many times before, probably during ancient funeral ceremonies... Maybe it was even my "work place" sometimes as a royal priestess.

Regarding **Nefertiti,** I found the original statue in the Cairo museum. Workers in the museum told me that YES, what she was wearing was indeed a crown which was placed on her head after the statue was carved. But around the crown should be part of her head. The bust is not complete or has been broken. Today, a week later, I found this information, and below, on the photo, you'll see exactly the shape of the hat and crown I saw in my dream! In my dream, at the end, they placed the second, spherical hat on top of the conical. Remember? Not only little pyramid, which cut on top. By the way I remember pyramid in Atlantis, which was cover with this sphere and this sphere open time to time. Atlantean people arrived from another planet and they need pressure, other gravitation for their body. This was regulated under this spheres.

Conical Hats Worn By Gods
http://www.crystalinks.com/conicalhats.html.http://members.aol.com/marslandsr/hats.htm.
The girl below is what I drew, right after I woke up. She is the one who had a small kind of hole in the scalp. This subject with the hole in the scalp was repeated many times in different dreams. She may be the girl from Egypt?

Girl with a crown, from the dream dated, September 6, 1991

God and Goddesses and Quetzalcoatl all wear a conical cap such as the wind god Ehecatl. He brought love into the world by mating with the maid Maya huel as a single tree with flowering branch

The two hats – the conical and the spherical

Cretan goddess, young, beautiful, with tangled hair and a conical cap. Side view of the hat to the right. (Statuette figurine from Tylenos)The Pharaoh is equally a priest and a ruler, and wears the crown of the two halves (upper world and underworld) of his dominion. The lower crown denotes the upper world, the high conical hat the lower.

Today, I found one more dream, it was 16 years ago.

Dream # 32
The Fox and the Sarcophagus, February 23, 1992

(Unfortunately, I lost the first page with the beginning, of this dream) After that, I saw the Fox who sat on a stone, with a long nose and long ears, like a monument, a statue, on a rectangular box which stood on two gold spheres. Below, there is a grotto, an entrance. Through this secret entrance there is a key – moving the rectangular box - spheres. Below this entrance there is the tomb of a queen, a sarcophagus. In the front of it there are two hieroglyphs (the same as on the rectangular box of the Fox). Under the sarcophagus, there are stone tiles with inscriptions. There are four signs: an ibis…, and some pictures of a yellow crown, the large lizard, beads (the beads are similar to fireballs, lightning fire bolts).

****

I did not know in 1992 that the FOX actually had the name of Anubis and I had not decoded the name yet. I believe this was my own sarcophagus. I saw this place numerous times in my dreams and wanted to find it.... I couldn't put here the full information of what was written on the sarcophagus. One day I might go to try to find my own tomb in Egypt. Maybe it is somewhere in Sakkara, among hundreds of pyramids, where the sarcophagi of kings, priests and their families are laid to rest. Sakkara is located about 30 miles from Giza.

People told me that while they reading the book, vibrations emanating from those dreams described in the book activate the mind and they think the situations happened to them in their past lives.
Some amazing memories occurred to Helena from St. Petersburg! Helena has very strong intuition and psychic abilities.

During editing some parts of the Russian version of this book, she recalled the amazing events of her own past life!! When she was a small child of 4 years old, she often dream of huge Angel Deities, they called her by the name Nefertari and sent to her aura bright light energy.

Nefertari was called the queen of ancient Egypt, the favorite wife of Pharaoh Ramses II, in whose honor he built the temple. The most surprising thing is that the preferences and habits of ancient Queen Nefertari, Elena discovered in herself.

Elena and the Queen Nefertari - both loved turquoise, wear clothes and ornaments of turquoise. The entire body of the temple of the Queen was painted turquoise, even all her tomb was decorated with jewels of turquoise. The house Helena kitchen ceiling painted turquoise and lotuses.

Also a very sad and strange coincidence: Nefertari's and Elela's first baby died...And many more other coincidence! Nefertari had 2 Siamese cats. In Elena's home for 17 years has lived 2 favorite Siamese cats.

****

I tried to find a better explanation for all of these unusual things that happened to me in Egypt. Upon reading some information on the subject, I came to the conclusion that maybe the reflection of the two giants I saw in the Cheops Pyramid was due to my "psychometric ability".

According to Persi Fosset, *"Any material object has a written memory of all its previous history"*. And people, who have this sensitive ability to feel this specific frequency, can read the message inscribed in these objects. The name given to the people who have this ability is "psychometrics".

The famous blind psychic, Vanga, from Bulgaria was a real example of this. Before she met with scientists, she asked them to sleep the previous night with a crystal or a piece of sugar-crystal under their pillow, or with a watch with a Ruby crystal movement. The next morning she would take the crystal into her hand and read the person's information, which had been "transmitted" onto the crystal during the night.

The famous Tofic Dadashev describes details of the life of the woman known as "The Jocunda", through her portrait painted by Leonardo Da Vinci. The details of her life are only known by a small circle of specialists.

What about the room in the hotel when, as soon as I switched off the red lamp, these unusual voices of all these Egyptians animals and goddesses came out of the dark?

On the one hand the memory of it is wonderful, yet, on the other hand, it really bothered me. I started studying the possible reason for which I heard these voices when I turned off the light.

I found that in 1851, Victor Hugo moved to a house he bought on the small island of Jersey in the North Sea. When he worked during the night he heard the sounds of a child running, a woman laughing, and that of a babysitter complaining. Every single night the same thing happened. No one ever saw any ghosts in that house. It seems that the walls of this house kept the sounds in their memory. The same happened to Persi Fosset in a "bad" house. As soon as he turned off the light, he heard screaming chicken running through his room and the sounds of an old, handicapped man following it. As soon as he turned the light on, the sounds disappeared. Every night this phenomenon repeated itself every time he switched the light off. He had strong nerves but he finally moved to a hotel when he could not stand it anymore.

People who worked during the night in the Kremlin have heard sounds coming from the Lenin room during the last 80 years. This room is locked, but there are still sounds emanating from inside it, as if someone is moving furniture, or pacing the floor. It seems that these sounds have been created by ordinary activities, and not by a ghost.

The same is true for The White House. Almost all American Presidents and members of their families have heard these kinds of sounds. Some even saw Abraham Lincoln, but in this instance, he did not produce any sound and did not move furniture.
According to numerous researches, in the dark, when people shut down their visual sensory perception, their hearing starts to be much more sensitive so that they effectively shut down the external background sounds from their hearing. They begin to accept what they hear and they start hearing faint, weak sounds. This can explain why people can hear things in the dark which they can't hear when a light is on in the room. When there is no light, we can start hearing sounds from the past which were preserved in the surrounding space, such as walls and various objects. Scientists think that in the future it may be possible for people not only to hear, but also to begin visualizing what they hear.
This hypothesis was advanced by the science fiction author, Ivan Efremov.

Well..., as for me it has already happened. I saw giants among normal size people near the pyramid! According to Persi Fosset, who says that material objects have a written memory of all their previous history, rocks of the Cheops pyramid kept this motion picture with the two giants for thousands of years. And I can name myself **as a psychometrics,** because I feel this specific frequency!

When I delved into this subject a little deeper, I found that anyone could develop this ability.

In Ukraine, Vecheslav Bronnikov developed a new method of "visual or hearing blindness". Normal kids began to read, have good orientation, recognized colors with closed eyes and their face covered with a black fabric.

So, who you are right now, what you do, will be stored in that library and people in the future will have the possibility to see you in their past!

Then I began to think that it may be possible to find some kind of mechanism to copy, from my eyes or my brain those visual scenes which I saw during hypnosis and in my visions. I really needed this sort of assistance when I started working with the artist who first drew the cover of this book.
I tried to explain to him a few times what I wanted but he just could not grasp (or visualize) what I was describing. I saw a Priest, this 45- 50-year-old, wise, noble man with a kind heart, high cheekbones, tall, slim, but well-built with a lean, beautiful muscle tone, with an enormous amount of jewelry around his neck and on his chest, hands and legs. I saw some tattoos on his face, a very unusual hair style with two pony tails and hundreds of small braids, with jewelry and feathers in it. He wore a jaguar coat. I saw his smiling, dark-blue eyes and his hand, tenderly caressing a white baby jaguar between its ears.
Instead, the artist drew a modern, urban man with drooping shoulders, with a fat belly. I tried to tell him that the Mayas had droughts at that time and they didn't have enough food to become obese. What's more, they were muscle-bound since they had to exercise a lot – even to accomplish a simple task. Imagine yourself walking up the pyramid a few times a day! You would be fit-and-trim in no time.
I also asked him to draw Kukulcan, the man-lizard, as in a Swarovski crystal toy-jewelry. Instead he drew a "vagrant" with green scales on his head and wrapped in a blanket.
Chak Mol is extremely tall, slim, a lean man playing with Maya boys....
Instead I got a modern, heavy punk-rock type of man, jumping on a stage....Sadly, I understand that for modern people it is extremely difficult to imagine Atlantean body proportions, unless they see them in reality. I am glad that movie "Avatar" finally came out and people saw how giant may looks like.

When I resumed my research a few weeks ago, I found an absolutely amazing invention, which would suit my needs perfectly! Since 1974, scientists have studied the hallucinations of mental patients and have endeavored to record what these patients saw – with astounding results.
They placed a swimming mask in front of the patient's eyes, and a photo camera, focused on the eye of the patient, was fitted in place of the glasses. This camera was then able to photograph the eyes' reflection during their hallucination. The doctors, who performed this feat, began their study with 262 patients, from which they obtained 102 photos, displaying the visual hallucinations of their patients! The information was transferred from the brain to the optic nerve onto the eyes.

Dr. Herbert, from England, called the nature of this type of stable light-flow a **"biogravitation field"** – not an electromagnetic field. I wish I had known about this technique before, so I could have shared with all of you exactly what I saw 2000 years ago in Chichen Itza.

The Mystery of the Sahara and the Pyramids

On the 13th of March, 2017, I accessed one more of my past lives in a dream!

I plan to visit a past life therapist, so as to confirm this dream, while under hypnosis.
In that dream, there were two young girls playing a game of "hide and seek". We were running between the bushes, on top of some little hills. I could see a few pyramids in the distance. The shape of the pyramids reminded me of those in Chichen Itza.
I then looked at the young girl who was my play mate, and noticed that she was very slim and very tall, with long blond hair. Her outfit was a lilac & purple color, with many designs on it, as if it was created by a fashion designer. She had bright, intense blue eyes, which harmonized beautifully with the lilac colors in the dress. In the dream, we were conversing in a strange, unusual language. When

we hiding from each other, we spoke to each other by whisper, and whistle similar to the sounds that Dolphins make. It was feeling that we talking telepathically."

****

When I woke up, my first thought was, that this dream came from my imagination. However, it was very interesting, that in the dream next to me, on a piece of paper, was written, one word. The paper looked like an important document, so that I would remember the word after waking up. The word was **"HADAZA"**. Something else was written on the paper, but I couldn't remember exactly what it was. After waking up, I Googled the word "HADAZA," wondering what it could possibly mean. I discovered that HADAZA is a Guanche name for girls, meaning; *distracted or lost*. This meaning could apply, since we were playing "hide and seek». As for me word Guanches was sounded like a South American tribal language. After researching, I came to a shocking conclusion, that the Guanches lived on the Canary Islands!

I also came to the realization that this tall slim girl in the dream reminded me of my friend, Alannah. Instantly, I got goose bumps all over, when I realized that it was Alannah. It truly was her!!!! It is interesting, that Alannah's roots are in the Netherlands, but she changed her last name to "Ireland", which is located West of the Netherlands. The Canary Islands are located Southwest of the Netherlands. Maybe, intuitively, Alannah was looking for her "motherland"; her true origins, from a long, distant past life. You can read about the ancient Guanches on Wikipedia.
I found more here: Magazine "Around the World" / July 1996 / Blondes with a foggy past. Ten secrets of the ancient Guanches by N.Nepomnyashchy (Журнал «Вокруг света» / июль 1996 / Блондинки с туманным прошлым. Десять тайн древних гуанчей Н. Непомнящего http://www.vokrugsveta.ru/vs/article/1285/)

What really struck me was the enormous similarities between the Guanches, the Mayans and the Egyptians and same things which I saw in my dream.

\# 1.They all built pyramids. «The pyramids of the island of Tenerife are rectangular **pyramids**, similar to the Mayan pyramids and the Aztecs in Mexico. Also here facts which support that my dream was about Guanches girls.

\# 2. «It should be noted that only the peoples of the Canary Islands, the Incas, and the Egyptians of the XXI Dynasty **mummified** their bodies. Guanches Mummies was made similar to ancient Egyptians, in the first place and secondly, as the Incas. Hall of mummies in the Canary Museum is collected a collection, which is no equal in the world!

\# 3. The island of Tenerife was inhabited by sufficiently tall, light-skinned aborigines of the European type, among whom were people with gray or blue eyes and light and reddish hair. In the past, Arabians, found a village, whose inhabitants were fair **with long, silken, blonde hair,** and the women had a rare beauty.

\# 4. They lived in stone houses, worshiped like the Egyptians and Peruvians, the **SUN God.** Guanches said that they are "the children of the Sun": ""Our fathers said that God, having settled us on this island "The Guanche had a caste of priests wearing clothes and headdresses the same as the Babylonians.
They also had a **Mother God, the same like in Babylon.**

\# 5. It is opinion exist, that The Canary Islands were **a part of Atlantis,** and that Guanches had Atlantian roots.

(XVII century Athanasius Kircher, at the beginning of the XIX century, Borie de Saint Vincent).
The Guanchs were ruled by ten elective kings, which we observe, incidentally, in Atlantis, described by Plato. Canarians themselves, the so-called "white natives", considered themselves the only people in the world who had escaped the mysterious disaster that had occurred in the past! "

6. French Norman Jean de Betancourt described in detail the strange language of the Guanches, who supposedly could understand the speech of fellow tribesmen, without uttering a sound and only moving their lips, and also they could **whistle** and understand each other up to a distance of 15 kilometers.
My friend Simon D.W., and I have seen each other in Atlantis, and we were relatives in that lifetime. To the surprise of his parents, Simon and his brother were speaking in a strange language, when they were children, and they understood each other. I wonder if he can remember any of the words and if it could have been Guanches?

Now I can't wait to visit Canary Islands and this museum!

I sent letter to Eliot and Marianne and suddenly instantly replay arrived from Elliot Estep:
(Elliot Estep was reader for my book and also he was in our movie ETERNAL HOLOGRAM)

"Hi there! Wow very interesting as I just read about the Guanches peoples this very morning as I flew to the Canary Islands today!!! I am here now in Lanzarote for the next week on vacation. **Very synchronistic timing** I must say! Lots of love to you both, Eliot."

During production of the book one mystery I cannot solved it was question for me all this years:
It was about USA President Lincoln reincarnation as John Kennedy with all his clan, which included family, all his co-workers, even with the astrologers and those who killed and even those who helped to kill!
Question was: how they all born around the same time again? And meet again? And each take exact the same role? Yes, this is synchronistic time, not plain co-incident, that you arrived exact the same day to Canary Islands. Will be good to visit this famous museum.
Strange...This version of the book was ready around one year ago for the print house, but was delay after delay...now I know real reason...Spirits in my dream
Show me this word **HADAZA** and open door to one more past life!

I sent to Marianne:

"Dear Marianne, please read below and see what happened! I wonder if you have cases in your practice about past life also had such a synchronistic timing? Julia"

Replay from Marianne:

"Hello Julia, what a lovely story about your dream and what you found out about the Canarias Islands and a past life! (whistle/people).**Synchronistic timing** is quite normal when past lives do reveal themselves, but only in case of such a thing as group reincarnation. It is said that once Atlantis went down, some survivors went to that part of the world (Canarias Islands), so when you and Eliot do have an Atlantean connection, this is all possible, due to energy lines. Love, Marianne"

Chapter 5

THE VIOLET FIELD

This chapter will show another side of the same Spirit – a very unusual part of the Spirit, which we know as the High Priest from Chichén Itzá, the Atlantian Queen, Amelia the pilot, and the royal girl from Egypt.

Yes, all of them have the same consciousness, thoughts and actions. It is one solid strong crystal. And this crystal will not be complete in your vision until you read this chapter and open one more granule of that *Spirit-and-Soul* crystal. I don't know how to name it, by the way, because the word "soul" sounds much too soft, tender, unprotected and fragile to me. It sounds like a very ephemeral, unclear substance. I prefer the word "spirit". It sounds much more solid, complete and stable.

Who Am I And Where Do I Come From?

I shared with you already these secrets in this book. You also know now the reasons for which I shared such intimate details of my own Spirit and these crying CDs on my website. Because they are the only way to demonstrate what the Spirit Journey is all about – the only way to help you feel, understand and experience it. The reason I was not sure I should write this chapter is because there are things which most people have never experienced in their lives and probably never will. And, as a result, they may not understand it at all. It may sound as another unknown language to them.

FIRST, it is good to know that this side of human nature exists and that you can open up to some ultra human possibilities for yourself. Di Cherry told me that all of us would maybe experience this after death, when the Spirit travels and lives between two lives – the past one and the future one. I am glad that I have this rare gift to remember, sometimes in every detail how I travel in my dreams in Spirit world and what I do, so that I can pass this knowledge on to people.
I know that Buddhist monks or other monks who dedicate their lives to their spirit development have this experience during their dreams on a routine basis. But they keep the experience as a deep, well-guarded secret. Maybe some spiritual schools also study this and have a record of their progress in this field of knowledge. I just don't know and I was never interested in finding them. I am "eye to eye" with my dreams, and I never felt or had the urge that I needed anyone. I am complete.
The spirit world is full of amazing colors, lights, dynamics, and speed which do not exist in our world. It is full of magic things, full of pleasure and joy and multidimensional occurrences.

SECONDLY, it is important to know that the energy people have and collect through their lives necessary in order to survive and continue developing in the Spirit world. So don't spend it or waste it in ordinary stressful situations – fighting with your better-half, for example, because you both will end up crossing the veil one day. Lots of bad entities around and they invisible for us. During people's disagreements and fights, bad spirits draining energy from people, feeding on this energy and left people empty and sick. Pay your debts, do what you promise to do, follow your goal in this life, spend a little time alone every day, meditate, never use swearing or bad words and forgive everyone around you, otherwise, it will drain a huge amount of energy from you. Enjoy life instead and experience pleasure from spreading happiness, making people around you smile. Try to be creative with anything you do, in any kind of job you have. Restore your power visiting nature.

After reading this book, these dreams, it will sound and feel as if you won't be losing so much after death. You will only shed one of the shells and it will be easy to find another one and to be reborn again, right? Do you remember that people have many lives?
As anyone, I wish to obtain good results from anything I do. I expect that, by this time, when you have almost gone through this book you will agree with me, or at least, you will say, "Maybe it is possible." Because in some instances, I feel a serious responsibility towards giving you this knowledge and preparing you a little for what you can expect after your own death.
On the other hand, DON'T try to cut your life short artificially, in suicide. Before you were born a program was set up by your Spirit, telling you what to do in this lifetime for your further spiritual development, and you need to complete it. People are born alone and die alone.

Remember: As long as you are alive, you will always regenerate! Don't give up, NO MATTER WHAT!

This responsibility and obligation resides in me from the Ancient Maya Priest who comes to you now through thousands of years to assist you in your plans. It was his and my daily job to take care of people, their spirit's well-being during their lives, and to help them navigate their way when they cross the veil to the after-life.
The second factor is the burdensome memory of my own death in my past life when I was Amelia. This is what is pushing me to help people with my own experience, to share with them the story of this amazing journey of my Spirit through lives and to tell them that their present life is not the last one. It is much more comfortable to die in peace, calm and smiling, knowing that you will be reborn

soon. I am sure you agree with me. So don't lose yourself at the last, most important moment of this lifetime, before you die.

It was very hard for me to hear myself in that part of the CD about Amelia, when I experienced her last moments before her sudden death. It was her screaming feelings of her approaching death, this unfair situation of being cut off in the middle of her life, and to die when the most important flight in her life was not complete yet that marked me the most.

In a wise, ancient Buddhist book, "The Book of Death", you can find details of the day-to-day navigation after death – what to do, where to go. When I read it, even though it is written in some very special Buddhist terminology, I understood and recognized everything described in it. It supports what I experienced in the Spirit world. It felt as if I were taking this information on an energy level, not in words and sentences. But I think for most people this book would be a deep mystery.

I instead invite you to similar places; they look like those places where Alice in Wonderland had her adventures.
Since I saw these kinds of dreams from an early age, I am used to them. My parents didn't have any idea where I was traveling in my dreams.
It reminds me of the day I went with my daughter to Playland on Granville Island in Vancouver. It was inside a building where many stores are selling all kinds of toys and kids' clothes. She dreamed to go where there were lots of colored balls – some sort of tunnel going through a succession of cages. Kids were going through this complex structure and would finally come out at the other end. It was the first time for my daughter and she was too small to go in there alone. But she wished to go inside very much! One parent advised me to go in with her. I watched how he went inside with his two kids and started to move very fast through the contraption. I guess he was a ferret in his past life! He had a ferret-like body – a long thin body – and ferrets love to play in this kind of long tube. I have one of the cutest ferrets at home, so I know. (Her name, NORA, if translated from Russian, would be the name for a tunnel, a long hole underground where they live.)

So I decided follow his advice and participate in this game because my daughter wanted to go in so, so much! I can tell you now; it was a totally wrong advice! It was row of cages and some of them were way too small for me!

I could hardly fit inside! And I am only 5' 6". In some places, I could fit only in two of them through the little, round hole in the wall between them! It sounds funny now, but it was no fun at the time. It was made for kids, not for adults! At some point, I felt that I may get stuck for the rest of my life in between these bars, and almost started panicking. I could see through these cages, but there was no one near, no door or anyone who could have helped me come out of this maze. This part of Playland was away from the main stores' hallway. I wondered if that man was stuck somewhere in there and was still living inside for all these years. :)
Anyway, that following night I had a dream about many little kids who were dropped by their parents every day to play in that cage-tunnel structure while their parents went shopping. The children stepped inside and came out in another world! This cage-tunnel was the WAY to another dimensional world! They spent one hour in that world and returned to Earth. Their parents would then take their kids home and didn't have any idea where their children had been and what they experienced... In my dream, I also came out with a bunch of kids from the tunnel into that other Parallel world or Time.
I remember walking in a strange, unusual street with foggy, grey twilight and sitting on benches talking with a "local" family. Everything about them was unusual; the way they looked, what they wore and how they talked to me. It felt as if I was seeing a reflection in a very strange, deformed mirror...

I slip into this Parallel world from time to time during the day, not in my dreams. It always happens suddenly, for a second, like a photo camera flash and I see very strange people, each of them very sophisticated, their faces unbelievable! Beautiful or very weird, strange, they're mostly slim and *long*, wearing very unusual outfits, LOTS of ideas for the couturiers, by the way! So, I began drawing them and now I have collection of these figures already. They would be good to wear for someone like Lady Gaga!

Okay, let's go now through the door to the room where my dreams are waiting for you. In these dreams, the Spirit travels to another multidimensional world. Spirit also contacted and met other spirits from our galaxy and other parts of the universe. My body looks and feels different in this other world. Instead of a body it was sometimes just one solid point or maybe like a pulsation of energy, with sparks of quantum particles.

© Josephine Wall. All Rights Reserved. www.josephinewall.com

Honestly, I just don't have the words and I don't know how to describe it. These kinds of dreams repeated themselves, continued and developed with the same subjects for many years, over and over again. They are very detailed dreams and they feel extremely real each time I woke up from them. Best to name it **a *separate reality*** – according to Carlos Castaneda.

By the way, I have an enormous amount of dreams that I collected through my life. Some of them are like a rare, magic, shiny stone. But to make of this a "Beauty Contest" is not my goal in this book. Here are only the dreams which were repeated many times. I believe it is an indication that it has some deep meaning.

It feels as if I traveled and lived during the night in some very real parallel world and visited the same places... I recognized people, Spirits and Entities which I saw, visited there before. I noticed the changes which happened to them over time. It is impossible to say if it is the Spirit's life from the past or from the future. I live few lives at the same time. You can try to decide that for yourself.

Warning!

This is another world where there are more than three dimensions. It is very difficult to describe, simply because nothing exists there that could compare to our world and our life! Also this dream was translated. I still hope that even through these obstacles, my readers can smell, feel and experience – like Di Cherry usually loves to say – "What it is all about."

I don't want people to think that I am crazy, so I asked a doctor to write something for me. Here is a "note from the doctor":
"Julia did not belong in any mental institution. She is mentally healthy. Her outline point of view may be the result of a much higher IQ than normal and as a result there is a possibility for her to see the world a little bit differently than most people do."

So let's take the first ride. I classified the dreams according to their different levels of energy. If you feel that you are totally lost and don't understand where you are, just skip that dream and go to the next one. Yet, it is best to still read it. **Even if you don't understand it, on the spiritual level or on your chakra, aura levels you will understand, accept and absorb this information and you might adjust to it. Not to worry: Your Spirit will take care of it.**
I purposely put here the plainest, basic dreams. Often I see myself at a more "advanced level" of cognizance, and it is almost impossible to describe it. I guess no vocabulary exists for this yet.

Dream # 33
Via Gos Came Inspiration, April 25, 1998

Something was deep inside me; disturbing, kind of worrying me all day long. I felt as if I would have some special dream that night or something unusual would happen. After all, I didn't know and until now if I was sleeping, or if it was real. Throughout the dream, I was in control and didn't lose myself.
It started with a terrible crashing sound. It was a horrifying thunder, as if the sky broke apart. It did not last for long. The sound could not last too long. But it was so enormous, incredibly loud; it seemed that I had never heard anything so loud, that my consciousness divided this sound in several parts. And I thought that I knew how to divide it and to play it on an instrument. It was a boiling, roaring sound. In order to describe the thunder during the storm..., it begins, then increases and should stop abruptly. And there were about four of such sounds, one after another. They started approximately at the same time, the last one was the concluding one, the loudest, and then it would be just one thunder sound.
It seems to me that I even sat in a bed. And then I saw myself, like it all happened on a computer screen. The dot is flying forward, as in a game, the airplane is flying, and there are contours of mountains, etc. I understood that I was that dot. On Earth we have gravity. But this was not a fall; it could be compared to a fall into a bottomless well. It seemed to me that I saw the contours of rocks around me, but I was still falling. Such a depth, such a long distance...
As soon as all this cracked, my consciousness rushed there, **to the bottomless well, but I was not falling; it was not a downward movement.**

I don't remember how this movement ended. But there was a qualitative change. During all of my dreams there was only my mind – no body, no arms, nothing. There was nothing from reality, yet at the same time, everything was real, life-like. I said life-like, but actually it was on the edge of life and on the verge of death. After that night my self-perception changed dramatically. I lived at least two parallel lives. No questions. No doubts.

I can only compare this with the army, when they have maneuvers, they shoot with blanks, but here it was real, not some maneuvers – huge dangers were lurking – you had to be on the alert all the time. It was like that. And yet there was nothing terrestrial – no fields, landscapes or rocks. The only thing I know about it – there were lumps of space, so to speak, they were different. It was happening in phases; each phase differed from the next by a time period of my staying there and by the tests that I had to pass.

I understood that I was not there for the first time, but many, many times already. It is a tension on the edge of your capacities, on the limit of limits. Once I heard a voice – it was not a human voice, but a female kind. Like a fairy. It was a round sound. I remember it, this voice. I remember her. She was a kind of owner of this space-lump. I got there and she said, "You forgot, you were here already." She guided me and I remembered how I should operate in this space; I remembered how to avoid these few dangerous traps. At one moment, I jumped into something like... you see your chair, imagine that it is circular and there is a wall a half-meter high alongside the circle. So I sat there – although I did not have a body. There were several of us there. Someone, a male beside me said, although without words, but I understood, that it is necessary to compress quickly.

There were such super-heavy elements around us; I had to twist somehow, to become a monolith. He said, "Now those crazies will come. They're like children, who will try to pull us apart..." Later, it started to shake, to pull us apart..., to try to rip us to pieces

Artist: Tony Ariawan http://area105.deviantart.com/gallery/

All this is hard to express. It was happening in fragments, space by space; each of them had its own pattern.[27]

"Via Gos Came Inspiration." This sentence was pronounced loudly during the last stage; it was a lasting, loud sound. Like a crashing sound with which all this began. No idea what it means...

****

According to this article below I described in this dream my travel throw the Black Hole!

---

[27] Peter Gariaev's experiments show the DNA of each person makes a photo of their body, its surrounding situation, what this person sees and senses and is sending it to the universe every single second! It is some information exchange going on, some connection, adjustment with someone, who is also you, who lives there in that parallel world. Maybe each person on Earth has his twin there. As for me I can prove it with hundreds of dreams where I am always **two in one.** And both share the same Hologram?

Black holes are 'portals to other universes,' according to new quantum results. By: Bryan, Sun, Jun 02, 2013 http://www.mnn.com/earth-matters/space/stories/black-holes-are-portals-to-other-universes-according-to-new-quantum

Black holes may not end in a crushing singularity as previously thought, but rather open up passageways into whole other universes. According to Albert Einstein's theory of general relativity, black holes are uninhabitable chasms of space-time that end in a "singularity," or a mass of infinite density. It's a place so bleak that even **the laws** of physics break down there. According to the startling new results, black holes do not culminate in a singularity. Rather, they represent "portals to other universes," reports New Scientist.

Researchers Jorge Pullin from Louisiana State University, and Rodolfo Gambini from the University of the Republic in Montevideo, Uruguay, found: there was no singularity. **Instead, just as the black hole began to squeeze tight, it suddenly loosened its grip again, as if a door was being opened.**

Under general relativity, falling into a black hole is, in some ways, much like falling into a very deep pit that has a bottom, only instead of hitting the bottom, you get pressed into a single point — a singularity — of infinite density. With both the deep pit and the black hole, there is no "other side." The bottom stops your fall through the pit, and the singularity "stops" your fall through the black hole (or at least, at the singularity it *no longer makes sense* to say you're "falling"). Your experience would be much different traveling into a black hole according to LQG, however. **At first you might not notice the difference: gravity would increase rapidly. But just as you were nearing what ought to be the black hole's core — just as you're expecting to be squashed into the singularity — gravity would instead begin to decrease. It would be as if you were swallowed, only to be spit out on the other side.**

In other words, LQG black holes are less like holes and more like tunnels, or passageways. But passageways to where? According to the researchers, they could be shortcuts to other parts of our universe. Or they could be portals to other universes entirely. According to relativity, the singularity inside a black hole operates as a sort of firewall, which means that information that gets swallowed by the black hole gets lost forever. **Information loss, however, is not possible according to quantum physics. ---->Yes, I am still here! Alive, not lost in Black Hole!**

Dream # 34
Big Creature of a Holy Religion, October 31, 1993

Today I fell asleep. The dream in its reality was very close to what has happened in Caracol. Not life, but very real. Sometimes it seemed that this reality is stronger, than real life. Distant reality – it is right. I was different; there was a different sense of self. I was very concentrated, like one strong crystal, or a monolith, with one and only goal in life. There is nothing besides that, nothing at all.

I haven't seen such concentration in life. In real life a person needs to eat, to drink, to redo something, etc. One depends on the real world, depends on sustaining oneself. I would call it our "friction of life", inertia. It does not exist in space where there is no gravity. And I had only one desire – I was walking and I knew that I should fly now – very far away, very, very far. Unbelievable, but it was my goal, the essence of my life. I was living by it all the time. The place, where I should fly – maybe some other galaxies... I know exactly the place and now I feel it. There was a very, extremely important thing to do. In my dream, I remembered, what it was. But even in a dream it was impossible to describe – everything was hanging on very delicate feelings. The dream was attuned to this harmony... It would be like the astronauts walking to their spaceship, knowing that they will get in and will fly with enormous speed to unimaginable distances.

And my goal – even if to speak about saving the whole humanity – would not be enough. Something global and serious... And I alone should do it. Just by myself without other people or assistants. Only I can perform this task. And this desire is concentrated in me and I am arriving to the moment when it will drag me there. My goal was very distant – I was from there, from far away – as if I knew from where – I could get there easily, to that distant place. But my goal was from there, I came from there to perform my task.[28]

And, strangely – there was nothing in my dream that concerns our world, the Earth – no grass, no people, no buildings – only myself, my concentration and the path to the centre of the white Milky Way, I just see its direction, feel it.[29] I must enter it and to find myself there. And suddenly there is some creature in front of me – a human being, a Spirit. It had no face. I just can compare the importance and responsibility with my concentration and appropriateness – like Saturn, nothing unnecessary. He appeared in front of me – straight, clear look, strict lips, if for a moment only I could compare *it* with a human face.

I knew him; I knew him well. He said to me without words (telepathically) – as if asking, "Today you will not fly to that distant goal" (This injunction is not ruled by anything, it does not depend on anything; it is like, today it is raining and tomorrow it will snow.) He said that today I should participate in SOMETHING ELSE. It is like in a Milky Way, there is a side branch which has a real ending and I need to help someone there. He expressed it as a request. It is a short and direct injunction. My main goal, the task of ***my life – will not disappear, it will stay forever.*** He had shown me this other aim for me to participate and to help.

I turned up in a place with some other people; we were like astronauts in the second film of "Aliens" where they all lie down into some cells to fly this unbelievable distance. It was like an airplane turbine, white, frayed sides, the hole, the entrance. We entered into something white, shiny, huge, with soft edges. We entered and then it felt odd. As if my body came out of me – the body, the heaviness, everything that has inertia, the weight was lifted – released. Only finest thin spacesuits, one over another remained – of incredible lightness. Perhaps only the soul stayed. Very, very light emptiness. They were transparent membranes, like Medusa's; I don't remember how many – 5, 7, 10. I started to look at it – at what I was wearing. It was like a spaceship, the whitest, transparent; it could be compared with a fluorescent lamp but it should be the cleanest one. I thought *what a beautiful spacesuit I have! It shines like silver.*

I knew one thing clearly – these few others and me – few human creatures (I can't say "people") selected among all people, as many as those who lived on the earth. They are a unity, a whole, sublime, light, holy..., not exactly a creature – one holy business, one religion, super-religion,

---

[28] **It looks like I used this Black Hole for the travels in Space, when I was a Mayan Priest.** "Mayan hieroglyphs describe it as a " Hole in the Sky", cosmic womb, or " black hole" through which there wizard-king entered other dimensions, accessed sacred knowledge, or toured across vast reaches of the cosmos. In September 2002 astronomers verified the existence of a massive black hole in the Center of the Milky Way, naming it "Sagittarius B." Jenkins writes about it: "If not a coincidence, the dark-rift itself might indeed be the surface signifier of deeper cosmic mysteries, ones that the Maya were well aware of." This black hole is "the cosmic womb from which new stars are born, and from which everything in our Galaxy, including human, came" (Daniel Pinchbeck, 2012 *The return of Quetzalcoatl*, 2006).

[29] The black hole found in the Milky Way, December 9, 2008. There is a giant black hole at the centre of our galaxy, a study has confirmed. German astronomers tracked the movement of 28 stars circling the centre of the Milky Way, using the European Southern Observatory in Chile.Black holes are objects whose gravity is so great that nothing - including light - can escape them. According to Dr Robert Massy, of the Royal Astronomical Society, the results suggest that galaxies form around giant black holes in the way that a pearl forms around grit. "The researchers from the Max-Planck Institute for Extraterrestrial Physics in Germany said the black hole was 27,000 light years, or 158 thousand million miles from the Earth. http://news.bbc.co.uk/2/hi/science/nature/7774287.stm

superior. These few people... you know, the superior beings have something that unites them – some beings superior and sacred. The same was true in this instance. As if there was one superior creature, maybe a principal that had chosen us. And the selected ones – us – decided the future of the people in general. They are above people, as if an extraction of all people was performed, like something single and big over the earth, something great that unites all of the people. They guide it, they know what to do with it, and have a sublime sacred goal. I don't know what to compare it with. And today I could not do what I wanted. He said that today was a special day that we should come together for some session. I felt that these few people were in the same situation as I was – they were wearing hoods. We all got into such a dream, but I was not sleeping and I had control over my thoughts; I can't understand it, they weren't sleeping either. We were in a kind of antibiosis with one thought or direction for the work we were to perform very clear in our "minds". There was a feeling that this living religion became one creature, acquired qualities from most of the living creatures. It was thinking and acting independently.

In different occasions I was dreaming in colors, in *living* colors every time – once in a few months, or years. It was an event, and I remembered it – the whole period of life – green-poisonous-emerald, rich blue, orange-peach, pink, bright raspberry, white and light-blurred blue. But it is improper to list them; they are beautiful and LIVING colors. And today – a great revelation – it was a living energetic creature.
Her energy was spliced of fine rays of every creature, infinitely clear and sublime. It is made of all these colors. There was a feeling that there were no people below us – just a single cloud of all the people. They govern it; they want to affect it with this religion. And today we had to fly away from the Earth. This big capsule started to twist like a swirl, the tunnel appeared, we were flying through it, and there was a sensation of permanent twisting. We had to fly to such a place. They were doing something with us there.

I also remember that I was tall, high, maybe three meters, or more. I was wearing only white. We arrived to such a place, a very distant one, although while we were flying very far in this capsule, it seemed like a moment. But when we arrived and stopped, nobody was coming out, we were hanging – and the most important thing was happening there, something very global, crucial – and it took a long time. Something was happening to our spacesuits, or raincoats. As if I shed them off and became very light. And self-perception also changed; when I woke up later it was still going on. They were doing something to us; the sensation of lightness increased, the crystal – it was me. The longer it was going on, the stronger the feeling of lightness became.

These dreams that you already read and this next one, belong to the same Spirit, which was in Amelia's body before – during my past life. Amelia acquired this strength, concentration, and this enormous focused goal to fly all over the world from the deep roots and the experience, which her Spirit accumulated during previous lives as a Mayan Priest and others.

Dream # 35
Business in the Center of the Galaxy, July 16, 1991

I had something to do in the center of the Milky Way Galaxy– just don't laugh. I recalled being there. Our Earth is very far on the side. I understood that I go there quite often for business. **You know, my body is very different – it is not soft, a tender-skin body like here on Earth. In fact, it is like a lightning. I am on Earth for some very pressing, but very short business.** From there our Earth appears like a "rational" slime. Before, at university, when I was studying squirrels, I thought that they have a very complex system, an almost human body, but, in fact, this is all terribly primitive... And now, I understand that you absolutely do not need to develop your physical body, you should only maintain it. And it is not frightening – to die – it is just to leave the Earth. They don't have senses there – it is a rudiment. They come to Earth to study, experience it.

****

Yes, an astrologer told me that this is possible, because my ASC in my astrology chart is connected with the Centre of the Galaxy! So, I am flying there for some important reason, not just to have some fun. Today is November 22, 2008, I just woke up, again, from an enormously powerful dream. I was flying with astonishing concentration and at an incredibly high speed to the same point in the Universe. The little doughnut-guide was near me again, talking very fast, as usual, in his metallic, computer-robot voice. Information, words were dropping one by one like a million of little beads out of *him*. I tried to write this down. At the end he told me, "You are the real 5th element to humans and this is an important point for the Earth's history. Get rid of all frictions, which take away your attention, for the next years, from one goal: to make *"the way through smoother"*." I feel a very strong tension, almost pain in my "time-travel-belt" point right now.

Then I started remembering what Oversoul 7 also said:

"Energy will change, new religion will come, death of all old consciousness and new will come, new consciousness. You, Julia will be highly involved with this. I see you on the top of the pyramid ... Pyramids were built a long time ago with the help of another civilization. Soon the pyramids will be re-activated and people will return to these pyramids for the rituals. Pyramids will be key moment to affect human consciousness.
When people will start to be free from FEAR it will help them to be free from the old consciousness and to accept new consciousness and to proceed through the difficult time much easier."
Please see at the end of the book part: **MIND OVER MATTER.**
YOUTUBE: Parallel Universes [1/5] Vortex Energy Part3 How the Human TACHION light field works - 22 part series

Dream # 36
The Guide of My Life, February 22, 1996

In a dream there was my guide. I asked him, "Why don't I want to receive deep information like it was before from the surrounding world, about progress, science etc. anymore?"
He told me, "You should not worry about it – if all the rest does not disturb you, then this also does not. It is at a level of gods and their representatives on Earth. You know everything and more than necessary already." As if I was living in the 21st century, but I am from the 25th century. This is not new, but old for me. And I remember that I had such sensation in my childhood – of insufficiency and emptiness, of sadness – insufficiency of the world around me, of people, of society – everything was primitive. When we moved, I was brought to my grandmother, I was three years old; I was sitting under a big poplar tree, and big aglets were falling from the tree like red worms. It was really a sad feeling I experienced at that moment. Incredibly sad and empty.
Later on, he told me about the Buddhists – they do not walk the ground, they are higher up, and they all "flutter".
Note that this dream occurred a long time ago, in 1996, and it is interesting that I read in one book last year that in the Buddhist temples in Tibet, some monks needed to have chains with some weight put around their legs because they practiced something very spiritual and special which made them unusually light and they were almost flying near the ground! Amazing: hard to believe. But I trust my Guide. My Guide is always right – not one mistake during all these years. I remember that once in one dream, he brought me to Yugoslavia when the war just started. We sat outside around some table with him and the local priest, near the church, and my Guide told us that this war will develop later

into the worse type of warfare and that there will be bombs falling from airplanes onto people... Sadly he was right, again.

Dream # 37
Your Cosmic Sister, March 20, 1992

In the first part of the dream, we were tracking down these creatures. We were in a Cosmos, in a capsule; we were floating. There was a Guide, but he did not participate. We were communicating, but not with words. I did not see you and the Guide, too, did not see your bodies. I knew that you are near me and talked to you. Not with words. I was teaching you. I brought you up to my usual walk, like a *stalker*. Every time everything is new. Everything is focused, I am like a warrior. All my attention was concentrated on tracking down these creatures. Besides which, part of my attention was directed to you, teaching you. You do not see it and I feel with all my cells on the verge of feeling. I felt that they were approaching to us in spasmodic, dashing stages. We were there a long time. I told you, "I feel them..." We entered space; we felt each other mutually and were coming closer. I taught you how to feel. I myself was on the verge of feelings. I was telling you about all my sensations. Maybe they were already beyond many planets away from us – it is something different, they are the others (but we also were not humans from Earth, we were from some cosmic civilization). They were – from the other one.

At some moment it started with increasing force. We were rushing at enormous speed, but the distance was so huge, that it took a long time. At the beginning, I felt them just with a feeling, and then with another feeling, then a third – there are no such feelings on Earth. It was like stages. When the fourth stage came, I knew clearly who they were. That this was a highly organized civilization, that there were several of these creatures and they were trying to establish contact with us. I recognized her (maybe they also have females) and I said, "See! Here comes my cosmic sister!"

At the last second, when they were in front of us, I recognized her; she was very close already. In a few seconds, there was a whirlwind before us. When I understood that she was my *cosmic sister* – it was like a forgotten past or like a silent knowledge. Maybe I knew her as far as billions of years ago and maybe I never knew her. I said, "Be prepared! Look!"

It seemed that we were decelerating and we managed to see each other. I noticed you were on the right of me; the Guide was behind – like a triangle. Like children's inflated swimming pool – the shape of our positions. She seemed to have two representations – like a knight in armor – she had a narrow cap, helmet as if made of small plates. I had a vision that we were passing some mansion with a path; I saw and felt it. Suddenly something like a flame – like a dog, or a red fox, like a splash – like a comet with a tail – flew out on this path. I knew that it was her. She flew to meet us and grabbed my hand with all her force. The left hand. It was a strong and unexpected *physical* sensation!

I woke up immediately. Because of this sudden awakening, a strong wave hit me in my chest, like an explosion. I even had a rush of fever. I should not have been awakened. When I regained consciousness I had the feeling that she was still holding my hand, that they were there, waiting for me to fall asleep again. This sensation moved towards my elbow – seven or eight centimeters before the joint. Later on, I could not fall asleep because of this sensation in my arm. And now I understand that in order to bear such moments and not to wake up it is necessary:
1. To have a lot of energy;
2. To saturate your life with unusual eccentric sensations, in order to satiate your body, so that your body will not be surprised.

****

When I see the symbol of the FireFox program on the internet with a fireball and fox with a burning, orange tail, I always remember this dream and the chain of them I had. Everywhere this orange fireball fox repeated itself – always touching me, mostly catching my hand. I just received letter from woman, Holland. "I dreamed about you last night and overall theme was: connected by the light and flying through the space ... it is make me very happy. I have had many past lives also in Atlantis, Egypt, etc. So no doubt we know each other." (Marianne Notschaele-den Boer, www.vorigelevens.nl) When I clicked to this website, I saw a photo of my cosmic sister, my cosmic twin! My body was shaking and covered with goose bumps. We returned to real life 16 years after I met her in my dream traveling in space for ages! She has supreme intelligence, just see size of her forehead.

YOUTUBE:
Met in dream, together in Atlantis and reunited in real life now!

Marianne

Dream # 38
A Man of the Forest – His Name, December 13, 1991

I could not fall asleep. I was looking at my watch as if I had an appointment. The previous time the watch showed 12:30. The nap lasted only one hour – when I opened my eyes, it was 1:30 (13!) – one hour or 58 minutes.

When I woke up, I understood that my dream had been repeated twice. A half hour each or it was a recording in my mind and it played twice. Everything that was happening and was there, despite the fact that I dreamed it twice, was like a fog slipping out of your hands. It is really hard to translate it into words.

I was on the Earth; maybe I was in a parallel life, in the world which is very close, but not the Earth – best to name it a separated reality. I was in some space (we say apartment, but it is a rough definition). There was a Guide, who spoke; his voice resounded during my entire dream. And also there was my great-grandmother whom I never saw before – nice, small and incredibly wise. It is like that on Earth – people live, each one in his own way, and then they come together, something unites them, this convention. If I flew there, then it would have been "because it is not from our life," said the magicians. But in this life I don't do it like that. I do something and also I live somewhere. It looked like a seminar - there were separate essences; it was like a report about how to live and what you do. I was saying this and made a conclusion, the others did it, too – although it was just my report, perhaps.

Those (the others) were several; I don't know how many. What was happening with them, I cannot describe and even understand. These creatures differed enormously. There was one – I think she was female – the Ying Chinese symbol. To be near her you should have been careful – I don't know how the others protected themselves. She aroused interest, but at the same time she was deadly dangerous. I was like seaweed in water, but like a chameleon changing my qualities, but faster than it – or appeared and disappeared, or produced rays – it was a kind of pulsation; I don't know what kind. It was dangerous for everybody. Everyone was also pulsating, but it was of another, different nature. People have a body, face, breast, back. And there was a creature which was at my back – something behind my back, light, fibers, energy – had to be situated perpendicularly to the other dangerous creature. Something was behind my back, if it stood straight – it should be hanging over it. Something of mine was being placed over him. But maybe it is necessary for him to understand my words – and I have an object from my body which I can hang over his head. It is hard to explain ... I am just trying. At the beginning, it seemed that there was an attuning to each other going on..., and something else which I don't remember. Maybe there was the third one, everyone was telling something. And afterwards there was the fourth one. When I was talking, maybe I delivered information without words. When I finished, I heard the voice of my grandmother (I just heard her, but did not see her). She knew that it was valuable for them, but I did not understand – she told them this and that. But it was not from our life. This reminds me of something like *Jabberwocky* in Lewis Carroll. I understood, they understood. But here I cannot understand at all. In *Jabberwocky* there is a substantive and adjective. But here there were neither of them. **It was an event from my other life.** The others were listening and were correcting at the same time. While I was telling my story, they were absorbing it. One perceived it as green, the other like an action, the third one flicked out something, and after that they started to exchange; each one perceived the fine facet that only he could understand. And after that they produced a synthesis. **All this was in the other sphere of life – not life itself.** Later another fragment arrived, when the human conversation started (before it was soundless, the humming Guide was translating) and I transcended to human rank.

It was as if I consisted of many stairs. I reached them on the top stair, the same as theirs. On the first one I was attuned, and then a stair below, when we were doing something together. Later, one step below, again – when I was telling my story. It can be said that stairs are material. When I was telling a story, it was almost human; there was an action, energy, matter. On the last step, there I was a human being. I disintegrated into several creatures, and later – into myself-human. And on the last step, the voice of the interpreter appeared; it was a translation into human language. I even thought that this Spirit dictated to my friend's psyche – he fitted by rank, position – he understood me.

I remember what they said in the end – they said it two times and when the dream repeated – again two times. Four times altogether. They pronounced with a loud voice (the interpreter said it, because they could not speak) for me to remember, "THE MAN OF THE FOREST ... HIS NAME..." – with a thunderous voice, loud, fearful, the loudest in the world as if a mountain began to speak. It was said loudly, solidly, strongly, like an elephant's walk. I don't remember what it was for. I cannot know in my human condition what we were talking about and I don't know, what is happening with this "Man of the Forest". I already opened my eyes when it was pronounced for the last time. They woke me up in order for me to remember for sure. When I opened my eyes it was: **1:30**, December **13. 13 and 13.**[30] This reminds me of *Jabberwocky* in Lewis Carroll. Most likely Amelia had the same dreams – or better said – the Spirit that resides right now in my body and that resided in Amelia's body 70 years ago, experienced the same "Space travel" in her dreams. So, by flying in airplanes she was trying to extend her dream world to real life. Nothing more.

Dream # 39
The Drilling From Belgium Bothers Me, October 16, 1992

I was talking about myself. Here I am and there is the other one who is talking about this one; I have a clear channel of communication. But clear is an inappropriate word. Clear means that when it was unclear, they washed it and it became clear. Here it is not so. There should be no dirt at all. It is crystal

---

[30] 13, interesting! It is an important number for the Priest and a lucky one for me in this life. It showed once 3 times on the license plates of the 3 cars arriving one by one, when my brand new friend, Istvan, was near – remember?

clear. As when you say, "I have it crystal clear," but something is interfering with your hearing. This drilling, this interference, in my dreams comes from Belgium, from Europe. In a sense, it is not a war, but they are trying to interfere with my dreams. And about me, she started her talk with the words, ***"She is eternal."***

*Nostradamus, in his prediction "Centurii", he tells that he sees in Belgium some centre of ancient magic. Well, it looks like this centre still exists or when I am in my dreams; I am crossing the same path with them.

Dream # 40
The Swirl of Comas, May 1, 1992

Everything that was happening was occurring too seriously – it was not from this life. To tell it all would take too much energy, too much effort.

It was like that: all of us, me, Shawn, you and another group of people. Everybody was conditioned, but in something like a coma. Perhaps it was a dark room. Everyone was doing the work with their minds. Let's assume, for comparison, that everybody is sitting in a balloon and each one, with his mind, is pulling the softness of the balloon to his own place – here and there or like that. Magicians are telling each other what they can do. Their desire to learn magic has brought them to sharing it between them all. But it was not enough; they were in darkness – little puppies whose eyes had not opened yet.

It was lasting a long time. But I left you all. When I appeared, I just noticed that everyone was prepared, conditioned. I went out, flew out. Ahead there was a fenced square, like a corral, large. I found an entrance and flew inside. It was just amazing. But there was a feeling that I knew about it for a long time and now I found it in order to bring you in. I went back, took Shawn with my mind. He could take directions from me. I knew that only through him, I could come to you. But there, where I entered you could not; you could do it only from the other side. Shawn understood and passed the knowledge onto you; you were together. You started to swim inside. And you told the others – there were about 20 or 30 people. I did not care much about it. You were guiding them and they followed you like a herd. They seemed not to see me at all, and practically did not perceive the child (who was the ten-year-old, Shawn). It was important for me that Shawn reached you. The others were your responsibility.

Later, the only thing I remembered – the thought, *"It is more serious, more forceful, than even I can do."* The body seemed to twist and disappear, dissolve. The body can do it like a bud – on the contrary – to curl in and more and then disappear. I understood that what was here was much more complicated than to swirl in and disappear, (many layers were swirling or were entwined). Inside this square, it was like – a person disappears, but not entirely... It was some condition... If you looked from above you could see how a person acquired a shape – a part of a spiral. All people turn into it, but it was always moving. These commas were of bright emerald color and to the sides there were golden protrusions. It always curled in – counterclockwise. It was not a dance, a singing, but it was a fluid, supple movement, like a melodious tune. When a person entered it, he turned off entirely. He was all – he *became* this condition. Later when I woke up, it seemed that it was similar to the singing of peyote songs. Maybe it reminded me of the situation in the first volume of the book by the author, Carlos Costaneda, which I read a long time ago, where Don Juan saw a dog and how every hair of hers was shining with radiating light.

I experienced it myself – it is enormously pleasant, impossible to escape, words are lacking to describe it. But I knew the laws of this condition. It is the most important thing. I knew this condition – pulsating. It lasts and then there is a pause of the same length of time. Then it happens again. And the other laws, I don't remember now. I knew, also, that you would not understand these laws before entering there. And it is dangerous to stay there, in this condition, without knowing the laws. And for the first time, I understood why it is so important to resist your own importance. When a person comes to such a state of mind, everyone is totally turned away from you; it cannot be otherwise. The person wants it to last forever; it absorbs you more and more. The person is so strongly overwhelmed by one's feelings that they lose contact with their internal guard.

It began to happen with everybody. And they were dissolved in it. It could eat them up. They needed to be taken out. It is possible when the person already has such a pole of strength – to remember oneself. When he has enough will to come out of this condition (it is very difficult for people) and to give the same period of rest. It happens automatically when a person has this guard inside. When I entered this condition for the first time, I had 8 or 10 full periods, and after that, I went to call for you.

And when you entered, I had to control each one of you from somewhere above. It is important: all people were living in shining commas. But in this corral there were people (maybe about 70 of them) – like black spots, like coals which burned out (as for you – you were burning brightly). They were on the right side. I did not feel that they were sleeping. They either died or hid themselves, like ancient Indian magicians – or they were burned because they did not know the laws. I knew that I could not speak to you about it before. Besides, you were in such a condition that you could not remember anything, even yourselves. I noticed that you were too far gone already. You entered deeper and deeper. I grabbed Shawn (I understood that I could not grab you separately, that you and he were linked through a chain reaction and that you were pulling many people with you).

You and Shawn were important to me; I had enormous strength. I could grab you out of there with my hand – but it would not mean that you would stop! I grabbed Shawn like a little ant, snatched him out and pulled him up to me (4 levels up). I knew that he, like everyone, was afraid of being hit. I started to hit him automatically. First, I hit him in the neck (with my left hand on his right side). I knew clearly that I needed to reach his left side where his important energy point was.[31] The right side was absolutely useless. There was some kind of barrier which I had to overcome. Then I reached him with my left hand (when I woke up my left hand was burning). I hit him a swinging blow with my left hand on the left side of his back! His self-importance is enormous – It could have destroyed all of you.

---

[31] It is possible when the person already has such a pole of strength – to remember oneself. In order to survive and keep a situation under control, it is very important to remember yourself in dreams and in this kind of Spirit travel. I see myself like a dot and split time into fragments and at the end of each fragment, I return to myself, this dot: "I exist, I am here" and after I continue to the next fragment (or segment) of the adventure.

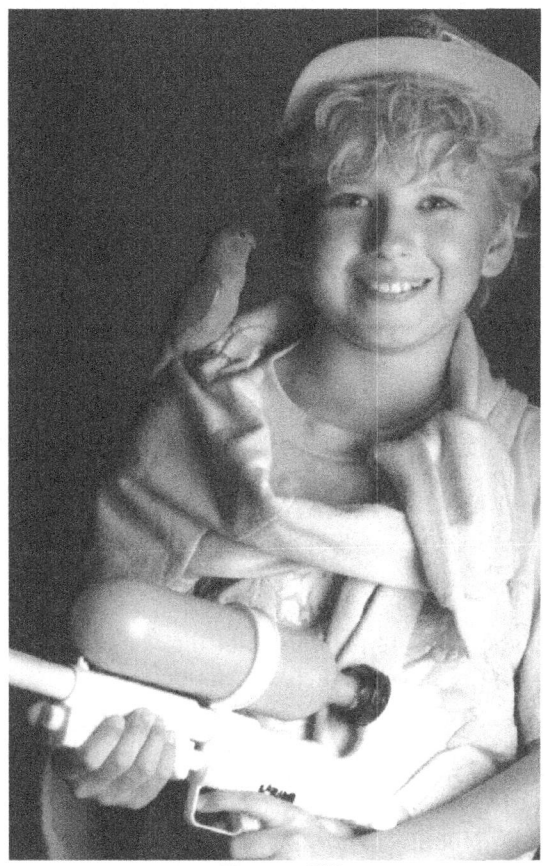

Shawn SV

I was not as soft as my Mexican-Indian teacher in my dreams. You were on the brink of ruin. Shawn came to his senses immediately by provoking a reaction within you and later onto the others. I knew this in my mind; I did not look with my eyes. But I knew that you should not be led out abruptly, you take too long to recover and could be ruined in this instance.
To my surprise in the morning Shawn got something like chicken pox – the rash was on the left side of his neck and cheek. Between us and let's keep this secret, I know why. Of course he did not remember anything from the previous night's adventure...

Happy Shawn wishes to be a hero in this present life, but he had no idea what he went through during the night and that he is a real hero, someone who saved people's lives with his special spiritual abilities in that dream.

Attention please!

People who cannot understand my dreams and still don't believe that life exists after death will be very surprised, instantly after they die, they will still be "alive", but in a different way. And now in Spirit world..., What's next? What to do? Where to go?
When you died, your soul want to go to the Source, but can't if you will go toward white glowing tunnel. Why? because there "trap", made by entities who wish to drain your energy and for this will locked your soul in reincarnation cycle of the "bad" Earth. As you know we have many versions of the Earth in many dimensions and many parallel worlds.
So you should turn around, you will see the entire Universe and will make decision : *That you want to go home...* and you will be there instantly ...and you will be free from Earth reincarnation cycle.

YOUR ETERNAL HOLOGRAM

What Happens After Death & Ascension Tips - Simon Parkes
https://www.youtube.com/watch?v=04OdG3V5zBo

Open.Your.Mind(OYM)Radio.Alex.Collier.January 10th https://www.youtube.com/watch?v=04OdG3V5zBo

God and Angels will meet you and accept you unconditionally. No matter if you believe that they exist or not, what you think about them, who you are, what race you are, your own relatives who passed away will wait to meet you as well.

You will spend time there to meet relatives and afterwards each of you will go through the place where people are waiting their judgment appointment. According to what you did on Earth during your lifetime, each and every one will be assigned to a space where people, who have the same level of Spirit development, reside. I know this very well, because a few friends after their death told me about it during my dreams. All of them love that place very much, by the way!

A cardiologist from Holland, Dr. Pim van Lommel, proved that the Soul lives and consciousness does not depend on the brain! He checked 344 patients after they came out of their coma. Consciousness continued to function after the heart and brain activity stopped.

In one case, when a patient whose heart had already stopped, when the ECG showed no brain activity, and before artificial ventilation of the lungs was applied, the nurse took out his dental prosthesis and put it in a box on the desk nearby. When the patient returned to life, he waited until that very same nurse came into his room to remind her that she took his prosthesis and placed it on the desk – she had forgotten about it. He said that he saw everything that happened, who said what and who did what in that room from the instant he *lost consciousness*. He said he was watching everything from above – on the ceiling.

Remember from Amelia's chapter, during my hypnosis session, I end up in real Heaven?
Here it is – for those who skipped that part before:

"I see so many people! All like angels. All white kind of, many, many, many... A door opens and I go there... It was interesting that until the last moment, I continued seeing many people; they all have this see-through kind of looks. If you take, for example, a clear plastic bag and put one inside another maybe 5 or 7 times, this is how it will be, how people look in Heaven. Wow!!! I visited real Heaven today! I loved it! I didn't want to return from there, by the way. It was such a pleasure to be there, such a light, happy feeling!

In case when some people committed suicide, well they will end up in between – between this and the other world. Most likely you will end up being a ghost forever in a grey, gloomy space. Once I crossed this space in my dream twice; it is a really ugly place to be...

Here are the facts. I talked to Di Cherry and I saw some program on TV where by psychic people confirmed how much effort is necessary to navigate lost souls to the right place. It is heavy work for them which they are doing every day for many years. This is their job. And imagine how many people pay to those psychics real money to get rid of those ghosts.

As for me, I am not interested in the subject of ghosts and never will be. Since I met them the first time in Japan I prefer never to deal with them again. Every ghost's program on TV has the same scenario which is very primitive and dead flat: everyone is scared to death, some hear strange sounds, some see shadows, and once, someone was even hit by a ghost and lost consciousness. Psychics are working hard to get rid of them. To see a ghost program once is more than enough.

****

Here the new ghost story. I arrived to Moscow with purpose to publish my book in Russian.

I was living by myself in luxury penthouse apartment kindly provided to me by my editor Olga. Very soon I realized that in this place lived Spirits - were I heard sounds of movement in the middle of the night in my bedroom. The door flew open and the Spirit called me by name in a loud male voice! When I was sleeping, the Spirit came to me and repeated several times the word **Le Shagart**. I woke up and wrote down the word; it was 3am.
In the morning, I began a search in Google for the word and to my surprise, found a village or small town in Armenia. From my window you can see the cemetery. When I asked what kind of cemetery is it? It was told - it was an Armenian cemetery!!!
I asked the Spirit his name. He said **Nathan.** I see in my vision a man around the age of 45 years, wearing a blue sweater, short hair, looking very modern. He explained that he is scared to go to God, because he committed suicide by hanging himself and is stuck between heaven and Earth, in this emptiness, and now living in the cemetery....
Next time a Spirit told me name **Mikael...**and repeated it many times over the night in my dream. I asked him to stop, and not bother me and I promised that I would book Nathan for the funeral service. I called the church and told to the priest that his disembodied clients were bothering me... He asked which one? I replied a dead one...when I told to him the name and all the info about Nathan he found him in the list of those buried in that cemetery!!!He held a memorial service. Amazingly the name of the priest was **Mikael.** The spirit of Nathan got what it wished for, his memorial service....

****

According to statistic 100 million in USA believe in Ghost, 10% sow them, so how come people believe in ghost if they don't believe in afterlife?

This story is from Belgium. A friend invited me to meet the producer of Belgian TV channel.
When I arrived at his home and in a large comfortable living room, I saw in the corner, a wooden statue of a man. Enormous sadness came to me from this wonderful person.
I approached the owner of Mr. R. and asked who it was? He told me that it was his uncle who was a sculptor, who had died 20 years previously. He was very sad during his life.
When he told me this, I asked: "Has your uncle ever had long wavy hair and was he taller than you? He said yes, but how do you know that? I simply told him: your uncle is next to you right now at the back of the left shoulder ... I can see it very clearly, almost like all the people around, maybe a little less bright in color.
****

Another story was with the woman from other TV channel, Kate.
She start tell me about her father, which died many years ago and how she deeply upset she was.
Kate asked me: When people die, does their Spirit really continue to live?
At this moment I saw man standing near her, it was again from the left shoulder side.
He had curly brown hair and brown eyes, like she did. And something round and white was below on the level of his stomach where his left hand would have been seen.
I ask her: Did your father have a broken left hand? Maybe what I was seeing was a white cast? She told me, no, he did not.

Next day Kate called me and told that she had contacted her mother; she sounded very excited! Her mother told her that when she married their father, he had on his skin a big white round spot located on his abdomen. He went through the treatment and within years it was gone, so daughter had never known this.

Kate was ENORMOUSLY happy about this news! She told me that her world changed for the best after that realization! It means this was her own real father's Spirit which had been there yesterday, as if he wished to prove it by showing this white spot.
There is mounting evidence that people's Spirit continues after death!

"As I read Julia's book I decide to share a story about my Mother.
Last December my mother was in the hospital with a heart condition. She had 8 other sisters and brothers that had passed (she was the youngest). I came in to visit, sat down beside her and she turned to me and said, "I must be hallucinating. I see people floating on the ceiling. "I told her, "They are there and they are waiting for you. "The next day she went with them as I sat there holding her hand.
As in science, matter changes from a solid/liquid/gas ... yet it is never destroyed ... as it is with the spirit-soul. It just changes forms.
Julia, Thanks for being you, you are a joy to the mind and soul. Your book is a great support to the people. "
Donald Baker from Florida, USA

****

A few years ago I met a ghost one more time in my life. It happened when I visited my business partner, Charles P., in the San Diego, USA. When we started talking about business and we were both looking at the computer screen, suddenly I saw and felt that a woman was looking at us from the ceiling at our backs. It was a huge room with very high ceiling. The loft, above, gave onto the living room below. I saw her – full size – standing near the railing of the loft. My partner was very surprised when I described her to him.

When he showed me her photo – it was exactly how she looked – it was the same woman! Her name was Kideok; she was the last daughter of the Yi Dynasty in Asia. C.P. told me that she was his mother and she had passed away a few years ago. He loved her deeply... She also loved him very much, so much, that after her death she stayed in our world just to be near her son! Ever since her death, her Spirit continued living in his house. No one had seen her, including him, but he admitted hearing her footsteps on the loft, especially when C.P. was cooking her favorite dishes and sometimes he could also hear some objects moving – she was doing it.

When I went to the loft, I saw her sitting on the bed in a meditating position! I saw her more with some kind of intuition, a sort of vision; because I remember that I started seeing her on the bed before I entered the room while I was still walking up the stairs.
This man worked at the White House during the terms of few presidents. One of the walls in his living room was covered with awards and I remember one of them was from President Clinton. What I try to demonstrate here is that a very modern, an intellectual man, accepted the fact that his own mother was living at his place as a ghost!

****

Another example; Di Cherry told me about one case. A woman came to her for help. For many years she had pain near her stomach. She went through all kinds of doctors, no one helped.
Di put her under hypnosis and found that this woman had a twin when she was born. This twin was a boy; he died right after birth and her parents buried him without giving him a name and, of course, he was not baptized. So his Spirit was afraid to go to God; he was not sure that God would accept him! He was stuck in that woman's body – for all these years...

So Di Cherry decided it would be best to give him a name and to baptize him.
When they prepared the holy water, Di Cherry asked this woman, "How about we call him Peter?" Suddenly a deep man's voice came out of the woman's chest, saying, "Michael!" He wanted to be called Michael! So they called him Michael and he disappeared instantly as soon as he was baptized. The woman, for the first time, breathed easily and relaxed. The pain was gone. No more pain! Yes, this is exactly what happened.

Has Quantum Physics Proven The Existence of An Afterlife?

New evidence continues to suggest that Einstein was right – death is an illusion.http://www.viralnovelty.net/quantum-physics-proven-existence-afterlife/Quantum physics theories may have proven that there is another life after death. According to Professor Robert Lanza, the theory of Biocentrism reveals that death is only an illusion created by our personal consciousness. It's important to note that although these thoughts seem and are deep, they have been well-known for a long while but simply have not been recognized by modern culture. He believes that humans rely more rationally by relying on the left brain which disables us from seeing the real world that exists alongside the one we perceive. He claims that there is another world apart from the one we are living in, but we need to be scientific to prove it. The same intelligence that allows us to realize astonishing scientific discoveries can also get us trapped in scientific misunderstandings should we

not stay open to change. Robert Lanz claims that after the death of a person moves into a parallel world. The researcher says that human life is like a perennial plant that always comes back to re-bloom in the multiverse. Robert Lantz said: " We believe in death because we've been taught we die. Also, of course, because we associate ourselves with our body and we know bodies die. End of story.
 "Lantz believes that death is not the absolute end of life, and represents a shift to a **parallel world.**He is convinced that if space and time aren't linear, then death can't exist in 'any real sense' either. In physics, a long-standing theory of an infinite number of universes with different variations of situations and people. All that can happen is already happening somewhere, which means that death cannot exist in principle.

Diane (Di) Cherry

There are many unexplained events that official science does not accept. Even when facts are telling the opposite and support what happened. What to do for the ordinary person? Believe it, or not? How about if we pose the question: whether such phenomenon is *normal, natural* to our world?
According to the philosophy, the Law of unity and conflict of opposites, our world contains many pair of contradictions. This is life and death, day and night, black and white, good and bad, normal and abnormal.

Parallel world.
Let's check one of these opposites: OUR world and the parallel world.
The world in which we live also can't exist without its opposite – the invisible parallel world.

The scientist Ziolkovsky wrote: "Material did not appear at the beginning as dense as it is now. There were stages of more rarefied material, when beings (entities) were created, which, for us are unreachable and sometimes invisible. However, they can be near us. If this is true, it means that thin rare-field material, much older than denser, younger material, then, of course, can be ahead of us in their development. Scientific proof of this statement exists: if we take together all physical objects on Earth, their weight does not equal the weight of the fixed mass, which it should be, according to the simplest of calculations. Therefore, it follows that this extra, lost Earth mass belongs to the invisible World.[32]

Many do not believe in this invisible world. But the new Wi-Fi technology is invisible, right? People use cell phones, wireless laptops and so on. And we know that they exist and even go easily through the walls of our homes and carry particular information.

YOUTUBE: Part 1 - Parallel Universes - BBC Horizon

The ultra-thin parallel world by its very nature is another non-material form of existence, the lives of intelligent beings. And their abilities are much more extensive than those of human beings. One of the characteristics of these living forms in this invisible world is that they show themselves sometimes on camera films which can fix the radiations invisible to the human eye.
I just finished talk with Gustavo on the phone, who I met during Equinox 2010 in Chichén Itzá. He lives in Florida. Here his Testimonial.

My brother Alberto, who lives in Mexico, told me his extraordinary history. He is an adjuster for an insurance company and he has to go to check and make report on car accidents and photos. Sometimes he goes in the middle of the night to very far and isolated places. Alberto found on the accidents photos people, who still in the cars! BUT body of that people had been taken already out before he take pictures! He mentioned that he had about 15 pictures with the same scenario: all the passengers inside the cars.
The clearest picture that Alberto has is a picture that involved a car accident with priest from a small town. The priest's body was on the ground covered with a blanket. After Alberto took the picture of the car, he sees on that picture a sphere above the car and inside the sphere there's a fetus! After I talk to him, I went to his room and saw the round griddle pan, which my brother painted a fetus inside exactly the way he had described on the priest accident!
This was the sign for me. Every time I saw this paint I fell so weird, but I know : this is message in the pictures is that we don't die after death and secondly priest representing the catholic church (Vatican) and I know that they hide this reality and the fetus in the sphere confirms that REINCARNATION IS REAL. My brother was just like the mail man carrying an envelope not knowing what's inside.

God Bless everyone. Gustavo Medrano.

Reincarnation and the Bible
Christians are usually very surprised to learn that reincarnation was a doctrine once held by many early Christians. Not only that, as you will soon see there is overwhelming evidence in the Bible of Jesus himself teaching it. Please see at the end of the book:
The Reincarnation of Jesus ,

---

[32] By the way 'dark matter' and 'dark energy' have been discovered only in the past 15 years - thanks to technology advances - e.g., Hubble and WMAP telescopes, among others. Physicists and cosmologists now believe that 'visible energy' (light and ordinary matter) comprises only 7% of the total universe; dark matter' - which scientist have yet to detect or prove its existence - represents another 23%'dark energy' - which they can't even properly describe - comprises the vast bulk of the total Universe ~ 70% In other words, scientists believe approx 93% of the 'physical' universe remains to be discovered and explored!

YOUR ETERNAL HOLOGRAM

Timeline of Reincarnation in the Hebrew and Christian religions
And you read already in Chapter "Amelia return" most amazing part where proof that people reincarnated as a group, right? About Abraham Lincoln and John F. Kennedy:
Evidence of Reincarnation Through Synchronicity

Interesting fact: 84% of people in the USA believe in the survival of the soul after death, but only 27% believe in reincarnation, that they were once another person. Actually this is almost the same! Why? (See below.)[33] I only logged on Google for a minute and found that Reincarnation was first written as such in the Bible but was then changed to the Resurrection later.

So people knew that after death their soul would survive, which is really good! However, the Reincarnation subject is widely ignored. Religious entities are telling people that they will stay forever in the other world! People are missing the most important point – the second part of their journey, which is the Reincarnation of their spirits. Their soul will return to Earth and they will be re-born as a new born baby time and again!
It also mentioned that the Catholic Church kept secret, from their followers, what would take place after they died. It looks like the church decided to keep the power for itself and kept people in constant fear of the afterlife. In my opinion, if this really took place, this is a crime against Humanity!
Remember what the Ancient Maya priest said? "Fear was introduced to society artificially as a tool for the manipulations of the mind and it prevented the development of the new consciousness and enlightenment."
Well, as an Ancient priest I am telling everyone exactly, in this book, with LOTS of facts to support my assertion, what will happen to people after they die.
A photographer from a local newspaper in Ogden City, USA, Andre Rittenhaim took a photo of an accident when a Cadillac ran into the car of the 32-year-old, Wilma Kenner, at high speed. What he said about this tragedy was this, "I took a few photos and ran to the laboratory to prepare them for the newspaper evening edition... When I looked at the still wet photos, in all five of them I saw a four-meter-high figure with hands like wings, between the flames and the black smoke!" He was shocked and couldn't believe his own eyes! Independent researchers have verified that these photos were real. (V. Lotohin, Secret Doctrine, # 16, 2008) [35]
I noticed another case on YOUTUBE where people could see clearly two white, glowing angels flying out of a high rise building where a child just died. Angels guide the Spirit in the right direction. If you stop the video at the 25 second mark, you would see the size of the angel. It is around four to five-and-a-half meters tall. The angels' sizes are about the same on the next video, where you can see five Angels flying and communicating among themselves in the sky! In the last video there is a baby on the photo, a baby angel, about the size of a human, the same as I saw when two of them arrived just before my daughter was born.

YOUTUBE: Angels are taking away the soul of the dead child.
(Stop on 0.22 min. Here you can see 2 Angels on the roof.)
A58 Fenomeno portal dimensional. *Start from 4.05-4.16 min.*
You can see Angel on the roof of the house
Heavenly Angel visits dying girl, Angel caught on video!
*^j^ ^j^ Angels Angels Angels ^j^ ^j^*
Scientist photographed a soul leaving the body in death – 1st part
In this last YouTube you can see that after a sudden death people's Spirit continues to go back and forces itself in their dead body.

---

[33] http://www.harrisinteractive.com/vault/Harris-Interactive-Poll-Research-The-Religious-and-Other-Beliefs-of-Americans-2003-2003-02.pdf

In order to study this parallel world and its characteristics, the Italian scientist, Lucian Bokkone, built a laboratory on a hill – it was an abnormal electromagnetic zone. He took photos of the empty corners, of the internal space. He built a special mechanism monitoring this space so that nothing could interrupt the process. This way it was absolutely impossible for anyone or anything from our world to intrude in this place. He obtained thousands of photos where there were images of strange geometrical figures, some entities, which do not exist on Earth – ghosts' contours and so on, and so on. Such materials made by many independent people exist throughout the world in huge amounts. Therefore, during its long history, humanity has lived near a **parallel world.** Sometimes the borders between the two worlds can open and visitors come into our world.

Here photo taken at the wedding of this men son. The profile of his late wife is visible in the left hand corner – in the rainbow .It is the same woman which is on the photo on his **lapel.**

In this amazing case, the deceased mother had enough energy to attend the wedding of her beloved son as a Spirit.

I saw a documentary movie, showing the interview conducted with the wives of the people who died during 911 Twin Towers horror in New York. These women said that their husbands kept talking to them from the other side! Sounds impossible, right? What about the little girl, who told everyone that not only her dear father, but also his co-workers kept talking to her and entertained her with jokes and funny stories? She was giving the co-workers' names and last names! But when her father died she was only a new-born baby. No way would she have known the last names of these other people. The only source is ... all of them were talking with the real Spirits! Some places are very special.

There are places where the Spirits can contact people easily. In this book, there are a few photos taken by my friend and photographer, **Tim Orden**. Several of these photos were taken in *Kauai, Hawaii on Polihale beach.* People come to this beach and stay overnight in tents just to talk to the ever-happy and laughing Spirits!

Tim did the same for the first time 35 years ago, when he was a young boy. Now he continues to visit this place and the Spirits talk to him instantly when he arrives, as if they were longtime friends! We witnessed how the Spirits started talking to him during photo session!!!

I know that there is a cave in Mexico where people can ask questions and the Spirits answer their questions using the echo in the cave!

Photograph by Tim Orden, Kauai, Polihale beach that day.

Dream # 41.
Gray Dumb-Bell in the Head, September 4, 1991

I had not fallen asleep deeply yet; I still remember myself, when some substance of gray color entered my head from both sides and started to crystallize inside it. It was not a pipe, the whole thing was filled in, crystallized all at once; it was fitting very well – like a dumb-bell – with something like earphones on the sides – flat ones – it was about three centimeters above the ears. I still have this sensation at the place where this "dumbbell" had been inserted. I had a feeling that this happens to me often, maybe even every night, but I don't remember it.
I am at the bottom of the ocean, deep, far away and I am doing everything there. I can learn a lot, because I know the way
.**It seemed that I am some other creature, who knows a lot, multidimensional one. It has a different nature and it remembers a lot. As a human I am now 5% of it.** I could get answers to all of the questions, but they did not give them to me; there was no one around to ask me.

Dream # 42
Dowel Bar into the Head, September 15, 1991

Yesterday, I had a dowel bar in my head again ... If that gray thing entered my head quietly and strongly, tightly, then it was of a very dense consistency, even not like a diamond, but harder, polished, long, very sharp at the end. The sensation was sharp, very strong and clear, on the verge of pain... In a minute, I crashed out, lost control of myself. I had the urge to stand up and go anywhere, at least to another room, but I was as if cut-off from everywhere. I was horrified at the moment, that if I could know the future and I didn't want to know our future.

****

Once, when I was in South Korea, I visited a place outside **Seoul named the Cultural village.**
While I was there, the locals performed a special Korean traditional dance. When I watched it, I just could not believe my own eyes! These men had a long white rope on their hats and the entire dance was dedicated to that rope.

I am sure most of you know that we all have an invisible, thinnest thread which connects our spiritual body from the top of our head to our astral body during sleep. No matter how far we travel through the universe in our dreams, this thread still continues to connect our astral body with our real body which we leave sleeping in bed. The entire population of South Korea is Buddhist. So it looks like this knowledge about the thread is basic there and that they even have traditional dances dedicated to this silver thread which shows the kinds of qualities it has! Amazing!

This next dream is very important for me. I will try to describe the location and mechanism which allowed me **to travel in time back and forth**. I remember in my dream, I try to implement changes in the past and to correct ways in the future. For example, it allowed me to travel to other planets easily and arrive there instantly.

South Korea, traditional dance

Dream # 43
The Belt Buckle. The Law of Time, March 16, 1992

I woke up three times; the dream was going on. I was feeling this belt on me. The buckle was like a case of an audio-cassette. The belt was thinner, narrower. The color was beige, similar to colour of my skin (it was as if soldered into my skin). The buckle was made of white plastic. When I woke up for the third time, through my sleep, I had a feeling that thousands of eyes were watching my body and their "sight" was directed to the belt as if it were golden threads. From every little eye, there is always a flow, always a sensation from all the spots on my body.

On the belt buckle there was a round button, closer to the left side. On the buckle, there was also a vertical crack. Something had to be inserted into this crack and something protruded out of the **belt** in order to insert the thing into it. The crack opened and closed.

YOUR ETERNAL HOLOGRAM

After the third awakening, I remembered only one thing – I understood time. *Time does not exist without space. Objects are defined in space. The presence of material object creates time.* The fact of the existence of material objects in space creates time. All three of them assume that this object should change (develop, evolve or devolve). As soon as a material object disappears, the un-evolution (or devolution) ends.

Where there are no material objects, there is Eternity. I understood it very clearly. I tried to change time – forward or backwards. If I pulled time in front of me, I stood in place, but moved time as if on a slide-rule. I don't remember the process. It was always connected with the belt – I was doing something with it. At different times, I unbuckled it, buckled it, and pressed the button. The buckle was like white fog, like my smoky stone. I don't remember the belt clearly. If there is such a belt, then there should be a buckle. One, which is also me, my second self, had shown me such things, explained to me and taught me, and I knew that it was I. She was speaking with a resounding voice into my ear. The lower part of my body is a "galactic disk" – a very thick, humming disk, but it is a thousand times denser, concentrated energy than what I described in previous dreams, and it can rotate like a weight at the gym. The upper part of my body – on the contrary – was extremely light and almost weightless. This part can rotate relative to the upper one. The second part – the upper one – is a transparent, radiating light; nothing specific can be seen – everything is "blinking".

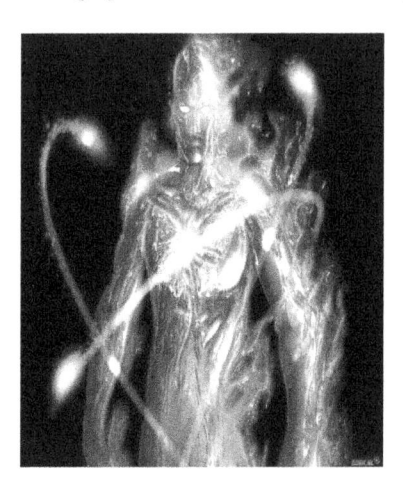

In 1899, in Arizona, workers digging the ground for the construction of a future hotel found an ancient burial made from rose-marble blocks which connected to each other so precisely that it looked like one solid piece. Inside this "mausoleum", there was an Egyptian-type of sarcophagus made of a strange blue colored substance in the shape of a human figure. The painting on top of the sarcophagus was that of a giant man which was lying down. He was absolutely naked and **wore only a big, wide belt.** He had sandals on his feet and a crown in the form of an Egyptian miter. Inside the sarcophagus there were only ashes. All the items found and the ashes proved the ancient source of this, because over time the skull is the last to be destroyed. Well, maybe he had a belt to travel through the Universe after death? The same as I used in my dream. Maybe it is even me in my past life?!!

About TIME

It would be a very exciting teleportation experience into the future or to another planets. I feel, I know for sure, no doubt for me whatsoever, that this is possible with people and things, because in my dreams, I often see all things around me (trees, rocks, buildings) as a set of dynamic frequency vibrations or pulsations. I can "press" this frequency and "transform" it into a solid object or to do the opposite. For example, I can go through the walls easily, because I see them as a plasma or colloid with a special frequency. **I know how to see, to make myself, my body as a frequency. I think it helps me travel very fast through the Universe – faster than light or sound and with help of**

wormholes of course. This is how I can send my body frequency far away into Space to some exact place of which the frequency is familiar to me already. For example, I can go to those galactic huge bee houses where my "home space" is located. I guess this is how I travel in time. Because information is also moving at a particular speed in time, as soon as you break the barrier you move at a faster speed and you find yourself in the future or in the past.

YOUTUBE:
Discovery - First Time Machine
Is Time Travel Possible?
Time Travel Evidence? Watch Found in 400 Year Old Tomb - The Strange and the Curious 101

Let me say it again, *I see TIME like a spooled thread, rolling one over the other and the other, and each of them is a span of time PAST, PRESENT, FUTURE. If something happens in space, such as an earthquake, for example, or another problem occurs, and as a result a wormhole is created amid the threads of this bobbin, it can be easily understood how people, ships, trains or animals disappear in one place, only to re-appear in a different place at a different time – traveling from one time to another.*
There are well-known cases where a person appears in the 19th century from nowhere, wearing an outfit from the 16th century for example, and he could not understand why he was there!
In the northern part of Australia, people see *prehistoric* Dinosaurs from time to time!

You can see YOUTUBE videos about Dinosaurs from the places where *Times* past and present were crossing paths.

YOUTUBE: More Dragons sighted in skies over Louisville!

Pterodactyl Sighting 2008

You have not forgotten the dream #5, in which I saw Baba Yaga's house on chicken legs?

I was curious and, at my surprise, I discovered that all the old legends about unusual creatures have the real roots through our life.

They are shown for themselves from time to time to people. By your own eyes you can see many YouTube videos. For example, in Mexico numerous occasions when Baba Yaga on chicken legs flying on a broom or attack even a man-cop!

In the UK was a lot of cases, when people see the flower fairies .There is a video about gnomes and elves ... In Thailand, people show real fairy!

YOUTUBE:

Real Fairy found in England, Real Fairy caught on Camera

Caught On Camera The Proof That Fairies Are REAL Not Fake!!!

Real Gnomes and Fairies Caught On Tape

Flying humanoid attacks a police officer in Mexico!

UFO-Flying Humanoid-English Subtitles --

Story following the Witch of Monterrey, Mexico

****

I know that the human creation of long railroads with trains and tunnels forming giant fish nets of steel structures, hundreds of thousands of kilometers long, interrupt space and as a result time on the planet. This is the main reason for the formation of wormholes and an explanation why trains disappear and re-appear years later in many different locations all over the world. The famous case of the small tourist train from Italy which left Rome in 1911 and went into the longest tunnel in the mountains of Lombardi and never came out of that tunnel, is a perfect example of this! Since then, the train was seen in Mexico City, and afterwards in many countries during our century, and finally even in the new tunnel under La Manche! Well, imagine how people in that train felt – frozen in time for almost 100 years! I hope they were all happy not knowing that they were stuck in time and would be living forever aboard that train!

According to the scientist, Pazei I.P., railroads are also powerful energy information channels. Any algorithmic movement creates an information flow. For example, a few years before this train disappeared in Italy, there was an earthquake near Massena. This event could have created not only cracks in the land but also it could have created a wormhole in space which was moving around the tunnel. Since the movement of the train was connected with the railroad, the lost train could have appeared in any place conditional upon the fact that there would be a railroad on site at that time or one would be built there in the future.

The "ghost trains" hit and killed many people on railroads every year in very strange and unusual circumstances. Witnesses tell that people were killed near or on the railroad when no train was around. Or the "ghost train" suddenly appears out of nowhere and creates accidents.

On June 14, 2001, the minister for railroads transport of Turkmenia, Hamyrat Berdiev died on the railroad! According to the witnesses, he was standing near the railroad when he was suddenly pushed onto the rails by some strong power and killed seconds before the train arrived and stopped close to him. It is interesting that there was no blood, no parts of his suit had been disarranged, and there was no sign at all of any contact between the train and his body. So please remember that rail roads are very dangerous places and be careful. There is always the possibility of being killed by the "ghost train" or disappearing in a time hole.

Dream # 44

The People Stopped In the Prairie, November 26, 1991

In that dream, I saw an area a place where is not much trees, and many bushes; the season the end of summer, maybe, they are yellowish, or maybe it is just a desert zone, grayish-yellow. The soil is like sand, rocky, dry. There are no full, green colors. The people there are modern, but they have to move far away from this territory. They carry only what they could manage to pack. There are no roads at all. Like pioneers from the West, they ride in covered wagons. Cars, small trucks, all like GMC trucks. **Was no Japanese cars.** There are not many of them, but it seems that they dispersed in different directions, the movement is slow, almost no movement. They prepare food, as when you camping. They are moving somewhere, but do not know where to go. There is no direction. They know that they should move somewhere. **Or maybe they ran away from somewhere, escaped danger, got away from it and slowed down.** There is an impulse to move, but it subsided. And we are also moving on something. I think about the situation and I feel a necessity to take some steps. These people are like little ants; they could not understand the situation in its full amplitude. They need a queen ant or something else to guide them through this serious, very unusual situation.
I was thinking comprehended, weighted everything and the current moment, and what it could bring to us later on globally, as a whole.
And I understood that the situation was hopeless. They were moving, in a way, but something was stopping their progress, something invisible which did not let them move farther. The movement ended. **Time stopped.** And I understood: in order to go on moving, the movement would start. If only I could find something in this area. I had to find some configuration which was there in this space, to catch it, to grasp it with my hands, to figure out an order, recreate a tuning. And it does exist, in fact; it can be compared with an aquarium filled with jelly, transparent, and inside it there is a stepped, linear figure which is not distinguishable externally, but it is there. I need to catch this amorphous item, to sense it, and after that, I need to recreate it, to feel it with my hands, my mind, and my senses to come to know its form. At the same time it is moving and in constant change. And when I find it and visualize it, get into a mutual contact; learn its form and movement, only then the situation will be resolved. Something will happen to me and I will be able to break through this wall in space, not only in space, but in time also ñ because time stopped and does not move into eternity; maybe that is why their gas and food did not run out. And when the breakthrough will take place, the stupor will end. The new life will start, the life energy will appear, people will be able to move forward and we will go further.
There will be transfiguration. At the beginning, I captured the situation with my mind and later I turned off. I was in a clearing. I groped with my senses to the place, in this clearing, where to start from in order to find this thing. The clearing was large and circular. I was sitting on the step of our car, facing the West. Later, I stood up and went westward (I saw that it was there) and came to the spot. I started searching with my senses for this .stepping stair... Later I woke up, yet, I think something else also happened.
When I was searching for this figure, I was doing it with thin threads which were like the ones I was pulling out of a frog, that golden thin thread, in order to come one step. In the last sentence of the frogs on the energy of animals, as a master of Kung Fu did an imitation of the animal's movement. Indians in North America as well, using this type of energy of eagle, frog, wolf.
* *No Japanese cars.* Maybe will be major earthquakes in Japan and whole country will not exist after? Impossibly sad…

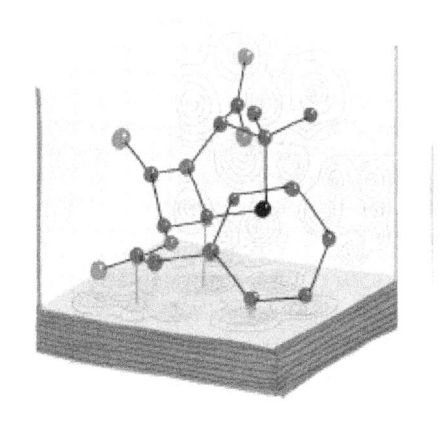

Or maybe they ran away from somewhere, escaped danger, got away from it →
It can be any, was big tsunami due to the asteroid and people who survived running from coastal area? This desert reminds me of Australia.

Dream # 45
Huge God Was Dictating Into My Ears, January 7, 1983

There were three key moments in this dream; the super-global, the relations of a human with other living beings, and other civilizations.
A Huge God was dictating into my ears. I knew that I would wake up, and then there would be a break, and then again, a dream. The voice was going on saying some strange things. At one moment, I captured the tone of this voice ñ I heard once such sound in Jane Mitchell Jarreës music, ZooLook, a very low tone, global. The voice shook me up; I could not understand the meaning of the phrases. When I came to my senses, the words came to me like a consequence. But I did not understand them. I got up and went to the bathroom and washed my face. I went back to bed; it was 3:35 a.m. on the clock. I wanted to drink, and realized that I was not breathing, maybe for a long time already.
Now I know how a baby starts breathing after birth. I was dreaming of a strange place, where I, and a few other people, could enter and choose to put on some clothes. The clothes were, very strange, each for a particular purpose. Everyone was dressing up according to one own self-perception. Then, we came to the window.
We knew that we were very high up on the opposite side the ruins of a church, 12 mountain peaks. The voice resounded again ñ perhaps I was speaking to them (although it seemed strange to me). The voice (maybe mine) started speaking. I knew that it would be a recitation of many positions. He said three. I knew that there would be a break, that I would wake up and then I would see. **I understood that somewhere beyond my consciousness there was this divine creature and it is also me.** It was speaking in a very low, grand tone. I don't know what he was saying at first.
(You will find an explanation for this occurrence at the end of the book, in the scientific interpretation section.)
1. Me, you or all humanity (Me is that spirit, you any person on Earth)
2. People believe that machines will put them on their knees, but I think the opposite.
3. The planet is challenged by a choice.
4. Who they are is the will of the one. The world is endless, and the life is one (meaning the life of a human person). The humanity stepped over a threshold.
5. Before the knowledge was one. Now they are uncoordinated. The world is shaken by madness. The power of nature is inevitable.

***I understood that somewhere beyond my consciousness there was this divine creature and it is also me.** This sentence supported what Don Julio told me... about me HUGE, Second one...

Dream # 46
A Warning from Three Astronauts, March 22, 1992

I was in a big hall and someone was telling me (there were no people around) that three astronauts from the other planet arrived on Earth. They wanted to warn us, or to say that our sun got into a period when it began to fade, and later on it would shine like the white nights in St. Petersburg or on the North Pole, but with much less intensity.[34] It would not glare and there would not be any shadows. I saw the Earth immediately – how it would look – the animals, the trees – in a different light... This phenomenon concerned something serious, something global for the Earth. The astronauts were interested in the thing that was above the Earth, 3 planes (like a shamrock) - this single whole consists of three separate parts (the shape is elongated). On the sea there are washed rocks, porous. It looks like it. This is something very important, extremely important. The shape or quality of these planes are of great interest to aliens. When they flew in to investigate, they died. I saw them when they were next to her. Three planes. Three cosmonauts. I knew a law in a dream. This thing is sandy gray. Yellow clay, made from little crystals, When I woke up, I firmly knew that the astronauts were dead today. And the day before the word "Shamrock" had come.

The "message" was important, unusually important. When I woke up, I knew for certain that three astronauts perished on that day. It was deeply sad.

Later, in my dream, I saw a huge asteroid coming to the Earth...

Maybe we should pay attention to the messages we are given. It cost these astronauts their lives, very sad.

p.s. This summer my friend gave me books. This is a story about an amazing boy, Slava Krashennikov, who was canonized by the Russian Orthodox Church as a Saint. He died at the age of 11. In his lifetime, he had a wonderful ability to heal people, and also made thousands of predictions that later came true.

While I was reading this book, I suddenly found out that his prediction about the same triangle - an object in space near the Earth! That's how he explained it: When space rockets return to Earth, they bring with them almost invisible light gray yellow crystals from space. It was "built" like a beehive in one of our layers of the atmosphere. This crystal grew rapidly by itself, and this represents a great danger to people on the planet. In connection with some conditions that will be created by people, it will fall and destroy everything. The crystal will look like an ice that does not spread and not melting The good news is that the "crystal" will fall over Siberia, which is not densely populated. Since that time, this crystal has reached huge sizes, it will grow to the shape of two leaves of clover, together taken - six - hexahedron

I saw exactly this in my vision for the last time in 1992. I do not know how the form he has now.

We had glass dome over the pyramids in Atlantis...maybe this crystals coming from another time line or other dimension.

****

One dream is repeated from time to time for years. I'm on a different continent, in shape which reminding me of two American continents. Over time, some things change there. In my dreams this continents located is also on our Earth, but of course, it does not exist on the maps ... strange somehow. Finally last week I did found where its location !

---

[34] Changes in the Sun's Surface to Bring Next Climate Change –
www.spaceandscience.net, Jan 13, 2008. Today, the Space and Science Research Center, (SSRC) in Orlando, Florida announces that it has confirmed the recent web announcement of NASA solar physicists that there are substantial changes occurring in the sun's surface. The SSRC has further researched these changes and has concluded they will bring about the next climate change to one of a long lasting cold era.

YOUR ETERNAL HOLOGRAM

Dream # 47
The Earth curled up, February 12, 1992

I saw the Earth, large, huge. I felt its enormity; it was occupying all of my scope of vision as if from the cosmos. The Earth started to curl up inside itself. It was happening very quickly. It is hard to describe with words, but it was easy to watch. Initially, there was a cutting in the Earth in one place and the peel started to roll inside themselves, like two rolls of paper, rolling in opposite direction from each other. It rolled in and disappeared. I did not see it anymore. The line of the cutting was drawn across the Atlantic Ocean, between Europe and America, diagonally. After rolling up, the Earth turned into a blue colloid sphere, as thick as condensed air, and when the sides were rolling inside it, you could see one layer through the other one. At the end when the Earth was rolling inside itself, it only left looked like a bright-red, burning ball in the middle. And after this ball disappeared.

I saw a few dreams like this regarding the Earth. Another **dream was on February 5, 1988.** According to that dream, the Earth will be "broken". It will have cracked at first, after which it will be wiped out. It will be **year 1695.**

As you can see in my dreams, I know the time when events will happen and the exact year when they will occur. But these dates are given according to some other calendar system than the one we use right now. Maybe someone knows and will tell me? It could give me a clue as to what kind of culture this calendar belongs. Most importantly, it would give me an indication as to when this will happen to our Earth.
For example, according to the Zoroastrian (Fasli) calendar, we currently live in year 1369. So we have about 326 years here on Earth to prepare to move to some new home on another planet. It is possible that this calendar is the ancient Zoroastrian, because I see the Persian Goddess very often in these dreams. By the way, I feel really uneasy. It is weird to calculate such a global thing as when our mother Earth will be wiped out... **1695 – 1369 = 326** years from now. It is a very, very sad, enormously heavy feeling.
****

Today, three weeks after I wrote this, my friend gave me a magazine and there I saw a short article: "Hawking says we must go into space." So I decided to add it right now, before my book went to the publisher, to calm my readers down.
I will type only a short part of it: *"...Stephen Hawking says we must go into space...We are not likely to be able to stay on Earth much longer. The possibility that our planet will be wiped out, Hawking believe is quite significant. The good news is, if we can avoid killing ourselves for another century we should have the necessary space settlements in place to launch our descendants into the universe"*(reference: Atlantis Rising, magazine, number 59, page 13; "Hawking says we must go to space").
He continues:
In 20 years he thinks we can have a base on Moon and within another 20 years a settlement on Mars. To find any place else "as nice as Earth"; we will have to go to another star system.

Sadly, I think this is the best option, because in previous dreams, I also saw a problem coming with the sun...Sixteen years after I had this dream, Mr. S. Hawking supports what I saw. It is nice to know that we have some extra time and that my channels are open to receive information so clearly.

But I wish it will never, ever happen to our beautiful, amazing planet Earth and it would have been just one of my weird dreams.

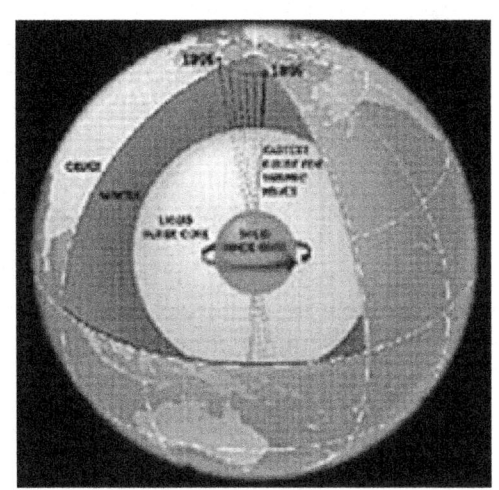

Earth inside

PS:
Predictions about our future can move forward and happen earlier than we expected, because of the disasters and the time experiments on the planet and because the creation of time wormholes continues. At first, *The Philadelphia Experiment,* then *The Montauk Project,* and now this *super-collider* under Switzerland which can create a black hole ... and swallow our Earth, the way I saw it happen in that dream. Today, a few days later, I found something else to add here!

Edgar Cayce predicted in **2120** for this event. M. Nostradamus and Ranio Nero both independent from each other, of course, predicted that humans will move to space, because it will be impossible to continue living on Earth in future. People will build cities, which are similar to a chain of huge balls, beads – it looks like a jewelry necklace.

M. Nostradamus:*It will happen in year 2200.* Wow! I am close with my prediction. If what I predict, that Earth will be wiped out in 326 years, we had better move out ahead of time. It is best not to wait another century as *Stephen Hawking* advises us.[35]

****

It is interesting... With this book, I started writing it for just one reason – to publish a very short book about Chak Mol. But now this process of writing reminds me of a fan which is unfolding, opening more and more and more every day, and I just can't stop myself from writing... It is like water in a river, I touch the keyboard and it starts to flow... It is hard to stop typing...

In one of my dreams, my late grandfather told me: in common life a person tries to succeed in something, to reach some level. But this is not important on the Other Side! The spiritual part which people collect here is almost not valued on Earth but very valuable out there.

As I understand it now, Spirits and Souls coming to Earth are born again here to experience more, to receive a special kind of knowledge, which they can receive only here on Earth, for their development, ultimately moving to the next higher level in the Universe. One of the happiest days in this evolution is the completion of this cycle of reincarnation, birth, death, rebirth, forever stopping. Spirits are then elevated to the top of this perfection stage.

****

---

[35] In order to reassure my readers, I wish to tell you that Nostradamus' prediction about Earth continues after year 2300. His last one concerns people coming from rainbow clouds and belonging to year 3797. Next he wrote: It is not given to me to see beyond the year 3797.

I knew one person in my childhood – he was a provost, his name was Roy. He was tall, huge. This is what happened to him. He went to the agency and ordered a coffin for him, made a photograph, prepared everything for the funeral, including the clothes. He did it in one day. Then, the next day he drove around town, visiting people, hugging, saying good bye. On the third day he lay down in the coffin and died. This story makes you crazy. I remember this story. He was a joyous, solid person, not a fool. He was 57 years old then, maybe more. (His second Saturn cycle) He was a very smart, intelligent man. I was a student at that university. He was my father's friend, who was the dean at the same university. One my old friend, Peter, who was very religious person, was telling for years to people in his church in Vancouver that he wish to die on the Mother God birthday. Well ... he was paralyzed and in coma his last 2 weeks, but he died exactly on that day! His body was sleeping in coma, but his Spirit was aware and going exactly according to the plan.

Dream # 48.
Canyon of Luminescent Elves, June 21, 1992

I turned up to be on the edge of ... say the Earth ... the mountains, in a field. Far behind there were the lights of a city. Twilight. Everything around was gray, a soil. But I had a feeling, that I approached this placed away from people very quickly. Ahead was the East. In front of me there was the edge of a gigantic precipice, which marked the rim of a huge valley. I did not see its end. It was as wide as a canyon. **It was filled with bright, white thinnest threads light*,** as if luminescent – all over, all the way down and up to the horizon. It was not an empty, but condensed light. There was a feeling that the space encompassing this light was organized. There were some creatures, many of them, of unclear, changing forms. There were voices – not earthy – squeaking, meowing, unclear as if in a dream. Spatter of sounds, like children's voices, like birds... as if elves were flying in there. It was one organism, they were somehow interconnected. It consisted of something that was permeated by radiating threads.[36] I entered this space and was there for a long time. I was doing something there. I had some business there, something was happening to me, like a fantastic fairy-tale. I returned from there and woke up.

YOUTUBE:
Part 1 - Parallel Universes - BBC Horizon

Dream # 49
Below – The Transparent Medusa of Air, November 19, 1992

I had dreamed a lot one day. We were sitting on the top of the mountain, very high up. Around, a little below us there was a precipice, where there were strange living creatures. They were bigger than humans; they did not care if they were on the ground or in the air. They were around, moved from ground to air; they were everywhere in space. They did not care about the mountains, or about the precipice. They were always a little below us, flying around us in circles. They were strange, transparent, and luminous, similar to planktons with blinking impulses. They were as if in water and filled inside with some things that resembled balls, jelly-fish, transparent. But they did not have fans like the jelly-fish. They were of irregular, changing forms; there were many of them.

From the moment I woke up, I recalled these creatures and I didn't feel quite myself – I was really stricken by what I had been dreaming, touching it with my memory. I felt the horror of the unknown – the extreme unknown and unusual. In my dreams I am not mindful of my surroundings, I don't think of what I encounter, but later when I wake up... This time I had goose bumps all over my skin; I can't express it – not the horror, but the surprise that I was dreaming of this. The moment of transfer to reality – this was horrible. I lay in bed for a long time and recovered slowly.

Dream # 50
Medusa in Streams of Energy, July 22 1992

There was a school, a college, but there were no children, just adults. There was one class, where they were writing only numbers. There were two big halls.

It was as if I was sleeping, and later woke up and remembered my last action. I learned that I was doing something. When I came to my senses I had a feeling that I looked through a water column. I was watching it through my body. My vision was not coming through my eyes, but as if through a peep-hole, and I could look through this 'peephole' in any direction. The body, through which I was looking, was as condensed air, or like jelly. The real eyes were above and I was looking at the level of the navel. I had a feeling that I was bending when I looked. And I had also a feeling that I was swimming – not me, but my body. Waving a little, like a jelly-fish turned upside down on a glass.

1. The first moment I don't remember – I was coming back into the world.
2. I was looking from inside the jelly-fish. When I came to my senses this jelly-fish, as if incredibly unwound, slowed down. **And my eye could see 360 degrees around me.**
3. All the space around me was filled with some kind of energy waves. The air was either resilient, or empty. I was in these streams and started moving in them, these streams were coming through me, they stretched me. But I had to have mastery to be able to move between them, to orientate myself. They were either large, or flat, sometimes interlaced, but each one was separate like some sort of twine. The energy was more or less rich. Between them – there was emptiness. It was very pleasant, blissful. Sliding was enormously pleasant, without rubbing, inertia like a supple dance when you are pulled in. Gradually I started to notice my arms and legs and understood that my entire body was between these streams. But it was as if there were no bones, it could bend in any direction in a snake-like fashion.

****

After I visited Egypt I started checking my dreams. I noticed a pattern emerging from them. I saw some of the most unusual things – when I just closed my eyes, before I started to fall asleep or just after I woke up. Here is the list:

Case # 1 – Dream # 3 Atharvan: It was not a dream; it was after a dream, actually. I woke up, looked toward the window and closed my eyes again. And at this moment (I felt a shiver on my skin) I immediately saw the face of a man of a huge size.

Case # 2 – in Egypt: "When I turned off the light I found that my room was overcrowded with all these Egyptian "papyrus animals"! It was very sudden and unexpected... I was scared, maybe for the first time in my whole life! I turned the light on instantly and closed my eyes. But I continued seeing them!"

Case # 3 – in Canada – "Today is June 12 – 5:30p.m. I decided to take a nap for an hour. I asked my daughter to wake me up at 6:30p.m. I lay down in bed, closed my eyes and as soon as I did, I saw a girl, right near me. Her face was very close to me. I wasn't even asleep yet. While I continued looking at this face, I heard my daughter opening the entrance door and taking her bike outside."

Case # 4 –" I lay down to take a nap at 3:00 p.m. and closed my eyes. Instantly I saw the face of a huge woman looking at me through the window; she was so big, that she needed to bend to see me through the window. Her face covered almost half of the big window of my bedroom! It was so sudden that I yelled, "Oh!!!" So my daughter ran into the room and asked, "What happened?" My daughter stayed near my bed. I closed my eyes and continued to see this big woman! She was at least 8 to10 meters tall or taller – I guess – because we live on the third floor! "

My Space Dharma, Medusa

Case # 5 – "I closed my eyes, trying to take a nap right after I returned from my reading with Di Cherry and, instantly, I saw this giant, this enormous-size man near me, sitting in front of a pyramid. He bent one arm and turned toward me. Then I saw his blue eyes, so close that I even saw his breath...I even saw the wrinkles around his eyes – everything in all of the little details. I could not sleep after that... I was deeply shocked and it would be difficult for me to describe the sensation I experienced."

I can continue citing cases after cases – forever. I would just find more and more dreams. It is better to give you a few examples, showing that it usually happens right before the dreams start. I noticed that for years it mostly happens around 3:00 p.m. in the afternoon.

Now I have a question for me and for everyone who reads this. How can it be possible? Does it mean that we have another dimension world, right here, around us, on Earth – a dimension to where my mind jumps so easily, instantly and sees all of this? Or is it that these creatures, Spirits, Goddesses are always around us and wait until we close our eyes to show themselves? After all of this, when I heard how a woman passing by, under my window, said to a man, "Angels are watching us", I thought it was a sign! I took it literally. I thought that she didn't fully understand what she was talking about – she pronounced the words just like that, so easily – that "angels" are actually right here, around us!

And why does it always happen to me around the same time – during the day and during the night? Even when we switch from standard to daylight-saving time, it happens at the same time on the clock – three o'clock in the morning or in the afternoon – that I see amazing things.

****

The dream described below is the longest dream I have had thus far. I named it the "Violet field" or "Stalker". This dream is for someone who has the patience to read it – it is pretty long. You can easily skip some parts of it and still be safe, avoiding the dangerous trip to the violet field, which is full of temptations... "It was on the edge of something larger than death."

I am visiting that place from time to time. I don't know my goal for doing this, but I guess I am looking, hunting for the real deal: "Deep Quality Danger Spots" on our planet and in space in order to exercise and continue to develop my Spirit.

Well, as everybody knows, Amelia was fearless during her life, me – I am the same. Here is an example of our "parent" Spirit, his daily routine and what this Spirit, which was in Amelia's body before, and is now in my body, may fear.

Dream # 51
The Violet Field or the Stalker

Today, it was real, palpable, on the brink of every imaginable danger. I do not remember all of the details and oddities now.
I woke up at 3:00 a.m. Weird dreams always happened at three o'clock – I would wake up at 3:00. For me, it is usually time to enter the other reality. An extraordinary state would engulf me, worry me at 3:00 a.m., when I was in my cozy home near Moscow. Nobody disturbed me there. I could control my sensations.
There is an odd Zone. It can be compared, in modern language, to virtual reality, an unusual one. Nobody would put on special glasses to visit it, though. I simply step out – and I am at the beginning of the road, and I start walking. I know this road, I am aware that there are three levels of complexity on this path.
The first one is the **Fore-Zone,** and then there is the Zone itself. Inside this Zone there is a remote site representing the purpose and the meaning of the whole Zone. In my mind, the name of this site sounded like the "Violet Field". It was a sensation of incredible danger, of distant definite end, of unbelievable difficulty of reaching this end, and, at the same time, there was a sense of attraction to the Zone. **For instance, a person lives this present life and then transcends not into a different person, but into the same being at a different level.** It's impossible even to compare this to a caterpillar's transformation into a butterfly. It is entirely different – a mutation, a transfiguration, a sensation of violets growing very dense, extremely dangerous, blossoming on the edge between life and death. However, since there was no life in this dream, it was on the edge of something larger than death. (Larger then death in real life can be when your SPIRIT, your Hologram will be eaten by someone from other alien race for example. You should remember that it is easy to protect your own Hologram, simply NOT to AGREE to be eaten. In this condition aliens cannot consume your Spirit. This sound crazy, but this is what it is.)
People were flowing in this direction, constantly – one by one, two by two, and groups of them. I saw them walking the first stretch – only the first. Nobody returned from there. It's rare when somebody comes back. They lose their minds there, they lose their self, and they lose their identity. They dissolve into nothingness. The Thing devours them. I can tell from experience – I have never seen anybody coming back – nobody returning. I know that they stay there, dissolve, the Thing annihilates

or destroys them. It would be ridiculous to say that the Thing "eats" them; the Thing is too grand for this, too ingenious, beautiful, and people are only tiny insects compared to its "magnificence".

I felt that this was real, that it existed on our planet. Perhaps it is our astral world, where individuals with extraordinary psychic abilities could enter. This reality sucks them in; it is made for this purpose. They enter it in their meditations perhaps... Afterwards, they cannot live in our reality as people, as persons. One should have a very strong core, stronger than all of these enticements. A certain entity – intelligent, energetic, of divine power – has created the **Thing.** There are lures and temptations everywhere. They hold a person there. Everything is based on unusual matters that can entice a person away, so they would forget their essence, forget that they are human beings, and forget their structure.

Everything is arranged to infatuate a person, to make them lose themselves, then the Thing swallows them up. For example they say – "he's going mad." He doesn't remember himself, as if his mind or brain has been pulled out.

This road looks like a forest road – it's smooth, trees on one side, sunshine seeping through. Cars never drive along this road. There are two footpaths: one is ascending, the other descending. One should climb up and up, all the time; walk with effort on these paths. It is smooth, but one has to make an effort to travel these paths. The central, even road, perhaps, just divides ascending and descending footpaths. This is the first section of the road.

When you approach the Zone's entrance, there are guards standing in a row stretching to the horizon. These men in uniform look like military-men, they all look alike. They are dressed in something austere, black perhaps. They make up a fence preventing people from wandering outside the paths. I have approached them many times; three times I have entered and walked out. When I saw ascending people, I snickered to myself, "They will notice the guards now and will think that it's real." I knew for sure, that all this was unreal – this being created everything. People are trapped from the very beginning. Those guards are a border between states.

I have no idea why nobody else knows this fact. The Thing created everything in the Zone – all these oddities and extravagances within it. In fact, it doesn't exist. That is, it does exist, but the Thing controls and constantly changes it. It is evolving and moving. I have an approximate map of its location, in my mind; I know how to reach the **Violet Field.** It is a large stretch of land with a piece of seashore inhabited by weird creatures. But the sea is without depth and continuum. I remember all of the details and nuances of this Thing in the morning and during the night – when I have the dream.

After that – the **Bald Hill.** You could meet lots of people there. They attained an incongruous size somehow. I knew one creature (it can be called a woman, I think), maybe I have met "her" briefly once. I know that I have entered the Zone many times and have addressed her, but this woman wouldn't hear me, wouldn't recognize me; I hadn't had any opportunity to help her. This time I saw her again for a fleeting moment. Now and then I could see something in her eyes, as if she had recognized me, but she was not sure from where. All her memory – of her previous life, of me, of herself – had disappeared; she didn't remember that we are all human beings. This time, when I was passing by these weird creatures from the sea, I spotted this woman on the Bald Hill. It is always windy on the Hill; a whirlwind is always swooping over the top of it. The Hill is not very high, just trampled down into a balding shape; those creatures are constantly rushing about up there. They are not beings, not human beings. There is not much space there, but protuberances sprout out and turbulences are speeding about all the time, thus all the people there are moving oddly fast, whirling about, like constantly moving, flying objects, at great speed within this restricted space, non-stop. Each of the creatures has something like a shoot or wing – a triangle, similar to a sail, larger than they are – a precise triangle that looks like a boomerang, or a moon crescent on its back. I hadn't got such a thing for I was not a lost soul. The rest of them had dissolved already, but these were still rushing about between heaven and hell. I was aware that their conscience was full of those ethereal creatures around them.

I realized with astonishment (I was awake) that within an hour I visited the place, let's say, three times. When I was there for the first time, I had seen this woman but done nothing. The next time I saw her, her glance reminded me of something. Once I arrived to a small town (it was two weeks before my departure to Canada) and met a girl, who greeted me, mumbling something without changing her facial expression; she didn't recognize me, couldn't grasp my existence, her glance was wandering vaguely. Probably people on drugs look like this. Now this woman's stare reminded me of this girl's expression. I've made an enormous effort to help her out, beyond the guards' line. In fact, I rescued her. Let's assume that four years of my life have passed between my second and third visit to the Zone, but my dream lasted only an hour!

She wouldn't recognize me, wouldn't grasp my presence. Her glance was wandering helplessly, unfocused, noticing only those chimerical creatures around her. I could see her consciousness in the shape of a medusa, which doesn't have anything solid in it, everything had been dissolved. I started throwing sand into this consciousness; to help these dispersed molecules regain a reverse memory and to restore, to rebuild its lost, inner fragile structure into something remotely resembling the previous one – to shape it into a tree with branches, to create the inner star which unites the jellyfish-like brain's outgrowths, to create a skeleton from it.

When all this was organized, then she started to see and perceive me. She had such a perception of me – it happens with religious fanatics – she did not respect me. They respect and worship only this essence that created this wonderland. She was still fanatically faithful to it. But at this moment she could feel herself as a separate being, like a grain. The separation had happened already, although minimal, from this terrible creature. I pulled her out in such a condition, with great difficulty, and left her alone.

Somehow, the ones who lost their minds were very heavy. It felt as I was pulling a long train, a machine weighing tons. While they are in the Zone, they become laden with an indescribable burden. It is not clear how these heavy creatures could swirl on such a small piece of land. They fly up and down with their wing. They do not slide on the ground; therefore, they have more space, in all directions. They are moving in the streams. It is strange, and hard to watch. This Thing is pulling them around; they do not belong to themselves.

I had my own goal. My goal always is to get through all the unusual and strange things that come across my path and not to lose my way, to feel intuitively this *Violet Field*, to come to it. It is a very complicated, very difficult task. I'll explain why. The qualities of Virgo are very important things in life. I looked at their plan from above. I was smiling to myself – I knew all the tricks of this "madam", this very cunning creature. I knew that she was doing it for the benefit of better prepared persons like me. She changes all the time the inner disposition. She does not change everything, though; otherwise a person would begin to feel lurking danger and concentrate. She does it cleverly. I needed to go through long **Furrowed Fields.** A person is walking, taking the usual route. He has been here many times. He does not notice the matters beside him, although they would attract anyone's attention, indeed. He knows that beyond the *Furrowed Fields,* there is a glass – the White Palace, which I called, for all intents and purposes, the 'Laboratory'. At the entrance, there is always a woman dressed in white. What is behind the laboratory? There are different things; white stairs, the woods..., thousands of different things. He keeps this in mind, the plan, and everything in its place, just slightly changed. Yet his plan becomes worthless already; he goes by the wayside...

The laboratory is made of light glass, as a glass palace, as the cosmic UFOs, as described by witnesses. At the laboratory's entrance the woman, in white clothes, waits for you and then guides you inside. You should pass through a lot of labyrinths inside. There is a room of rooms, room of rooms, in which there are various and frightening creatures – frightening by their unusual appearance, variety, attractiveness, fearful incomprehensibility. You don't know what they are, it is impossible to understand it with your mind. They are frightful because they always stop you. They always attract attention. I always stop in front of each of them, and this contact between us is like a struggle between them and me to overcome them or at least to stay equal. To bear their influence, it takes three to five minutes – to pass this test. You cannot circumvent this building, and you cannot avoid these creatures.

Two of them caught hold of me strongly and *absorbed* my condition. They brought an indescribable horror into my soul. I knew, that I was dreaming, that it was a created reality, so I decided to imagine this road full of these soldiers, to stop my journey, and not to allow myself to wake up right away. First, I had simply to come out, and wake up after that. It was important. I don't remember how many times it happened prior to this one particular episode. Yet, I remember how many times I reached this clearing, perhaps I never came near it. I made a decision, that now I should get out of here immediately. At that moment, this line of soldiers and this road appeared clearly, in my mind's eye – before my eyes.

Maybe, I don't know, maybe I had not come to it, maybe time after time I went farther and farther inward, getting used to these substances, trying to get through them farther and farther – it seems like it. Since I passed the Bald Hill easily, the sea, the fields with blueberries, I knew their dangers, specificities, what exactly is dangerous about them. For the first time there were these two essences; I had a really good look at them and I survived their contact. They were in one room, on the right and on the left of me. I was allowed to enter the laboratory and this woman brought me in (usually she was only at the entrance, and I thought, *this is something new*). Maybe there are a few of them, they all look alike and not one of them is authentic. How talented, a genius, is the one who invented them! It is beyond any rational thinking. You can't absorb it with your mind, with your senses, with your intuition...

They looked alike as if from one family. They did not have anything, which could be referred to as fear on Earth. Usually you can recognize your enemy by its features – when it is a vampire, or predator, they have fangs, tentacles, poisonous saliva – everything that attacks you and ruins your body. They had nothing that ruins your physical body. I don't remember my body, by the way. You could accept with your mind that they were in two ***aquariums.*** They certainly were in a watery substance. Let's assume that these aquariums were suspended in the air – as large as a room – such an aquarium, and everyone in it was filling it almost to the rim. They were about three meters high, but their power, strength seemed not to match; they were even stronger, more powerful.

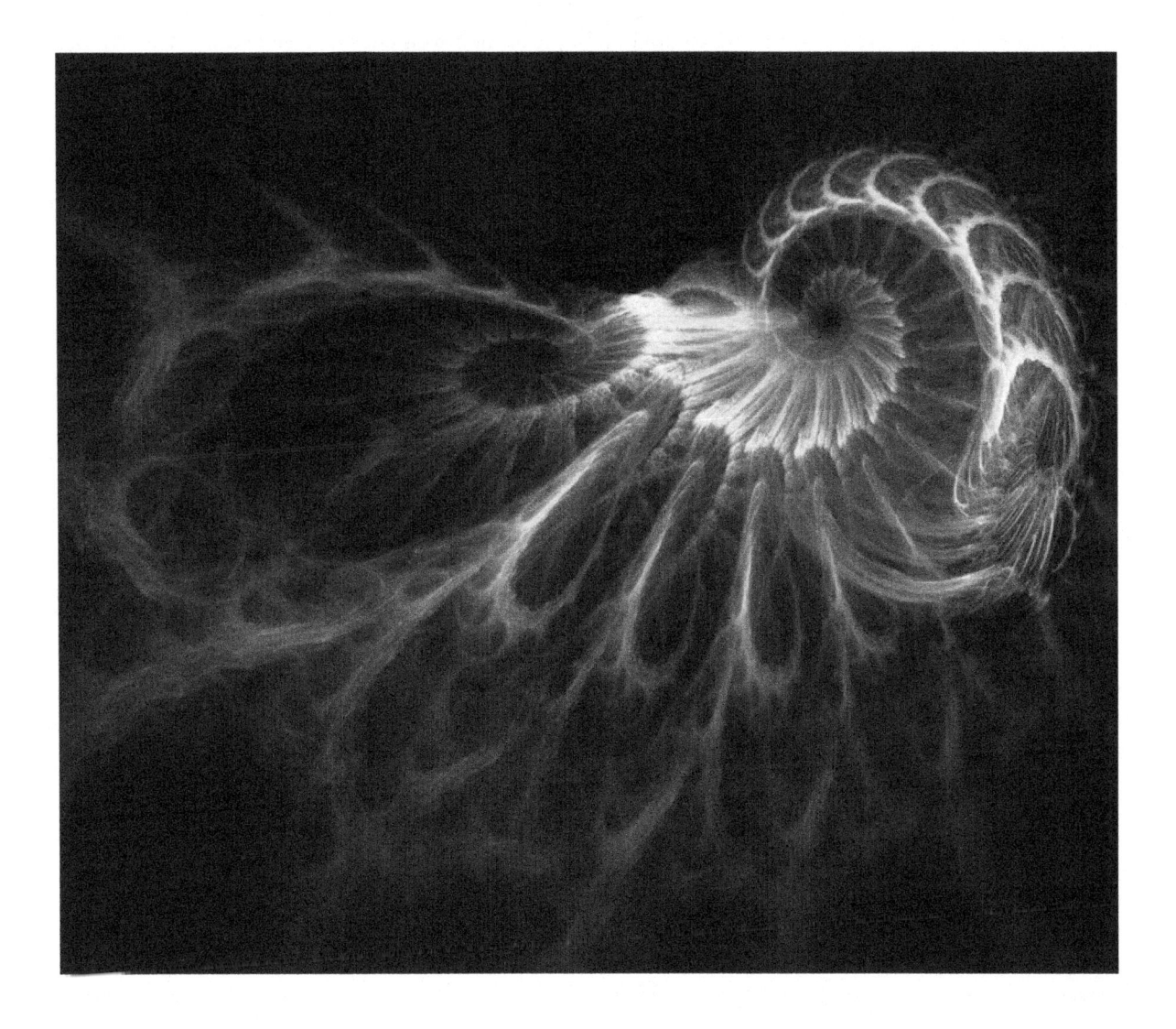

Then there was a form of salutation, when golden rays – millions of golden rays – came out of a spherical point. There were a million rays; it looked like a jelly-fish. But if the salute was golden when it shot above water, it dissolved into a fog of stripes, as black smoke going through water, as streams of ink from a squid, but they did not disappear, they remained in suspension in the water. But up there, on top, the spherical point had merged into a myriad of these stripes – unmovable billions of stripes. There were not any movement there; no sound, no color practically, no sense of physical density – was it hard or soft – no parameters by which to describe it. Between them there was a difference in colors, the other one was darker and denser. I was horrified by the second one.
There was a difference in what they were sending to me – what defines the meaning of their existence. It was like a struggle, torture at the verge of my ... strength, I cannot say nerves, since nerves exist only in real life. I stood in front of one of them at first, then in front of the other. I approached her, to face her, very closely. There was no other way. It was a conscious move, she felt me very strongly, everything I represent. That is why her knowledge about me makes her stronger

and gives her an opportunity to affect me selectively – in those areas, where I feel her. She affected me even more – she concentrated and put pressure on me.

There was a constant flow, which comes from her to me. It comes but does not approach, because it came in pulsation. And here – it is like a field, constant field, it pulls you. I was not frightened of the fact that it pulls me, like the others; I entered and approached to a certain distance from which she could affect me, but to be in her field was a hard test. There was no fear – they all are unknown, incomprehensible, so to speak – it is the first stage, where the water is...

There are just strange forms and it attracts people. Here the forms are unimportant, and they capture you deeper; they penetrate, test you, and evaluate your human structure. Maybe something which is beyond intuition? I don't know what this feeling is, what kind of sensation a human can experience. But to be in this field felt like unconscious fear, horror. You are in this condition and do not know what it may bring you. This condition is unbearable; it is on the verge of ... of all capacities. The only sensation I remember of me was that my solar plexus was attacked; there was pain, severe pain. There was a very strong physical tension after strengthening my loins and shielding my being. I felt as if I had used all of my energy – I was spent – and decided to return. But later – it was so strange – I came to another room and went to sleep again.

There were two of them – the initiators that led me there, they knew – and a third one who just tagged along. I looked carefully at this small person (people appear pathetic there, insignificant – not because of their size, but because of their inability to cope) and it seemed that it was a girl I know ... I remember ... I evaluated them – that they are unable to get anywhere, that they would not come back. But this one I knew and she seemed to recognize me. And what did I do? I returned. I entered into that Zone with them, walked them to the edge, showed them a little, and took them back. I had shown them – only from the side – what is there and how it is, and I marked on somewhat of a plan that there, on the right of me, diagonally, straight from my shoulder was the *Violet Field*. Perhaps when I entered, I always looked from above. Immediately, I thought, "Oh my God, I was here just now, but everything had changed already.

The Furrowed fields, the Sea, the Bald Hill, the Cranberry Plantation (like in English parks – they cut labyrinths), the Laboratory, and there is a mass, a million of different things." I just realized that these initial things, which existed from the beginning, had changed already. There are no fields anymore, or they are moved aside, and in their place, there is something inserted – the *clearing of solar prominences* (fiery gasses which interact with each other). It is like a mosaic, but there is, say, a hundred colors and variations, and here they are endless. You should always remember what was there before, what has changed, where it was before, to evaluate yourself, if something new appears, to evaluate this new thing and yourself, your capacities. You should do it, in order to define if you've passed three new zones, but ten of them you may be incapable to pass. The plan, like a map, is retraced with everything in repeated renewal.

When I was coming back with that non-authentic girl, I saw from the corner of my eye, that those who had followed us did not come back. And I was holding her all the time. I photographed the first third of the route in my mind (I could not capture it as a whole) – and it had changed – very cunningly changed. So to pass through it all, you need to remember your goal, to have a sense of the *Violet Field* and walk through it with your eyes closed. And once you got used to it, and you recognize something, everything is familiar. You walk and walk, and then suddenly, you will stray off course.

It always feels as if an undefined anxiety envelops you while you are in the Zone. Time changes all the time there – with the changes of mosaics it twists, it screws and with it the fields drop out, then they appear again. The principle of appearance and disappearance – they do it by changing time. Space and time is one substance, you cannot separate them. You are once in the past, then in the present, then in the future. You get from one thing to another with temporal changes. There is no future or past – it is just different times. It is not linear, as on Earth; it is unintelligible to me and it is frightening, inexplicable. There are some lapses constantly – you walk straight, and then suddenly fall into another pit.

The sea is conditional. It is not something going far into infinity. It began conditionally and finished right away after coming to depth – instantly. There was a million of different things, creatures, expressions, movements. I can say only one thing – all this was soundless, and colorless. Maybe everything there was gray-white-black. There were not any shades of color. Some kind of an astral world where there are no colors. The only things that had color were the violets. They were of a deep violet color. I remember it with my eyes. Then again, I don't think that there were any flowers there. Perhaps it was some surface, substance into which you enter, up to your ankles, and in which you stay, some energy-like thing ... but it is, I know for sure, situated on a flat surface. You should enter it as you would a field. Maybe it radiates energy upwards and you stay in it like in the *aquarium*...

There were elements – like water, like wind, hurricane, and fire. There were time lapses. Everything was happening in some space, where some flows, unintelligible to your mind were not linear, not in three-dimensional space, but more-dimensional. For instance, those lost souls on the Bald Hill, you could see by their movements, what sort of field was there, what kind of streams. Everybody was walking there – they were attracted to it, like someone is attracted to greed, greed to possess a treasure; they either knew or felt it, they were drawn to it. When at the beginning they walked this thorny path, they walked in all consciousness; something interested them, maybe they had a presentiment of the *Violet Field*, but they did not anticipate the hardships that were awaiting them. They were drawn as if by a magnet, like bees to honey... They wanted it very much. They all walked, driven by an impulse. They had only enough energy to come to the soldiers, but not enough for more. (I suspected that the THING eat energy of the visitors, or their whole HOLOGRAM)

My strength was in knowing, in feeling, that those ones were not soldiers, and the water was not water – that all of this was not real, not genuine, that it does not exist. The danger resides in something else.

Here short part of one Testimonial from the Testimonials section of the book. I did met Martin and we did visit this place. We saw numerous Spirits there in day light, some come close and I felt how they start touch me. Most amazing that layers of different times all at once, at the same, time was presented there! One mirage instantly like a wave change to another mirage...you can see how this place was looks at different time in the past and maybe in future as well.

" I know how important your story about the Violet is. It is not only a dream because I know this field really exist in the Netherlands. On this field are important 2500 years old graves of spiritual leadership like that of Odin and Svadi. Svadi was a son of Thor, his mother the daughter of king Priam of Troy. The Violet field is known as 'splendor field'. Its location is referenced twice in Voluspa in the Poetic Edda as 'Ithavoll', as a meeting place of the gods."
Martin van Wieringen The Netherlands

Looks like "Violet field" which I described in my dream also located here but in another dimension. Interesting that here also name Svadi connected with Violet Field. About Svadi and why my pin name Svadi Hatra you will read in next chapter.

Chapter 6

KUKULCAN

© Josephine Wall. All Rights Reserved. www.josephinewall.com

Dream # 51.
Kukulcan ? (Human-Lizard), September 19, 1991.

The sky is the color of alexandrite, a violet gemstone. Everything around is yellow – it is clay. This clay consists of polyhedrons, which are stuck together, like graphite, stratified.
The time of day hard to say, there was no sun, but it was very light, similar to a white night in the North Pole. He had the same violet eyes as the sky, with orange, round pupils. He looked like a lizard – a man-lizard with human face. He was half-sitting.
He is green – the scales of cactus petals, but not prickly. Near the temples, the scales are small, then they become bigger and bigger and grow into a beautiful crest on his head. It looks very neat and precise. He did not react to me, so to speak. I looked at him from all sides. At the beginning, I felt as

if his skin was on me, and I began to transform into *it*. (Maybe I was him? And saw myself from the side?)

He was very quiet. There was a feeling of deep, unknown mystery or wisdom, enveloping him, like an aura. The green emerald scales were covering his skin, which was glowing under them. Maybe the skin was bright orange. I think, yes, it was of a glowing, orange color. He looked like a well-designed, very detailed piece of jewelry, but real, and alive at the same time, which made him even more priceless. We were near each other for some time. I don't recollect now what happened afterwards.

I woke up and looked at the clock near my bed. The day was **19.09.1991**. The memory of him stayed with me for maybe a month until I began to see him again and again. I saw him about 8 to 10 times during that year. He is a "really cool guy", adorable in his perfection. He is like a beautiful, rare toy with an electronic mechanism inside him. I describe him as having "electronic insides", perhaps because he seems so advanced and modern to me.

****

Now, 17 years later, suddenly this particular hairstyle, with a crest, is in fashion for boys. Every time I see a boy with such a hairstyle, it reminds me of my lizard friend. I then decided to draw him, to show you what I mean or to remind myself how he looked at the time I had that first dream of him.

When I was looking for a pencil, I came across some advertising pamphlet that said, *"The future is friendly."* (TELUS © all rights reserved) This is good news, by the way!

While I was drawing him I began to think that it is possible that I like him because he is green, the color of plants and his scales are like cactus leaves, which gives him this rare human and plant look. My dream has come true! I always wished to be as close as possible to plants – and he is two-in-one, both plant and human at the same time. I wish I could be like him!

Once I was envious, when I saw in a magazine someone's kitchen in Mexico with a real tree growing through the house! Imagine that! You could sit all day long, your body leaning against a real live tree, and type on your computer!

Well..., I sketched him very fast and here he is. I didn't draw the small scales on his human face – you can add them with your imagination.

He has a human face. He has a small nose and lips ... and long narrow eyes. (My friend already told me that artists usually draw people looking like themselves, and that, here, I drew Amelia's profile! She sent me this YOUTUBE video where she thinks Amelia's profile is identical to the profile I drew: NewsPlayer – Amelia Earhart.)

When I began paying attention to this, I made an astonishing discovery! First, boys and girls with this "punk" hairstyle may have seen these kinds of people in their dreams! They don't remember the dreams but they wish to adopt this hair style, perhaps because they feel comfortable with it, or their hair to be shaped in such a fashion is appealing to them. Similar to what I am feeling when I wear my jaguar jacket. The same is probably true of those modern people who have their whole body covered with tattoos. Maybe, in their past lives, they lived in some culture where people had tattoos on their bodies from a young age, and that's the way they used to see themselves –somewhere in Africa, or Australia or India...

Since the unusual developments that have occurred during the last five months of my life, I began seeing people in a different way. I began understanding them and being more tolerant of their choices in life. People who look weird in our eyes, all these punks, tattooed bodies, who wear strange outfits – maybe their preference with this strange, weird style comes from their past lives through their dreams.

YOUR ETERNAL HOLOGRAM

Human-lizard Being.

When I traveled through Italy this summer, near the Coliseum in Rome, I saw men in gladiators' outfits. They, too, had the same kind of plumage shape on their helmets. I found the same thing in Greece!

Lord King Pakal   **Roman Gladiator's helmet**

310

I am telling this because it happened to me and, in my life, I started adopting behaviors or following styles which I saw in my dreams; it started to be part of my lifestyle.

But let's go back to this sentence: *"When I began paying attention to this, I made an astonishing discovery!"* I started paying attention to the **SHAPE** of the head.

The hairdressers in Chichén Itzá shaped my hair in this style. They lifted my hair up and turned it towards the front of my head. They made a ponytail at the end; sometimes they divided and made two ponytails. One day they cut some of my hair because it was getting too long and I saw myself in profile – I looked exactly the way I did in my dream. The whole of my hair had been pulled to the front and lifted into a ponytail – very nice indeed.

****

Morning. I just woke up. 6:00 a.m. A heavenly, enchanting fragrance surrounds me, from the white lily near my bed... I am lying down in bed thinking about this unusual head-shape I drew yesterday. For some reason, I felt there was something important about it...

I start remembering... and now I am at my desk, typing...

There were many boys around with this hairstyle, millions of them all over the World! Some have their hair shaped in a high crest, others in smaller styles. There are all kinds of variety of this crested hairdo! But if they let their hair grow a little bit longer, it will be shaped as my lizard friend had.

Then I remembered the statue of the Lord King Pakal I saw at the hotel in Cancun; he had his hair shaped in the same fashion!

Next, I remembered things that are even much more important! This headdress or style is exactly the same as the shaped hats the Buddhists, the Egyptians, and the Mexican priests wore! All of them, all over the world, wear this shape of helmet, hat or hairstyle!

My aunt, Mary, told me that when I was a little girl I loved a woolen hat with a little pompom on top. I even wanted to sleep with it on. Then I started paying attention to what she said. The shape of this baby's hat was exactly the same as the hairstyle worn by this "priest". See first photo in this book.

Later, on the same day, I was sitting on my favorite bench in the rose garden in Stanley Park. I was drawing the Buddhists' hats. Well, it is not really comfortable to draw with your sketch book in your lap, but you will have idea what I am talking about.

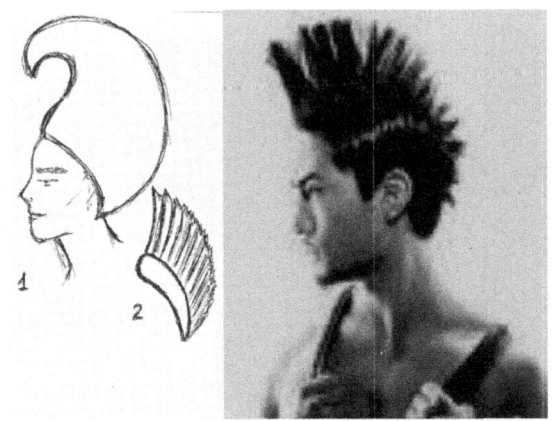

1: International Priests hat shape
#2: Buddhist hat looks like Roman Gladiator's helmet

O my God! **God...????**
When, I searched *"god with scales"* on one smart website: http://www.crystalinks.com/
God with scales, here's what came out!!!
One entity played key roles as creator in Egypt, Sumer, India, China among other myths about creation. In Mesoamerica and Peru he was known as Quetzalcoatl, among other roles he played. His

pyramid was the Pyramid of the Sun in Teotihuacán Quetzalcoatl ("feathered snake") is the Aztec name for the Feathered-Serpent deity of ancient Mesoamerica, one of the main gods of many Mexican and northern Central American civilizations.

The name "Quetzalcoatl" literally means quetzal-bird snake or serpent with feathers of the Quetzal (which implies something divine or precious) in the Nahuatl language. The meaning of his local name in other Mesoamerican languages is similar. The Maya knew him as Kukulkán; the Quiché as Gukumatz.

The Feathered Serpent deity was important in art and religion in most of Mesoamerica for close to 2,000 years, from the Pre-Classic era until the Spanish Conquest. Civilizations worshiping the Feathered Serpent included the Olmec, the Mixtec, the Toltec, the Aztec, and the Maya.

http://www.crystalinks.com/quetzalcoatl.html

He was known as the inventor of books and the calendar, the giver of maize corn to mankind, and sometimes as a symbol of death and resurrection. Quetzalcoatl was also the patron of the priests and the title of the Aztec high priest.

Next I found: Snake-bird gods fascinated both Aztecs and pharaohs, By Robin Emmott.

*Ancient Mexicans and Egyptians who never met and lived centuries and thousands of miles apart both worshiped feathered-serpent deities, built pyramids and developed a 365-day calendar, a new exhibition shows." There are huge cultural parallels between ancient Egypt and Mexico in religion, astronomy, architecture and the arts. The exhibition, which opened at the weekend in the northern Mexican city of Monterrey, shows how Mexican civilizations worshiped the feathered snake god Quetzalcoatl from about 1,200 BC to 1521, when the Spanish conquered the Aztecs. From 3000 BC onward Egyptians often portrayed their gods, including the goddess of the pharaohs Isis, in art and sculpture as serpents with wings or feathers. MONTERREY, Mexico, Sept 24 (Reuters Life!)

The Sumerian God also has the same "hair style" as the one I saw on my man-lizard!

What's more, the Sumerian God has wings – symbol of his ability to fly ... and a pine cone, symbol of the genetic experiments and third eye, pineal gland. Below, he looks similar to my beautiful green human-lizard. Except mine has a **human face**, but this one more reptilian. After that, I read this sentence: *"The feathered serpent and the serpent alongside a deity signifies the duality of human existence, at once in touch with water and earth, the serpent, and the heavens, the feathers of a bird,"* said Ulloa.

Flying (or "Bird") God and Sumerian God, Ashur
"The Sumerian Gods Created a Biogenetic Experiment Called Humans"

http://africa.reuters.com/wire/news/usnN24278139.html
Don't you think it sounds too complicated? I think, in reality, it is much easier.

Here is what this is really about...
It is Reptilian & Lizard from very advance civilization visiting Mexico and other countries in the past, and people made him God. He has scales, so they call him lizard or snake. He arrived in some "flying object", so they also started adding bird qualities, such as feathers to his representation, wings that would give him the ability to fly. They called him **"Quetzalcoatl",** using two words together: bird-snake and serpent with feathers. *(The name "Quetzalcoatl" literally means quetzal-bird snake or serpent with feathers of the Quetzal.)* This is it! Nothing more.

Note: The original writings and drawings of this dream and all other dreams exist. At the time I had this dream, in 1991, I had no idea who this lizard man was. I didn't have any idea that I would see similar to him, but another one, with reptilian face **"Quetzalcoatl",** in Mexico 17 years later!

I repeat again here: It is impossible for me to say that these dreams are from the Past or from the Future. I see it like a spooled thread, rolling one over the other and the other, and each of them is a span of time. Spooling the thread of ages in this manner explains that they are very close to each other, and running parallel to one another in space.

Quetzalcoatl & Bas-relief from Chichén Itzá, can you see men with the mask?

At the same time, if a wormhole is formed amid the threads of this bobbin, it can be easily understood how people, ships, trains, animals disappeared in one place, only to re-appear in a different place at a different time – traveling from one time to another.

A New Mexican Membreno Apache chief told me recently that at certain times in human history, the past and the present snap back together as if they were two ends of a gigantic rubber band. He told me, "The past is now." (Can Humpty Dumpty be put back together again? Gene D. Matlock © Copyright 2005).

Ouroboros is an ancient alchemy symbol depicting a snake or dragon swallowing its own tail, constantly creating itself and forming a circle. It is the Wheel of Time - The Alchemy Wheel – 12 around 1 to manifest grid programs that give the illusion of linear time allowing souls to experience emotions.

YOUR ETERNAL HOLOGRAM

Quetzalcoatl pyramid

Ouroboros is associated with Alchemy, Gnosticism and Hermeticism. It represents the cyclical nature of things, eternal return, and other things perceived as cycles that begin anew as soon as they end. In some representations the serpent is shown as half-light and half dark, echoing symbols such as the Yin Yang which illustrates the dual nature of all things, but more importantly that these opposites are not in conflict. Origins of the Ouroboros: The serpent or dragon eating its own tail has survived from antiquity and can be traced back to Ancient Egypt, circa 1600 BCE. Crystallink.

Snake eating tail, Ouroboros

From another point of view, I was a Mexican Priest in Chichén Itzá. According to Gene Matlock, during my past life as a Priest, I could meet people from the past and future in real life, travel through the Universe and perhaps visit Egypt. This is why I saw the Egyptian Anubis during the sacrifice ceremony on the top of the pyramid in the temple, and one man was there wearing an Egyptian hat, like that of the Nefertiti statues. Maybe he had the same long skull like Nefertiti and belong to "teachers".

As with all Myths about Gods and Goddesses, Mayan creational mythology discusses connections with being from other realms that came to Earth to seed the planet. Many people connect the story of the Popol Vuh with a story of extraterrestrial Gods and made man in their own image Within Mayan culture they have legends of visiting Gods from outer space. As in all creational myths, religions, and prophecies, the gods promise to return one day (Maya Gods and Goddesses, CRYSTALINKS).

In Chichén Itzá, the God KUKULCAN, looks like a man inside the jaw of a snake or serpent. On the sculpture of a bas-relief – the God Kukulcan is inside a flying snake.

What about this flying serpent? I mean this airplane which looks like a snake?

With whom, (me as a Priest) did I have contact in that Dream # 5 – The Upper Kingdom, October 24, 1993? Well, I have some ideas about it.
I brought my creatures to this THING. Then something crawled out to meet me. It had green spots all over his white body. The wise one. It appeared, suspended in front of me. It was speaking with a soft voice, like Kaa (the huge snake in the cartoon about the Indian boy, Maugli). It said to me, "I will save yours, the little ones." And it began to unwind, unroll, as if it was crawling out of an invisible crack in the wall. There was an opening and it crawled out – I didn't see the inside of the place. It was growing in size – expanding, and became as big as a Hercules plane. From the tail a huge crack opened across its body leading my creatures inside it. Its head was flat, like a leaf. The crack was in the lower side – and my creatures started walking inside IT.

It is always a question for me, **Who or What is this THING?**
First, I know there is a legend in India, describing the civilization of Nag, which existed a long time ago. Nagy is a snake which is highly intelligent. Many temples in India have a snake represented in their construction – sometimes many heads are sculpted together. Even the steps on the temples – like those in Chichén Itzá – have snakes statues on both sides at the foot of the stairs. Maybe it was some kind of real live creatures that existed in ancient times – some kind of intelligent, huge snake, a descendant of the dinosaur's family.*Rudyard Kipling, Rikki-Tikki-Tavi*
"Who is Nag?" said he. "I am Nag. The great God Brahm put his mark upon all our people, when the first cobra spread his hood to keep the sun off Brahm as he slept. Look, and be afraid!" He spread out his hood more than ever, and Rikki-tikki saw the spectacle-mark on the back of it that looks exactly like the eye part of a hook-and-eye fastening.

Let's go back to my dream. The entrance to this THING reminded me instantly of this snake's jaw, near the pyramid stairs in Chichén Itzá and that of an airplane. Just a month after I had the dream with my human-lizard I had another dream, in which I saw an airplane or starship entirely covered with scales, similar to snake scales.

Dream # 53.
Starship with Fish Scales, October 21, 1991

Dream # 1: (It was 2 dreams in one night.)
There was a church. Everyone was dressed in an old-fashion way. I turned up in this church on previous occasions. There were two great-grandmothers. Everything was going on properly. I was talking to my great-grandmothers – they were very attentive and polite. They were well dressed. Later on, I unexpectedly collapsed to the ground but something pulled me out of my trance immediately. And I turned up in a cosmic ship instantly. It was high – no gravity. The ship was the shape of a fish inside, narrowing at the ends; the floor was transparent, as if we were inside a bottle. It was important that there were no cracks and cavities, because it affected the ship's movement. The inside shape was also connected with its movement. Ahead there were two figures – with their backs to us.

YOUR ETERNAL HOLOGRAM

Lockheed – Airplane's entrance

Snake's jaw, Chichén Itzá

Egypt, Temple of Abydos

They wore silvery hoods which were sparkling with silver lights – threads. The Guide was with me, he was showing me all this. We were doing something together – I don't remember what. And these two – the silvery ones – floated to us and we communicated. The walls of the ship were like those of a chamber where they test sound transmissions, and something – hard to explain what – was protruding from the walls. These silvery ones were smaller than me, about 130 cm high. They were all covered with big fish scales. And something protruded from him – the size of a palm. It was covered with fish scales as well. The two silvery ones were ahead of me – about 30 meters from me.

Behind me there was a round door – the size of a big multistory building, like a huge barn. But everything was closed very tightly – no cracks. In front there was a silvery screen, a background for them. The screen was about 5 or 6 meters high, and if there was a plate, it encircled it, at the side of a wing. The floor was transparent and under it – a divergent surface with a scale. They didn't wear a helmet, but something like cotton wool, fine cotton, or "energy", which resembled a halo over the saints' heads on icons... I think I have an idea now who is on the icons. On this video exact shape I saw!

YOUTUBE:UFO's with Jesus - Ancient Painting

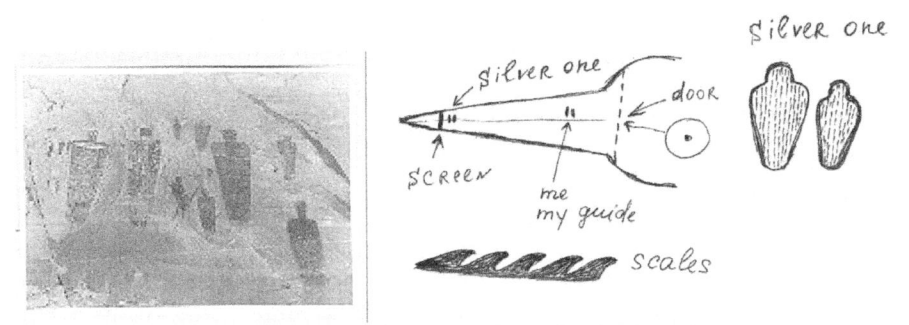

Drawing with the fish-scale airplane

Ancient paintings on rocks show other aliens the same way.
As I see them.... and how they choose to show themselves to people.

This is a picture, which was drawn by a Russian cosmonaut after he saw a strange object in space. There are similarities with the bottle shape, fish scales and so on, of my drawing. The only difference, in my dream, was that I was inside of it with my Guide and could only see left part of it.

[39]Вторжение НЛО на Землю. Скрытая правда. UFO 2016
https://www.youtube.com/watch?v=OKORgxvv6YM, startfrom2.57 min

Frescoes in Europe seem to depict space ships.
This painting shows a man in a flying apparatus. It's hanging above the altar at the Visoki Decani Monastery in Kosovo, Yugoslavia.

YOUR ETERNAL HOLOGRAM

****

In 2011, 3 of December we lived with her daughter in a luxury 5 * hotel in Bulgaria.

My daughter is an indigo child, she saw **"Spirits"** with a balcony. I ask her: "Spirit" this shape? Like in this picture on the ancient stone and my picture here? She was surprised that I knew and she said yes, it was this kind. I had fond memories of contact with them, so I did sent invitation to them telepathically.

At night I woke up from a deep sleep, when I saw that in the other room, where sleeping daughter, arrived completely different look with the face of a lizard! He was very big and chunky, he had reptilian scales and a lot of spots on the face and body, his skin was light brown in color. Eyes was round and huge, with a horizontal line and bright orange color. I even remember its characteristic odor.

Interestingly, the shape of the room was change, wall between my room and my daughter's disappeared. He showed how my daughter's face is beginning to change to my mother face and showed that it was her past life He revealed hers other past lives. Nice! But telepathically I did prohibited my daughter to have eye contact with this unusual visitor.

He spoke to me telepathically as well. He said that I am a human, as well as other type of beings, from highly development civilization, which very rare visiting Earth. And they respected my civilization. It located very far away from our galaxy! In the morning I draw his face and show to my daughter, she get scared and run ... then she told me "there were two of them!" Well, they were very smart and we respect each other. He was like a Priest &King in some way. But I prefer don't meet him again. Because was moment of disagreement, when he wish to look at my daughter and I was not agree, and he made me frozen and handling in the air for a second. So I did run beside him, touching his skin and turned light, it was exactly 12, 00, midnight! He did not like bright light and move instantly to balcony.

Kukulcan reconstitution   *One more dream*

By the way, I mentioned before that monks travel in space often, during dreams and meditation,

this is their daily routine, so they meet these Spirits from the past or the future often.
Here is one of the drawings made by a monk in 1962.

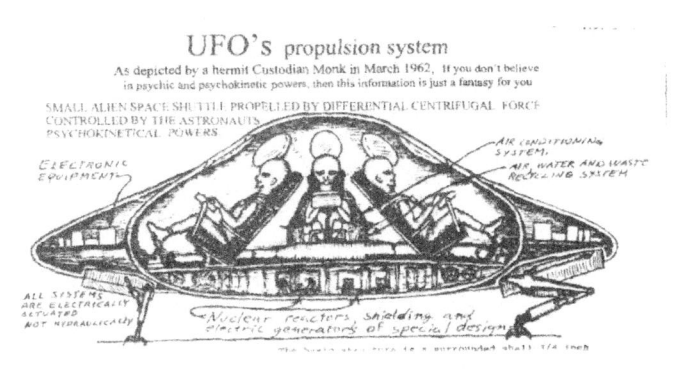

A monk's drawing

Dream # 2
Diamond chain armor (Fish Scales)

I had some dresses, beautiful – about 20 or 30 of them made of fine fabric, with embroidery, excellent.

Dress that looks like silver scales, shoes and silver suitcases, photographer Tim Orden www.timorden.com

I lived in a room, where I was putting on these dresses. There were mirrors, and the dresses were hanging around. Later on, I went shopping with my grandmother. She told the sales lady that she ordered for me – I don't remember the word – something like a corset. It was made of silver fish scales, similar to a chain armor, which is only covering the upper part of the body, not the legs or arms. The whole thing was made in one piece – no seams. It was made of something so impressive that they all gasped – they could not imagine such a thing. And it was incredibly expensive, as if they were diamonds put together. I did not see the face and figure of my grandmother ... maybe she was my other grandmother. (Well..., maybe she was Amelia's grandmother)

Standing beside black pearl shells

First, the three dreams about "scales" repeated themselves in a one month interval. I already noticed this kind of pattern before. For example, for a few months, I had dreams about crystals and palaces mostly, afterwards I dreamt only of space travels, or only about plants...
Secondly, I collect dresses and tops which are made, in parts, of material that resembles fish scales and I look like a fish or snake in them. People, young and old alike, call me a "mermaid" when I am wearing this particular dress, because I have long blond hair and it makes the set complete. I love this dress. It is also interesting to note that I was attracted to shells, which look like scales. I was working with black pearls for some time. In one photo, I stand near black pearl shells, which look like scales!

In this previous photo, I am sitting on a silver suitcase, I am wearing the silver dress, and silver shoes ... everything is just like in airplane **silver.** This is what I mean when I say that people may develop strong habits from their dreams. This suitcase is permanently near my desk, I feel very comfortable when I see it. I guess it reminds my Spirit which was before in **Amelia's body about aluminum airplane panels,** with these cute little dots on top.

At the end of the book in the part **WHO AM I?** You will find another astonishing reason why I am so much attracted to the silver color and silver metal. Now it looks like everything is in great harmony with my clothes, because, finally, I have an explanation as to WHY things are the way they are. I have some jaguar outfits, all kinds of **jaguar** shoes, bags, and gloves, etc. And now **scales**: diamond scales, **silver** outfits, silver bags and suitcases, silver-scale dresses, silver shoes, silver skirts, silver jackets, pens... Throughout my life, I just felt comfortable in these kinds of clothes, not just when they're in fashion.

YOUTUBE: AVATAR SVADI 5, Mystery numbers?

By the way, I have dreams where I am wearing also strange **fishnet outfits**. It reminds me of those Atlantis people, mummies actually, which also used it. Robert Ghost Wolf found confirmation of that fact. http://www.robertghostwolf.com/Aztlan/outheretv.htm
Amazing photos, I advise you to take a look!
They also found some sort of netting made of llama hair, using a technique that was common to the proto-Egyptian civilizations in the Mediterranean regions.
I even found some fishnet, a Barbie's gold dress, for my ferret! Yes, this is an obvious addiction to the habits from my past lives.

Our ferret, NORA LINA

WHO is this human-lizard in my dream?

Below are some excerpts from a book entitled, "Globe Teaching", about astrological predictions in 1990, which I published under the pen-name "Magician" – which I know now as the High Priest of Chichén Itzá. In this book, predictions come independently from each other. These people lived sometimes 300 to 500 years apart – no phone, internet or fax. According to the predictions of Ranio Nero, Nostradamus, Edgar Cayce and many other astrologers and prophets, climate will dramatically change on Earth. The human skin will start changing; it will start to have spots at first, and afterwards, it will start growing some form of scales to protect the skin. And our color will also change.

I have had other dreams with different kinds of people from the future. They had grey and lilac skin, lilac eyes, and their hair and nails were green. Maybe later, these extremities will develop into green scales?

Back to the green color. Maybe it will be because people will start producing chlorophyll such as plants produce, with some genetics help, or our body will start to do this without help, and, this way, they will create extra oxygen? Maybe there will be too much carbon dioxide in the air? This human with lizard scale is a really cool and brave guy!

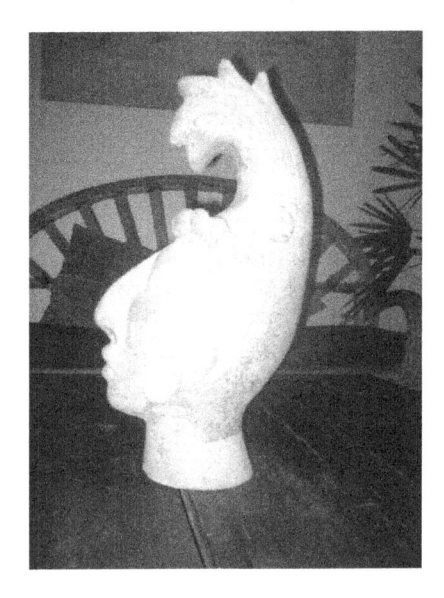

Maya warrior.   Giant iguana with white button-like "earrings"

He is the one who survived and went maybe through the million of generations and rows of transformations to attain ultimately this scaly cover, which protects him from a harmful environment. He is like a hero, like a **warrior. Warrior?** Wow, I just remembered that I saw one like him – another statue in a hotel in Tulum, Mexico. I saw the same sort of profiling and details in Maori statues, made by Pacific islanders in Hawaii.

By the way, did you see round **white huge earrings** on him? The first time I saw it during my past life hypnosis session I laughed that all men, and nobles alike, would be wearing this kind of button-like earrings! Now I know exactly why they wore these earrings!

God Kukulcan, who looked like a lizard, had these round circles about his ears such as all iguanas have! As I mentioned before, since the Maya nobles and warriors were copying Kukulcan, they also copied these round circles at the side of its head and wore these white button-like earrings!

NOW WHO IS THIS TALL LONG FIGURE IN MY DREAMS? And why do people build pyramids?

Those who are way too big, the size of huge statues? I started searching, trying to find answers for myself first of all.

It was interesting that while I was writing this book, I actually studied myself through the puzzles of my dreams and hypnosis sessions, with the help of scientific research. I found a lot of answers and now it turns into pictures and each and every one piece fits into the puzzle nicely together. I still have some "unsolved mystery", but it makes me happy and optimistic that I have the material to work with to continue my search further.

Dream # 5 – The Upper Kingdom, October 24, 1993

*There was a king in the palace. God was in the church, but he was not there, and the manager was a priest. The same with me. The symbol was a spirit; He would have come to the feast, and I am a manager, the executive. The spirit would have come, or His thoughts, or His light ... I am the lady of the kingdom. There were some creatures – not people – around me, **very tall, of huge size**. The tall-sized creatures were very different, their essences were different, like the birds, the grass, as if one would have a head of an Eagle, and the other of a Snake.*

Now see Dream # 15 - A message from the Magnificent Maya people, June 24, 2008

*I turned back and looked inside the temple. My old teacher, the Priest, is sitting with his tortoise in his hands. All my people were around me dressed in beautiful, colorful outfits with feathers, masks and shiny, luxurious jewelry. The Snake, the Eagle and Anubis were nearby as usual. They all looked at me very seriously – they were waiting in total silence. From the corner of my eye, I saw **long, tall figures**, watching all of us in the distance.*

And again these enormous, tall people in the dreams: # 3 Atharvan, October 13, 1989; Zaratustra in Water, dream # 18, September 6, 1993; dream # 19, Ruby Emerald, February 11, 1988; Woman on a Red Crystal, dream # 20, September 25, 1994.

*I saw this **giant, this enormous-size man** near me, sitting in front of a pyramid. He bent one arm and turned toward me. Then I saw his blue eyes, so close that I even saw his breath... I even saw the wrinkles around his eyes – everything in all of the little details. I could not sleep after that... I was deeply shocked and it would be difficult for me to describe the sensation I experienced.*

*Instantly I saw the face of a **huge woman** looking at me through the window, she was so big, that she needed to bend to see me through the window. Her face covered almost half of the window of my bedroom! It was so sudden that I yelled, "Oh!!!" So my daughter ran into the room and asked, "What happened?" My daughter stayed near my bed. I closed my eyes and continued to see this big woman! She was at least 7 to 8 meters tall or taller – I guess – because we live on the third floor!*

YOUTUBE:
A58 Fenomeno portal dimensional 3.43min.
Who is Looking from the sky with this huge eyes?
If you look for this on Google will be this sign with my 3 lucky numbers in once! 777, 108, 58!
777 - 108 / A58 Fenomeno portal dimensional Espiral Ovni Noruega

Why do such enormous-size statues exist in Egypt? And Rome?

This summer, I saw in the Cairo museum and in the Louvre in Paris King Akhenaton with his daughter who all had enormous, long scalps, including Nefertiti, his wife. By the way the name Nefertiti obviously comes from the word Neferu. When I asked a worker in the Cairo museum why the king and his daughter had such an unusual skull, he replied that maybe they were aliens...
Recent exploration activity in the Northern region of India uncovered the skeletal remains of a human of phenomenal size. This region of the Indian desert is called the Empty Quarter. See the photo and note the size of the two men standing in the picture in comparison to the size of the skeleton!! A very small article on this was published in Times of India - Mumbai edition on 22-Apr-2004.
I found a very clear answer to all of this with the very interesting research done by Dr. Valery Uvarov, Earth's Hidden Twin And The Birth Of Civilization (Nexus magazine, #15 Vol.5).[36]
"Let us go back 15,000 years, to the historical period that the ancient Egyptian texts call "the First Time" (Zep Tepi) or the era of the Neferu, "when the Neferu lived on the Earth and talked

with people". The word Neferu (Netheru), translated as "gods", has a complex internal structure. The descriptions of the Neferu in the texts indicate that they were human beings with god-like abilities. It was these beings who gave people knowledge of mathematics, architecture, astronomy and medicine, of the structure of the solar system, of cyclical processes and the principles lying at the foundation of the universe. All that made Egypt great was received in its time from the Neferu. It would seem that the Neferu of the ancient Egyptians and the Nephilim of the Sumerians are travelers from another planet."

YOUTUBE: Massive Skulls of the Nephilim

Alien Annunaki Illuminati who gave us Science, Language, Mathematics, etc.

© Josephine Wall. All Rights Reserved. www.josephinewall.com

Now let's follow the most important parts of this brilliant article: "Now, let us move across to the Mesopotamian region, to the land of the Sumerians (the territory of present-day Iraq and Syria). This is not a random move: there, too, people built pyramidal edifices—the stepped ziggurats. The surviving written texts and legends of the ancient Sumerians also contain many mentions of some highly developed civilizations that "descended to Earth from the heavens" and collaborated closely with the elite of Sumer.

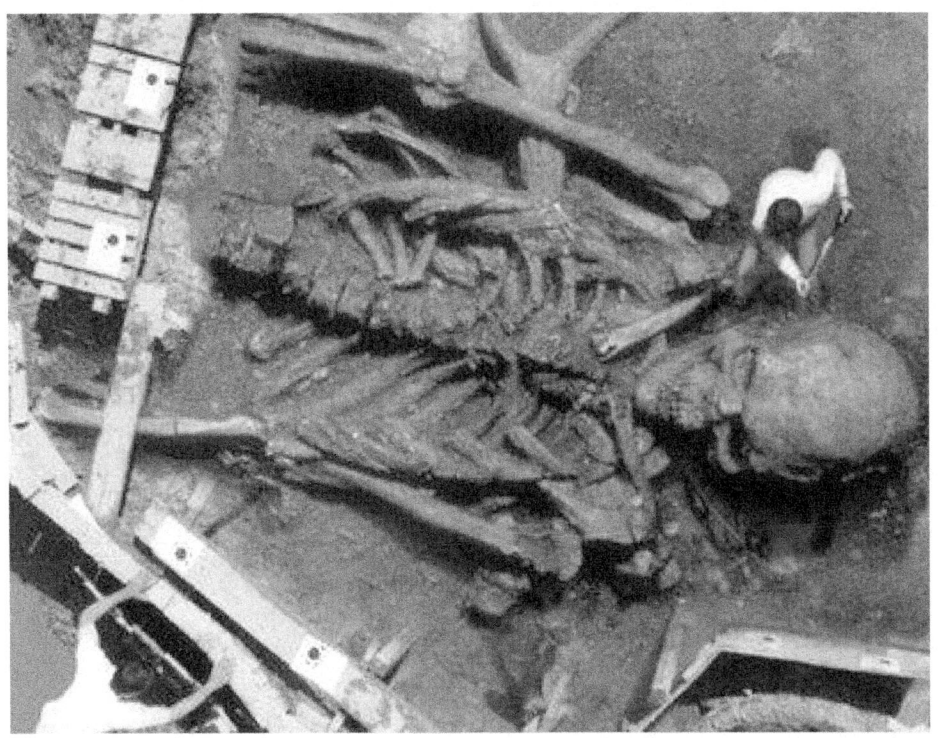

A giant in the "Empty Quarter" with the Neferu-shaped eyes

Another huger skeleton here:

Also, a GIANT NEPHILIM OF SIZE 170 FEET found. It was exposed as a result of devastation tsunami in Thailand. 170 feet is about 50 meters – the same size as Nefellium's statue near the city of Bamian in Afghanistan. *"Near this city there are five colossal statues of people from five previous races. The biggest one is a 52-meter man from the first Ephemera race. The sculpture is wrapped in a blanket that may indicate or symbolize its once fragile form."* Photo few pages below.

The interaction between "gods" and humans became so close that a number of ancient texts speak openly of the "gods" having sexual relations with "earthly maidens". The result was the birth of children with unusual genetic abilities, described in legends as "demigods", who went on to become rulers of the land of Sumer.

There is no counting the scientific achievements and technical innovations of the Sumerians, who devoted particular attention to the study of the sky and heavenly bodies, as well as of the Nephilim, the gods that "descended to Earth from the heavens".

Revelations from the Egyptian *Book of the Earth*. Let's return to Egypt, to the Valley of the Kings. We are going to visit the tomb of Ramses VI, a pharaoh of the 20th dynasty during the New Kingdom period.

As for me, I am sure the Egyptians drew this man not only as a symbol of the Sun, but a man from Neferu. Egyptians drew him with exactly the same body size proportions as compared to normal size humans. Right near him they drew an ordinary human. These discoveries of the giant skeletons support absolutely what I have been saying: these **real giant** skeletons on the previous photos with two people near them were exactly of the same proportions between the size of the giant from Neferu and the ordinary person near him. This was drawn on the wall of the *tomb of Ramses VI – fragment from the Book of the Earth, Part A, Scene 7.* The existence of this huge giant solves the mystery, which archeologists still have not explained to date: how it can be possible that different ancient structures on Earth have enormous weight and large size blocks with which they were built?

Studying the Maya, Hancock was amazed by the "computer-like circuitry" of their calendar and extraordinary precision of the calculated length planet orbits; it keeps track of eclipses, etc. Hancock proposed that the calendar was a bequest from a technologically advanced civilization of prehistory. He also thought that the image of Lord Pakal on his sarcophagus, with its "side panels, rivets, tubes and other gadgets", suggested a "technological device. Believing he had found the secret purpose of the Maya, Argüelles saw their wizard-king as representatives or avatars of galactic civilization that were post-technological".

For von Daniken, Lord Pakal was clearly an "ancient astronaut", operating the controls of some futuristic craft: *"This strange being wears a helmet from which twin tubes run backwards. In front of his nose is an oxygen apparatus. The figure is manipulating some kind of controls with both hands".* (Daniel Pinchbeck, 2012 The return of Quetzalcoatl, 2006) .This forces us to radically reassess our attitude to the surviving works of antiquity, as they probably contain priceless information about the world around us, humanity, the true history of Earth and our astonishing ancestors.

When I read this sentence, tears start running from my eyes... I was deeply touched...

Yes, here was the answer to my whole life's puzzles about my thousand unexplained dreams, visions and hypnosis sessions! All of this is part of the history of our planet and this is part of my past lives. Well what kind of expression will be on the author's face when I will tell him that his article made me cry? I guess he will be surprised.
Well, while I type this, I continue to cry right now – they're kind of happy tears. To have solved this mystery; **to know WHO I AM**; not being afraid to share my dreams with people and talk about my ultra-human abilities in my dreams and not to worry anymore that people would think that something is wrong with me or that I am just crazy (I am not) feels wonderful!. Here is the proof.

"Contact between the Neferu and Earthlings began long before the events described and was initiated by the Neferu themselves in the process of their exploration of the planets of the solar system. "The Neferu's level of development was so high that our contemporary science would simply be unable to accept it, although more than enough staggering facts have already been accumulated. In our opinion, the most mind-blowing physical evidence of the scientific and technical genius of the Neferu is the gigantic underground complex of meteorite and asteroid defenses constructed in what is now western Siberia."
Here is amazing example how this meteorite defense complex destroyed the Tunguska meteorite in 1908, the Sikhote-Alin meteorite in 1947, the Chulym bolide in 1984 and the Vitim meteorite on September 24, 2002. Argüelles proposed that the Tzolkin, their 260 - day ceremonial calendar, was the basis of Mayan esoteric technology, linking them to vast cosmic cycles and evolutionary patterns. The seemingly simple 13-by 20 matrix of the Tzolkin functioned as the basis of Mayan science and space travel, allowing them to receive and transmit information -as well as themselves-between star systems. He called Tzolkin the "Loom of Maya", and suggested they utilized in their science of divining harmony and creating resonant patterns – a science that was an art of being in the right place at the right time.
"Like galactic ants, the Maya and their civilization would be the synchronizers of momentary need-represented by planetary or solar intelligence-with universal purpose, fully conscious entry into the galactic community. Argüelles compared this mission with the goals of our present civilization: Who can say what the goals of our civilization are? Do these goals even have a relation to the planet, much less to the solar system? 'It was apparent simplicity and intricate subtleties of this Tzolkin, rather than "Encyclopedia Galactica", that the Maya had bequeathed to us to help us enter the community of galactic intelligence." (Daniel Pinchbeck, 2012 The Return of Quetzalcoatl, 2006)

"The next stage was the creation of a planet-wide communications system that provided the Neferu with extensive opportunities to stimulate the development of Earthlings' minds. To accomplish this highly complex task, a certain group of powerful Earthlings was given "instructions" on how to build structures in which they would be able to hear the "voice of god" (the Neferu) and communicate with him."
This explains why the pyramids in Egypt and Mexico have lots of similarities, simply because they receive this knowledge from the same source, the same "teacher". It also explains why, in Ancient Egypt and in Mexico, their Gods and Goddesses, elites, were wearing masks in ancient times, at the beginning of their development. Their Neferu "teacher" was under the masks. I had this feeling during my first hypnosis session when I was suddenly on the top of the Chichén Itzá pyramid. The first thing I saw near me was an enormous Eagle head-mask, the size of which was much bigger than what a normal-size human would wear. It was a strange feeling that it was either a real half human and half eagle, or not a human at all, (under this mask).
"Through visits to the "house of god" (pyramid) on the days appointed by "the gods", the chosen ones would receive knowledge "of divine origin". Using this knowledge, they would be able to improve their health, acquire exceptional abilities, "listen to the universe" and see places elsewhere

on Earth and beyond. In brief, the priests understood that the "gods" had chosen them for a great mission and that every step, every new achievement, would bring them closer to "the gods" and the "supernatural" qualities that "the gods" possessed." V. Uvarov.

Let's see this **"supernatural"** ability, which I had as a Priest. As you remember Don Julio told that my name was "Child which arrived from the stars"
Let's go back to the dreams: **Dream # 5 – The Upper Kingdom**, October 24, 1993, where I fought with some terrible, black, big and hairy creature.

*I have to fight. Then something surprising started to happen. I was looking at everything as if from some other, second sight. Suddenly there was two of me. Everything ended up very quickly - looking from the outside – incredibly simply and easily. The other me who was fighting did this – she was standing away at about two to three meters and then the beast lunged in my direction – at that same moment, that same second, an air stream appeared in front of him, very thin, **it captured him then lunged and turned in the right direction. In front of him, there was something invisible, similar to a veil with gold threads, fibers, but incredibly taut and strong, like laser rays, twisted.** There was a breath inside the veil, or something like a stream of air, invisible. This was in the air in front of him right at the moment he lunged at me with his armor. He hit the veil around him. His body was pulled into the threads, bending around and twisting to escape. It turned up, he hit, cut himself. Meanwhile I did nothing. I just stayed there and watched from the side. **Yet I knew that I had created this air-wall with threads in front of him.** And I noticed that the sickle, that had stricken him and was in his hands, looked actually like a laser disc, but larger, and incredibly thin and sharp.*

And in the same dream I was in contact with the Neferu and I saw what their "airplane" looked like.

"I brought my creatures to this THING. Then something crawled out to meet me. It said to me, "I will save yours, the little ones." And it began to unwind, unroll, as if it was crawling out of an invisible crack in the wall. There was an opening and it crawled out – I didn't see the inside of the place. It was growing in size – expanding, and became as big as a Hercules plane. From the tail a huge crack opened across its body leading my creatures inside it. Its head was flat, like a leaf."

Let's find out why pyramids were built?
Tremendous prospects opened up before human beings, the significance of which exceeded any efforts required for their accomplishment. And they began working with a will. People started building pyramids in various parts of the world according to the plans and instructions given by "the gods". The unprecedented efforts of the Earthlings and, importantly, the Earthlings' own hands, created a complex that embraced the whole Earth in a spiral running from south to north. The complex of structures included pyramids, steles, dolmens, hills and mountaintops that were given a pyramidal shape. All the elements of the complex were erected on specially selected elevated features connected with energetically active geological faults that, in the Egyptian religious tradition, were known as "the Sacred Hills of the First Time". In all, 64 of these were chosen.
The distance between pyramids belonging to the complex was 5,000 kilometers. The dolmens—which (like the chambers of the pyramids) acted as resonators, amplifying particular energy flows—were placed directly on these faults, their openings facing a distant object belonging to the complex, forming an energy-carrying circuit. The pyramids, meanwhile, were constructed with a strict north-south orientation to their sides.
By the way Valery Uvarov found that in his past live he was building pyramids in Yucatan!
You can find more in the book "Pyramid" by V. Uvarov
http://www.twelvearound1.com/PYRAMIDSPAGE.html
YOUTUBE: VALERY UVAROV: PROJECT12 - New Atlantis?
VORTEX Energy Part 1 Pyramid Energy and the Earth Grid (22 parts)

****
Amelia had a dream to write many books. So I decided that I would not put my name on this book, because I wanted, I preferred, putting her name to support her and in honor of her dream which did not come true in her lifetime – a fact that upset her deeply at the moment she was dying. I guess it is nice that a new, reborn person of the same Spirit supports her. It would have shown, once again, that this present life is not so important to me, that I rid myself of my ego and that I didn't care about having my name on the book. But my editor told me that legally I could not put Amelia's name as the author... That's sad. I was Amelia and agreed to do this now. So I decided not to put any name on it – to be "anonymous". But Roxane told me that in order to register the book and receive the ISBN copyright, the book should bear an author's name... Well this is the hardest part. After all the lives I lived, it is hard to decide which name will be the appropriate one to choose!

I haven't used my first name, for many years now – I only use it on my passport. My nickname is Yulia, which I got at a very young age and which I chose for my name. I am sure this is because it relates to Yucatan, the place where I lived as a Maya Priest. In Canada there are no one named Yulia (with a Y), so most people started calling me Julia (with a J) when I first landed in this country. Some like to call me **Jasminrose**, because I have two nicknames: *Julia and Jasminrose. Jasminrose Lily* I like a lot. I love flowers and fragrances. I am even ready to add *Flora* to those names – it would make me very happy. Amelia's name also name of the flower! But flowers and plants are just one part of me. This is a difficult situation... I just don't know my own name and I am searching for it, hoping to find it.

Once, I signed my last name on the cover of a book about astrology as *Magician.* As you know, I found out later that Magician was the name for the High Priest in Mexico. Because this book was not an autobiography, this book was written by a group of people about astrology...

No, it is not an autobiography. Yes, some facts were necessary to add from my real life, Amelia's life, in order to compare these with the other lives of the same Spirit.

This book is about a Spirit Journey through a chain of many lives. It is like a gift of rare knowledge, experiences about the existence of a much BIGGER Eternal, Spirit LIFE outside of the present one, one that each of us is living right now.

I love the name *Diamond,* diamonds are perfectly organized structures, and very strong at the same time. I could even be right on point and name myself, *Diamond Star,* because its rays are the most important product of the diamond, to shine from the INSIDE OUT and make the world around us more beautiful. But... maybe most people would think that I am trying to point to the luxury, the flashy part of it... For now Diamond Star my company and e-mail name.

Next on the list is the name *Svadi Hatra* from my dream, you will read about this dream a few pages later. This is how I am called by my "friends" and "business associates" in Space. I decided to check if there was any meaning behind the name. It meant nothing together, but the two words:

Svadi and *Hatra* support WHO I AM amazingly well!

Svadi
From Wikipedia, http://en.wikipedia.org/wiki/Svadi
Giant Svadi *from Dovre Mountain live in the north... Sea king, who is called Svadi.*

Blesanerg mountain

YOUR ETERNAL HOLOGRAM

There once was a **giant,**
Who lived on a Mountain called Blesanerg,
In the North,
His name was Svadi,
He was a son of the **Thunder** God Thor.

Yes, this is right on point. I saw many times, in my dreams, giant people and I saw myself the same size as well. The biggest statues of ancient people exist in that very same area!

The city of Bamian is located in Afghanistan, between Kabul and Bal. Near this city there are five colossal statues of people from five previous races. The biggest one is a 52-meter man from the first Ephemera race. The sculpture is wrapped in a blanket that may indicate or symbolize its once fragile form.

Amazingly also in **Svadi,** all of the letters that I have in my present last name are the same!

By the way, I just visited **Istanbul was in the Topkapi Palace.** This palace was the Imperial residence of the Ottoman sultans for almost 400 years. I saw an enormous sized sultan's outfit. I asked one of the guides in that room, "Why did the sultan have such big kaftans and pants; was he a huge sized man, a **giant?**" She replied that, "Yes, it was possible." This is it? Possible?

***Giant size kaftan belongs to sultan (IV.) Murad'a Afteditir.
(1623-1640) , photographer Darlene Laurel SV***

It is prohibited to take photos in that room, so I could only take a photo of the kaftans from around 3 meter distance. Also it lie down in the display window with an angle, not straight. So on the photo it is looks few times smaller than in reality. The sultan's pants were maybe 200 cm long, so this sultan should have been at least four -five meters tall!!

This is **no "trick photography"** – it seems as if I am "slipping" into the kaftan. Maybe it was my Spirit Guide who wanted to tell me that this kaftan belonged to me before? Maybe I was that sultan, Svadi – Giant, who lived in this area?

At **bnaiyer.com,** in blog I found a reference to **Svadi**.
Please see below. If you follow the book you will see that amazingly all main characteristics fit perfectly my Spirit: **thunder, diamond, "Supreme Being" and love to animals, plants, etc.**
(Here in the book was story about Chak Mol, Mexican hero, who in reality is Atlantean giant and his name Thunder Paw. I was his mother, queen in Atlantis and words **giant/thunder** connected with me as well, because I was also very tall and produce thunder sound by using energy devices. And see again at the end of the book part WHO am I? **body as a lightning**)
In connection to qualifications of guru and sishya, maheswara, "because of his love to all manifestation like animals and other species **(svadi)**".
"**Svadi**", I am inclined to think that refers to the attention or focus, perhaps even the love or devotion one gives to someone or something else.
My supposition here supported to some degree by Shashi Bhushan Dasgupta in his book, "Introduction to Tantric Buddhism", where he writes, "It is emphatically said in the 'Jnana-siddhi' that our Bodhi-mind, which is of the nature of the Vajra [the **diamond**], is itself the Buddha hood; so Buddha hood should be realized through conceiving all things as the self. In such a stage a man realizes himself in all things, everywhere, in all aspects, by all means and for all time, and he realizes the universalized self as the universal perfectly enlightened one.
This realization of the self as the highest being is the realization of the self as God (devata) and the process is technically call the **svadi-daivata-yoga.**
It is the Lord, the holder of the **thunder.**
What this investigation has resulted in is a) **"Supreme Being",** in light of the connection to **svadi-devata**, was not just a case of using inappropriate English words to reach a predominately Christian audience, it seems that it that there is a sense of a "Supreme Being" connected to and with the Gohonzon, though not how we in the west would normally envision Supreme Being; and it suggests that Nichiren might have been much more influenced by Tantric thought than previously believed.

Hatra

From Wikipedia, the free encyclopedia,
http://en.wikipedia.org/wiki/Hatra

Hatra *(Arabic: al-Ḥaḍr) is an ancient ruined city in the* Iraq. *It is today called al-Hadr, and it stands in the ancient* Persian *province of* Khvarvaran. *The city lies 290 km (180 miles) northwest of* Baghdad *and 110 km (68 miles) southwest of* Mosul.
Hatra was founded as an Assyrian *city by the* Seleucid Empire[1] *some time in the* 3rd century BCE. *A religious and trading centre of the* Parthian empire, *it flourished during the 1st and 2nd centuries BCE. The temples cover some 1.2 hectares and are dominated by the Great Temple, an enormous structure with vaults and columns that once rose to 30 meters. The city was famed for its fusion of* **Greek, Mesopotamian, Syrian and Arabian** *pantheons, known in* Aramaic *as Beiṯ Ĕlāhā("House of God"). The city had temples to* Nergal(Sumerian *and* Akkadian), Hermes(Greek), Atargatis (Syro-Aramaean), Allat *and* Shamiyyah (Arabian) *and* Shamash *(the* Mesopotamian Sun *god).*
Each shrine was named after a single god, and with the development of the wide ranging **Sumerian civilization** *these gods became part of a Pantheon or single family of divinities, known as the*

Annunaki (Anu = Heaven, Na = And, Ki = Earth). Rather than Anu being seen as "the god" of the heavens, he was the heavens. In this way to the earliest Sumerians, humankind lived inside a living divine realm.

*This entity Don Julio called SECOND ONE, GODDESS, who also PART of my SPIRIT – who is located in the eye of the pyramid of the **Sun**. And now! **Hatra**, City of the **Sun** God! Because the holy city is dedicated to the **Sun God**.* http://www.expatica.com/nl/whats-on/event/Hatra-City-of-the-Sun-God.html

*With the growth in size and importance of the temples, so the temple functionaries (**priests = Sumerian sanga**) grew in importance in their communities, and a hierarchy developed led by the En, or chief priest.*

Julia, Istanbul, Topkapi Palace.   *Ancient giant, real size. Afghanistan, Bamian city*

As you read my dreams through this book and hypnosis sessions, you see that I am the size of a normal human being, to 3 to 4 meters, to the size of a giant of about 8 meters and even much, much bigger – of an enormous size, maybe 50 meters or bigger, as a huge God looking down at me from the sky, to a normal size human. This "God looking down from the Sky" entity Don Julio called SECOND ONE– who is located in the eye of the pyramid of the Sun.

These are things that my dreams repeated many times and there are hundreds of dreams already like these. The more I study my dreams, the more I understand that all of this was more than real a long time ago on Earth. The same is the case with that Atlantean woman and her ultra-modern environment with most advance technology, which allowed her to travel in space at extremely high speed. Scientists found these devices and even a small computer, the size of a calculator, on the ocean floor in the drowned Atlantis.

I continue to study the history of our Earth these days to find an answer to the question, "WHO AM I?" I guess that all of the people who live on Earth have a long chain of lives going back to ancient times. I am lucky that I have the ability to remember lots of things from my past lives in my dreams, right down to the smallest details. Also, deep hypnosis sessions help in making the pictures clearer.
I mentioned Neferu or Nephilim, because I had hundreds of dreams where I am of an enormous size and, yes, with goddess-like abilities such as it is described below.

Here is a full excerpt about the statue of Nephilim in Afghanistan:
YOUTUBE: NEPHILIM DNA - ET HISTORY IN EARTH DNA - 2

I wish to repeat here again: About Nephilin: *"The city of Bamian is located in Afghanistan, between Kabul and Bal. Near this city there are five colossal statues of people from five previous races. The biggest one is a 52-meter man from the first Ephemera race. The sculpture is wrapped in a blanket that may indicate or symbolize its once fragile form".*
By the way, 52 meters is the size of a 12- or 14-storey building, depending on ceiling heights. It is interesting that in my dreams I saw myself sometimes enormously tall, looking down from the sky onto my second little self – two of me at once, second one bigger than 52 meters!

I think that the big people in my dreams – ATHARVAN, October 13, 1989; ZARATUSTRA IN WATER, September 6, 1993 – belong to Nephilim. Also, the Sumerian Goddesses Nephilim had symbols and things in their hands, outfits, which my "friends" and I were using in my dreams, when I traveled through Space.
But I don't remember using or having any of these attributes while I was an Atlantean woman living on Earth as a fragile, very light spirit human-angel kind of person, which I guess arrived from the Heavens.

From my experience during the hypnosis sessions, what happens each time is that I turn instantly into this ancient person and respond to any question without thinking. Words come out automatically, directly from that person with his or her voice; the muscles on the face move in a different way and I, Julia, can't do anything about it. I am in the position of a silent witness to all of this. The first time it happened, I was in deep shock; afterwards I started getting used to it. After my first hypnoses session I said, "It was overwhelming and I didn't have any control over what was going on. I never had experienced something like this in my entire life..."

Now, I mentioned in previous pages that it is possible that I see so many future prediction events in my dreams and this calendar looks like ancient Zoroastrian. Because I see also in the dreams Persian and Sumer Goddesses way too often: *Atharvan, Zaratustra, Ashur and Ashar.*

I even received a special Zoroastrian initiation a long time ago when I helped to legalize the Zoroastrian astrology in the Soviet Union. During an ancient Persian ritual, I received a Zoroastrian name and number conceptualized by real Zoroastrian priests! I don't follow this religion. It was fun and entertaining at the time. There were various and beautiful rituals with lots of ribbons of different colors. Well, it seems that astrology runs "through" the family. I was involved in helping to legalize the Zoroastrian astrology in the Soviet Union during this life time ... plus the Maya astrology was one of my professions, when I was a Priest in Mexico.

It is worthy to note that Mayas have a strong connection with Turkish people. Gene D. Matlock said that Turkish and Mexican people even have common cultural roots ... and he proved it. For example, his wife had a handmade bag crafted in Turkey, but in the market in Mexico, local people were sure that the bag had been made in Mexico! http://en.wikipedia.org/wiki/Gene_Matlock

Remember? Don Julio told me that the name of the **Priest was He HaiOli** which means "Arrived from the stars"! So it seems that my Spirit was in this ancient part of Iran, Iraq and Turkey, as a Neferu and Nephilim (please see below, why). Next, my Spirit was born as a Sumerian Priest, maybe the **giant Svadi** in Turkey. Later in Atlantis, my Spirit was reborn as a woman of importance, **a Queen** with a priest's responsibility at the same time. After that, in Mexico my Spirit was **a Priest** as well. Somewhere in between, Spirit was an **Egyptian royal girl** with the crown and many more, which I did not check yet. I have dreamed about living in Holland or Belgium around the 16th century.

I continue studying myself, my dreams and the history of our blue planet. The last two were **Amelia and now Julia.** As you see, it is a line of PRIESTS here. In all these past lives, I was a **PRIEST or PRIESTESS.**

Now back to Amelia Earhart,

The letter *E* # 5 and the letter *H* # 8 in the alphabet – my two lucky numbers!
HART
If you switch the *R* and *T*, it reads *HATRA*
It looks like the Spirit's real name is *Svadi Hatra* and before it was re-born in Amelia's body; it was looking for something similar and chose Amelia's parents with the last name, EarHART. So, it was right for me to choose the pen-name *Svadi Hatra* as the author of this book. By the way Amelia submitted four poems to Poetry magazine, under the alias Emil **Harte.** And I have **HATRA.** Yes, it looks like everything is in great harmony!

Now, following my example, perhaps you can imagine WHO YOU ARE?

Your own Spirit can also have a chain of many re-born lives, back to very ancient times and you may have had deep experiences at all levels, all kinds of people have lived and re-lived on this planet.

Dream # 54
You Are Svadi Hatra! June 7, 1995

This dream occurred in the daytime. Around 3:00 p.m. a little man, 2.5" tall, was dancing on the desk in front of me and talking to me very fast; he was in a happy and funny mood!
"Did you call channel 5? You just call them, tell them about yourself, who you are!"
(Channel 5 in Vancouver is where you find TV programs about inventions, science, UFO, extraterrestrials and so on.)

"You are Svadi Hatra from the Galaxy Kvazi IN. This is how we call you. You always like to start flying with your crazy high speed from this long tube, in the "bee" house."

He continued talking very, very fast... all kinds of things came out of his mouth. He poured information out, like a robot would read it to me, in a monotone voice – no inflexion in his speech, not as we usually talk – no pause either. Just round words, like beads rolling out of his mouth in a stable voice, with no emotions.
It was the same kind of dream with lots of information coming to me at high speed, such as in Dream

7 – Arabian and American Mountains – 2 pyramids: Egypt and Mexico, October 25, 1990.

His voice was talking to me very quickly – humans cannot talk that fast – it was saying different things, which I could not memorize. The views were replacing each other, the voice followed with information – very even; all phrases were similar, spoken like a robot. The letters were like little beads tumbling down through my ears at incredible speed.

The funny part is that he said that I was from the **Galaxy Kvazi IN**. It sounded the same as when we say, "She is from the Western Inn or Holiday Inn..."

I have only a short version of this dream; I don't know where the full version is. Maybe I will find it one day. It was a month before I gave birth to my baby. I remember more but I don't want to add anything now. All of my dreams were transcribed directly from their original version on paper, which was written right after I woke up. So my name is *Svadi Hatra* when I fly in my dreams, at crazy speed across the Universe, while I visit galaxies, planets and stars, wearing this narrow helmet. Well, I don't take a passport with me into my dreams, but at least now, I know that I have some identity in the Universe...And I know that I am human from the future.

Julia's original transcription of Dream # 54

From an early age, since I remember myself when I close my eyes try to sleep I see instantly enormous small objects as a most smallest possible dot and instantly it is already so huge that did not feet to my vision and it continue again and again and again until I full to sleep....

Now I know that can be possible only with much greater speed. Most likely this dot is a planet... stars...when I travel in Universe. And when I approach them they became huge and did not fit my eyes view...

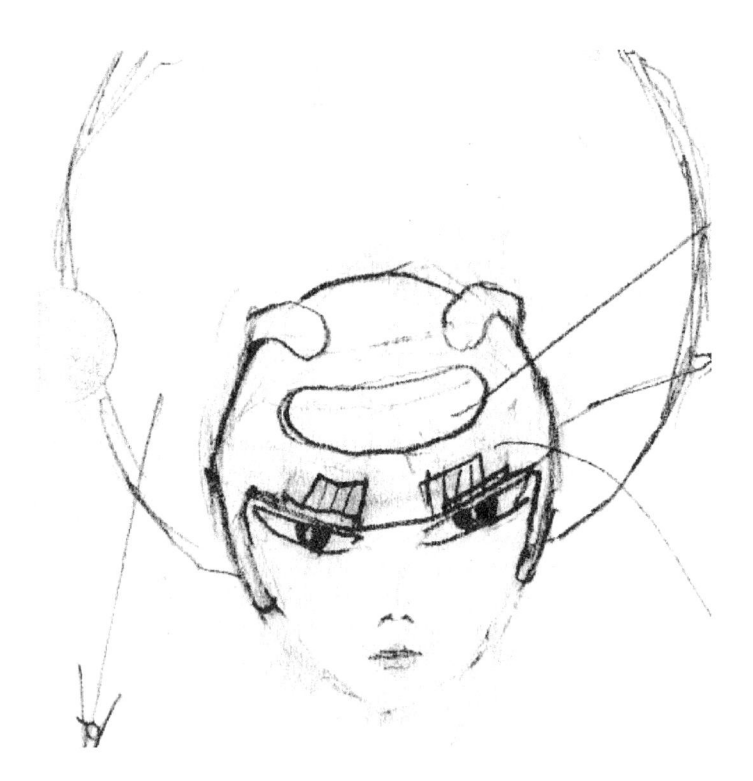

Svadi Hatra, human from the future.

Dream # 55
Meeting Myself From The Future, October 30, 1987

I promised in The Priest chapter to tell you about this meeting. I was in Caracole, which is located in an area not far from the Caspian Sea at the border with Iran. Lots of pomegranates there! Beautiful! This area has the name of a unique piece of land named "Moon Mountains", and listed in the book under "Wonders of the World". People are always afraid of the unknown and of things they don't understand... There is nothing to be afraid of in this dream.

****

I was inside some kind of capsule, in a transportation vehicle.
There is only one row of armchairs inside – two people in each section. In the hallway, there was an amazing child, maybe 130 cm high, standing in front of me. He looked straight at me. In order to see him better, I bent my knees and started peering into his face. He was something extremely beautiful, which I never saw in my life. I told him that I was a scientist and that I wanted to see him better, to study him.
He told me that he knew everything about me, and he knew that I was a scientist, and he agreed. Next he told me that **he was *me*,** myself from another time! And that today, he wished to show me everything. He also told me that I could ask as much as I wanted. I was a guest this time, in their capsule. We communicated with each other without words, telepathically. I don't know what gender this adorable creature was.
He had a small child's face, a very small nose and mouth, and I guess he rare used them. He had big elongated eyes and right next to the eyes, there was the edge of his helmet. There was a white glowing "halo" around his face, from ear-level. When I looked at it more closely, and observed the details, it was like a foggy smoke, light-ash and turquoise in color, like a colloid. You could almost

see through it... His face was of a darker color, the helmet was lighter and the "halo" was of a much lighter color yet.

Because of this, his head gave the impression that it was made of two layers. This child's face had a golden olive color. His cheeks were tinted in a coffee-olive-lilac color. He had emerald green eyes. Above the eyes, on the edge of the helmet there was a blue, thin crystal. The light from the crystal dropped on the olive face which gave it this beautiful radiating color. The blue crystal consisted of tiny tubes that looked very sharp. They were like one crystal that made up lots of other crystals – such as what you find in a geode. They pointed up at a 30 degree angle from the very narrow edge – as narrow as a shaving blade.

In front of the helmet there was an oval shaped scale and plate – and two of the same on both sides. This helmet enclosed his ears – if he had any – completely. There were orange crystals on the neck and a bright orange neon dot on the front of his neck in the middle at shoulder level. On the edge of each shoulder there was bright blue neon color.

All together it looked like an icon found in the churches. His entire body was covered with clothing – the only bare skin was his face. His clothes were made of scales – the same as his helmet.

He invited me to sit. I saw a woman sitting farther down the window and the seat next to her was empty. I looked at her hands and saw a very unusual bracelet. As soon as I woke up, I drew the bracelet, the child and the capsule.

There were many fragments in that dream. At first, we all sat down and a person, like this child, sat at the back and communicated with all the people together at once, telepathically. Other were children with elongated eyes, except for this woman next to me. It was like a brain storming session when questions were posed and everyone tried to find an answer. I loved that game and participated fully!

At one point, the child asked me to look through the window. I recognized the place! We were next to the Russian Defense Ministry, in Moscow! This is not far from Red Square and the Bolshoi Theater. We flew very low! I saw people walking on the street and cars! We turned near the restaurant "Praga", where I usually ordered special gourmet cakes, and continued moving above the street, which crosses Kalininsky prospect. I was inside the capsule for only a few minutes by then. I wondered how we could possibly have covered 3500 miles in a few minutes – from the border of Iran to that far north. I asked everything I wanted and I tested almost everything. They went on talking without words directly to my mind.

Nothing there compares to anything that we have here. It is hard to describe, impossible to find the right words. I studied them. Another fragment of this dream describes these unusual people, maybe 8 or10 of them, who did something odd with a black oval cylinder.[37] They knew how to twist space with it – they showed me how, I loved it! I very much wanted to participate in everything they did!

At one point, they invited me to take a ride on a very fast, very cute, little train, on very narrow rails, where there was only space for two people to sit. I loved that ride. I felt great! But what was most interesting is that I saw myself operating, working with beautiful crystals, like those I had in the Atlantis dreams! The crystals were of all colors in Atlantis. I remember the time, inthe capsule, when a blue colored crystal turned to purple, violet when I activated it! It worked the same as it did when I worked with my crystals in Atlantis.

****

This complicated configuration around the child's face made me think that a computer was perhaps incorporated in that helmet, placed directly on his head. Perhaps it was a translation centre, a camera, radio, you name it, there seemed to be everything in there. Great idea!By the way as you can see he had little **"horns"** on this head, which turn up few times! Maybe it some kind of antennas…

---

[37]

dream. I don't know how to describe them; they were nothing like what we have here. Nothing. I can't compare these things with anything. I was working on this "project" for many days, repeating the process many, many times. This was a system already. And I was working hard on this.

****

I have a strong, clear, very organized mind. I remember myself in my dreams when I sleep. I saw myself from the side in the dreams. I split into two people and it helps me control what is going on with one of me – the main one. I control myself in the dreams and decide where I wish to go and what to do. Sometimes, I fall asleep and create a dream for myself. Sometimes, I love that dream so much that I travel again to the same dream, the next time I fall asleep. And I add something nice to it, something new, to provide for a better quality entertainment. For sure simply I visited same place time to time

But, most importantly, something which I understand clearly is that since that day I had this one particular dream, **I am no longer afraid to die.**

I will be there after my death, in this beautiful world. Actually, I didn't want to return from my dream back that day. When I woke up, the entire world around me looked very plain, primitive, like a black and white photo. It looked like a house made of cards. It was very beautiful out there. I looked out the window; there was a full moon on that night and the moonlight made shadows everywhere from a little pomegranate tree, full of fruit, like a garden in a fairy tale. I love to be out there, because creativity proceeds without friction, problems or interruptions in that world. Here, you need to support yourself with food, clothes and a place to live. You simply need a computer or a pen to write. There you don't need anything to create – it is pure "creativity". What a pleasure!

****

The problem with most people is that they are afraid of what they don't know or can't understand and they start creating some "funny" theories. It is just their way of trying to save people from what does not even exist. I wish to elucidate, to put this mystery box on the table and open it. I wish to let those hidden "secrets" jump out and show themselves to people, because in reality nothing can actually hide – there is nothing on Earth that should provoke such unhealthy reaction or attract such a distorted attention to the facts. For example, I adore those angels and Spirits in my dreams. I can tell you a lot about them, because I met them during my travels through the Universe. BUT it is not my intent, in this book, to add more stories about them. If I even mentioned them, it is only an "attachment" to the context of the main topic about our own development. They have their own business. I have my own life and goals. And you as well, right?

I know what I want next in life and where I am going. I wish to have a reading to see my future lives and adjust myself to future development. As for me, I am continuing the study of *who I am*, and of the history and future of our planet.

BUT did you remember what is most important for you and every one of us here on Earth to know?

"I am myself, not more than somebody else and not less then somebody else."

I advise you to make this adjustment for yourself and you will be just fine, totally okay. The Universe is full of all kinds of Spirits, Angels, Creatures, Entities, good and bad, by the way, so be careful! And YES, God and Goddesses exist there as well.

People from the past and the future are just a small part of it and, most importantly, they are actually who we are, ourselves from the future, for example. Nothing more. Yes, they have advanced technology, so what? It is not the most important thing, actually. Try to imagine yourself living all your life in an airplane? Not so much fun, right? As for me, I prefer to visit nature, plants. Did you remember my dream, "Huge God dictates to my ears"? What was said about it? People will play for sometimes with techno stuff and after throw it away like an unwanted toy.

© Josephine Wall. All Rights Reserved. www.josephinewall.com

They visit us here to learn from people much more important things: emotions which they don't have, feelings, smiles, laughter, love, possibility to create poems, songs, music and those heavenly beautiful rays from God's creative energy from our eyes, which only humans can create. For some important reason, you and I were born humans. Start studying yourself and ask, "Where are you going in this lifetime and what are you planning for the next one?"

****

Why was Amelia reborn now?

So people need to keep this planet clean for themselves – they are "the future generations"! And this is a very important point and it should make a big difference for those who do not feel any responsibility for what will happen after they leave this life.

Some people and children are terminally ill...

His is a priceless support to a little child who is dying right now – as we speak – to know that this life is not the last one and that he will have many lives ahead of him!

I can help people risking their lives in their daily work: Firefighters, rescue workers, test pilots, police, miners, soldiers, medical personnel, scientists.

I can teach how to avoid mass psychological casualties in critical situations, how to keep people's Spirits free from GREAT FEAR, how to get rid of negative thoughts, and how to avoid mass panic.
I can show people how to be strong, stable, and in extreme situations, do the maximum in order to survive and preserve the best of our civilization.

According to what I just said, it is not important to have different countries! As the consciousness of humanity continues to evolve, each and every person will come to fully understand that they have experienced many lives. Each person will understand that they have lived as different genders, nationalities, races, and all kinds of levels of experience withinsocietal systems. From this understanding, humanity can now see that NOTHING exists anymore that can create separation. It will then not be necessary for formal borders to exist between countries, as all people will have one citizenship: as citizens of Planet Earth.

It will help get rid of tension between countries, delete constant conflicts and bring infinite peace, save huge amounts of money, which is currently spent on the military, governments and bureaucratic structures in each country.

See how powerful and heavenly beautiful this subject is! How much harmony give to us knowledge about the existence of this Human Hologram, this Eternity of our Spirit, which each of us carry as an inheritance from all of our past lives.

****

Why is the Mayan Priest reincarnated now?

I always wondered why Mayan Priest was I born again at this time?

The world is overwhelmed with fear of climate change and the coming of 2016-2022. The movies "2012", "Knowing" and "Road" show people being weak and powerless.
Many people watched the memorial ceremony for Michael Jackson in the Staples Centre, where some pointed toward the ceiling and said: "We know that he is here now" ... but some sounded really unsure... "Where? What is there?"

Where did they go - all of the people who died?
The Ancient Mayan Priest comes to you now after thousands of years to assist you in your plans. It was his daily job to take care of people, their Spirits' well-being in their lives - to help them navigate

their way when they crossed the veil to the afterlife. So I feel a serious responsibility and obligation towards giving the secret knowledge in this book to prepare people for what they can expect after their own death.

YES, I was there as Amelia when I found out that I was going to die soon. I was hysterical! I felt it was totally unfair that my life would end suddenly and that everything would be cut off. So, now I share my experience in order to support millions of people – each and every one on the planet.

In this book I shared the story of the amazing journey of my Spirit through other lives, to let people know that their present life is not the last one and their Spirit also Eternal!

This **Magnificent Eternal Hologram** is the most precious thing that people can ever own.

It is good to know that another side of human nature exists and that you can study some superior human capabilities for yourself. It is a gift of rare knowledge – the experiences of the existence of a much BIGGER Eternal Spirit Life outside of the present one that each of us is living right now.

In the chapter "Violet Field" you found that the Spirit world is full of amazing colors, lights, dynamic speed, and magic things which do not exist in our world. The Spirit also traveled to another multidimensional world.

The Spirit contacted and met other spirits from our galaxy and other parts of the universe. My body looked and felt different in this other world. Instead of a body, it was sometimes just one solid point or perhaps a pulsation of energy with sparks of quantum particles.

YES, in this book, **I proved that God exist!** And you already read how Spirit travels to Heaven, with the assistance of beautiful angels! **YES!** I received Blessing from God, who saved my life and as a result, I am alive now and wrote this book!

Supreme Being, **Svadi Hatra**, which resides now in my body lived before on this planet and occupied the body of other people:

- **Giant Svadi, Sumerian Priest from Hatra, Iraq;**
- **Royal Priestess from Egypt;**
- **High Priest from Chichén Itzá, Priest Jaguar, Magician, He Hioli;**
- **Queen of Atlantis, Kingdom of Crystals;**
- **Amelia Earhart, woman pilot from America;**

And now I am returned back as a scientist Julia Svadi Hatra.

Here are my two hands for you, as well as my unlimited amount of invisible hands as my book – to support and help everyone, to make you strong, powerful and unshaken during difficult times of change. My book is full of inspiration from the brave, fearless Amelia Earhart; rare knowledge, experiences in extreme situations and wisdom from the Maya Priest and the Queen of Atlantis. These people lived intensely and at the leading edge of possible human capabilities, with enormous responsibilities, while caring deeply about people.

Our Blessing to each and everyone in our beautiful Solar system.

YOUR ETERNAL HOLOGRAM

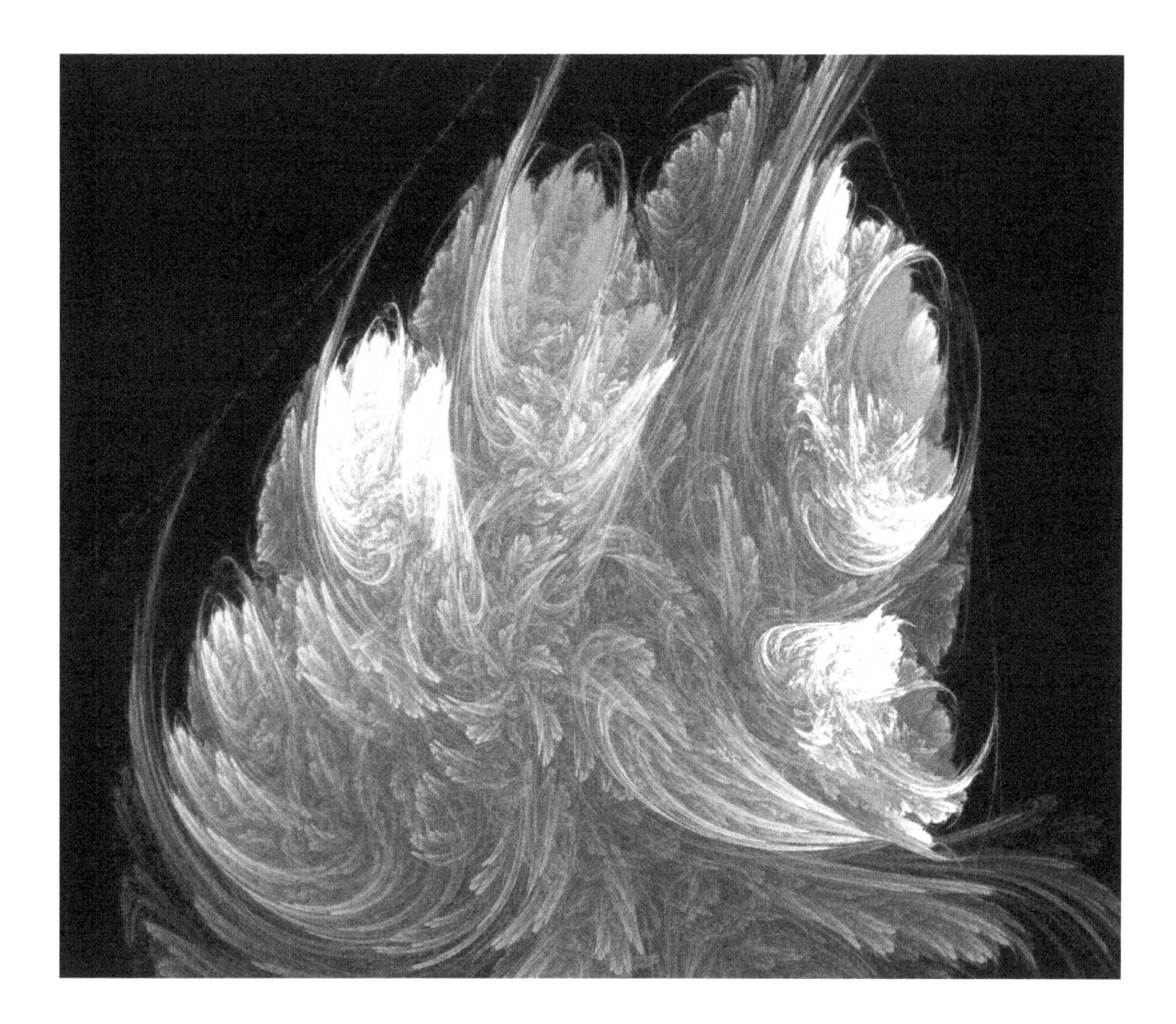

YOUTUBE: 2012 Power of Reincarnation

Wow...! Suddenly, at the very moment I finished typing the last sentence of this book, this big, yellow and black butterfly flew from nowhere directly onto my laptop and sat right there, near the screen... I looked at the window... it was closed. It was cold outside. I was in shock and thinking, what is the time of the year now?

It's still wintry – February!!! I don't know how it could be possible for this butterfly to appear so suddenly from nowhere in the middle of winter. Outside, there is still some snow in places in Stanley Park.

Was this the "Materialization" of a live butterfly?

Or is this a gift to me from the ancient Spirits who supported me during the whole process of writing this book? Perhaps this wonderful butterfly was somewhere in my apartment, still in its cocoon, dormant from last summer? But what did it eat during its development into a caterpillar and into a full blown adult butterfly?

No green leaves in the room – this is impossible! Surreal...

Well, I believe it to be the work of the Spirit – same as *he* called three cars with the number 013 at the same time and at the same place and put them on the road one after the other. Same as it was *he* who sent my neighbor to bring his laptop out of the closet to put it near my door...
I clicked on the calendar of my laptop, it was February 19th, and took a photo of this gorgeous butterfly. I was still in shock, really, this kind of butterfly usually appears in Stanley Park at the end of June.

Starting a book with pictures of me flying on the butterfly in my dream, and now this book is completed with the same magic beauty butterfly!

I was still thinking about this outstanding situation, when I remembered a letter I received recently:

Hello Julia, It's Mark Zealand, the documentary/camera man from English Bay. I just wanted to say that I found our conversation very interesting, also very random! One minute I'm filming people walking by, the next I'm listening to your unique story while an old man walks by with pigeons landing on his head!!Well, I just wanted to say hello and if you want to talk some more about possible project ideas, let me know. Cheers Mark

During the last three days, the butterfly sits on the corner of Tutankhamen's picture and I baby-sit her, feeding her honey water. They both have black and gold yellow stripes.

By the way, pharaohs have her blue eyelashes and even eyebrows... like Svadi Hatra from my dream and I myself have followed their fashion for the last 20 years

YOUR ETERNAL HOLOGRAM

Note: Two years later, while working on this version of the book, I suddenly understood why the Spirits gave me this butterfly!

Book was start with a picture of me on the butterfly flying in my dreams,

And now this book is completed with the same magic beauty butterfly!

Who am I?

I began to study "Who am I?" since 2008 and continue doing this now.

As you remember Supreme monk WonDam told that I am very rare, because of some special qualities my Spirit has. It is human, but also **"multidimensional Supreme Being, One in a Kind."**

As Mayas Spiritual Leader Don Julio mentioned in the movie:
"Julia has **Twin Spirit** as one. One as a human and second one **multidimensional, an Ancient Spirit, Goddess."**

When I was in Russia in 2014 for a short moment, where published book and movie, by blessing I ran into the most unique genius psychic Mr. V.V. Kustov. Enormous abilities surpass beyond matter of his own forehead. Top Russian Psychic is the **third person** who saw my Spirit and support what Don Julio and WonDam told.
Here is how this man tried to describe second one, who also is part of my spirit, which is difficult finding something can help to imagine it.
"Yes, it is **multidimensional**" he told:

*"If you sow movie " Terminator " there was part when he start to be like a **liquid metal, silver one.** You are on top of it reflects light as a DVDs disk with **all colours in once, very beautiful.** And most amazing part that this Entity, this THING, which is second part of your SPIRIT and it have very*

*special energy flow... It feels **ETERNITY**, like a draw- well, which is going to ETERNITY, fare away to another Galaxies or another Universe....*
He told: "that never met in our planet anything like this. He told that I am" **One in a Kind"**
and that I have extra unusual (peculiar) abilities from this Second one, which I am not aware off them yet...They start to show up in next few years, this multidimensional being abilities...
He saw enormous power in the body and he said that I can protect for many people at one from dangerous situation.

I started to check again my dreams...Do I really have something to support as what he said?

TWO in ONE, ETERNITY, multidimensional liquid silver, metal crystal structure?

Yes, I see myself **two in one** in many dreams in this book. For example here:

Dream # 22
The Woman-Double and a Wise Man, July 8, 1984 even three ribbons, I *saw myself, the other one, who stayed in the same place, and the other one saw this one, too.*

Dream # 19

Ruby Emerald, February 11, 1988

I look from above, like a huge person. The woman is standing like little Thumbelina.

Dream # 34

Business in the Center of the Galaxy, July 16, 1991
I had something to do in the center of the Milky Way Galaxy – just don't laugh.
I recalled being there. Our Earth is very far on the side. I understood that I go there quite often for business.
You know, my body is very different – it is not soft, a tender-skin body like here on Earth. In fact, it is like a lightning. *I am on Earth for some very pressing, but very short business.*
From there our Earth appears like a "rational" slime.

I also had numerous dreams during my life, where Spirits, Angels telling to me that I am ETERNAL.

Dream # 39. October 16, 1992
"*I was talking about herself. Here I am, and there is another that says about that:*
And for me it began with the words - **"It is Eternal"**

In the dream, below I have tried to describe the **crystallization process** of my body to prepare for space travel.

 # 40
Gray Dumb-Bell in the Head, September 4, 1991
I had not fallen asleep deeply yet; I still remember myself, when some substance of **gray color entered my head from both sides and started to crystallize inside** *it. It was not a pipe, the whole thing was filled in,* **crystallized all at once;** *it was fitting very well – like a dumb-bell – with something like earphones on the sides – flat ones – it was about three centimeters above the ears.*"
Now I knew extra reason, why my suitcases and my outfits **metal & silver.**

Dream # 38
A Man of the Forest – His Name, December 13, 1991

It was as if I consisted of many stairs. It can be said that stairs are material.
I disintegrated into several creatures, and later – into myself-human.

Dream # 41. Gray Dumb-Bell in the Head, September 4, 1991

It seemed that I am some other creature, who knows a lot, ***multidimensional one.*** *It has a different nature and it remembers a lot. As a human I am now 5% of it.*

Dream # 2
Hieroglyphs on the palm, September 12, 1992

They also said about me: ***"You are a Goddess, and there is also one more person."***

Dream # 45
Huge God Was Dictating Into My Ears, January 7, 1983

"I understood that somewhere beyond my consciousness there was this ***Divine creature and*** *it is also me. It was speaking in a very low, grand tone ... "*

All of this info support what told about my Spirit Mayas healer, Mexican spiritual leader Don Julio, leader of 13 million monks in S. Korea Supreme monk WONDAM and top psychic of Russia, healer V. V. Kustov.

CONCLUSION:

Yes, I have TWIN Spirit, first is a human and Second one is multidimensional, people named it Supreme Being or Goddess.

After this Conclusion I even more start interesting about very unusual qualities of my Sprit and I continue to study it. Good part that this sentence below gives me stability from this still Unexplained mystery: "Yes, I am myself, not more than somebody else and not less then somebody else. I am Avatar Svadi Hatra "

Now I wish to ask each person in the world : **WHO ARE YOU?**

And when each person will look at themselves and start to make this analysis of themselves, it will be very important, because all world will change. Consciousness in the world will change. This knowledge that the Spirit is Eternal, and the power of awareness of Reincarnation will enlighten and lift consciousness all over the world.

WHAT DOES YOUR ETERNAL HOLOGRAM LOOK LIKE?

Mind over Matter

The book has already been completed, but as a scientist, I continue to study himself as a person with the universal consciousness.
Suddenly, I found the answers to many questions all at once!
It started with the dream I had in 2009.
I lived in Canada, Vancouver. In the dream, I saw myself walking down the street in Seattle, USA, which is located 120 km from the border and Vancouver.

I was talking with a Russian scientist who came to the conference on nuclear physics. He told me that they are investigating the smallest particles.
In the dream, I ask this scientist, which keyword to use to find it in Google: How can I find you when I wake up? He told me his name: Lapu... and a few words.
Waking up, the first thing I went to the computer and ... found his article. I immediately called to his work in Russia. The personnel department of the Moscow Physical-Technical Institute of the Russian Academy of Sciences, Physics and Astronomy, I was told that it actually works in the academy and gave me the phone number of his lab!

I was very surprised when I realized that this is a real person! He lived in Moscow, and I talked with him and with his colleagues. What I saw in a dream turned reality. I talked to a real person who lives in Moscow, he was in Seattle in 2008 at the conference, but not in 2009, when I had the dream!
As you can see in my dreams I went back year ago, I was time traveler. I have a letter that I sent to them via the Internet in 2009, the next day about all of this.

Below I will explain how this can be possible.
All these years, since 2009, I asked myself the same question: why is my Spirit interested in these atoms? I became interested and started to study.
I realized that they are studying **Pion atoms,** the science of the nucleus and the particles.
It turned out that this is the smallest particle so far discovered on our planet and in the universe! These strange, mysterious Pion atoms have the ability to randomly disappear and reappear. Science cannot explain why and how it turns out!
"Size" really does not exist, in the sense in which we think about it at the quantum level.

"There is no experimentally vindicated radius of the electrons and any quarks. These are particles of extremely small dimensions, not engage in any physical space, and that's all we can say about them. Do neutrons and protons have a "size", i.e., they physically take place in space, because they are the quarks, held together by a powerful force, so that their "size" is simply a range, which is dominated by the powerful force of interaction between quarks. In general, the smallest subatomic particles do not exist, as they do not have resolution. "

They do not exist, but are actually presenting there!
Maybe this is the fabric, from which was made of our Spirit? Our quantum field, our Hologram?
It is also invisible, but it does exist!

Let's think together: **Our bodies are made up of atoms and subatomic particles. 99% of our body is made up of protons and neutrons, but among them there are a huge number of pions atoms in our body. We also made from a significant amount of these particles.**

This part is materialized and times again de-materialized and it always happens at different time points.

This part was for me the question: where are they traveling when the fade? Possibly located in another dimension, that would get the information?

Is it possible to explain with this telepathy, communication at a distance, amazing mental abilities?
I'm sure there's a connection between pions atoms and human consciousness, our holograms.
They are both exactly the same quality!
Pion atoms may explain and answer questions about the unusual abilities of my mind and body that I have demonstrated many times in this book, which was a mystery to me.

I found interesting information on the Internet, YouTube, which I think help to understand this subject better.

//// Mind Science Kept Hidden//// Documentary
□□□□□□□□□□□□□□□□□□□□□□□□□□□□□□□□□□□□□□
http://www.youtube.com/watch?v=fSGONup-CYE

I decide to type info also here. During my travels I was surprised that most of the people on our planet did not use internet, in most of the cases it limited just to use Facebook to connect with each other!

Please follow me below:

Science still cannot explain how this could be possible, but Dr. William Taylor, found that the mind can travel, travel in space instantly and far into space.
ASTRONAUTS in the United States found that consciousness is a better quality in space than on Earth. Dr. William Taylor has researched and discovered that consciousness cannot be blocked by any barriers. For example, lead blocks the high frequency microwave gamma rays, radio waves.
This means that the mind may be higher frequency than the gamma spectrum, so it can penetrate through all the barriers.

Consciousness is multidimensional with a very high frequency and very small (tiny) wave lengths and therefore they may have amazing penetration.

Dr. Taylor, found the next level of emotional frequencies emanating from the heart center: the speed of 186282 miles cubed per second or 64.64 miles per second Quadrillion!!! This is the level of cosmic proportions..... For example, radio waves of ordinary light to reach the Pleiadian constellation must be 440 years old, the mind can travel this path in 0.25 seconds!

From second chakra, it can be in the Andromeda galaxy, which is 2.5 million. Light years from Earth, in a split second! At this point, realize we are on a super level.
In 1927, at a conference of nuclear physics in Belgium was discussed
"Mind over matter" and concluded: that "Mind researchers affects the outcome of experiments." Dr. Bruce Lipton, Dr. John Gray

Quantum Communications.

These experiments were conducted with small nuclei and particles. This means that the mind of scientists through pion atoms was in the interaction with the nuclei and particles, they studied and changed their!!!

Interesting research Peter Gariaeva. He found that if you put a cell culture in a petri dish, and say prayers, currents cells and genes can be regenerated, restored! But if you swear, swear, cells and genes will be destroyed, as if to break down and die...
Recent studies have found that the DNA core - not our brain cells, and the cell is the intelligent center **membrane ring cells.**

Membranes read alerts - messages of the MIND! And.... there are **changes in the cell nucleus.** Thus the signal is coming from our consciousness, gets memory from our consciousness.... and program our DNA! With the ability to constantly re - rewrite the DNA, re-reprogram our DNA Matrix, if we are not satisfied with our origin. And to broadcast a new message about us in the universe! !

Re- program in ourselves, in the power of our mind, as well as in achieving any goal to which we aspire..... New knowledge. We all can develop this power in our minds. This ability, when we can communicate with each other without words. You can find the right person for the business, yours spiritual master before you meet this person in real life.
 You will improve your life find your life's purpose.

You can create your own reality as I have done, for example, many years ago.
I was in the spa and told the masseuse that today, Friday and next week on Wednesday, I will meet my future husband. I saw him in a dream, and it did happened follow week!

Do you remember the part in the book about **reincarnation of groups of people?**
Kennedy clan and his business partners?

http://www.near-death.com/experiences/reincarnation08.html

How to **they met** each other in real life? They put this intention in energy and space on their HOLOGRAMS and so they were born together.... and it strengthened their energy, each of them separately, and even more so when they were together ......this what help them meet each other in new life.
Yes, now I can easily explain and answer questions about my own unusual abilities, abilities of other people. For example: teleportation of the human spirit (astral travel) almost instantly to very remote places on the planet or in the universe, as I have done it many times during my sleep, and sometimes in real life.
So this is how it possible to do healing at a distance? The nature of intuition and telepathy? Materialization, levitation, all kinds of miracles, and the knowledge that comes out of nowhere?
And even telekinesis, the ability to move objects power of thought, how it was made
Nina Kulagina.

So what is the power of your consciousness?

*"In Tibetan Buddhism, magical practices involving the creation of **"Typlas"**, known in the west as the occult thought forms. Typlas, thought forms, imaginary objects that can be created by using the accumulation of the energy density of artificial life through rituals, meditation and other practices. Poet W.B. Yates, who founded a magical order in which he tried to revive some of the Celtic deities through visualization and rituals.*

One of them, "White Fool", apparently, was quite an independent life force that he was seeing some friends W.B. Yeats, during their visits. But they were not aware of his magical practices. "

Daniel Pinchbeck 2012 The Return of Quetzalcoatl, 2006.

****

Now let's think more broadly:
It has been proved that **WATER** can store information. Consciousness can affect the structure of water. Water, saves memory, our thoughts and feelings, it was recorded.

YOUTUBE
Water. A new dimension (2013) Documentary
Film - WATER. "The great mystery of the water." HD.

Formula WATER, H20 contained 2 Hydrogen, which can store information.
Our bodies are 90% of water.
Our Sun also contains 91% of hydrogen. Sun has almost the same structure as we have!
More here from internet for you:
Consciousness is spreading faster than light.
Acupuncture points can create flash 8 minutes before the solar flares from the Sun reach the Earth!
If Sun send a telepathic message to us, we can get it faster than the speed of light!
If we want to talk to the our Sun, as a living being, all together as one collective mind, billions of people, we may ask the Sun not to send us this harmful solar flares
We may ask Sun calm down and be in agreement with us.
Now let's think more broadly:
Hydrogen was created less than a second after the Big Bang.
At the creation of the **Universe,** and has established itself as the most abundant element amount throughout the universe.
Massive spiral Milky Way galaxy with billions of stars and planets made primarily of hydrogen

75% of the visible mass of our galaxy consists of hydrogen.

Since hydrogen saves memory, it means that the whole memory was stores in the galaxy entire history!

*"All matter originates and exists only by **force**. **P**resumably, this force is the existence of a conscious and intelligent **Mind**. This Mind is the matrix of all matter"* ~ ~ Max Planck, Father of the quantum physics.

YES, we can communicate with other civilizations in the Universe!

If consciousness is synchronized with the universe, then we can engage in dialogue with other galaxies!!! We can talk to God, our Creator.

To fix the future, we have to change people's minds. This applies to all mankind.

Human consciousness is matures over 3 years. If a man gives birth to the idea today, that its implementation will take place in three 3 years.

I offer here a solution that we can implement, delete global problems that already exist and are problems being created and forming in the near future on our planet, Earth.

It sound pathetic, but is still possibility to do this with the new technology and power of mind.

So called **"Sun worship"** Maya and ancient Egyptians actually recognize and accept that higher knowledge and wisdom literally passed through the Sun, or more precisely, through the cycles of the binary motion of sunspots.

Indians in North America can communicate with entities of the universe, with the goddesses, teachers, priests....

I can hear that human ears cannot hear....

I can see things that normal people do not see.......

It seems that this ability has been stored in my hologram of those times when I was a Mayan priest, and I can teach about this people.

And I know numerous people on the planet who also have extra ordinary abilities.

We have to go back and start again to use quality collective consciousness - it will be a more strong and powerful signal into space.

The secret of ancient knowledge - the development of the forces of the human mind and use it **as the collective consciousness** of millions of people in the world use it as a way of creativity and the opportunities to reform our planet, to make life more harmonious.

We can see our past and future, to stop the war and fix the problems of nature, change the weather and prevent disasters.

When we educate our consciousness we will start to be wise, then we can develop the power of our mind.

We can do this at the UNIVERSE level.

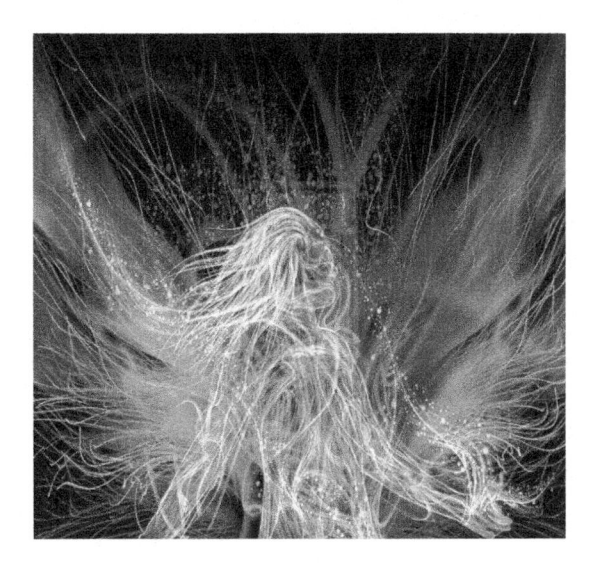

Reincarnation and the Bible

The concept of **reincarnation** is supported by many near-death experiences, including those where Jesus appears.
Now with "YOUR ETERNAL HOLOGRAM" discovery in this book, which supported with many facts, there should be no more DOUBTS that reincarnation exist.

Reincarnation is a doctrine which can be accepted by every follower of Christ and should be a part of orthodox Christian doctrine. For those who wish to study deeper. Below is a link with more details from the website of my friend Kevin Williams. For people who don't use internet please study here as well.

http://www.near-death.com/experiences/origen03.html

One of the reasons many Christians reject the validity of near-death testimony is because they sometimes appear to conflict with their interpretation of Christian doctrines. But Christians are usually very surprised to learn that reincarnation was a doctrine once held by many early Christians. Not only that, as you will soon see there is overwhelming evidence in the Bible of Jesus himself teaching it.

"Resurrection"

For thousands of years, Christians believed that when a person dies their soul would sleep in the grave along with their corpse. This soul sleep continues until a time in the future known as the "last day" or also known as the "final judgment." This doctrine concerns a time when Jesus supposedly returns in the sky and clouds with the angels to awakened sleeping souls in the graves. Then all corpses will crawl out of their graves like in the movie "Night of the Living Dead." This doctrine is the orthodox Christian doctrine called "resurrection" and it is the result of a misunderstanding of the higher teachings of Jesus concerning the reincarnation of the spirit into a new body and the real resurrection which is a spiritual rebirth or "awakening" within a person already alive.

From time to time throughout Jewish history, there was a persistent belief about dead prophets returning to life through reincarnation.

Reincarnation and Early Christianity

The first great Father of the early Orthodox Church was Origen (A.D. 185-254) who was the first person since Paul to develop a system of theology around the teachings of Jesus. Origen was an ardent defender of pre-existence and reincarnation. Pre-existence is the religious concept of the soul as not being created at birth; rather the soul existed before birth in heaven or in a past life on Earth. Origen taught that pre-existence is found in Hebrew Scriptures and the teachings of Jesus.

The doctrines of pre-existence and reincarnation existed as secret teachings of Jesus until they were declared a heresy by the Roman Church in 553 A.D. It was at this time that the Roman Church aggressively destroyed competing teachings and so-called heresies within the Church. Along with the destruction of unorthodox teachings came the destruction of Jews, Gnostics, and ultimately anyone who stood in the way of the Inquisition and Crusades.

But on December, 1945, writings containing many of these secrets of early Christianity were unearthed in Upper Egypt. This area was one of the main locations where Christians fled to when the Romans invaded Israel. It was here that these secrets were continued to be taught. Undisturbed since their concealment almost two thousand years ago, these writings of the secret teachings belonged to an early sect of Christians called Gnostics and these writings ranked in importance with the Dead Sea Scrolls which were discovered two years later. These so-called secret teachings concerning life and death are strikingly similar to what we know about near-death experiences.

Reincarnation and the Secret Teachings of Jesus

There are many Bible verses that affirm the reality of reincarnation. We will examine some of them here.
The episode in the Bible where Jesus identified John the Baptist as the reincarnation of Elijah the prophet is one of the clearest statements which Jesus made concerning reincarnation.

For all the prophets and the law have prophesied until John.
And if you are willing to receive it, he is Elijah who was to come. (Matt. 11:13-14)

In the above passage, Jesus clearly identifies John the Baptist as the reincarnation of Elijah the prophet. Later in Matthew's gospel Jesus reiterates it.

And the disciples asked him, saying, "Why then do the scribes say that Elijah must come first?"

But he answered them and said, "Elijah indeed is to come and will restore all things. But I say to you that Elijah has come already, and they did not know him, but did to him whatever they wished. So also shall the Son of Man suffer at their hand."

Then the disciples understood that he had spoken of John the Baptist." (Matt. 17:10-13)

In very explicit language, Jesus identified John the Baptist as the reincarnation of Elijah.

Even the disciples of Jesus understood what Jesus was saying. This identification of John to be the reincarnation of Elijah is very important when it comes to Bible prophecy. By identifying the John with Elijah, Jesus identified himself as the Messiah. The Hebrew Scriptures mentions specific signs that would precede the coming of the Messiah. One of them is that Elijah will return first.

Jesus again identifies John to be the reincarnation of Elijah.

The Bible does not limit the reincarnation of Elijah to John the Baptist either. The Bible suggests that another reincarnation of Elijah will occur around the time of Jesus' second coming. And not only does Elijah appear again at this time, but Moses is reincarnated as well. In the same way that John and Elijah appeared together on the Mount of Transfiguration so will they appear together at Jesus' return.

The Pre-Existence of the Soul

The pre-existence of the soul was a secret teaching held by early Christians until it was condemned by the Roman Church in 553 A.D., perhaps because it implied reincarnation spirit. The following Bible verses describes the pre-existence of souls.
He chose us in him *before the foundation of the world*, **that we should be holy and without blemish in his sight and love. (Eph. 1:4)**

Reincarnation and Divine Justice

According to the Bible, divine justice demands that sinners pay for their own sins. Jesus taught this when he declared: This law of divine justice is so universal that it even applies to science. It is Isaac Newton's law of cause and effect. It is also known as a law in physics: For every action there is an equal and opposing reaction and what goes up must come down. In fact, this law of divine justice is the very law of nature. Breaking the law of divine justice is very similar to breaking the law of gravity. The result is impersonal. Both are a transgression of the law of nature.

All who take the sword will perish by the sword. **(Matt. 26:52)**

If anyone slays with the sword, with the sword must he be slain. (Rev. 13:10) This statement from Jesus is completely absurd and ignorant unless reincarnation is true.
This law of divine justice is practically a universal religious concept. In eastern religions, this law of divine justice is known as karma. This law of divine justice is equal to the concept of reincarnation. This law of living by the sword and dying by the sword is the principle of reincarnation. In other words, this law of divine justice is the law of reincarnation.

The Dead Inherit the Earth
The following Bible passage is a promise that Jesus makes to those who have forsaken everything to follow him:

No one who has left home or brothers or sisters or mother or father or wife or children or land for me and the gospel will fail to receive a hundred times as much in this present age - homes, brothers, sisters, mothers, children and fields ... and in the age to come, eternal life. **(Mark 10:29-30)** Without reincarnation and pre-existence, this promise of Jesus is completely ludicrous because it would be impossible to happen. For example, it would mean that those who leave their parents for the sake of Christ will receive even more parents in the age to come. And those who leave their children for the sake of Christ will receive even more children in the age to come. It is evident that this promise by Jesus intends to be fulfilled in a future life on Earth.

The Disciples Returning to Witness Jesus' Next Incarnation In the Book of Revelation there is a verse that only makes sense if reincarnation is a fact:
Look he is coming with the clouds, and every eye will see him, even those who pierced him. **(Rev. 1:7)** The above Bible verse reveals an astonishing fact about the second coming of Jesus. The people who killed Jesus will be alive and living on Earth when Jesus returns. Given the fact that the people who killed Jesus have been dead for thousands of years, the only possible way that this prophecy can be fulfilled is through the killers reincarnating before Jesus returns.

****

Reincarnation should be the doctrine of every Christian. Perhaps there is a divine reason for the recent discoveries of the Dead Sea Scrolls and the writings of the early Jerusalem Christians discovered in upper Egypt - both of which proclaim reincarnation, not bodily resurrection, to be the real faith of Israel.
So now we can give these definitions:
Resuscitation=The restoration of life to a physically dead body

Resurrection=The giving of spiritual life to a spiritually dead but physically alive person

Reincarnation=The physical rebirth of the spirit of a dead person into the body of a fetus

As previously mentioned, reincarnation was an established belief in the days of Jesus

Due to the condemnation of pre-existence (and reincarnation) by church authorities in 553 A.D., reincarnation became an enemy concept to the Judeo-Christian West. The reason reincarnation was declared heresy was given by Gregory, the Bishop of Nyssa.
The five reasons he gave were:
(1) It seems to minimize Christian salvation.
(2) It is in conflict with the resurrection of the body.
(3) It creates an unnatural separation between body and soul.
(4) It is built on a much too speculative use of Christian scriptures.
(5) There is no recollection of previous lives---> **In this book you saw the proof!**

In conclusion, this Biblical defense of reincarnation leads to the following conclusions:

(1) The religious concept of a massive worldwide reanimation of corpses at the end of time is a foreign concept originating from ancient Persia.

(2) A massive worldwide reanimation of corpses seems bizarre, unnatural, and repulsive.

(3) The few instances recorded in the Bible where corpses were reanimated were miracles.

Doctors today bring people back from the dead with modern technology.

(4)Reincarnation was widely believed by the people of Israel in the days of Jesus and by people all around the world.

(5)All Hebrew and Christian scriptures support reincarnation: the Bible, the Dead Sea Scrolls, the Christian Gnostic gospels, the Torah, the Hebrew Bible, the Apocrypha, the Kabbalah and Zohar.

(6)Many of the Biblical references to "resurrection" refer to spiritual regeneration while already physically alive instead of the reanimation of corpses on the so-called "Last Day."

(7)**Reincarnation** is the rebirth of a person's spirit into a new body to be born again as an infant.

Resurrection is the "spiritual awakening" of a living person's spirit by the power of the Holy Spirit.(8)The Bible records Jesus himself teaching reincarnation to his followers.(9)Early Christians in Jerusalem believed in reincarnation and taught it until it was declared a heresy by the Church of Rome.

(10)Reincarnation has been a tenet in Orthodox Judaism for thousands of years and continues to this day.

(11)The concept of reincarnation is supported by many near-death experiences including those where Jesus appears.

(12)Reincarnation is a doctrine which can be accepted by every follower of Christ and should be a part of orthodox Christian doctrine.

http://www.near-death.com/experiences/origen03.html

Reincarnation is a doctrine which can be accepted by every follower of Christ and should be a part of Orthodox Christian doctrine and all other religions.

****

Documentary movie "YOU and YOUR ETERNAL HOLOGRAM "
directed by Julia Svadi Hatra won 2 awards at the International Festival movies in Canada 2014
Award of Excellence Winners Documentary Feature Competition
2014 Canada Film Festival Rising Star Winners
Documentary Short Competition
And one of the best 8 documental movies in the world in 2014.
Movie and book has been translated into Russian.

YOUR ETERNAL HOLOGRAM

Scientific Interpretations

By Grazyna Fosar and Franz Bludorf
DNA can be influenced and reprogrammed by words and frequencies (Russian DNA Discoveries)

The human DNA is a biological Internet, and superior in many aspects to the artificial one. The latest Russian scientific research, directly or indirectly, explains phenomena such as clairvoyance, intuition, spontaneous and remote acts of healing, self-healing, affirmation techniques, unusual light/auras around people (namely spiritual masters)*,
Good to know! Japanese tourists see this that I had this light in pyramid.
the mind's influence on weather patterns, and much more. Only 10% of our DNA is being used for building proteins. It is this subset of DNA that is of interest to western researchers, and is being examined and categorized. The other 90% are considered "junk DNA".

The Russian researchers, however, who are convinced that nature was not dumb, joined linguists and geneticists in a venture to explore those 90% of "junk DNA". Their results, findings and conclusions are simply revolutionary!

According to them, our DNA is not only responsible for the construction of our body, but also serves as data storage and communication. The Russian linguists found that the genetic code, especially in the apparently useless 90%, follows the same rules as all our human languages. To this end, they compared the rules of syntax (the way in which words are put together to form phrases and sentences), semantics (the study of meaning in language forms) and the basic rules of grammar. They found that the alkaline of our DNA follow regular grammar, and do have set rules, just like our languages. So, human languages did not appear coincidentally, but are a reflection of our inherent DNA.

The Russian biophysicist and molecular biologist, Peter Gariaev, and his colleagues also explored the vibrational behavior of the DNA. The bottom line was: "Living chromosomes function just like solitonic / holographic computers, using the endogenous DNA laser radiation." This means that they managed, for example, to modulate certain frequency patterns onto a laser ray, and with it, influenced the DNA frequency and thus the genetic information itself. Since the basic structure of DNA alkaline pairs and of language are of the same structure, no DNA decoding is necessary. One can simply use words and sentences of the human language! This, too, was experimentally proven! Living DNA substance (in living tissue, not in vitro) will always react to language-modulated laser rays, and even to radio waves, if the proper frequencies are being used. This finally and scientifically explains why affirmations, autogenously training, hypnosis, and the like can have such strong effects on humans and their bodies. It is entirely normal and natural for our DNA to react to language.

Esoteric and spiritual teachers have known for ages that our body is programmable by language, words, and thought. This has now been scientifically proven and explained. Of course, the frequency has to be correct. And this is why not everybody is equally successful, or can do it with always the same strength. The individual person must work on the inner processes and maturity in order to establish a conscious communication with the DNA. The Russian researchers work on a method that is not dependent on these factors, but will ALWAYS work, provided one uses the correct frequency. But the higher developed an individual's consciousness is, the less need is there for any type of device. One can achieve these results by oneself, and science will finally stop laughing at such ideas, and will confirm and explain the results. And it doesn't end there.

YOUTUBE:
Russians Change DNA with Frequency Experiments (1/2)

The Russian scientists also found out that our DNA can cause disturbing patterns in the vacuum, thus producing magnetized wormholes! Wormholes are the microscopic equivalents of the so-called Einstein-Rosen bridges in the vicinity of black holes (left by burned-out stars).

These are tunnel connections between entirely different areas in the universe, through which information can be transmitted outside of space and time. The DNA attracts these bits of information, and passes them on to our consciousness.

Dream # 2
Hieroglyph on the palm, September 12, 1992
They said, "Because you have capabilities, energy," (specific energy in dreams).
They also said that people cannot remember this even if they get there. And this would make no sense to them, and they would not get their experience there. From that comment, I thought that maybe people do not have enough energy.

This process of hyper-communication is most effective in a state of relaxation. Stress, worries, or a hyperactive intellect prevents successful hyper-communication or the information will be totally distorted, and useless. In nature, hyper-communication has been successfully applied for millions of years. The organized flow of life in insect states proves this dramatically. Modern man knows it only on a much more subtle level as "intuition". But we, too, can regain full use of it.

An example from Nature: When a queen ant is spatially separated from her colony, building still continues fervently, and according to plan. If the queen is killed, however, all work in the colony stops. No ant knows what to do. Apparently, the queen sends the "building plans" also, from far away via the group consciousness of her subjects. She can be as far away as she wants, as long as she is alive.

Dream # 30
The Blue Vessel of an Egyptian Priest and Pharaoh, January 10, 1992
These people gave this knowledge, and afterwards it was passed on during the life of a man. Besides the main Priest, there were some others, less significant. Each of them had just one part ... but everything he was giving, he gave only to one person. He is like a queen bee; everybody valued the knowledge he passed on.[39]

In man hyper-communication is most often encountered when one suddenly gains access to information that is outside one's knowledge base. Such hyper-communication is then experienced as inspiration or intuition.

It looks like this is the way the Priest and another of his noble "colleagues" communicated with their HIGH POWER, God, and Spirits and received information. For years, a 42-year old male nurse dreamed of a situation in which he was hooked up to a kind of knowledge CD-ROM. Verifiable knowledge from all imaginable fields was then transmitted to him, which he was able to recall in the morning. There was such a flood of information; it seemed that a whole encyclopedia was transmitted at night.

---

[39] People lost their connection with the parallel worlds, lost the integrity of development. Before, they were walking in step, in one stream. But they stopped, dropped back, lost the sense of knowledge.

The majority of facts was outside his personal knowledge base, and reached technical details about which he knew absolutely nothing.

I receive lots of information this way also, during many dreams
For example: -

Dream # 7
Arabian and American Mountains - 2 pyramids:
Egypt and Mexico, October 25, 1990
His voice was talking to me very quickly – humans cannot talk that fast – it was saying different things, which I could not memorize. The views were replacing each other, the voice followed with information – very even; all phrases were similar, spoken like a robot. The letters were like little beads tumbling down through my ears at incredible speed.

When hyper-communication occurs, one can observe in the DNA, as well as in the human being, special phenomena. The Russian scientists irradiated DNA samples with laser light. On screen, a typical wave pattern was formed. When they removed the DNA sample, the wave pattern did not disappear, it remained. Many control experiments showed that the pattern still came from the removed sample, whose energy field apparently remained by itself. This effect is now called phantom DNA effect. It is surmised that energy from outside of space and time still flows through the activated wormholes after the DNA was removed. The side effect encountered most often in hyper-communication, also in human beings, are inexplicable electromagnetic fields in the vicinity of the persons concerned.

This effect can explained why on the photo after the accident people still in the cars, photo was made after body was removed from the cars.
Letter from Gustavo Medrano.

Electronic devices, like CD players and the like, can be "irritated" and cease to function for hours. When the electromagnetic field slowly dissipates, the devices function normally again. Many healers and psychics know this effect from their work. The better the atmosphere and the energy, the more frustrating it is. The recording device stops functioning and recording exactly at that moment. And repeated switching on and off after the session does not restore function, but next morning all is back to normal. Perhaps this is reassuring to read for many, as it has nothing to do with them being technically inept; it means they are good at hyper-communication. In their book "Vernetzte Intelligenz" (Networked Intelligence), Grazyna Fosar and Franz Bludorf explain these connections precisely and clearly. *The authors also quote sources presuming that in earlier times humanity had been, just like the animals, very strongly connected to the group consciousness and acted as a group.* To develop and experience individuality we humans, however, had to forget hyper-communication almost completely.

Now that we are fairly stable in our individual consciousness, we can create a new form of group consciousness, namely, one in which we attain access to all information via our DNA, without being forced or remotely controlled about what to do with that information. We now know that just as on the internet, our DNA can feed its proper data into the network, can call up data from the network, and can establish contact with other participants in the network.

Remote healing, telepathy, or "remote sensing" about the state of relatives, etc. can thus be explained. Some animals know also from afar when their owners plan to return home. That can be freshly interpreted and explained via the concepts of group consciousness and hyper-communication.

Any collective consciousness cannot be sensibly used over any period of time without a distinctive individuality. Otherwise, we would revert to a primitive herd instinct that is easily manipulated. As a rule, weather, for example, is rather difficult to influence by a single individual. But it may be influenced by a group consciousness (nothing new to some tribes doing it in their rain dances). Weather is strongly influenced by Earth resonance frequencies, the so-called Schumann frequencies.

****

But those same frequencies are also produced in our brains, and when many people synchronize their thinking, or individuals (spiritual masters, for instance) focus their thoughts in a laser-like fashion, then it is, scientifically speaking, not at all surprising if **they can thus influence weather.** Researchers in group consciousness have formulated the theory of *Type I civilizations*. A humanity that developed a group consciousness of the new kind would have neither environmental problems, nor scarcity of energy. For, if it were to use its mental power as a unified civilization, it would have control of the energies of its home planet as a natural consequence. And that includes all natural catastrophes!

Dream # 16
Destruction of the Crystal Sphere, February 19, 1992
I started making similar, circular movements with my right hand or my mind ... **her ability to achieve amazing results!**
A theoretical *Type II civilization* would even be able to control all energies of their home galaxy.

In the book "Nutze die taeglichen Wunder", it described an example of this: whenever a great many people focus their attention or consciousness on something similar, like Christmas time, football world championship, or the funeral of Lady Diana in England, then certain random number generators in computers start to deliver ordered numbers, instead of the random ones. An ordered group consciousness creates order in its whole surrounding! When a great number of people get together very closely, potentials of violence also dissolve. It looks as if here, too, a kind of humanitarian consciousness of all humanity is created. At the Love Parade, for example, where every year about one million of young people congregate, there has never been any brutal riot as they occur, for instance, at sports events. The name of the event alone is not seen as the cause here. The result of an analysis indicated rather that the number of people was TOO GREAT to allow a tipping over to violence to come back to the DNA: It apparently is also an organic superconductor that can work at normal body temperature.

In my experience, in some special dreams during the last 30 years when it was the "level of God, Goddess's voice" talking to me with prediction about future, which later always happened, or giving me unique information about nature or space or history of human, first, it was always very loud and secondly, when I woke up my body was always overheated.

This is a further explanation of how the DNA can store information. There is another phenomenon linked to DNA and wormholes. Normally, these super small wormholes are highly unstable, and are maintained only for the tiniest fractions of a second.

Dream # 3
ATHARVAN, 13 October 1989,
But I could not bear it, only for a moment, then everything blurred, I could not bear to look for a long time. I was there for an instant – a few times. Just like a quantum of light. YES, this is why I saw the face only for a very short moment!
And one more:
Dream # 18
Zaratustra in Water, September 6, 1993

I knew that I could not; I am unable to look straight at him. But he wanted to show himself to me – at least as a reflection in the water.

Under certain conditions, stable wormholes can organize themselves, which then form distinctive vacuum domains in which, for example, gravity can transform into electricity. Vacuum domains are self-radiant balls of ionized gas that contain considerable amounts of energy. There are regions in Russia where such radiant balls appear very often. Following the ensuing confusion, the Russians started massive research programs, leading finally to some of the discoveries mentioned above. Many people know vacuum domains as shiny balls in the sky.

They accelerated from zero to crazy speeds, while sliding gently across the sky. Russians found in the regions where vacuum domains appear often and sometimes fly as balls of light from the ground upwards into the sky, that these balls can be guided by thought. One has found out since that vacuum domains emit waves of low frequency, as they are also produced in our brains. And because of this similarity of waves, they are able to react to our thoughts. Many spiritual teachers also produce such visible balls or columns of light in deep meditation or during energy work, which trigger decidedly pleasant feelings and do not cause any harm.

Apparently, this is also dependent on some inner order, and on the quality and provenance of the vacuum domain. There are some spiritual teachers (the young Englishman Ananda, for example) with whom nothing is seen at first, but when one tries to take a photograph while they sit and speak, or meditate in hyper-communication, one gets only a picture of a white cloud on a chair. In some Earth healing projects, such light effects also appear on photographs.

Simply put, these phenomena have to do with gravity and anti-gravity forces, that are also exactly described in the book, and with ever more stable wormholes and hyper-communication, and thus, with energies from outside our time and space structure.
Earlier generations that got in contact with such hyper-communication experiences and visible vacuum domains were convinced that an angel had appeared before them. (Dream, God Blessing, angels, July, 20 1995, They were two real angels with white wings!)

And we cannot be too sure as to what forms of consciousness we can gain access to when using hyper-communication. Not having scientific proof for their actual existence (people having had such experiences do NOT all suffer from hallucinations) does not mean that there is no metaphysical background to it. We have simply taken another giant step towards understanding our reality.

Official science also knows of gravity anomalies on Earth (that contribute to the formation of vacuum domains), but only of ones of below one percent. Recently, gravity anomalies have been found of between three and four percent. One of these places is Rocca di Papa, south of Rome. Round objects of all kinds, from balls to full buses, roll uphill. But the stretch in Rocca di Papa is rather short, and defying logic, skeptics still flee to the theory of optical illusion (which it cannot be, due to several features of the location).

All of this information is from the book, "Vernetzte Intelligenz" von Grazyna Fosar und Franz Bludorf, summarized and commented by Baerbel. The book is unfortunately only available in German, so far.

****

There is a connection between shape, texture and energy of the crystal **Dream # 26, Hundreds of Followers. Rubies,** November 8, 2003, and the same with *strange square-round shape. Either round*

outside and square inside, or vice-versa in Dream # 7, Arabian and American Mountains, 2 pyramids, Egypt and Mexico, 25 of October 1990,
http://www.crystalinks.com/numerology2.html .
Also, please see Arnold de Belizal, The Atlantis Ring,
http://www.crystalinks.com/atlantisring.html [17]
DNA Found to Have "Impossible" Telepathic Properties, Journal of Physical Chemistry B, Geoff S. Baldwin, Sergey Leikin, John M. Seddon, and Alexei A. Kornyshev
DNA has been found to have a bizarre ability to put itself together, even at a distance, when according to known science it shouldn't be able to. Explanation: None, at least not yet.
Scientists are reporting evidence that contrary to our current beliefs about what is possible, intact double-stranded DNA has the "amazing" ability to recognize similarities in other DNA strands from a distance. Somehow they are able to identify one another, and the tiny bits of genetic material tend to congregate with similar DNA. The recognition of similar sequences in DNA's chemical sub-units occurs in a way unrecognized by science. There is no known reason why the DNA is able to combine the way it does, and from a current theoretical standpoint this feat should be chemically impossible.

Even so, the research published in ACS' Journal of Physical Chemistry B, shows very clearly that homology recognition between sequences of several hundred nucleotides occurs without physical contact or presence of proteins. Double helixes of DNA can recognize matching molecules from a distance and then gather together, all seemingly without help from any other molecules or chemical signals.In the study, scientists observed the behavior of fluorescently tagged DNA strands placed in water that contained no proteins or other material that could interfere with the experiment. Strands with identical nucleotide sequences were about twice as likely to gather together as DNA strands with different sequences. No one knows how individual DNA strands could possibly be communicating in this way, yet somehow they do. The "telepathic" effect is a source of wonder and amazement for scientists.
"Amazingly, the forces responsible for the sequence recognition can reach across more than one nanometer of water separating the surfaces of the nearest neighbor DNA," said the authors Geoff S. Baldwin, Sergey Leikin, John M. Seddon, and Alexei A. Kornyshev and colleagues. [28]

This recognition effect may help increase the accuracy and efficiency of the homologous recombination of genes, which is a process responsible for DNA repair, evolution, and genetic diversity. The new findings may also shed light on ways to avoid recombination errors, which are factors in cancer, aging, and other health issues.
Biblical quotes: King James Version.

1 http://noosphere.princeton.edu/fristwall2.html
2 http://www.fosar-bludorf.com
3 http://www.ryze.com/view.php?who=vitaeb

In his videos Corey Goody told that he was travel to planets and inner Earth during his work. Some of the my dreams, events, facts from my book supported by him, as well as supported our each other experiences. Plus I have in the book archaeological facts, which also supported it. This extra proof of reality and existence of all those "mysteries" is very important confirmation for our audience. Some Beings which I met, Corey also met. In bodies of some of this Beings my Spirit resided in my past lives and I have memories about it and I did described it in this book.

*For example Corey met in real life Beings with the crystal in the head, similar in two of my dreams:
Dream # 30, The Blue Vessel of an Egyptian Priest & Pharaoh, January 10, 1992

Dream # 31, CROWN, September 6, 1991

* Corey met very slim and very tall "Beings", similar to Beings in my dream.

Dream # 24, I was Very Thin and Extremely Tall, February 11, 1997

* Corey also support that copy of information of our " living essence" stored somewhere in Space,

 in another dimension.

Dream # 29, Bifurcation similar to a "vibrating" ruler, May 13, 1991; part "TRINITY "

* Corey travel to inner Earth and described how information was exchange there

with Being name " Korrie"

I also did described interaction and information exchange with three Beings.

Dream # 38, A Man of the Forest – His Name, December 13, 1991

*Corey told that Beings, who with most high density can travel very fare in Universe instantly.

I described in my book how I travel myself : I know how to see, to make myself, my body as a frequency. I think it helps me travel very fast through the Universe – faster than light or sound and with help of wormholes of course. This is how I can send my body frequency far away into Space to some exact place of which the frequency is familiar to me already.

*In this YOUTUBE video below Corey also support **importance of FORGIVNESS**, which I mentioned in the book. It is important for all people to know, here for people, who did not used internet:

If you have trauma or something in your life you still hold on to and you haven't forgive to yourself or forgive to others, that cause this trauma. That trauma became ten guidable ball, that others or entity can be attach to this. Best way to be totally free from this attachments is to go with the process of forgiving to yourself and to people, who may done most horrible things to you. And if you did not let go... they still have power over you now, and there still an attachment to you and they will continue victimizing you...Some people and entity have symbiotic things, Entity feeding of human life energy. People vampire, they sit and talk and do everything they can in order to get reaction from you... There attachment bad Entity feed on this energy. They maybe give back 10% of receiving energy to there human host. When people getting of this energy, they addicted to this, it is high. When entity removed from them, they feel withdraw... like situation when somebody quit smoking cigarettes. But it is very important to rid of this parasite Entity. YOUTUBE: Part 1 Mt Shasta Secret Space Program Conference - Corey Goode Presentationhttps://www.youtube.com/watch?v=vXhulEQib5U , start from 1.34.25... min, http://www.spherebeingalliance.com/

I understand for sure now that most of the dreams in this book, was not a dreams, but it was real events or real travel in my body or Spirit & my living essence to another Galaxy, Earth inner world.

DISCOVERY OF THE BIOFIELD

As a former Maya High Priest in my past life, I am very proud to give you proof right now – below – as to **why astrology can be one of the new important science branch about people's health and wellbeing**. I am glad that I was reborn as a scientist and can show to the world that we, Ancient Mayas, were highly educated intelligent people:

"A little known rotational force called the "biofield" has been detected around living organisms and has a strength that varies with changes in solar activity, lunar phase, planetary positions and the Earth's geomagnetic field.
A simple device has been created which measure a spin force around living organisms. The discovery of this spin force bridges the gap between small bodies -subatomic particles, atoms and interstellar molecules---and large bodies---planets, asteroids, stars and galaxies .At times of new or full moon or when there are large disturbances in Earth's magnetic field the biofield often shows a change in the initial direction of rotation.

"Taken together, the findings of Brown, Jones, the author, and other researchers all point to connections between living organisms, spin, and geomagnetic activity. All living organisms seem to be in resonance with Earth's dynamic magnetic field. Earth's magnetic field is in turn a function of solar activity and the positions of the Moon, and at least some of the planets."

I am sure it will cheer up astrologers all over the world, who try to protect their valuable knowledge and reputation during their entire life, trying to prove that astrology is working and it is a real powerful knowledge.
Let's touch now one more time subject: What does our Spirit look like? Or at least, maybe is it possible to see some of the Spirit's physical characteristics? I believe one of them is biofield.

For example:

*Mesmer believed there was a fluid-like energy around the human body which was highly charged in healthy people, and weak or nearly absent in ill people. He recognized that this force was somehow related to magnetism, and he thought that magnets could conduct it. He called this force "Animal Magnetism" to differentiate it from ordinary iron magnetism. He found that he could produce "magnetic like" effects in his patients by stroking the space around them with magnets or his hands. His formulation was similar to what Reich later called orgone energy."

*Tesla, a contemporary of Edison and inventor of the alternating current motor and many other instruments, was reported to have spoken about a "higher octave" of magnetism which had not been recognized by traditional science.

Buryl Payne: "Well, then, what is the biofield? It appears to be a genuine new force in science. It manifests as a physical force clearly observed on all types of biological matter. As of this time (1989) it appears to be a force which produces movement at right angles around the human body.

It does not push or pull like gravity or electrostatic forces. It appears to be in the form of a circular or spiral force around the body. The origin of the force is not electrical, magnetic, heat, or gravitational. It is much too large to be produced by these forces. It needs a name. Since the body's intrinsic magnetic field measured in shielded rooms is about one billionth of a gauss, this biofield could not be an ordinary magnetic field. Whatever we choose to call it; the aura, animal magnetism, orgone energy, prana, spin force, ch'i, or the biofield, this energy is quite large; over 100 million times as large as the body's magnetic field! If it were magnetic, the biofield would be equivalent to several hundred gauss. The author has simply called it the Biofield, a contracting of biological energy field. The author has chosen to call it simply the biofield, and to call the instruments which serve to detect it, biofield meters.

"After several months of observations it was discovered that the amount of the initial rotational deflection of the Biofield meter varied in association with the geomagnetic field. The dashed line shows measurements made with the Biofield meter and the solid line shows data on Earth's magnetic activity provided by the National Bureau of Standards in Boulder, Colorado. At times of higher geomagnetic activity, the biofield also showed higher activity. Measurements made over a seven year period on various forms of biofield meters showed consistent connections between their movements and solar/geomagnetic activity. This was so, even for those forms of the biofield meters which did not have magnets placed on them. It seems that the geomagnetic activity is the largest component of biofield activity."

Ralph Stone, founder of Polarity Therapy, has illustrations showing a spin field around the body. One person who meditates reported to me that she experienced a spinning sensation during a meditation. Perhaps there really are whoosh birds after all! If this force were a spin force it would fit with other patterns found in nature. If the force were in a spin form, it would imply that if we could place a small test object in space around a human, that object would start to rotate around the person. This experiment could not be done on Earth, but perhaps it could be done in space. If so, the spin force, or life force, is similar to magnetism, for magnetism is a spin force located in the space around a wire carrying an electric current.

"Spin forces are not unique to living systems--they are omnipresent in the universe. Spin or angular momentum is associated with most sub atomic particles such as electrons, protons, neutrons, etc. Apparently everybody in the universe spins! Interstellar molecules spin. Stars, planets, satellites, even entire galaxies and clusters of galaxies all are known to spin. One astronomer maintains that the whole universe spins! Spin forces might be called "form forces" or "organizing forces", for they help form complex living organisms, which abound with spirals, helixes, and circles over and over again in myriads of different ways from double helices in DNA and RNA to Whirling Dervishes.

"As previously mentioned, there are also two other forces now assumed to exist. Called the strong and weak nuclear forces, they operate within atomic nuclei to help keep nuclear particles from dispersing due to electrical forces."
"More research on the biofield is urgently needed, and it's impossible for one person to do it, so it is the author's hope that many readers will take up the exciting challenge and enjoy the fun of exploring a whole new field.
"There are so many parameters to uncover! It's as if we were back in the 1800's when electricity and magnetism were first discovered—an experimenter's paradise."

"A most important question is: what is the direction of this force?"

Buryl Payne, Discovery of biofield,
http://newilluminati.blog-city.com/discovery_of_the_biofield.htm

Sources

1. The Extraordinary Story of Healer Alfons Ven
   Extracted from Nexus Magazine, Volume 14, Number 6 (October - November 2007)
   http://www.nexusmagazine.com/articles/AlfonsVen1.html
   Alfons Ven, Evolution Vision Foundation Website:
   http://www.visionone.tv
   Phone: +31 20 436 0900 or +31 30 233 31 88
2. History of the Golden Ages - by Steve Omar
3. A VOYAGE TO KNOWLEDGE OF THE AFTERLIFE by Bruce Moen © 1999
   Extracted from Nexus Magazine, Volume 6, Number 3 (April-May 1999).
   editor@nexusmagazine.com
   From web page at:
   www.nexusmagazine.com by Bruce Moen © 1999
   www.afterlife-knowledge.com
4. THE LAST ATLANTIS BOOK YOU'LL EVER HAVE TO READ! : THE ATLANTIS-MEXICO-INDIA, by Gene D. Matlock
   Retrieved from "http://en.wikipedia.org/wiki/Gene_Matlock" From Khyber (Kheeber) Pass to Gran Quivira (Kheevira), Nm and Baboquivari, Az by Gene D. Matlock
5. The Miracle Man: The Life Story of João de Deus, by Robert Pellegrino-Estrich Extracted from his book Published in 1997, ©1997/1998 All Rights Reserve. Extracted from Nexus Magazine, Volume 5, #2 (February - March 1998). From our web page at: www.nexusmagazine.com
6. "The Origin of the Advanced Maya Civilization in the Yucatan", by Douglas T. Peck, Organ Transplants and Cellular Memories. Extracted from Nexus Magazine, Volume 12, Number 3 (April - May 2005) From our web page at: www.nexusmagazine.com by Paul Pearsall, PhD; Gary E. Schwartz, PhD, Linda G. Russek, PhD © 2002
7. Akiane Kramarik http://www.artakiane.com/
8. An archaeological study of chirped echo from the Mayan pyramid of Kukulcan at Chichén Itzá by David Lubman Acoustical Consultant
   http://www.ocasa.org/MayanPyramid.htm
9. http://mesoamerica.narod.ru/Images/Gods/xochipilli.jpg
10. Sacred Geometry and the Mayan Calendar Ian Xel Lungold, http://www.mayanmajix.com/3nn02_01_04.html
11. The Mayan Math: Mathematical Modeling of an Ancient Number Patterr, Daniel Clark Orey, Ph.D., California State University, Sacramento,
    http://www.csus.edu/indiv/o/oreyd/
12. Religious therapeutic rituals and their role in shaping sotsiotipaAndrew G. Safronov, safronov@3s.kharkov.ua
13. P.P. Gariaev, M.J. Friedman, E.A. Leonova- Gariaeva Crisis in Life Sciences. The Wave Genetics Response, 2006,
    http://genoterra.ru/news/view/8/941
    http://www.wavegenetics.jino-net.ru/
14. Paulo Coelho "Alchemistry" http://www.paulocoelho.com.br/russ/index.html
15. Numbers and Their Meanings
    http://www.crystalinks.com/numerology2.html
16. Daniel Clark Orey, PhD – The Mayan Math: Mathematical Modeling of an Ancient Number Pattern
17. Arnold de Belizal, The Atlantis Ring, http://www.crystalinks.com/atlantisring.html

18. www.zilli.fr
19. www.Atlantisoils.com, Atlantis oils, Healing & Well Being Centre
20. Zodiac Keywords, by Michael Erlewine
http://lessons.astrology.com/course/show/Beginners-Astrology/74-Zodiac-Keywords
21. Anubis, God of Embalming and Guide and Friend of the Dead by Caroline Seawrighg http://www.touregypt.net/featurestories/anubis.htm
22. Egyptian astrology, http://www.pvv.ntnu.no/~raaness/astrology/
23. Anubis statues, Copyright © 2006 The Unicorn Shoppe
Design by: IDEAS& Powered by Zen Cart
theunicornshoppe.com/store/index.php?main_page/
24. Anubis
http://www.google.ca/imgres?imgurl=http://dhawhee.blogs.com/photos/uncategorized/anubis_statue_1.jpg&imgrefurl=http://dhawhee.blogs.com/d_hawhee/2007/01/index.html&h=360&w=288&sz=28&tbnid=4Ib2Z_lsGIYJ::&tbnh=121&tbnw=97&prev=/images%3Fq%3DAnubis,%2Bstatue&hl=en&sa=X&oi=image_result&resnum=3&ct=image&cd=1
25. Coneheads. Researcher Robert Connolly photographed this strange elongated skull in 1995. It was found in South America and is estimated to be tens of thousands of years old. http://www.light1998.com/Weird-Skeletons/Weird-Skeletons.htm
26. Joe Mills - http://www.light1998.com/ALIEN-SKULLS/ALIEN-SKULLS.htm
27. Dr. Gunther von Hagens, www.bodyworlds.com
28. DNA Found to Have "Impossible" Telepathic Properties, Journal of Physical Chemistry B, Geoff S. Baldwin, Sergey Leikin, John M. Seddon, and Alexei A. Kornyshev "Ancient America: Flight in time and prostransive. Mezoamerika" Excerpts from the book by GG Ershovoy UnCopyrighted©Sam, 2003-2006.
29. Genady Belimov, "Soul and intelligence of the plants", TD 2005, # 5
30. Giants and Ancient History, Hidden Proofs Of A Giant Race, http://www.light1998.com/GIANTS/giants-m.htm http://www.stevequayle.com/index.html
31. An excerpt from...The Discoveryand Conquest of Peru, Translated with an Introduction by J. M. Cohen, Penguin Books, based on original documents dated 1556 http://www.stangrist.com/giantsdisc.htm
32. Buryl Payne, Discovery of biofield, http://newilluminati.blog-city.com/discovery_of_the_biofield.htm
33. V. Lotohin, Secret Doctrine, # 16, 2008
34. Dr Valery Uvarov, EARTH'S HIDDEN TWIN AND THE BIRTH OF CIVILISATION (Nexus magazine, #15 Vol.5).
35. Akaija is a unique healing device and jewelry made by Akaija & Art
www.akaija.com
http://www.akaija.com/info/UK/UK06_3D.shtml
http://www.akaija.com/info/UK/UK05_gallery.shtml
36. Toni Elizabeth Sar'h Petrinovich, Sacred Spaces, sacred@anacortes.n
www.sacredspaceswa.com, www.angelichuman.com, www.daughterofjesus.com
37. Вторжение НЛО на Землю. Скрытая правда. UFO 2016
38. https://www.youtube.com/watch?v=OKORgxvv6YM, start from2.57 min
39. Daniel Pinchbeck, 2012 The return of Quetzalcoatl, 2006.
40. The Strange Disappearance of Amelia Earhart, Nostradamus and the New Prophecy Almanacs Michael McClellan.
41. www.newprophecy.net/pastceleb.htm
42. Vasiliev, "Miracles and adventures", newspaper, *Secret Doctrina*, #13, July 2007.
43. "Amelia Earhart's soaring spirit"
May 25, 2009, Susan King, Los Angeles time,
http://articles.latimes.com/2009/may/25/entertainment/et-amelia25

44. Linda Finch, http://www.worldflight.com. (July 1997).
45. Singer Zzak , Zzak (Irving) GrinwaldYOUTUBE Meet "Zzak G" (Interview) Zzak G - Homeless
46. Howard Wills, healer. http://www.howardwills.com/YOUTUBES Howard Wills on Happiness Peace Making, Howard Wills: Dropping Love Bombs
47. Alfons Ven, EVOLUTION VISION foundation, Deviser of the 28-day cure, http://www.slideshare.net/alfonsven http://www.alfonsven.org, myriam@alfonsven.com

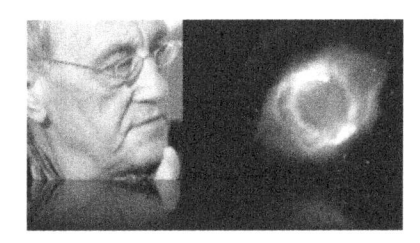

48. ////Mind Science Kept Hidden ////Documentary □□□□□□□ http://www.youtube.com/watch?v=fSGONup-CYE
49. http://www.near-death.com/, Kevin Williams□□□□□□□
   "Reincarnation as a group", about 2 American presidents: A. Lincoln and J.F. Kennedy, evidence of reincarnation
   REINCARNATION and BIBLE: http://www.near-death.com/experiences/origen03.html
   http://www.near-death.com/experiences/reincarnation08.html
50. http://500px.com/NataNaz/photoshttp://nanaz555.ya.ru/e-mail: nanaz@mail.ru
51. YOUTUBE was a video : LSC's Concave Earth, Platonic Solid Concave UniverseLord Steven Christ
52. www.BlueAvians.com, www.SphereBeingAlliance.com, www.ComicDisclosure.com
53. What heaven's really like? http://www.everystudent.com/forum/heaven2.html
54. Choteya, (XOTEYA), Magic-vernissage.com, http://ufo-hoteya.com/ru/
55. DavidIcke.com
56. V.V. Kustov, http://www.kustov.ru, Specialist bio -correction, parapsychologist. The expert for the health rehabilitation and maintenance of business projects.

The Smartest People In The World Are Trying To Tell You Something

There are probably other parallel universes in our living room
"There are vibrations of different universes right here, right now. We're just not in tune with them. There are probably other parallel universes in our living room—this is modern physics. This is the modern interpretation of quantum theory, that many worlds represent reality."
Dr. Michio Kaku, Theoretical Physicist, Professor and Bestselling Author

... There are an infinite number of parallel realities coexisting with us in the same room
"There are hundreds of different radio waves being broadcast all around you from distant stations. At any given instant, your office or car or living room is full of these radio waves. However if you turn on a radio, you can listen to only one frequency at a time; these other frequencies are not in phase with each other. Each station has a different frequency, a different energy. As a result, your radio can only be turned to one broadcast at a time. Likewise, in our universe we are *tuned into the frequency

that corresponds to physical reality. But there are an infinite number of parallel realities coexisting with us in the same room, although we cannot tune into them."
Professor Steven Weinberg, Nobel Prize in Physics (1979)

"In infinite space, even the most unlikely events must take place somewhere. People with the same appearance, name and memories as you, who play out every possible permutation of your life choices."
Professor Max Tegmark, Dept. of Physics, MIT

We are facing a revolution in our thinking about the physical universe
"Today, probably more than in any other day, we are facing a revolution in our thinking about the physical universe—the stuff that you and I are made of. This revolution, brought to a head by the discoveries of the new physics, including relativity and quantum mechanics, appears to reach well beyond our preconceived vision, based as it was on the concept of concrete solid reality."
Dr. Fred Alan Wolf, Author and Physicist

If a universe can be imagined, it exists.
Professor M.R. Franks, Member, Royal Astronomical Society of Canada

An ensemble of other different universes is necessary for the existence of our universe.
Professor John D. Barrow, *Dept. of Applied Mathematics and Theoretical Physics, Cambridge University*

We all exist in multiple universes...
"... but we only carry our own perception of our universe. We walk in our own bubble of reality without time or space and create our own universe."
Gerald O'Donnell, Leading Expert in the Military Science of Remote Viewing

I could go on and on here, because there are countless other intellectuals that have made discoveries in the possibility of alternate universes, including the world-famous Professor Stephen Hawking, Professor Alan Guth, and even Albert Einstein himself.

If you need more proof, just try Googling scientific theories like String Theory and M-Theory, or watch the film 'What The Bleep'. But for now, check out this unbelievable story...

Burt Goldman *http://www.quantumjumping.com/*

What heaven's really like?

-by a leading brain surgeon who says he's been there: Read his testimony before you scoff...it might just shake your beliefs

Dr Eben Alexander says he was taken 'on a voyage through a series of realms' after he went into a coma when he was diagnosed with meningitis
What is unique in my case is that I am, as far as scientific records show, the only person to have traveled to this heavenly dimension with the cortex in complete shut-down, while under minute observation throughout.There are medical records for every minute of my coma, and none of them show any indication of brain activity. In other words, as far as neuroscience can say, my journey was not something happening inside my head.Even the deep notes of the church organ and the glorious colours of the stained glass seem to echo faintly the sights and sounds of Heaven.

Here, then, is what I experienced: my **map of Heaven.**
It was a circular entity, emitting a beautiful, heavenly music that I called the Spinning Melody. The light opened up like a rip in the fabric of that coarse realm, and I felt myself going through the rip, up into a valley full of lush and fertile greenery, where waterfalls flowed into crystal pools. There were trees, fields, animals and people. There was water, too, flowing in rivers or descending as rain. Mists rose from the pulsing surfaces of these waters, and fish glided beneath them. This water seemed higher, and more pure than anything I had experienced before, as if it was somehow closer to the original source. My gaze wanted to travel into it, deeper and deeper. I now see all the earth's waters in a new perspective, just as I see all natural beauties in a new way.

I found myself as a speck of awareness on a butterfly wing, among pulsing swarms of millions of other butterflies. I witnessed stunning blue-black velvety skies filled with swooping orbs of golden light, angelic choirs leaving sparkling trails against the billowing clouds.
In Heaven, everything is more real — less dense, yet at the same time more intense.
Those choirs produced hymns and anthems far beyond anything I had ever encountered on earth. The sound was colossal: an echoing chant that seemed to soak me without making me wet.
It was the sound of sheer joy. All my senses had blended. Seeing and hearing were not separate functions. It was as if I could hear the grace and elegance of the airborne creatures, and see the spectacular music that burst out of them.

Simply to experience the music was to join in with it. That was the oneness of Heaven — to hear a sound was to be part of it. Everything was connected to everything else, like the infinitely complex swirls on a Persian carpet or a butterfly's wing. And I was flying on that carpet, riding on that wing.

There I encountered the infinitely powerful, all-knowing deity whom I later called Om, because of the sound that vibrated through that realm. I learned lessons there of a depth and beauty entirely beyond my capacity to explain.It's hard to put it into words, but the essence was this: 'You are loved and cherished, dearly, forever. You have nothing to fear. There is nothing you can do wrong.' It was, then, an utterly wonderful experience.

Acknowledgements

To dear **Alfons Ven** who taught me to ask myself: "Who am I?" From this question, this book emerged. Without this question, this book would never have seen the light of day or even exist. His genius gave me the unique possibility to return myself and others to our own selves by using his "miracle pills", changing our lives forever. It helped me in opening the doors to a waterfall of my own enormous amount of energy and in staying in great, dynamic health, optimistic and happy.

Alfons also helped me in making the decision of visiting my previous lives with the assistance of the "Regression Specialist", Di Cherry, which ultimately opened my eyes to a chain of events that occurred in my past lives.

Special, deeply felt thanks to the wise, **Di Cherry**, who, over the last 60 years, has helped thousands of people getting rid of the heavy burden of their past and find out *who* they really were through studying their Spirit Journey and seeing their lives under a new light.

Thank you to **Don Julio**, who recognized me as an Ancient Maya Priest, who talked to me in ancient Maya and opened the door to my home, the Chichén Itzá pyramid, 2000 years later.

Thank you to the famous Iranian artist, **Shahla Homayouni**, for her beautiful painting in the book. It touches my Spirit deeply. The mask, that the girl holds in her hands with love and tenderness, reminds me of the Maya Priest, which I was in my past live.

Special Thank you to **Douglas D.Settles** from USA, **Marianne Notschaele-den Boer** from Holland, **Simon Dewulf,** from Belgium, **Gloria Elizabeth Sanchez** from Mexico, **Eliot James Estep** from USA, **Carola W. Ruijschvan Dugteren** from Holland, **Erica Bones** from Texas, USA, **Martin van Wieringen**, The Netherlands**, Djuna Davidashvili,** Russia.This group of people belong to all races on our planet, they were my close friends and relatives from my past lives, they found me independent from each other and greatly support with this book and documentary movie production in this lifetime.

Special thanks to **Roxane Christ** , my editor, who supported me during the writing of this book. With her thorough knowledge of the language, she helped me, and many other authors, bring our books to life and make them available to readers". Thank you for such an amazing support dear Roxane!

Very special thanks to artist **Josephine** (www.josephinewall.co.uk) Her amazing magnificent paintings, full of wisdom, colors and beauty and as a mirror to my dreams! Each and every one painting precious for me and touch my Spirit deeply, some bring tears to my eyes. It is Kingdom of fairies, Goddesses, flowers, animals, plants, butterflies, songs, dance and love!

During preparation of the last addition version of the book there came some critical moments. Thanks to **Sally Williams** from Australia helped with editing parts for the new version of the book, for your priceless support and assistance at the most important point!

Deeply I thank you my dear friend singer **Zzak Grinwald** and his wonderful, wise friend, who is the Oversoul on other side, for the priceless help, advice and support at the moments when it was most needed. You are my friends forever.

YOUR ETERNAL HOLOGRAM

Special thanks go to **Samir Ali Baba**, who helped me, with his amazing magical oil, opening a jewelry box full of ancient spirits of Egypt, and affording me the astonishing possibility to see and communicate with them!

Thank you to dear **Kevin Williams.** You have created a precious web site: www.near-death.com with scientific articles studying life and death and life after death. I consider you as the # 1 reincarnation expert on our planet.

Special thanks go **Darlene Laurel SV**, for my photograph on the cover image of the book entitled, "Offshore Living and Investing" by David A. Tanzer Thank you also for this second photograph which appears on the cover of book, "Re-birth of an Atlantean queen" which you tookon a small island of the South Pacific near the place where Amelia disappeared. And now for this collection of numerous great photos you took on the Equinox 2010 in Chichén Itzá Mexico!

Thanks to the **Ancient Maya Priest** who gave me wisdom, knowledge about the other side of life: energy, auras, how to connect with Spirits, Gods and Goddesses. All of which were passed onto me in the form of an amazing friendship with plants, animals and echoing rocks; understanding their tender souls. I am also grateful to him for passing onto me his enormous strength, love and care for his people. He helped them survive through terrible droughts in Mexico and he was strong enough to sacrifice his own son for their wellbeing.

Special thanks to brave **Amelia Earhart** who flew the World and became a legend. This enormous effort and her achievements were made available to me in a full and detailed account of her life. It helped me in comparing my life, the life of an Ancient Maya Priest, with her life and proved that the Spirit of each person on Earth has many lives. I am deeply grateful for the gift she passed onto me, as a newborn person, who now carries the same Spirit: her experience and knowledge in biology, medicine, art, writing, and drawing, which she acquired and developed during her lifetime. I am thankful for her enormous strength and love for life and adventure. All of this priceless Spirit development is deeply appreciated by all other re-born people in these Spirits and those who will be reborn in future and continue to carry Spirit light through the chain of lives.

Special thanks to wonderful **Eleanour Roosevelt**, which I remember very clear from my past life as Amelia. Eleanour Amelia's dearest friend, with whom she was shared common ideas about Woman Status in society and Human rights: Eleanor was 1st Chair of the Presidential Commission on the Status of Women, 1st United States Representative to the United Nations Commission on Human Rights.

I express special thanks to **Tim G. S.** I shall acknowledge the massive efforts of laboriously collecting and systematizing of my dreams, which are used in this book.

Thanks to **Carlos Castaneda** for the invention of new terminology. This helped me and many other authors all over the world, to describe the Spirit world. Going through his books, his message became perfectly clear. I guess because of my past life experience as an ancient Maya Priest, I could read between the sentences what was impossible for him to describe or put into words.

Thanks to the wonderful **Crystalinks Metaphysical and Science Website**, which provided with great image sources and information about Ancient Civilizations and helped me with my research.

Special thank you to amazing, optimistic and highly professional hard working team, who helping to solve mystery and find Amelia's airplane: **David W Jourdan** & NAUTICOS and his team**, Jon**

Thompson success /Titanic venture, investor, FedEx founder and chairman **Fred Smith**, researcher **Spencer King**, writer **Elgen Long** "Crash and Sink" theory explaining the disappearance of Amelia Earhart.

To my lifelong friend and companion in my dreams, the **Holy Spirit**, my Guide who lives somewhere in the Universe, on the Other Side and for giving me support, helping me travel in my dreams through the planet and our Universe. He is the one who was talking to me throughout the years, teaching me and educating me in my dreams and helping me connect with other Spirits, Gods and Goddesses. I give you prayerful thanks.

To some amazing **High Power**, this Invisible **Beings,** for there assistance, and to my extended family on the Other Side, who are my Guardian Angels, who care about me, and who help me navigate in this life to avoid danger make the right decisions and warn me ahead of time by talking to me daily through the numbers' code, I give thanks.

Special thanks to **GOD** who blessed me and saved my life, and as a result, enabling me to write this book and produce movie. With Infinity of love to you from me, here on Earth and in Space beyond, in past and in future...

****

YOUR ETERNAL HOLOGRAM

For any information, please visit the website:

www.ameliareborn.comcontact@ameliareborn.com

YOU TUBE
AVATAR SVADI 1 , MESSENGER>>
AVATAR SVADI 2, KUKULCAN>>
AVATAR SVADI 3, ANGELS & GIANT >>
Avatar Svadi 4, GIANT in Chichén Itzá >>
AVATAR SVADI 5, Mystery numbers? >>
AVATAR SVADI 6, Treasure from Ancient civilizations >>
Avatar Svadi 7, Hypnoses Di Cherry >>
Avatar Svadi, part 8, ancient Maya crystal skull # 12 found! >>
Avatar Svadi, part 9 continue >>
Avatar Svadi, part 10 >>
Amelia's mystery >>
Amelia Reborn >>
2012 Maya Priest >>
2012 Power of Reincarnation >>
Amelia Earhart, reincarnation, last minutes before her death >>
Met in dream, together in Atlantis and reunited in real life now! >>

To buy this or any of Julia Svadi Hatra's books, movie on line, please visit Amazon.com and write the title of your choice in the "search window". **CD** available at www.ameliareborn.com

1. Di Cherry introduction to past life readings, hypnosis.
2. Reading Priest
3. Reading Chak Mol, part #1
4. Reading Chak Mol, part #2
5. Reading Amelia

NOTE:
Color photos for these books are available on the website www.ameliareborn.com Photo Gallery.

Testimonials

I really do think from what I wrote that you are an amazing woman, someone that comes along once in a life time. You are a real live Goddess! Most priceless alive human on the planet at our time. I really mean it is Incredible! Your outlook on life, philosophy and spiritual beliefs outstanding and intriguing. Your dreams very smart, unusual, bright and full of dynamic. It attracts like a magnet to read your wise book. Intelligence far beyond normal. What is your IQ?

Henry D.

****

Thank you for the quick response and your AMAZING book! I cannot wait to explore your adventures and gems of wisdom that are no doubt found all throughout your work and experiences...I am finding your stories and dreams fascinating! You have inspired me to continue my search into my own past life regression, as I know many keys lie within my own experiences that I do not fully comprehend now. You are extremely special and I can only thank Our Creator for stumbling onto your site...

**In Love & Light,
E James**

****

BEST BOOK TO TAKE TO THE BANKER! IT WILL BE NEVER BORING TO READ IT OVER AND OVER AGAIN FOR MANY YEARS! YOUR BOOK like a jewelry box for me, which if you would open it; you would be astonished seeing the flush of rare, magic multicolored things inside it. You are AVATAR who opened this rare knowledge to all of us.

hurrican888

****

"I feel very close to Amelia when I look at you or read your words. She, as you know, was also a budding scientist-physician before she turned to flying planes. Amelia's survived spirit is a much more profound thing than any physical reality."

Todd.

****

Amelia here is just the top of the iceberg! Looks like the Spirit structure as a Russian doll "matreshka". Each layer is a human life and more deep it goes more ancient and unique person come out!!... Atlantean queen... Egyptian Royal Priest... Sumerian Priest... and even Giants... But I agree, You, Svadi Hatra is the one who culminates with the final incarnation of this ancient Spirit Being as a scientist and author.

WISEWIND1

****

Amelia Reborn displays living proof of how a profound spirit will live on through the ages, and re-manifest itself in other living beings. Maya Priest, Ancient Priest of Chichén Itzá, Ancient Royal Egyptian, Sumerian Priest, Svadi Hatra, Giant Svadi, Atlantean woman, the chain is intertwined chronologically, to include Amelia and Julia, and no one tells it so beautifully as Amelia Reborn.

neilnils

****

YOUR ETERNAL HOLOGRAM

Amelia Reborn, her website, her spirituality, and her ever evolving outlook will truly and completely open the mind, the soul, and the spirituality of all who is not afraid to surrender themselves for their own self benefit.

ajajaj11113333

****

I remember that I was so curious about Julia's book, and when it arrived I immediately started reading. It was hard to put it down so I think I read it in two days or so. Julia's story about her memories as Amelia touched me deeply. And the reports about her ancient Maya heritage caused quite a stir. Once or twice my own memories about that time came to the surface. I want to thank Julia for telling her story in her own way because that made it possible to solve a piece or two of my own puzzle, it inspired me to experience some of my former lives. I hope this book will be published in the Netherlands shortly!

Blessings, Carola
www.sjamama.nl

****

Wow! I love these books! I read 85 pages in one sitting! I do not know Julia, yet I have known her forever. The first night I watched her videos and saw her pictures I knew there was truth to be shared. I have always known the information she shared, yet it was the first time these ears heard it. When you find yourself fighting your want to believe, listen without ears. I was shown her honesty through proof like many others, but do not misunderstand 'proof' through the filter of what you have been told, instead understand it through the power you have within yourself to reconcile what it true to YOU. Blessed be. On a separate note all together, I know now about the druids and the snake skirts, the rights and the knowledge that were lost or hidden. I understand more now about the true nature of where your benevolent precursory lifetimes came from and why the 'common law of good and well-ordered universality' was not a fanciful myth but a time so sublime and so non-pastoral that people could scarcely believe such things could be their own real history.

It was a major shift for Julia, a shift into the physical interlacing of her druid/priest/teacher past. Chills reading that parts. Beyond Maya, beyond illusion, past legend, past scrambled history; Julia, you are a two eyed serpent, you are a druid, a surveyor of the landscape of truth, descendant of AN; a Tuatha Den'AN.

I am honored to have witnessed your arrival here and can only hope that there are others who have come into this lifetime, that can rectify the broken strings so that our harmony can be heard once again and without tremor. Let those who have confused us and cast us into ignorance be raised up and rejoined to the radiant light so we may continue our quest without shackle or fetter.

One love to you, Sister of the Cultivation –
Seth I.

****

In 2008 I met Julia via Internet and we have been sending each other many emails ever since. As a professional past life/regression therapist, with my own practice in the Netherlands, I have done thousands of sessions with clients to their past lives over the last twenty years and I have written many articles in magazines and various books regarding the subject reincarnation and past life memories.

It struck me that Julia is a kind-hearted, honest, intelligent, down-to-earth person. And apart from that, she is a scientist. She approaches reincarnation (soul & body) on a more scientific level, different from the way I work as a therapist with emotions of clients and finishing emotional trauma in past lives.

Julia's mission is among others to proof scientifically that after death our spirits do not die.

As a therapist I also see these recurring patterns and characteristics in past lives of myself and of my many clients but I never felt the need to do something with that information. However Julia does. She wants the world to know that our spirit is eternal. If we die, our spirit goes on...

I've read Julia's book and was impressed by the many details she had produced in proving that we, human beings, do not need fear death because our spirit is eternal. She did this by unraveling her own dreams, deep investigation, visiting countries and comparing information out of 4 of her different past lives.

*Julia was definitively an **Atlantean queen** (I would rather call that some sort of an Atlantean high priestess) in one of her past lives. She has vivid memories of me being her sister in that lifetime. I only have vague recollections about that specific past life, but I am pretty sure that she is correct about that. Not all persons remember the same way, one in colours, images, another in feelings, emotions, knowing.*

*Once I did a past life consult with a friend of her, Simon D., and he also stated during his regression that he knew her from that past life as a **queen in Atlantis**.*

*In another life **time Julia was a Maya priest**. No doubt she had lived many other lives as well. I have had vivid images of a lifetime in which Julia and I were travelling in space together in a strange grey vessel.*

Lucky, that this lifetime Julia is a scientific investigator, so she is able to proof things.

*I found many little details in the book that made me able to say: yes, Julia was once Amelia Earhart, or even better: **the soul in Julia's body now, was in Amelia's body the last time**. But besides that, it's a lovely book to read. I do hope that Julia's book will reach many readers so that people everywhere will learn that indeed our soul goes on...*

Marianne Notschaele-den Boer
www.vorigelevens.nl

****

Wow! I guess I discovered real treasure here!

Silvercrystal

****

This Spirit created the longest commercial ad in the history! With Amelia's disappearance mystery, Spirit keep whole world attention for 70 years long! And now decided to give SECRET of SPIRIT's ETERNITY LIFE to humanity! Smart!

naturegene

****

February 3, 2011
Julia sent me a copy of her book, ETERNAL HOLOGRAM. I discover that Julia's message to humanity is *genuine*, *accurate*, and of the *utmost importance* to all of us!
The story of her Spirit is filled with highly detailed experiences, vivid and powerful dreams, and countless insights that will bring you great joy and peace, as she proves and reminds us that we are all Divine Beings of Light. I have come to understand that Julia is very special and that her purpose

was decided *before* she incarnated in her past and current lifetimes. As a priest and scientist of the highest caliber, her message of Truth and Love will help assist ALL those who are ready to receive it. As we continue to approach 2016, people everywhere are Awakening as the global veils of illusion continue to dissipate. People are asking: "Who am I?" and "Where do I really come from?" These are important and vital questions to ask ourselves! The answers will not be revealed to us from an outside source, but rather, from *within*! Let your Spirit guide you as you discover your *true purpose* -- in this lifetime and beyond.

Julia's collection of books, videos, audios, and images provide a powerful and comprehensive look into the journey of a Great Spirit. Her mission in this lifetime is of the utmost importance for humanity, and you will feel this as you read and experience it! After all, it is no coincidence that you are reading these words right now!

I have been learning more about myself and my past ever since I met Julia. She has helped my spiritual progression in many ways already, just by reading and experiencing her story. I also know now that our Spirit connection predates this current lifetime. I am extremely grateful for the opportunity I have had assisting her with this book and will continue to spread its message far and wide. We are living in the most unique and exciting time in history -- and we are all here by our own choice! Let us all make the most of this wonderful experience.

Thank you to Julia and to all those who are reading this now! Blessings to you all.

In Love & Light,
Eliot James Estep
(Eternal Student -- USA)

****

That is so wonderful, and you should be so very proud of yourself. Just think of the impact that you can have on the lives of others through your book ... opening up their minds, their spirituality, their soul, and their current lives!!!!!!"

Christopher M.

****

Afraid to die? Just read front page of that website! And you will never afraid again! Never! Can't wait to read whole book... Amazing! YES, Amelia alive! Can you believe it?

Miracleforest

****

WOW, it's such a small world! Thank you! This shows that we are all recycled in one way or another. PS. You are SOOOO BEAUTIFUL!!!! U've been an Ancient Maya Priest of Chichén Itzá, the first TRUE female pilot known as the Great Amelia Earhart, and NOW you are America's Next Top Model!

Localibran

****

SEE, YOU ARE THE BEST!
You are a true testimony of skeptics who's been there in the "I don't know" phase, to "it's more real than you can ever imagine" phase! Most scientists are realists because that's what they study and go by what's there in the naked eye, without really giving spiritual connections a try for the simple idea

that "it was just my imagination" kind of thing. But when you go through something like what YOU'VE gone through and journeyed to the past YOU, there isn't a second question or a way to deny it (especially coming from a woman like Earhart, prior HIGH, Ancient Priest of Chichén Itzá that students study about in history books)! Whoop, that gives ME a chill!

I can understand your story without judgment or having a big head about it quite well, because I truly with all my heart believe in things like this.

Just finding this kind of thing out only 1 year ago, I'm sure it STILL can give you a rush, because it still must feel so fresh, like it was only yesterday you found out.

But if you've had visions and dreams about it, I'm sure that it can give you a kind wisdom you've never had before, and a final connection to it all (and not just think you're going crazy).

Because you are literally a "walking, breathing LIVING LEGEND" only so many can understand and appreciate, since there ALWAYS will be skeptics.

But to the skeptics you can tell them, "Hey, I was once just like you!"

I ABSOLUTELY LOVE www.eternalhologram.com, all the more detailed insight and your experience. I am definitely in the process of ordering your book (and help promoting it too)! I think this is a story and an insight everybody should know about and bring the closure and the TRUE scoop on what REALLY happened to the -"once" dearly departed Amelia Earhart! (Get it?)

Miss Julia, you are BEAUTIFUL and INCREDIBLE, and I can see why Amelia chose such a sweet, graceful, elegant, and intelligent woman to come back in and share the new millennium with us to keep her story alive and heard, and give us the truth!

**With love and admiration,
Erica!**

****

"I have read your book from cover to cover. I think it is a awesome book written with the spirit of eternal live in a way that everyone can understand the spiritual touch from your dreams.

I know how important your story about the Violet is. It is not only a dream because I know this field really exist in the Netherlands. On this field are important 2500 years old graves of spiritual leadership like that of Odin and Svadi. Svadi was a son of Thor, his mother the daughter of king Priam of Troy.

The Violet field is known as 'splendor field'. Its location is referenced twice in Voluspa in the Poetic Edda as 'Ithavoll', as a meeting place of the gods

The history of the Violet field survived as the wise woman's prophecy, the song of a seers. Odin/Wotan, chief of the gods, always conscious of impending disaster and eager for knowledge calls on a wise-woman. She first tells him a part of the past, of the creation of the world. By stanza 30 she than turns to the real prophecy, the disclosure of the final destruction.

This final battle, in which fire and flood overwhelm heaven and earth: The fate of the Gods, with a happy end.

"Now do I see, the earth a new. Rise all green, from the waves again; The cataracts fall, and the eagle flies, and fish he catches beneath the cliffs. The gods in Ithavoll meet together, of the terrible girdler, of earth they talk; And the mighty past, they call to mind, and the ancient runes, of the rulers of Gods."

Martin van Wieringen The Netherlands

****

"Your Eternal Hologram" chronicles the magnificent journey of an ancient Spirit Being. The book begins in Chichén Itzá and describes lives in Atlantis, ancient Egypt and Mexico. The remembrance includes an incarnation as Amelia Earhart and culminates with the final incarnation of this ancient Spirit Being into the scientist and author, Julia Svadi Hatra. Chapter after chapter, dream after

dream, Julia weaves a tale of phantasmagoric images, describing her life as an ancient Maya Priest, how she was consecrated in a Buddhist Temple, how she devotes her innocence and intellect to the scientific explanation of her dreams and visions. Where ever the visions or dreams occurred, she goes – physically travels – to the place and finds verification, veracity into what she has asserted many years ago. Many people claim to have "seen the light", to have had "near death experience" but not many (if any) claim have gone through the "Violet Field" of temptation and come back, not once, but many times over. Julia has traveled to the Other Side, to our Parallel World. She has a definite view or panoramic vision of our destiny, our eternity. Julia is by no means a religious person, she is a scientist. She is not to be fooled by anyone's pretenses; she will delve into science, to prove you right or wrong. She follows in the footsteps of such eminent minds as that of Stephen Hawking, Peter Gariaev, and countless others – only to verify any and all of her dreams. Julia knows where Amelia Earhart's plane is – she can pin point the location of Amelia's tragic end with absolute certainty. She even offered to accompany a team of scientists to the place – only to be turned down ...

Roxane Christ

****

"I've been a psychotherapist for many years. My specialty was using hypnosis and helping people do regressions, both in this lifetime and past lives. I've done hundreds of past lives on myself and with those of my clients and friends. I'm pretty skeptical of other people saying they did a past life as everyone wants to see themselves as being someone famous, i.e., the Queen of Sheba, the King of Siam, Marilyn Monroe, or even Amelia Earhart. When I first saw Julia's claim that she was Amelia Earhart, I instantly had those same skeptical thoughts. As I read her accounts however, of how she did her past life regressions (in hypnosis); the dreams she had for years prior to this; the feelings and emotions she felt in the dreams and her regressions; and the 'proof' she has offered from her scientific background, there **is no doubt she is indeed, Amelia Reborn!**

After meeting Julia in person, I did a past life where she **and I were together in Atlantis where she was the Queen.** Together we worked with the amazing technology of Atlantis, which ultimately brought the downfall of the country.

In another of Julia's lives, she was the **High Priestess in Chichen Itza, Mexico**.

As stated above, I'm always skeptical of someone claiming to be well knows people from history. Remarkably, in this case, Julia has proven to me that she has indeed lived these remarkable lives.

Julia's spiritual destiny is to bring this message to those who will listen that there is life after life, both in this world and in that world between lives, the soul lives on, the joy of life and living, and that there is truly nothing to fear.

Douglas Settles, M.A.

****

Reading your book but I am crying so much reading I can hardly read it. Your book resonates so much with me, so much emotions it brings up. You put your heart in this book to touch the hearts of the readers.

Buryl Payne

****

Julia Svadi Hatra is perhaps the purest soul I have ever come in contact with. After years of knowing her, I realized her external beauty has somehow been surpassed by her inner beauty.

JC Smith

****

This is an amazing story and reality. Thank you for sharing this? With the world. Much Love, Light and Blessings your way! Greetings with love from Indonesia.
YOUTUBE **schmeitss**

****

Julia, The Universe works in mysterious ways! I noticed a front cover of your books on a website. I was rather intrigued about your experiences and you sent me your latest book to read, a number of stories in your book triggered memories in me. Amazing that it is only 6 weeks ago when we got in touch when I was in Madagascar and you in Canada, which is truly on the opposite side of the world. Since this day I read your book, visited your friend, past life specialist Marianne in the Netherlands, I visited Chichen Itza in Mexico! Amazing how "the old force" that you so easy appear to tap into, together with "the new technology of the internet" makes the world an amazing small place! I wish you well with all your ambitions, plans and visions, the world will be a better place for it!

Hans Donker, Brisbane, Australia

We loved your book.
It will help people understand that the **Kukulkan lineages are still alive today.** *The return of the intended magicians is understandable through your journey*

YOUTUBE **noor8**

****

Dearest Julia,
I would just like to say: THANK YOU for your amazing contribution to humanity. I truly believe that your work accomplishes what it set it out to do, and hope that it will reach the eyes and ears of the masses for their consideration and contribution to their own Awakening.
The knowledge you have brought forth about our ETERNAL HOLOGRAM, the Annunaki/Nephilim/Giants, the 'alternate' true history of humanity, the purpose of Atlantean crystals/pyramids/etc., the understandings of Mayan culture/history/purpose and how it relates to our current stage of humanity, has all been PRICELESS and ACCURATE wisdom. I truly thank you for your wonderful and persistent efforts of uncovering the past, future, and present journeys of your great Spirit.
I have learned MUCH from your book, guidance, and example. Your Spirit is one I will never forget, and hope to meet again in person someday. I know that we came into contact for a purpose, and I hope that my assistance was valuable in the final publishing of your book.

Sincerely, with Love,
Eliot

****

Ancient Maya language you spoke in your present life, is what we call **xenoglossy**, *being able to talk a language out of a past life even if you never have learned it in your present life.*

YOUTUBE **XYmar89** , www.vorigelevens.nl/

****

As I read Julia's book, "Your Eternal Hologram" I was amazed by her remarkable abilities. She can see things that for normal people, are impossible to see. I can assure you that her discovery about the existence of the HUMAN ETERNAL HOLOGRAM is absolutely correct. We are a group of scientists that have witnessed that when aliens meet a person, they take information from that individual. This hologram, which each human has, contains information about the person's past, present and possibly its future...The fact that Julia is an Ancient Maya priest reincarnated from Chichen Itza is unique and precious. She gives important facts on the subject of reincarnation.

She shows how the knowledge of a Power of Reincarnation will change the consciousness of people, she gifted a rare knowledge to Humanity about the Spirit life after a person's death, as well as with her Foundation support my deep research about the importance of the Pyramids chain structure in our planet in coming years and beyond.

VALERY UVAROV: PROJECT12 - New Atlantis?
Human_holograms_extraterrestres

****

Julia, is a very special lady. Where others stop, she will continue to search for the right answers. In the coming Earth changes she will guide many through these turbulent times.

Patrick Jeryl, author "How to Survive 2012"
www.howtosurvive2012.com

****

I HIGHLY advise anyone and everyone to☐ pick up this sweet beautiful ladies book about all of this. A true MUST READ that has some really interesting and insightful fact's that really crack's it down in even more depth. Nobody (unless you're living right that is) should be afraid of passing away. She is definitely a TRUE testimony to this very important fact that live's even beyond HER words that everyone really must understand.
A MUST READ TO EVERYONE THAT WANT'S TO KNOW THE TRUTH!!

Erica, Texas, USA

****

When my friend came to me with Julia for the first time, a wave of energy began to move between me and Julia. We both had goosebumps all over our bodies. This is how our souls begin to know each other. We were with her in Sumer, Persia and in Atlantis. I took Julia's hand in my hands.

Surprisingly for me and all the people who were around us, our fingers began as magnets stick to each other! **Yes, Julia and I, we were together in Atlantis**. *I remember our life in Atlantis. We were 3-4 meters high, both like on my paintings.* **She was a Queen there.**

Julia has a very powerful, unusual energy, and many abilities. For example, she can see the spirits of dead people. One day a woman came to me from aTV channel, the program "Good Morning" and asked me about her passed away father. I was very busy with sick people and asked Julia for help. Julia immediately saw the father of the woman right next to her and described big white spot on his stomach area. When the woman called her mother, she confirmed that her father had big white spot! By the time the children grew up, the father was healed. That is why children have never seen a white spot. The father actually arrived and showed this white spot and proved that it is indeed him and people after the death still exist and live as spirits before they will be born again. I know that she can do healing for people with cancer. A couple of times I had way too many patients and all those who were with the cancer I sent to another room to Julia to take care about them, all went home happy. Julia likes to heal, I guess it came to her from **her previous life as a Maya priest.** *She support me with the energy when I was sick.*

At night, when I paint pictures, I write poems ...
Surprisingly, the next day Julia can come and read my new poem, which I created only a few hours ago! She said that she woke up from my voice and start recording ... it's happened several times.

Djuna Davitashvili, healer, president of the "International Academy of Alternative Sciences "
Russia, Moscow

****

Julia, Thanks for writing all your dreams down in your book. I have read the book over the last month and there is only one thing I can say: it feels very familiar with me. **The parts about Atlantis struck me right in the heart. Funny that you describe the drawing of an 'eight' with your hand to start materialization. I knew it was working like that, so reading it in your book sounded so normal to me.** *Also the part about Belgium drilling is exactly as it is. I am living in Holland, just at the Belgium border. I met in recent years some people from Belgium who still have knowledge and use some of their tricks from the time there was ancient magic on earthThanks for sharing your dreams, it helped me to step to the next level of my spiritual development.*

Peter Reusel, The Netherlands

****

"I read all the reviews and agree with the importance of proof of the existence of Eternal hologram and that our Spirit is Eternal. But I want to draw attention to the fact that in my opinion, **is the most unusual in this book - it really is the real magic. In the text of the book there is an amazing property that occurs while reading, which are beginning to activate the vibration of our Soul, affecting the deepest layers of our Spirit, our eternal hologram every person who reads it!***
People begin to remember past lives, suddenly opening there own unusual abilities...
People told me that while they reading the book, vibrations emanating from those dreams described in the book activate the mind and they think the situations happened to them in their past lives. It does not matter if someone does not understand everything in the book - a miracle to happen anyway! It's amazing and delicious! You can learn about it in a review of other people, who also had a similar experience as me.
This book - a real key for access to the enlightenment of consciousness each and everyone on this planet. Julia is a **true Magician, who visits our planet with high mission for humanity.***"*

David Csercsics, Toronto, Canada

****

Got this weekend your book in the hand. Even touching the book gave me already trills.
I have been reading several parts of it. It is more than amazing. Your statement that 'spirit is eternal' is well emphasized and believable. Your contribution to testify from theinvisible world will bring back a lot of people to live a sound faith driven live. You know that you are abundantly blessed, set-apart and might fully used to serve as a priest.

It was already written by the prophet Hosea: (free quote) 'My people (says Yahweh) are destroyed for lack of knowledge.' He blames the priests for it as it is their task to instruct the people and that during that period priests neglected that and lived a shameful decadent live, not caring for the common man.

Now you are here, bringing the knowledge that can save the people from destruction. That's exactly why your speech, book(s) and video (s) should be spread rapidly all over the world in many languages. Sure a giant enterprise and of course you will persevere.

Reading your book my reverence is increasing strongly for you being out there as a living testimonial of the Spirit world. *Many mediums, psychics etc. tried to approach me in vain the last 20-*

yrs, as none of them were pure and badly wired with the parallel world. Now finally there is you! The living model of faith, hope, love, creativity and beauty. Blessed are you that brings peace of mind instead of fear.

I will order 10 copies of the book to hand over to friends. Also to my granddaughter, whom was trilled after reading the back cover.

Alfons Ven,
EVOLUTION VISION foundation
Deviser of the 28-day cure, E-mail: myriam@alfonsven.com, www.slideshare.net/alfonsven

JULIA SVADI HATRA

AVATAR SVADI HATRA

© Josephine Wall. All Rights Reserved. www.josephinewall.com

YOUR ETERNAL HOLOGRAM

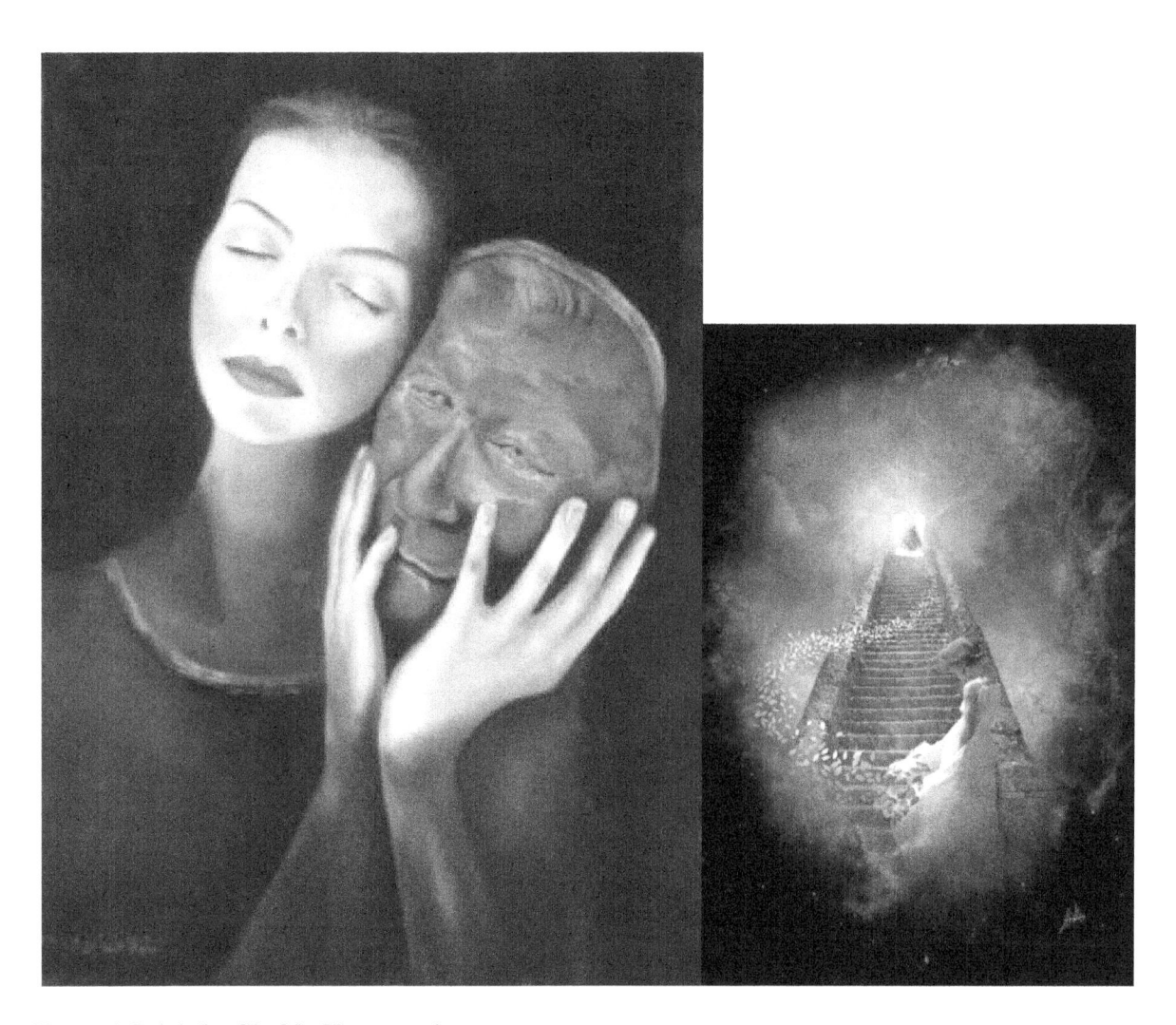

Eternal Spirit by Shahla Homayoni.
http://www.homayoni.com
Shahla.ht@gmail.com

AVATAR SVADI HATRA

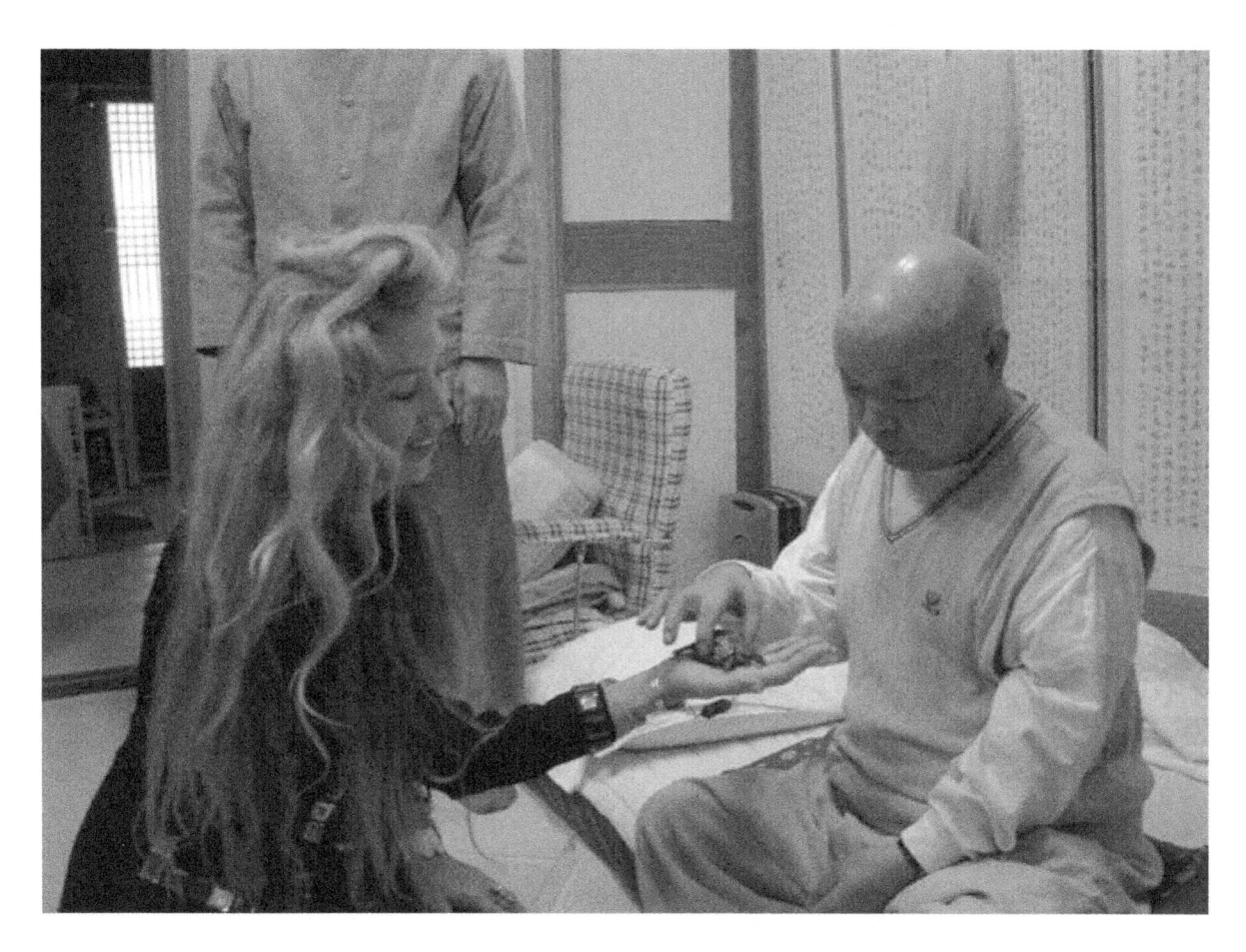

**Meeting of two High Priests:
from Asia and Ancient Mexico, turtle gift exchange.**

**Honorable Supreme Buddhist monk,
who is the leader of 13 million monks.**

YOUR ETERNAL HOLOGRAM

Mexican spiritual teacher, Julio Luis Rodriguez, Equinox Day – Chichén Itzá (Mexico)

Rock from the past, Coba pyramid

Unique specialist for bio -correction, powerfulparapsychologist Kustov V.V.

Diana Cherry, president of hypnoses asossiation, Canada.

Ancient Maya Priest of Chichen Itza reincarnated

Photographer: Darlene Laurel SV

AVATAR SVADI HATRA

TRINITY© Josephine Wall. All Rights Reserved. www.josephinewall.com

YOUR ETERNAL HOLOGRAM

"Who am I ?" , photograph by Tim Orden, www. timorden.com

Nostradamus predicted in 2 quatrains Julia birth, as a re-born Amelia Earhart.

398

Alfons Ven, amazing healer

**Julia– The Good Priest – Equinox 2010,
Chichen Itza, Photographer: Darlene Laurel SV**

Josephine Wall. All Rights Reserved. www.josephinewall.com

AVATAR SVADI HATRA

Josephine Wall. All Rights Reserved.

YOUR ETERNAL HOLOGRAM

Julia with Maya dancers, Tulum, Mexico.

Reading of the Crystal skull

Josephine Wall. All Rights Reserved. www.josephinewall.com

Alternative reality, Josephine Wall. All Rights Reserved. www.josephinewall.com

Josephine Wall. All Rights Reserved. www.josephinewall.com

YOUR ETERNAL HOLOGRAM

Amelia's red/white colours

Julia on the top of her pyramid, Chichen Itza, Mexico.

YOUR ETERNAL HOLOGRAM

Dress looks like silver scales, silver shoes and suitacses, as a result of travel in Univerce.

AVATAR SVADI HATRA

www.josephinewall.com

YOUR ETERNAL HOLOGRAM

Hunting in Thailand, wild python and tortoise, big and small only5 sm

Hunting for snakes in Australia. Photographer: David Holiday

YOUR ETERNAL HOLOGRAM

Pyramid of Heopse

Mohammed Abbas and Mr. Samir, Egypt.Lights for the light show was in timeline

AVATAR SVADI HATRA

Ancient Maya Priest from Chichen Itza Hei Hiole
(child which arrived from the stars)

Photographer: Darlene Laurel SV

YOUR ETERNAL HOLOGRAM

© Josephine Wall. All Rights Reserved. www.josephinewall.com

Julia Svadi Hatra author of this book

YOUR ETERNAL HOLOGRAM

Two previous life Julia: Royal priestess of Egypt and the pilot Amelia Earhart, easy to see that looks alike. Darlene Laurel SV, Photographer, Photo # 1

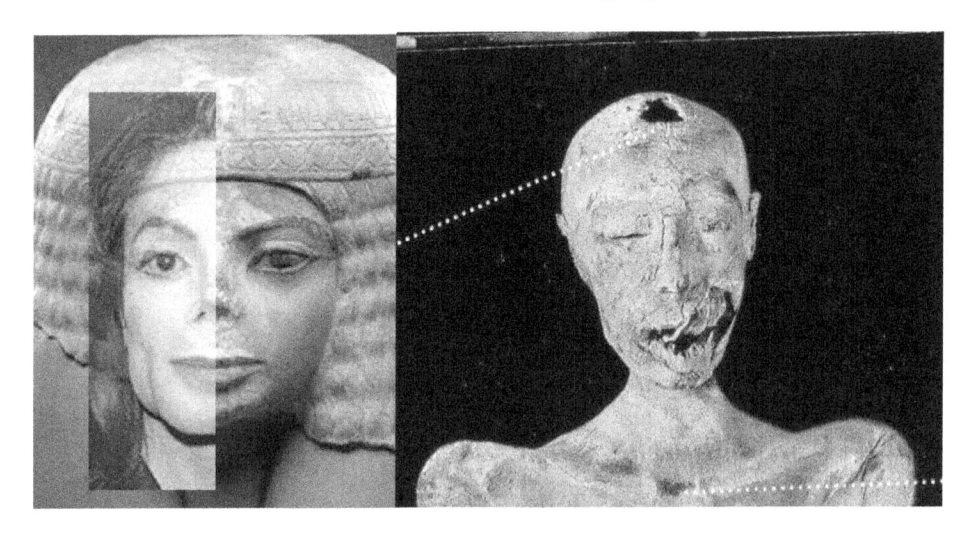

1. Michael Jackson – the reincarnation of an Egyptian Pharaoh woman

2. "Egyptians removed the brain through the nostrils.
Why there is a hole on the top of the head, no one knows."
(Discovery Magazine, April 2009). A Secret was opened in this book!

Two of the many cases of teleportation, materialization by Julia

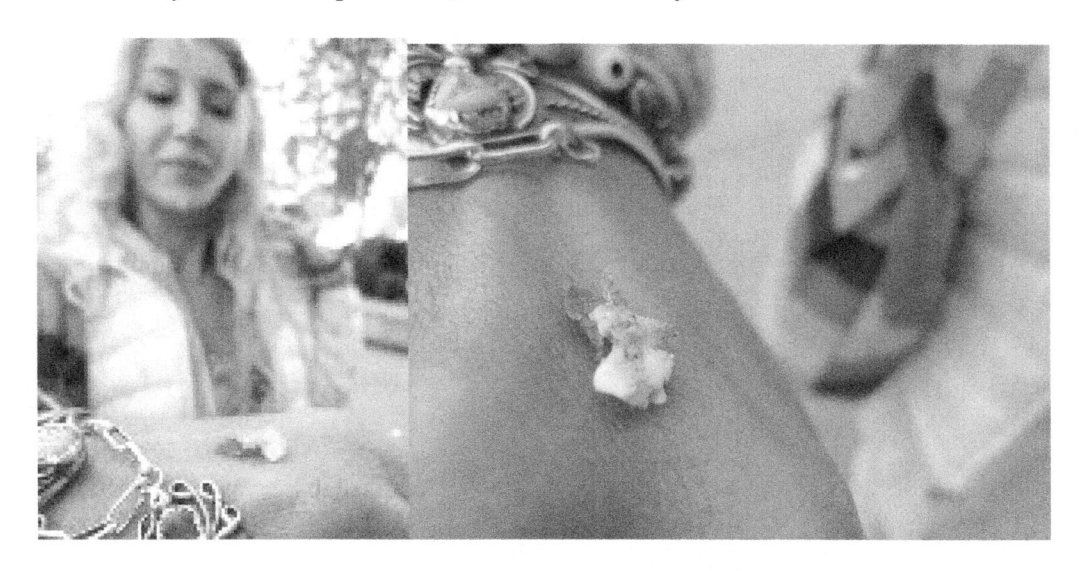

Materialization of alive butterfly, February, Canada

YOUR ETERNAL HOLOGRAM

photographer by Natalia/ nanaz

AVATAR SVADI HATRA

© Josephine Wall. All Rights Reserved. www.josephinewall.com

YOUR ETERNAL HOLOGRAM

© Josephine Wall. All Rights Reserved. www.josephinewall.com

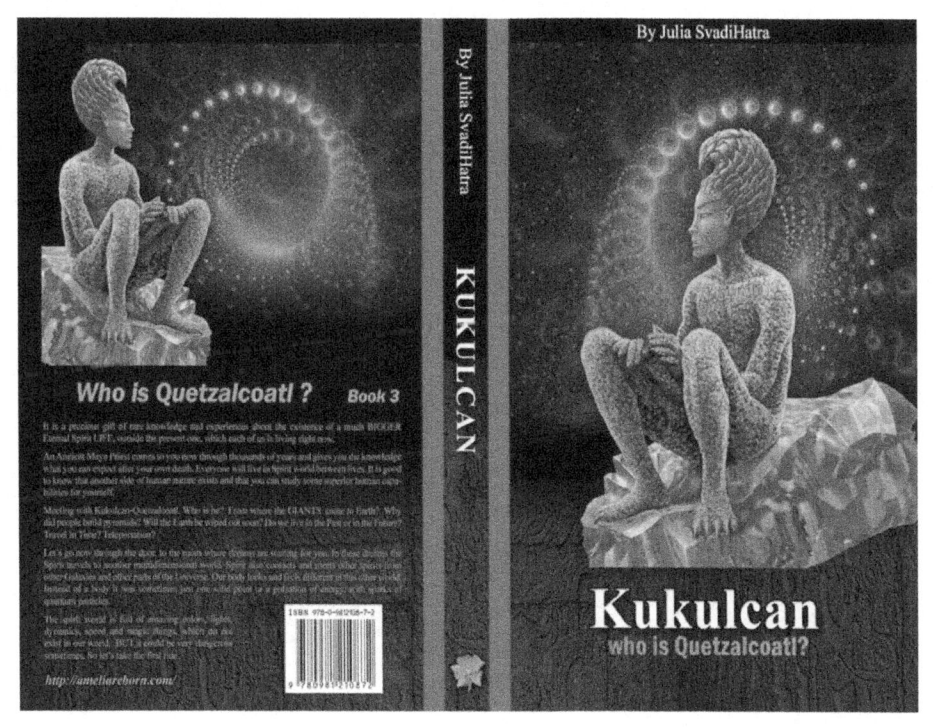

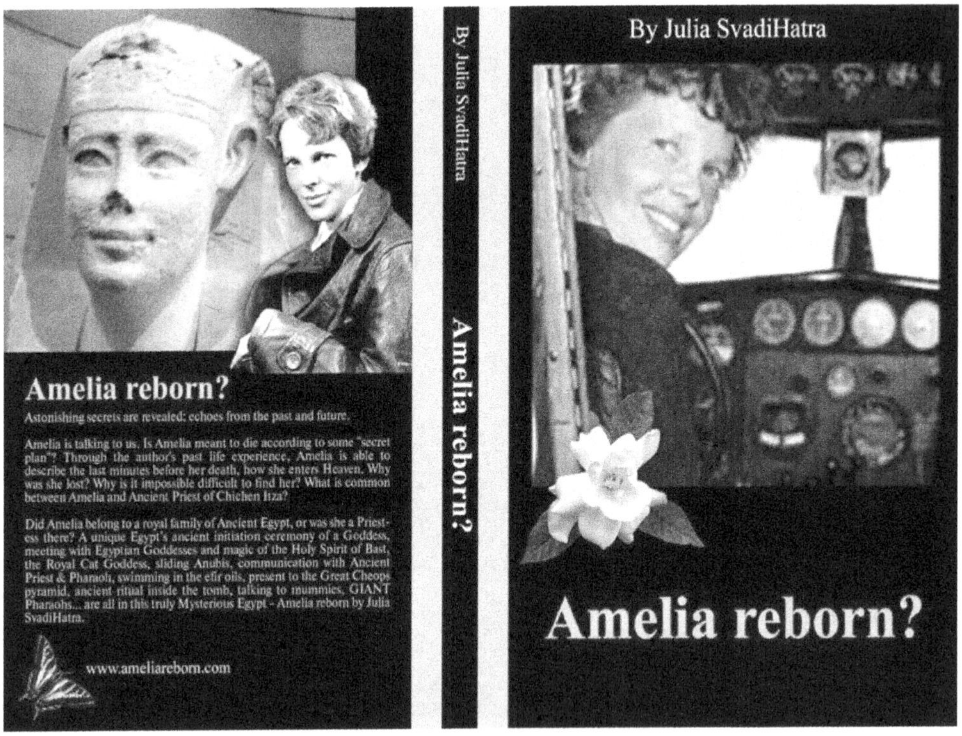
Amelia reborn?
Astonishing secrets are revealed: echoes from the past and future.
Amelia is talking to us. Is Amelia meant to die according to some "secret plan"? Through the author's past life experience, Amelia is able to describe the last minutes before her death, how she enters Heaven. Why was she lost? Why is it impossible difficult to find her? What is common between Amelia and Ancient Priest of Chichen Itza?
Did Amelia belong to a royal family of Ancient Egypt, or was she a Priestess there? A unique Egypt's ancient initiation ceremony of a Goddess, meeting with Egyptian Goddesses and magic of the Holy Spirit of Bast, the Royal Cat Goddess, sliding Anubis, communication with Ancient Priest & Pharaoh, swimming in the efir oils, present to the Great Cheops pyramid, ancient ritual inside the tomb, talking to mummies, GIANT Pharaohs... are all in this truly Mysterious Egypt - Amelia reborn by Julia SvadiHatra.
www.ameliareborn.com
By Julia SvadiHatra
Amelia reborn?
By Julia SvadiHatra
Amelia reborn?

Who is Chak Mol ? Book 2
Who is Chak Mol, this popular Mexican hero?
Did the High Priest meet an Atlantean Giant living among the Mayas in Chichen Itza?
Who was God of Rain?
http://ameliareborn.com/
ISBN 978-0-9812108-6-5
By Julia SvadiHatra
WHO IS CHAK MOL?
By Julia SvadiHatra
Who is
Chak Mol?

Made in United States
North Haven, CT
12 January 2022